APPLIED ECONOMETRICS

Applied Econometrics: A Practical Guide is an extremely user-friendly and application-focused book on econometrics. Unlike many econometrics textbooks which are heavily theoretical on abstractions, this book is perfect for beginners and promises simplicity and practicality to the understanding of econometric models. Written in an easy-to-read manner, the book begins with hypothesis testing and moves forth to simple and multiple regression models. It also includes advanced topics:

- Endogeneity and Two-stage Least Squares
- Simultaneous Equations Models
- Panel Data Models
- Qualitative and Limited Dependent Variable Models
- Vector Autoregressive (VAR) Models
- Autocorrelation and ARCH/GARCH Models
- Unit Root and Cointegration

The book also illustrates the use of computer software (*EViews*, *SAS* and *R*) for economic estimating and modeling. Its practical applications make the book an instrumental, go-to guide for solid foundation in the fundamentals of econometrics. In addition, this book includes excerpts from relevant articles published in top-tier academic journals. This integration of published articles helps the readers to understand how econometric models are applied to real-world use cases.

Chung-ki Min is Professor of Economics at Hankuk University of Foreign Studies, Seoul, South Korea.

Routledge Advanced Texts in Economics and Finance

For more information about this series, please visit www.routledge.com/Routledge-Advanced-Texts-in-Economics-and-Finance/book-series/SE0757

APPLIED ECONOMETRICS

A Practical Guide

Chung-ki Min

Routledge
Taylor & Francis Group

LONDON AND NEW YORK

First published 2019
by Routledge
2 Park Square, Milton Park, Abingdon, Oxon OX14 4RN

and by Routledge
52 Vanderbilt Avenue, New York, NY 10017

Routledge is an imprint of the Taylor & Francis Group, an informa business

© 2019 Chung-ki Min

British Library Cataloguing-in-Publication Data
A catalogue record for this book is available from the British Library

Library of Congress Cataloging-in-Publication Data
Names: Min, Chung Ki, author.
Title: Applied econometrics : a practical guide / by Chung-ki Min.
Description: Abingdon, Oxon ; New York, NY : Routledge, 2019. | Series: Routledge advanced texts in economics and finance ; 31 | Includes bibliographical references and index.
Identifiers: LCCN 2018049763 | ISBN 9780367110321 (hardback) | ISBN 9780367110338 (pbk.) | ISBN 9780429024429 (ebook)
Subjects: LCSH: Econometrics.
Classification: LCC HB139 .M555 2019 | DDC 330.01/5195—dc23
LC record available at https://lccn.loc.gov/2018049763

ISBN: 978-0-367-11032-1 (hbk)
ISBN: 978-0-367-11033-8 (pbk)
ISBN: 978-0-429-02442-9 (ebk)

Typeset in Times New Roman
by Apex CoVantage, LLC

Vist the eResources: http://routledgetextbooks.com/textbooks/instructor_downloads/

CONTENTS

10   Autocorrelation and ARCH/GARCH   203

11   Unit root, cointegration and error correction model   230

FIGURES

TABLES

PREFACE

This textbook is meant to be used in teaching practical uses of econometric models with minimal theoretical explanation. Based on my experience teaching econometrics courses in Korea, Hong Kong and the US, I have learned that most students are not interested in the theoretical explanations because they are *users* (not developers) of econometric models. To draw an analogy, users of mobile phones need only know how to perform functions such as sending messages and taking calls and will be less interested in the technology that makes those acts possible.

Uniqueness of this book

When I first started teaching econometrics, I found that all of the available textbooks were fixated on the theoretical aspects of econometric models and contained few applications. This is why I started writing a textbook which is both *user-friendly* and *application-focused*. To help readers apply econometric methods to real-world problems for their empirical research, I explain key elements of econometric models and illustrate the use of computer software (*EViews*, *SAS* and *R*) to estimate the models. I also cite relevant articles published in top-tier academic journals, providing excerpts that help the readers to understand how econometric models are applied to their real-world use cases and how the results are reported in publications. It should be noted that this integration of published articles is one of the unique strengths of this textbook.

Target readers

The target readers of this textbook are undergraduate and graduate students who major in accounting, economics, finance, marketing, tourism, etc. Based on the feedback from undergraduates, graduate students and also junior faculty members, I am confident that this *user-friendly* and *application-focused* approach is highly useful and relevant to empirical researchers. For this reason, I think that this book can be used as a main textbook, while other more theoretically focused books can serve as supplementary material.

Structure

Each chapter of this book consists of three parts. In the first part, I introduce econometric models with the minimum level of theoretical explanation required for comprehension. In the second part, I illustrate the use of computer software (*EViews* and *SAS*) to estimate the econometric models. Then

I explain how to interpret the computer results. For users of *R* (a free software package for statistical computing), the illustrations are available at the e-Resource Hub for this book. In the final part, I cite excerpts from relevant articles published in top-tier academic journals, using them to exemplify the real-world use cases of these models. The cited articles are from diverse fields, including accounting, economics, finance, marketing and tourism studies. These practical applications make the book an instrumental, go-to guide for solid foundation in the fundamentals of econometrics.

Software packages

To illustrate how to estimate econometric models, I use the following software packages. These companies have kindly permitted me to use the outputs from their software packages:

- *EViews*, IHS Global Inc.
- BASE SAS 9.4, SAS/STAT 13.1 and SAS/ETS 13.1, SAS Institute Inc., Cary, NC
- *R*, a free software environment for statistical computing and graphics.

ACKNOWLEDGMENTS

I started writing this book when I taught courses, Applied Econometrics and Empirical Research Methods, at the School of Accounting and Finance, Hong Kong Polytechnic University. I am grateful to Professor Ferdinand Gul and Professor Judy Tsui who invited me to the university and provided the hospitality for this writing.

I am also grateful to several people who have influenced and encouraged me to write this book: In Choi at Sogang University, Korea; Jeong-Bon Kim at City University of Hong Kong; Jinsoo Lee at Hong Kong Polytechnic University; Lai Lan Mo at City University of Hong Kong; and Deokwoo Nam at Hanyang University, Korea.

I received a great deal of help and suggestions from my colleagues at Hankuk University of Foreign Studies, Korea. I thank Sangmee Bak, KwanghoKim, Giseok Nam, Taek-seon Roh and Yong-jae Choi. Chanyul Park assisted me with text editing and graph drawing.

Finally, but not least important, I would like to thank my family for their endurance and support.

1 Review of estimation and hypothesis tests

Learning objectives

In this chapter, you should learn about:

- Sampling distribution and uncertainty/accuracy of estimators;
- Unbiasedness, consistency and efficiency of estimators;
- p-value and the extent of data evidence against a null hypothesis;
- Interpretation of hypothesis test results.

The goal of testing statistical hypotheses is to determine whether sample information from a population supports a statistical hypothesis postulated, or whether empirical evidence is strong enough to refute a hypothesis. I will use an example to introduce the basic concepts and to illustrate the test procedures.

1.1 The problem

An automobile manufacturer claims that a newly developed model gets at least 28 miles to the gallon. The Environmental Protection Agency (EPA) investigates whether the company is exaggerating the performance of its new model.

1.2 Population and sample

In this problem the **population** is the set of all automobiles produced by the company. In fact, we are interested in the average miles per gallon (MPG) of the population. However, it is practically impossible to test-drive all of the produced automobiles to measure their MPG. Instead, we select a small number of automobiles from the population, called a **sample**, and test-drive the selected automobiles only. Then, using the sample information we make a conclusion about the average MPG of the population; it is called the **statistical inference**.

Suppose that the EPA selected a sample of 49 automobiles of this model and obtained a sample mean of 26.8 miles per gallon. The population standard deviation (σ) is assumed to be 5 miles per gallon from the previous studies.

What conclusion should the EPA make based on the sample information? Because the sample mean is calculated using only a small number (49) of automobiles, it is not equal to the population mean. The population mean is the average MPG of all automobiles produced by the company. However, because the sample is obtained from the population, the sample mean is not far different from the population mean. To make a conclusion, we need to understand how different the sample mean is from the population mean; this is explained in what follows.

1.3 Hypotheses

The hypothesis of 28 MPG, i.e., $\mu = 28$, is called a **null hypothesis**, denoted by H_0. We set up a null hypothesis to test whether empirical evidence is sufficient to refute the null hypothesis.[1] In contrast, the hypothesis of $\mu < 28$ which competes with the null hypothesis, is called the **alternative hypothesis** and is denoted by H_1. In summary, the hypotheses in this example are

$$H_0 : \mu = 28 \quad \text{vs.} \quad H_1 : \mu < 28$$

1.4 Test statistic and its sampling distribution

Since we are interested in the population mean (μ), the sample mean (or the arithmetic mean of sampled observations) is a good **estimator** for μ.[2] Therefore, the sample mean is used for testing the hypotheses and called a **test statistic**.

Now, we predict what values the sample mean will take on when the null hypothesis (here $\mu = 28$) is true. The idea underlying the test procedures is that if the observed sample mean (here $\bar{Y} = 26.8$) is rarely probable when H_0 is true, we could say that the observations do not support H_0, thereby concluding that H_0 is wrong.

To do this, we need to understand the sampling distribution of the test statistic, that is, what values of the sample mean ($\bar{Y}$) will be observed from all possible samples of size 49. Before we implement the experiment, MPG of the 49 automobiles can be expressed using random variables. That is, let a random variable Y_i denote the MPG of the i th-drawn automobile (i = 1, 2, . . ., 49). Depending on which automobile is selected, the MPG value of the i th-drawn automobile can vary with probability. That is why Y_i is called a **random variable**.

The sample mean ($\bar{Y}$), which is the arithmetic average of 49 random variables, is also a random variable because $Y_1, \cdots, Y_{49}$ are random variables.

$$\bar{Y} = \frac{Y_1 + Y_2 + \cdots + Y_{49}}{49}$$

It indicates that the value of $\bar{Y}$ can vary depending on which automobiles are included in a sample. We need to know what values of $\bar{Y}$ can be observed from all possible samples of size 49.

In general, the **Central Limit Theorem** shows that for sufficiently large sample sizes (n), the sample mean $\bar{Y}$ approximately follows a normal distribution with a mean of μ and a variance of σ^2 / n, i.e.,

$$\bar{Y} \sim N\left(\mu, \frac{\sigma^2}{n}\right) \text{ or } Z_n = \frac{\bar{Y} - \mu}{\sigma / \sqrt{n}} \sim N(0,1), \text{ where } \sigma \text{ is the population standard deviation, as displayed}$$

in Figure 1.1.

This distribution is called the **sampling distribution** of $\bar{Y}$ because the values of $\bar{Y}$ obtained from different samples are distributed as such. The standard deviation of the sampling distribution, $\sqrt{\sigma^2 / n}$,

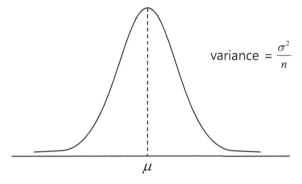

Figure 1.1 Central Limit Theorem: Sampling distribution of $\overline{Y}$

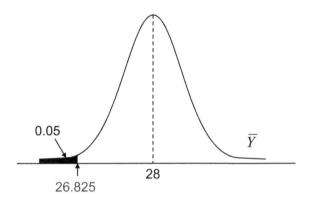

Figure 1.2 Sampling distribution of $\overline{Y}$ when $H_0 : \mu = 28$ is true

is called the **standard error** of $\overline{Y}$. The standard error measures the variability of $\overline{Y}$. With a small standard error, $\overline{Y}$ is likely to be close to μ no matter which sample is used for the calculation of $\overline{Y}$.

Suppose that $H_0 : \mu = 28$ is true. By the Central Limit Theorem, the sampling distribution of $\overline{Y}$ follows a normal distribution of $N\left(28, \frac{5^2}{49}\right)$. Remember that the population standard deviation σ is assumed equal to 5 in this example.

From the normal distribution table, we know that only 5% of all possible samples give sample means smaller than 26.825. Or, 95% or $100 \times (1 - 0.05)\%$ of all possible sample means will be greater than 26.825. Therefore, we may set up the following decision rule:

Reject H_0 if the observed sample mean is less than or equal to 26.825.

Accept H_0 if the observed sample mean is greater than 26.825.[3]

We chose 26.825 for the threshold value of the sample mean. We call this threshold value a **critical value** (denoted by C_α, here $C_{0.05}$, where α is the significance level as defined below). Using this critical value, we can set up a region (or an interval) to reject H_0, which is called a **rejection region**, here { $\bar{Y} \leq 26.825$ }.

1.5 Type I and Type II errors

Although sample means of less than $C_{0.05}$ are less likely to occur when H_0 is true, those small values can still occur with a probability of $\alpha = 0.05$. If that happens, our decision will be incorrect. The following table summarizes possible outcomes.

Decision	Truth	
	H_0 is true	H_1 is true
Keep H_0	Correct decision	*Type II error*
Reject H_0	*Type I error*	Correct decision

1.6 Significance level

In the above hypothesis test, we set up the rejection region such that the tail area is 0.05, i.e., $\Pr(\bar{Y} \leq 26.825) = 0.05$. With this rejection region, we will reject H_0 if an observed sample mean $\bar{Y}$ is smaller than or equal to $C_{0.05} = 26.825$. However, even when $H_0 : \mu = 28$ is true, it is still possible with a probability of 0.05 to observe $\bar{Y}$ values smaller than 26.825, as shown in Figure 1.2. If so, we mistakenly reject H_0. The probability of making this Type I error is called the **significance level** of a test, denoted by α (alpha). We often use $\alpha = 0.1, 0.05$ or 0.01 in testing hypotheses, but of course are not limited to the three levels.

1.7 *p*-value

In the above example, since the observed sample mean ($\bar{Y} = 26.8$) falls in the rejection region, we can reject H_0 at a significance level of $\alpha = 0.05$. However, we can also reject H_0 even at a smaller significance level and therefore provide stronger evidence against H_0.

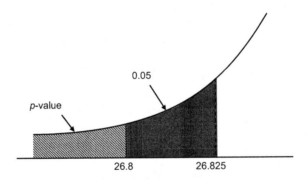

The smallest significance level at which H_0 can be rejected is called the ***p*-value**. It is more informative to report the *p*-value of a test than to say that H_0 is or is not rejected at a certain significance level. Given a *p*-value, we can make a conclusion about the hypotheses at any significance levels. That is,

H_0 can be rejected at significance levels greater than the p-value. In contrast, at any significance levels smaller than the p-value, H_0 is not rejected. For example, the p-value of the above example is 0.0465 as $\Pr(\bar{Y} \leq 26.8) = 0.0465$. It implies that H_0 can be rejected at $\alpha = 0.05$ but cannot be rejected at $\alpha = 0.01$.

The p-value might be interpreted as the extent to which observations are against H_0 or as the probability of making a Type I error when we reject H_0. The smaller the p-value is, the stronger the evidence is against H_0. If a p-value is 0.002, we can reject H_0 with a small probability (0.002) of making a Type I error. However, if a p-value is 0.29, we can still reject H_0 but with a high probability (0.29) of making a Type I error. Thus, any H_0 can be rejected, but the extent of confidence with the rejection is different depending on what level of significance is used (or what the p-value is).

The following explanation will help you understand the conclusion made by a hypothesis test. The observed sample mean $\bar{Y}$ is 26.8 in the above example. If the null hypothesis $H_0 : \mu = 28$ is true, it is very unlikely to observe such small sample mean of 26.8, as indicated by the small p-value of 0.0465. Therefore, we can confidently reject H_0 because the probability of making a Type I error is only 0.0465. In contrast, suppose that the observed sample mean $\bar{Y}$ is 27.5. Since it does not fall in the rejection region at the 5% significance level, we accept or do not reject H_0. The idea is that a sample mean of 27.5 is very likely to be observed when $H_0 : \mu = 28$ is true. However, it does not indicate that $H_0 : \mu = 28$ is true because a sample mean of 27.5 would also be likely to occur when $\mu = 27.8$ or $\mu = 27$. Thus, it is not possible to prove that a certain null hypothesis is true.

The main purpose of using a hypothesis test is to present strong evidence against an argument. Therefore, we set up the argument which we want to reject as the null hypothesis (H_0) and examine whether empirical evidence is sufficient to reject H_0. If we can reject H_0 at a small significance level, it indicates that evidence is very strong against H_0. However, if we cannot reject H_0 at a certain significance level, it indicates that the evidence is not strong enough to reject H_0 and that H_0 has to be kept until stronger evidence against H_0 is found.

1.8 Powerful tests

A hypothesis test is said to be **powerful** if at a chosen level of significance, it has the largest probability of rejecting H_0 when H_1 is true. In other words, by applying a powerful test we can maximize the probability of correctly rejecting H_0 when H_0 is not true. To do it, we need to accordingly set up rejection regions depending on the type of the alternative hypothesis. Below shown are three cases of the alternative hypothesis.

Case I: (one-tailed test)　　$H_0 : \mu = a$　　vs.　　$H_1 : \mu < a$　(a is a constant)

A rejection region is a collection of observed values of a test statistic (here $\bar{Y}$) which support H_1 more than H_0. Under this alternative hypothesis of $H_1 : \mu < a$, small values of $\bar{Y}$ are more likely to occur than large values. Therefore, the rejection region will include small values and thus appear only on the left-hand side tail.

Example 1.1　　$H_0 : \mu = 28$　　vs.　　$H_1 : \mu < 28$

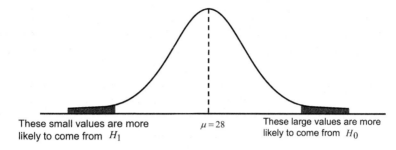

These small values are more likely to come from H_1 $\mu = 28$ These large values are more likely to come from H_0

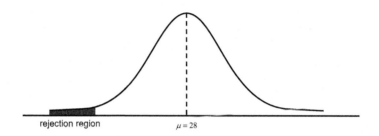

rejection region $\mu = 28$

Case II: (one-tailed test) $H_0 : \mu = a$ vs. $H_1 : \mu > a$

The question is whether an observed value is too large to come from the null hypothesis. Therefore, the rejection region will include large values and thus appear on the right-hand side tail only.

Example 1.2 $H_0 : \mu = 28$ vs. $H_1 : \mu > 28$

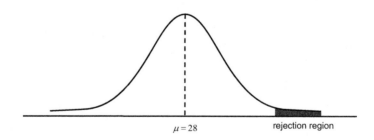

$\mu = 28$ rejection region

Case III: (two-tailed test) $H_0 : \mu = a$ vs. $H_1 : \mu \neq a$

The question is whether an observed value is too much different from a to come from the null hypothesis. Therefore, the rejection region appears both on the left-hand side and on the right-hand side because those values in the shaded area support H_1 more than H_0.

Example 1.3 $H_0 : \mu = 28$ vs. $H_1 : \mu \neq 28$

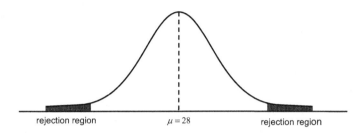

rejection region $\mu = 28$ rejection region

Example 1.4   A manufacturing process is supposed to have a mean of 224 mm. Do the following data give evidence that the true mean of the process is not equal to the target value of 224 mm?

Hypotheses $H_0 : \mu = 224$ vs. $H_1 : \mu \neq 224$

Data: (56 observations)

223 221 224 225 221 223 221 224 225 221
220 201 212 232 240 231 211 215 201 221
224 233 218 219 212 232 212 232 224 222
221 224 231 233 225 226 232 234 235 235
246 231 212 234 224 223 223 222 245 245
244 242 243 245 241 243

Computer output:

sample mean ($\bar{Y}$) = 226.768,
standard deviation (s) = 10.796,
standard error ($s.e. = s / \sqrt{n}$) = 1.443

t-statistic $\left(\dfrac{\bar{Y} - 224}{s.e.} \right) = 1.225$

p-value = 0.0602 for a two-tailed test $\left[= \Pr(|t| \geq 1.225) \right]$

Most computer packages including *EViews*, *SAS* and *R* produce p-values for two-tailed tests, i.e., for testing $H_0 : \mu = 224$ vs. $H_1 : \mu \neq 224$. In some cases, however, we can be sure that the population mean μ is never smaller than 224, but are not sure whether μ is significantly greater than 224. If so, you can make the p-value smaller by applying a one-tailed test, $H_0 : \mu = 224$ vs. $H_1 : \mu > 224$. The

p-value becomes a half of the two-tailed p-value, i.e., 0.0301 ($= 0.0602 \div 2$). You are now able to reject the null hypothesis more strongly (confidently) because the p-value is smaller.

Below is shown how the p-values are calculated. For $H_0 : \mu = 224$ vs. $H_1 : \mu \neq 224$, the p-value of 0.0602 is the sum of the two shaded regions.

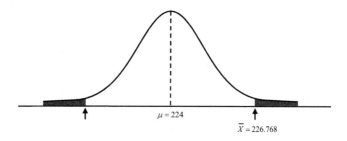

For $H_0 : \mu = 224$ vs. $H_1 : \mu > 224$, the p-value is 0.0301 because this is a one-tailed test.

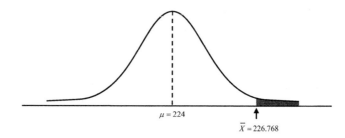

1.9 Properties of estimators

In testing hypotheses about the population mean (μ), we used the sample mean $\overline{Y} = (Y_1 + \cdots + Y_n)/n$ as the test statistic although $\overline{Y}$ is just one estimator out of many possible estimators for μ. However, the choice of $\overline{Y}$ was not made arbitrarily but was based on the theoretical results that $\overline{Y}$ satisfies desirable properties. In this section we introduce those properties.

In order for an estimator to be relatively good, it should have three properties: unbiasedness, efficiency and consistency. The Central Limit Theorem says that sample mean $\overline{Y}$ is centered at the (unknown) population mean μ which is to be estimated. In other words, the expected value of $\overline{Y}$ is equal to μ, $E(\overline{Y}) = \mu$. Then, $\overline{Y}$ is called an **unbiased estimator** for μ. In general, an estimator is defined to be unbiased if its expected value is equal to the parameter to be estimated.

Consider another estimator $A = \dfrac{Y_1 + \cdots + Y_n}{n} + 3$. Since $E(A) = \mu + 3 \neq \mu$, A is biased as shown in Figure 1.3. It implies that this estimator A aims at a wrong value while the sample mean $\overline{Y}$ correctly aims at the value (μ) we want to know. Therefore, it is expected that $\overline{Y}$ produces more accurate information about μ than A does.

There could be many unbiased estimators, though. For example, an estimator $B = (Y_1 + Y_2)/2$ is also unbiased, although it uses only the first two out of the total n observations. For any sample size greater than 2 (i.e., $n > 2$), the variance of $\overline{Y}$ (σ^2/n) is smaller than the one of B ($\sigma^2/2$). As Figure 1.4 shows, the estimator with a smaller variance is expected to provide more accurate information about the population mean.

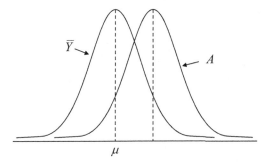

Figure 1.3 Unbiasedness: sampling distributions of $\bar{Y}$ and A

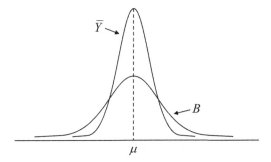

Figure 1.4 Efficiency: sampling distributions of $\bar{Y}$ and B

An estimator is defined to be an **efficient estimator** if it has the smallest variance among unbiased estimators. Thus, $\bar{Y}$ which uses all sampled observations is an efficient estimator for μ. This efficiency is defined for a given size of a sample.

We now consider what will happen to the sampling distribution as the sample size increases. This is called the *asymptotic* or *large sample properties* of estimators. Since the variance of $\bar{Y}$ is σ^2 / n, its variance converges to zero as the sample size n increases to infinity, thereby the sample mean $\bar{Y}$ converging to the population mean μ. That is, as $n \to \infty$, $\sigma^2 / n \to 0$ and therefore $\bar{Y} \to \mu$. Simply, we can say that the probability limit of $\bar{Y}$ is μ, i.e., *plim* $\bar{Y} = \mu$.[4] Therefore, $\bar{Y}$ is said to be a **consistent estimator** for μ, or an *asymptotically unbiased* estimator. It means that sample means $\bar{Y}$ obtained from infinitely many observations will be equal to μ, no matter which samples are drawn.

1.10 Summary

1   The objective of hypothesis test is to reject a null hypothesis at the smallest possible significance level. Failure to reject a null hypothesis does not support that the null is true.

2   In order to use a statistic for testing hypotheses, we need to know the sampling distribution of the statistic from which we can derive critical values and rejection regions for a given level of significance.

3   The *p*-value is the smallest significance level at which H_0 can be rejected. Thus, it is more informative to report the *p*-value of a test than to say that H_0 is or is not rejected at a certain significance level.

4   If an estimator is unbiased and efficient, the estimator is expected to produce the most accurate information about the parameter it estimates.

5   If an estimator is biased but consistent, this should be used with care for small-sized samples. For sufficiently large samples, however, consistent estimators can produce unbiased information about parameters; consistent estimators are asymptotically unbiased.

Review questions

1   (a) Explain what the Central Limit Theorem is.

     (b) Explain why the Central Limit Theorem is required for testing hypotheses.

2   It has been shown that the sample mean ($\bar{Y}$) is an unbiased estimator for the population mean (μ), i.e., $E(\bar{Y}) = \mu$.

     (a) Explain whether the observed value of $\bar{Y}$ is always equal to μ.
     (b) Using the Central Limit Theorem, explain how much the observed value of $\bar{Y}$ is different from (or similar to) μ.

3   In testing hypotheses, the *p*-value is defined as the smallest significance level at which the null hypothesis is rejected. Suppose that you obtained a *p*-value of 0.014 for testing a null hypothesis $H_0 : \beta_1 = 0$ against an alternative hypothesis $H_1 : \beta_1 \neq 0$.

     (a) Make a conclusion about the null hypothesis at a 5% significance level. Also make a conclusion at a 1% significance level.
     (b) If you use a different alternative hypothesis $H_1 : \beta_1 > 0$, what is the *p*-value? Make a conclusion at a 1% significance level.

4   It is said that the hypothesis test procedures have been designed to reject a null hypothesis, but not to accept a null. If a null hypothesis is accepted (or is not rejected), can we conclude that the null is true? Explain.

5   If a null hypothesis of $H_0 : \mu = 28$ is rejected against $H_1 : \mu < 28$, then a null hypothesis of $H_0 : \mu \geq 28$ is always rejected against $H_1 : \mu < 28$. Explain why.

6   It is expected that the most reliable information about a parameter can be obtained from an estimator which is unbiased and efficient. Explain why.

7   An estimator $\bar{Y}$ is a consistent estimator for μ if $plim\bar{Y} = \mu$. Explain why this consistency matters for obtaining accurate information about the parameter μ.

8   It is possible for an estimator to be biased but consistent. What caution do we have to exercise when we use such an estimator?

9   Consider an estimator ($\hat{\mu}$) for the population mean μ. It is known that its sampling distribution follows a normal with mean $\mu + (1/n)$ and variance σ^2 / n, i.e., $\hat{\mu} \sim N\left(\mu + \dfrac{1}{n}, \dfrac{\sigma^2}{n}\right)$.

     (a) Explain whether $\hat{\mu}$ is unbiased.
     (b) Explain whether $\hat{\mu}$ is consistent.

Notes

1 By following the hypothesis test procedures, we are able to present strong evidence which rejects a null hypothesis. However, as explained in what follows, we cannot prove that a null hypothesis

is true. Thus, a hypothesis test is designed to reject a null hypothesis at the smallest possible probability of making an error.

2 An estimator is a formula that assigns a value to each possible outcome of a sample. And the value assigned by an estimator is called an **estimate**. For example, $\bar{Y} = (Y_1 + \cdots + Y_n)/n$ is an estimator for μ and the sample mean 26.8 calculated using the 49 observations is an estimate.

3 Accepting H_0 does not mean that H_0 is true. The given data will not be able to reject other hypotheses (e.g., $\mu = 27.9$) which are slightly different from the null hypothesis. Thus, the hypothesis test is not designed to prove whether a certain null hypothesis is true. Instead, it examines whether empirical evidence is sufficient to reject the null hypothesis. Therefore, instead of "accept H_0," more correct phrases are "fail to reject H_0" or "keep H_0 until we find strong evidence against H_0."

4 Formally, $plim\bar{Y} = \mu$ means that for every $\varepsilon > 0$, $\Pr\left(\left|\bar{Y} - \mu\right| > \varepsilon\right) \to 0$ as $n \to \infty$. This is also called the law of large numbers.

2 Simple linear regression models

> **Learning objectives**
>
> In this chapter, you should learn about:
> - Uses and limitations of simple linear regression models;
> - Estimation of a linear relation between two variables;
> - Assumptions under which the least squares method produces unbiased, consistent and efficient estimators;
> - Linearity in parameters vs. in variables.

2.1 Introduction

2.1.1 A hypothetical example

To understand what the regression models are, we use a hypothetical example. Suppose that there is a small town with a total of 74 households. Since Table 2.1 contains information about all of the households in the town, it is the *population*, not a *sample*. We observe that the annual consumption level in the population is quite different across households in the town: the minimum is \$36,000, the maximum is \$99,000 and the average is \$67,568.

One question of our interest is why their consumption level is so different, in other words, what factors determine the consumption. According to an economic theory, consumption is positively related with income, provided all other factors affecting consumption are held constant. The other factors could be age, location, the number of household members, etc. In this chapter we focus on income only, but will consider other factors as well in the next chapter when multiple regression models are introduced.

Following the consumption theory, we also consider information about their income in addition to their consumption. Table 2.1 indicates that households with higher income tend to consume more than the ones with lower income. To clearly see the relation, we calculate the conditional average of consumption in each income level, i.e., $E(Y|X)$. Figure 2.1 shows a linear relation between income (X) and the conditional average of consumption, $E(Y|X)$.

2.1.2 Population regression line

From the plot in Figure 2.1, the conditional average consumption can be modeled as a linear function of income,

$$E(Y \mid X) = \beta_0 + \beta_1 X \tag{2.1}$$

This line is called the **population regression line** which gives the conditional average of Y (*dependent variable*) corresponding to each value of X (*independent* variable).[1]

In Eq. (2.1), β_0 and β_1 are parameters and are called **regression coefficients**. The slope coefficient β_1 measures the difference in the conditional average of Y per unit difference in X.[2] That is,

$$\beta_1 = \frac{\Delta E(Y \mid X)}{\Delta X}$$

Table 2.1 Consumption and income of all 74 households in a town (unit: $1,000)

Income (X)	50	60	70	80	90	100	110	120
Consumption (Y)	36	46	52	60	67	78	83	94
	37	47	52	61	68	78	86	95
	38	47	53	63	70	80	87	95
	39	48	53	64	72	80	87	95
	40	48	55	64	72	80	88	96
	40	49	56	65	72	81	88	96
	40	49	56	65	73	83	88	96
	42	50	56	66	74		90	98
	43		60	68	75		91	99
	45		61		77		92	
			62					
Number of households	10	8	11	9	10	7	10	9
Conditional average $E(Y\mid X)$	40	48	56	64	72	80	88	96

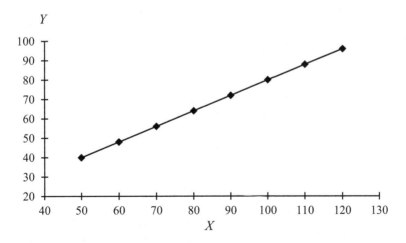

Figure 2.1 Plot of income (X) and the conditional average of consumption $E(Y\mid X)$

In reality, because we cannot observe the population of the 74 households, we will not be able to calculate the conditional averages shown in Table 2.1 and Figure 2.1. In what follows, we will learn how to estimate the regression coefficients β_0 and β_1 when only a part of the population (i.e., a sample) is observed.

2.1.3 Stochastic specification for individuals

Table 2.1 shows that an individual consumption is not necessarily equal to the conditional average corresponding to its income level. In other words, even when households have the same level of income, their consumption could be different. Let's take an example of an income level of 70. According to Table 2.1, there are 11 households whose average consumption is 56. Although the 11 households have the same income, their consumption level varies from 52 to 62. The reason is because other factors than income have affected their consumption.

In order to model for such possible differences in the dependent variable, we add one more term known as the **error term** or **disturbance** (u). For the 74 households in the population, each household's consumption can be expressed as the sum of the conditional average corresponding to its income and an error term.

$$\begin{aligned} Y &= E(Y \mid X) + u \\ &= \beta_0 + \beta_1 X + u \end{aligned}$$

(2.2)

The error term u is a proxy for all omitted variables that may have affected Y but are not (or cannot be) included as independent variables. The variance of u, denoted by $\sigma^2 = Var(u \mid X)$, measures the extent of consumption differences in each income level and thus the uncertainty of the regression relation. A large variance implies that the omitted variables play an important role in determining the dependent variable. In contrast, for an extreme case where the variance is zero, the value of Y has a deterministic relation with X; i.e., the consumption is entirely determined by the income only but nothing else.

There always exist some omitted variables in any model. In the example of the consumption function, there could be a myriad of variables affecting consumption and it is not possible to include all of them in a regression model. Facing the possibility of omitted variables, we need to know whether these omitted variables distort our regression analysis. Since the error term represents the influence of omitted variables, it is natural to examine the error term. The idea is that we extract as much useful information as possible out of the given observations. If we have done it, the error term should not show any systematic pattern at the minimum. Section 2.5 in this chapter explains what is meant by no systematic pattern of the error term.

2.2 Ordinary least squares estimation

If the population is observed, it would be easy to find the population regression line. Using the observations on the population in Table 2.1, we can calculate and connect the conditional averages for various income levels to obtain the population regression line: $E(Y \mid X) = 0 + 0.8X.$[3]

In almost all cases, however, the population itself is not observable. Therefore, we will have to rely on a sample from the population to get information about the regression coefficients β_0 and β_1. Suppose we have randomly selected a sample of 20 households out of the population. An example of sampled observations is shown in Table 2.2 and Figure 2.2; these observations are called *cross-sectional data*.[4] For each observation i (= 1, . . . , 20), the linear regression model is expressed as

$$Y_i = \beta_0 + \beta_1 X_i + u_i$$

(2.3)

Table 2.2 Consumption and income of 20 randomly selected households (unit: $1,000)

No. (i)	Income (X_i)	Consumption (Y_i)	No. (i)	Income (X_i)	Consumption (Y_i)
1	50	39	11	90	67
2	50	42	12	90	70
3	60	47	13	90	72
4	70	53	14	90	75
5	70	55	15	100	78
6	70	56	16	100	81
7	70	61	17	110	87
8	80	61	18	110	88
9	80	64	19	110	91
10	80	68	20	120	95

Filename: 2-cons-sample.xls

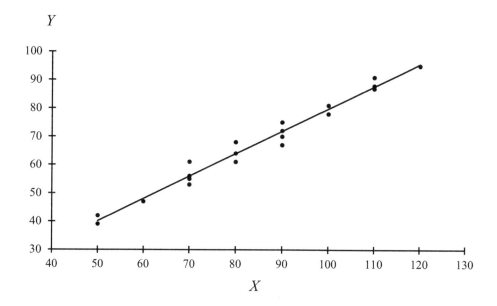

Figure 2.2 Scatterplot of income (*X*) and consumption (*Y*) of the sampled households

Using the sample information, we need to infer the population regression line, more specifically the values of β_0 and β_1. However, it is not possible to draw a straight line which passes through all points in the scatterplot. Alternatively, we look for the line which is *located closest to all points*. The criterion for this is that the line should minimize the sum of the squared residuals; the residual is measured by the vertical distance between an actual value (Y_i) and its fitted value ($\hat{Y}_i$) and is denoted by $\hat{u}_i = Y_i - \hat{Y}_i$ in Figure 2.3.[5] Therefore, this method is called the **ordinary least squares (OLS) method** and the line is called the ordinary least squares (OLS) line. In sum, the OLS method finds $\hat{\beta}_0$ and $\hat{\beta}_1$ which minimize

$$\sum_{i=1}^{n} \hat{u}_i^2 = \sum_{i=1}^{n} \left(Y_i - \hat{Y}_i\right)^2 = \sum_{i=1}^{n} \left\{Y_i - \left(\hat{\beta}_0 + \hat{\beta}_1 X_i\right)\right\}^2 \tag{2.4}$$

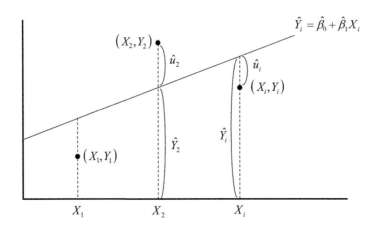

Figure 2.3 Ordinary least squares (OLS) line

By differentiating Eq. (2.4) with respect to $(\hat{\beta}_0, \hat{\beta}_1)$ and setting them to zero, we can derive the following **normal equations**.

$$\sum \left\{ Y_i - \left(\hat{\beta}_0 + \hat{\beta}_1 X_i \right) \right\} = 0$$
$$\sum X_i \times \left\{ Y_i - \left(\hat{\beta}_0 + \hat{\beta}_1 X_i \right) \right\} = 0 \tag{2.5}$$

The solution to Eq. (2.5) is the OLS estimators for β_0 and β_1 :

$$\hat{\beta}_1 = \frac{\sum_{i=1}^{n} \left(X_i - \bar{X} \right) \left(Y_i - \bar{Y} \right)}{\sum_{i=1}^{n} \left(X_i - \bar{X} \right)^2} \tag{2.6}$$

and

$$\hat{\beta}_0 = \bar{Y} - \hat{\beta}_1 \bar{X} \tag{2.7}$$

where the bar over a variable denotes its sample average; $\bar{X} = (1/n) \sum_{i=1}^{n} X_i$ and $\bar{Y} = (1/n) \sum_{i=1}^{n} Y_i = (1/n) \sum_{i=1}^{n} (\beta_0 + \beta_1 X_i + u_i) = \beta_0 + \beta_1 \bar{X} + \bar{u}$. Since $\left(Y_i - \bar{Y} \right) = \beta_1 \left(X_i - \bar{X} \right) + (u_i - \bar{u})$, we can rewrite the OLS estimators as

$$\hat{\beta}_1 = \frac{\beta_1 \sum_{i=1}^{n} \left(X_i - \bar{X} \right)^2}{\sum_{i=1}^{n} \left(X_i - \bar{X} \right)^2} + \frac{\sum_{i=1}^{n} \left(X_i - \bar{X} \right) (u_i - \bar{u})}{\sum_{i=1}^{n} \left(X_i - \bar{X} \right)^2} = \beta_1 + \frac{\sum_{i=1}^{n} \left(X_i - \bar{X} \right) u_i}{\sum_{i=1}^{n} \left(X_i - \bar{X} \right)^2} \tag{2.8}$$

$$\hat{\beta}_0 = \left(\beta_0 + \beta_1 \bar{X} + \bar{u} \right) - \hat{\beta}_1 \bar{X} = \beta_0 + \left(\beta_1 - \hat{\beta}_1 \right) \bar{X} + \bar{u} \tag{2.9}$$

where the last equality in Eq. (2.8) holds because $\sum_{i=1}^{n} \left(X_i - \bar{X} \right) \bar{u} = \bar{u} \sum_{i=1}^{n} \left(X_i - \bar{X} \right) = 0$.

Output 2.1 OLS estimation results: 2-cons-sample.xls

Dependent Variable: Y
Method: Least Squares
Sample: 1 20
Included observations: 20

Variable	Coefficient	Std. Error	t-Statistic	Prob.
C	0.460039	2.547578	0.180579	0.8587
X	0.793372	0.029368	27.01486	0.0000
R-squared	0.975929			

These expressions will be later used to understand the statistical properties of the OLS estimators. However, it is not necessary to memorize the above formula because we can obtain the calculated values of $\hat{\beta}_0$ and $\hat{\beta}_1$ using econometrics computer packages such as *EViews*, *SAS* and *R*. Output 2.1 shows the OLS estimation results obtained using *EViews*.[6] The OLS line is

$$\hat{Y}_i = 0.460039 + 0.793372 X_i$$

The calculated value of an *estimator* is called an *estimate*. The expressions in Eqs. (2.6) and (2.7) are the OLS estimators for β_0 and β_1, and the calculated values of $\hat{\beta}_0 = 0.460039$ and $\hat{\beta}_1 = 0.793372$ are the OLS estimates.

2.3 Coefficient of determination (R^2)

2.3.1 Definition and interpretation of R^2

The value of the dependent variable Y_i can be decomposed into two parts: one is the value predicted by the OLS line ($\hat{Y}_i$), and the other is the residual ($\hat{u}_i = Y_i - \hat{Y}_i$). From $\hat{Y}_i = \hat{\beta}_0 + \hat{\beta}_1 X_i$, the predicted value $\hat{Y}_i$ represents the component in Y_i which is correlated with the independent variable X_i, while the residual $\hat{u}_i$ is the component uncorrelated with (or orthogonal to) X_i. Squaring each component and summing them over all observations, we obtain the following relations[7]:

$$\begin{aligned}
& Y_i = \hat{Y}_i + \hat{u}_i \\
\Rightarrow\ & Y_i - \bar{Y} = \left(\hat{Y}_i - \bar{Y}\right) + \hat{u}_i \\
\Rightarrow\ & \sum\left(Y_i - \bar{Y}\right)^2 = \sum\left(\hat{Y}_i - \bar{Y}\right)^2 + \sum\hat{u}_i^2 \\
\Rightarrow\ & TSS = RSS + ESS
\end{aligned} \tag{2.10}$$

where *TSS* (total sum of squares) measures the total variation in Y_i[8]; *RSS* (regression sum of squares) measures how much of *TSS* is explained by the least squares line; and *ESS* (error sum of squares) represents the unexplained portion in *TSS*.

For an OLS line to be useful in understanding why the values of Y_i vary across observations, its *RSS* should be big enough. The coefficient of determination (R^2) measures the *goodness of fit* of an OLS estimated line.

$$R^2 = \frac{RSS}{TSS}$$

R^2 lies between 0 and 1 and is unit-free.[9] R^2 is the proportion of the total variation in Y explained by the OLS line and thus measures the goodness of fit. If all observations lie on a straight line, the regression model will provide a perfect fit to the data, thereby $R^2 = 1$.

The usefulness of R^2 is somewhat limited, however. Remember that in order to use R^2 as a test statistic, we need to know the sampling distribution of R^2 under a null hypothesis. Since the sampling distribution of R^2 does not follow a standard distribution, particularly in finite samples, R^2 is rarely used for testing hypotheses.

One more thing to note is that when the dependent variables of two regression models are different, it is improper to compare their R^2 values. Consider the consumption example in Table 2.2 where Y is used as the dependent variable. If another model uses the logarithm of Y as its dependent variable, i.e., $\log Y_i = \alpha_0 + \alpha_1 X_i + v_i$, its TSS will be different from the one of the original model $Y_i = \beta_0 + \beta_1 X_i + u_i$. Since the denominators in the R^2 calculation are different, their R^2s are not comparable.

2.3.2 Application of R^2: Morck, Yeung and Yu (2000)

It is believed that stock returns reflect new market-level and firm-level information. The extent to which stocks move together depends on the relative amount of market-level and firm-level information capitalized into stock prices. One widely used *measure of the stock price synchronicity* is the coefficient of determination (R^2) from the following linear regression.

$$RET_{jt} = \alpha_j + \gamma_j RET_{mt} + u_{jt}$$

where RET_{jt} is stock j's return in period t, and RET_{mt} is a market index return. A high R^2 in this regression indicates a high degree of stock price synchronicity because a large proportion of the total variation in RET_{jt} is correlated with the market return RET_{mt} which is common to all stocks in the market. This regression is similar to the classical capital asset pricing model (CAPM). While the CAPM is often used to quantify risk and to translate the risk into an estimate of expected return, the above regression is here used to decompose the types of information contained in stock prices.

Morck et al. (2000) find that stock prices in economies with high per capita gross domestic product (GDP) move in a relatively unsynchronized manner, implied by low R^2 values. In contrast, stock prices in low per capita GDP economies tend to move up or down together, yielding high R^2 values. A time series of R^2 for the US market also shows that the degree of co-movement in US stock prices has declined, more or less steadily, during the 20th century. These observations indicate that the stock price synchronicity declines as an economy develops.

Morck et al. (2000) propose that differences in protection for investors' property rights could explain the connection between economic (or financial) development and the R^2. First, political events and rumors in less developed countries could cause market-wide stock price swings. Second, in countries that provide poorer protection for public investors from corporate insiders, problems such as intercorporate income shifting could make firm-specific information less useful to risk arbitragers, and therefore impede the capitalization of firm-specific information into stock prices. This effect would reduce firm-specific stock price variation, again increasing the stock return synchronicity and thus the R^2.

However, Jin and Myers (2006) point out that imperfect protection for investors does not affect the R^2 if the firm is completely transparent. Some degree of opaqueness (lack of transparency) is essential for the observed pattern of the R^2. Suppose that outside investors can observe only a small part of firm-specific information although they can observe all market-wide public information. This opaqueness allows insiders to exploit firm-specific information for more cash flows. As a result, the firm-specific variance absorbed by outside investors in the stock market will be lower when the opaqueness is more serious. Since macroeconomic information is presumably common knowledge, outside investors can absorb all market risk. Thus, the ratio of market to total risk reflected in the stock prices is increased by opaqueness; the more opaque an economy is, the higher the R^2 is.

2.3.3 Application of R²: Dechow (1994)

Dechow (1994) compares the ability of earnings relative to net cash flows and cash from operations to reflect firm performance. Net cash flows have no accrual adjustments and are hypothesized to suffer severely from timing and matching problems. In contrast, earnings contain accruals that mitigate the timing and matching problems associated with firms' operating, investment and financing cash flows. Therefore, earnings are predicted, on average, to be a more useful measure of firm performance than either cash flow measure (*Hypothesis*). Dechow compares the association of the accounting variables with stock returns (*RET*, the benchmark measure of firm performance), and judges the one with the highest association to be a more useful measure of firm performance.

Employing three simple regression models, Dechow compares their coefficients of determination (R^2) to produce evidence for the hypothesis.

$$R_{it} = \alpha_0 + \alpha_1 E_{it} + u_{it}^E$$
$$R_{it} = \beta_0 + \beta_1 CFO_{it} + u_{it}^{CFO}$$
$$R_{it} = \gamma_0 + \gamma_1 NCF_{it} + u_{it}^{NCF}$$

where R_{it} is the stock return (including dividends) for firm i over time interval t; E_{it} the earnings per share; CFO_{it} the cash from operations per share; and NCF_{it} the change in the balance of the cash account on a per-share basis. These accounting variables are scaled by the beginning-of-period share price. Since the dependent variable is the same in the earnings and cash flows regressions, their R^2 s can measure the relative explanatory ability of earnings and cash flows. The empirical results in Table 2.3 show that the R^2 is larger in regressions including earnings relative to the other regressions including cash flows (*CFO* and *NCF*), supporting the hypothesis.

Table 2.3 Tests comparing the association of earnings and the associations of cash flows with stock returns for a quarterly interval: $R_{it} = \alpha + \beta X_{it} + u_{it}$

	Independent variable (X)		
	Earnings (E)	Cash from operations (CFO)	Net cash flows (NCF)
Intercept (α)	−0.016	−0.008	−0.007
Coefficient (β)	0.742	0.022	0.036
R^2 (%)	3.24	0.01	0.01
		$R_{CFO}^2 / R_E^2 = 0.003$	$R_{NCF}^2 / R_E^2 = 0.003$

Source: Adapted from Dechow (1994, Table 3 on page 22).

2.4 Hypothesis test

2.4.1 Testing $H_0 : \beta_1 = 0$ vs. $H_1 : \beta_1 \neq 0$

In the regression of $Y_i = \beta_0 + \beta_1 X_i + u_i$, the null hypothesis $H_0 : \beta_1 = 0$ implies that X has no relation with Y; in other words, the information on X does not help us understand the variation in Y. The alternative hypothesis $H_1 : \beta_1 \neq 0$ implies that the coefficient for X is different from zero, indicating that X is useful for understanding the variation in Y.

Using the sample of 20 households shown in Table 2.2, we obtained the OLS estimate of $\hat{\beta}_1 = 0.793372$. Someone might ask why we need to test the hypotheses when the OLS estimate $\hat{\beta}_1$ is obviously different from zero. As explained earlier, the population regression line is not observed and the value of β_1 is therefore unknown. Alternatively, we use sample observations to get information about the population regression line (i.e., β_0 and β_1). Since the sample information is not complete but only a part of the population, the OLS estimate $\hat{\beta}_1$ is not guaranteed to be equal to β_1. Depending on which sample is drawn, the value of $\hat{\beta}_1$ would vary. Therefore, we need a logical and scientific test method which can incorporate the uncertainty associated with OLS estimates.

Using the *p*-value

The **p-value** is the smallest significance level at which H_0 can be rejected, as explained in Chapter 1. Therefore, H_0 is rejected at any significance level greater than the p-value, but is not rejected at any significance level smaller than the p-value. For example, a p-value of 0.0465 implies that H_0 can be rejected at $\alpha = 0.05$ but cannot be rejected at $\alpha = 0.01$.[10]

EViews, SAS and R produce p-values for two-sided tests, i.e., for testing $H_0 : \beta_1 = 0$ vs. $H_1 : \beta_1 \neq 0$. When you have a prior information that the coefficient β_1 is not negative (or not positive), you can apply a one-sided test (e.g., $H_1 : \beta_1 > 0$ or $H_1 : \beta_1 < 0$) to get a smaller p-value; the p-value for a one-sided test is half of the p-value for the two-sided test. Remember that the smaller a p-value is, the stronger the evidence is against the null hypothesis $H_0 : \beta_1 = 0$.

In Output 2.1, the p-value for the X coefficient is 0.0000 (shown under a column name "Prob"), indicating that the slope coefficient is significantly different from zero at any significance level larger than the p-value (0.0000). In contrast, the p-value for the intercept is 0.8587, indicating that the intercept may be zero; in other words, the null hypothesis $H_0 : \beta_1 = 0$ is not rejected at a usual significance level of 0.05 or 0.1.

Using the sampling distribution of $\hat{\beta}_1$

For testing hypotheses, it would be enough to use the p-value. However, it is useful to understand how the p-value is calculated, what the sampling distribution of the OLS estimator $\hat{\beta}_1$ is and what the standard error indicates about the accuracy of estimates.[11]

By the Central Limit Theorem, the OLS estimator $\hat{\beta}_1$ is known to follow a normal distribution of mean β_1 and variance $Var\left(\hat{\beta}_1\right) = \sigma^2 / \sum_{i=1}^{n} \left(X_i - \bar{X}\right)^2$, where σ is the standard deviation of the error term u_i, $\sigma = \sqrt{Var\left(u_i | X_i\right)}$, as displayed in Figure 2.4.

$$\hat{\beta}_1 \sim N\left[\beta_1, Var\left(\hat{\beta}_1\right)\right] \quad \Rightarrow \quad \frac{\hat{\beta}_1 - \beta_1}{\sqrt{Var(\hat{\beta}_1)}} \sim N(0,1)$$

The denominator $\sqrt{Var(\hat{\beta}_1)} = \sigma / \sqrt{\sum_{i=1}^{n}(X_i - \bar{X})^2}$ is called the **standard error (s.e.)** of $\hat{\beta}_1$, Since the population standard deviation of the error term (σ) is unknown in most cases, we substitute for σ a sample estimate $\hat{\sigma} = \sqrt{\sum(Y_i - \hat{Y}_i)^2 / (n-2)} = \sqrt{ESS / (n-2)}$ to obtain the following t-statistic which follows a t distribution with $n-2$ degrees of freedom, as displayed in Figure 2.5, where *ESS* is the error sum of squares, the unexplained variation in Y_i.[12]

$$t = \frac{\hat{\beta}_1 - \beta_1}{se(\hat{\beta}_1)} \sim t_{n-2}$$

The denominator is an estimate of the standard error of $\hat{\beta}_1$ which uses a sample estimate $\hat{\sigma}$ for σ, i.e., $se(\hat{\beta}_1) = \hat{\sigma} / \sqrt{\sum_{i=1}^{n}(X_i - \bar{X})^2}$. This standard error measures the accuracy of the sample estimate $\hat{\beta}_1$. [13] A small standard error indicates that the estimate $\hat{\beta}_1$ is likely to be close to β_1.

If $H_0 : \beta_1 = 0$ is true, then the ratio $t = \frac{\hat{\beta}_2 - 0}{se(\hat{\beta}_1)} = \frac{\hat{\beta}_2}{se(\hat{\beta}_1)}$ should follow a t distribution. You may refer to any statistics book about how to find a rejection region using a t table. However, when you conduct research, you don't need to use a t table because all computer packages for econometric analysis produce standard errors, t-statistics and p-values, along with coefficient estimates.

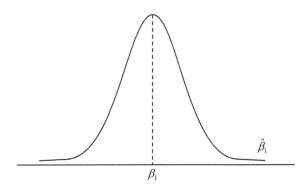

Figure 2.4 Sampling distribution of $\hat{\beta}_1$

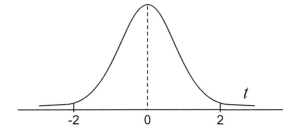

Figure 2.5 Distribution of the t-statistic

The OLS estimation results in Output 2.1 show that the standard error for $\hat{\beta}_1$ is 0.029368 and the t-statistic is 27.01486 (= 0.793372/0.029368).[14] Since the p-value is the significance level when the observed t-statistic is used as a critical value, the p-value is calculated as $\Pr[t \geq 27.01486]$ plus $\Pr[t \leq -27.01486]$, which is 0.0000. Therefore, we can reject the null hypothesis $H_0 : \beta_1 = 0$ and conclude that the slope coefficient β_1 is significantly different from zero. Similarly, the standard error for $\hat{\beta}_0$ is 2.547578 and the t-statistic is 0.1805789 (= 0.460039 / 2.547578). The p-value is calculated as $\Pr[|t| \geq 0.1805789] = 0.8587$, implying that the intercept is insignificant at a usual significance level of 0.1 or 0.05.

The above testing procedure can be understood in terms of confidence interval. When we infer about the unknown value of β_1, we often allow for sample variation and construct a confidence interval, e.g., $\left[\hat{\beta}_1 - 2 \times se(\hat{\beta}_1), \ \hat{\beta}_1 + 2 \times se(\hat{\beta}_1)\right]$ for the 95% confidence level. The uncertainty (or accuracy) associated with a sample estimate $\hat{\beta}_1$ is measured by its standard error. If the standard error is large, the estimate $\hat{\beta}_1$ is considered little reliable, thereby leading to a wide interval for β_1 to satisfy a given confidence level. In contrast, as a small standard error indicates that the estimate $\hat{\beta}_1$ is relatively accurate, a tight interval can satisfy the given confidence level. Related to the hypothesis testing, if the confidence interval does not include 0, we can reject the null hypothesis of $H_0 : \beta_1 = 0$.

2.4.2 Testing $H_0 : \beta_1 = c$ vs. $H_1 : \beta_1 \neq c$ (c is a constant)

Suppose that we test $H_0 : \beta_1 = 1$ against $H_1 : \beta_1 \neq 1$. If the null hypothesis is true, the sampling distribution of $\hat{\beta}_1$ is $t = \dfrac{\hat{\beta}_1 - 1}{s.e.} \sim t_{n-2}$. So, we need to calculate the p-value associated with the t-statistic of $\dfrac{\hat{\beta}_1 - 1}{s.e.}$. However, the computer output from the OLS estimation function gives the t-statistic and the p-value only for the case of $H_0 : \beta_1 = 0$, i.e., $t = \dfrac{\hat{\beta}_1}{s.e.}$. For general types of a null hypothesis (e.g., $H_0 : \beta_2 = 1$), you need to follow one more step in computer packages such as *EViews*, *SAS* and *R*. See "Appendix 2 How to Use *EViews*, *SAS* and *R*."

2.5 The model

Until now, we have used the OLS method to estimate and test for regression coefficients. It means that we have implicitly assumed that for a given regression model, the OLS estimator is most desirable among all possible estimators. In this section, we explain under what assumptions the OLS estimator is unbiased, efficient and consistent.

2.5.1 Key assumptions

These assumptions are about the disturbance (u_i) in a simple linear regression. The idea is that the disturbance should not show any systematic pattern in their relation with themselves and with the independent variable X.

The population linear regression model relates a dependent variable Y to an independent variable X.

$$Y = \beta_0 + \beta_1 X + u$$

To estimate the parameters (β_0, β_1), we use data on Y and X. For each sample observation i $(= 1, \cdots, n)$, the linear regression model explains the determination of Y_i.

$$Y_i = \beta_0 + \beta_1 X_i + u_i$$

[Assumption I] Zero conditional mean $E(u_i | X_i) = 0$ for all i

This assumption, called the *zero conditional mean assumption*, requires that the conditional (on X_i) average of each disturbance u_i be equal to zero. This means that the Y_i values corresponding to each value of X_i are distributed around the conditional mean, $E(Y_i | X_i) = \beta_0 + \beta_1 X_i$. If $u_i > 0$, the Y value is greater than its conditional mean; if $u_i < 0$, the Y value is smaller than its conditional mean.

If this assumption is satisfied, the conditional expected value of u_i is not a function of the independent variable. In other words, the independent variable X_i is not correlated with u_i and is called an *exogenous* explanatory variable.[15] If $E(u_i | X_i) = f(X_i) \neq 0$, then X_i is correlated with u_i and is called an *endogenous* explanatory variable.[16]

Unbiasedness

The value of an OLS estimator $\hat{\beta}_1$ can vary depending on which observations are included in a sample. The distribution of all possible values is called the sampling distribution of $\hat{\beta}_1$. If the average of all possible $\hat{\beta}_1$ values (or the expected value of $\hat{\beta}_1$) is equal to β_1, i.e., $E(\hat{\beta}_1) = \beta_1$, then $\hat{\beta}_1$ is said to be *unbiased* and is expected to provide fair information about the unknown parameter β_1.

For the OLS estimators to be unbiased, Assumption I has to be satisfied. Taking the expectation of the OLS estimators in Eqs. (2.8) and (2.9), we can show that $\hat{\beta}_0$ and $\hat{\beta}_1$ are unbiased.

$$E(\hat{\beta}_1) = \beta_1 + \frac{\sum_{i=1}^{n}(X_i - \bar{X})E(u_i)}{\sum_{i=1}^{n}(X_i - \bar{X})^2} = \beta_1 \tag{2.11}$$

$$E(\hat{\beta}_0) = \beta_0 + \left\{\beta_1 - E(\hat{\beta}_1)\right\} \cdot \bar{X} + E(\bar{u}) = \beta_0 \tag{2.12}$$

Notice that if the conditional expected values, $E(u_i | X_i)$, are equal to zero, then their unconditional expected values, $E(u_i)$, are equal to zero. Then $E(\bar{u}) = \frac{1}{n} E(u_1 + \cdots + u_n) = 0$ in Eq. (2.12). From Eq. (2.8), the variance of $\hat{\beta}_1$ is

$$Var(\hat{\beta}_1) = E(\hat{\beta}_1 - \beta_1)^2 = \frac{E\left[\sum_{i=1}^{n}(X_i - \bar{X})u_i\right]^2}{\left[\sum_{i=1}^{n}(X_i - \bar{X})^2\right]^2}$$

$$= \frac{\sum_{i=1}^{n}(X_i - \bar{X})^2 E(u_i^2) + \sum_{i=1}^{n}\sum_{j \neq i}(X_i - \bar{X})(X_j - \bar{X})E(u_i u_j)}{\left[\sum_{i=1}^{n}(X_i - \bar{X})^2\right]^2}$$

$$= \frac{\displaystyle\sum_{i=1}^{n}\left(X_i - \bar{X}\right)^2 E\left(u_i^2\right)}{\left[\displaystyle\sum_{i=1}^{n}\left(X_i - \bar{X}\right)^2\right]^2} = \frac{\sigma^2}{\displaystyle\sum_{i=1}^{n}\left(X_i - \bar{X}\right)^2}$$

where $E\left(u_i u_j\right) = 0$ because Assumption III to be introduced below indicates that $Cov\left(u_i, u_j\right) = E\left[\left\{u_i - E\left(u_i\right)\right\}\left\{u_j - E\left(u_j\right)\right\}\right] = E(u_i u_j) = 0$.

Strict exogeneity

The theoretically correct expression of Assumption I is that $E\left(u_i \mid X_1, \cdots, X_n\right) = 0$; the expectation is conditioned on all observed values of the explanatory variable. If so, the conditional expected value of u_i is not a function of the explanatory variable in every observational unit. We say that such explanatory variable is **strictly exogenous**.

If observations are independently collected (e.g., random sampling as in most cross-sectional data), then u_i will be independent of X_j for all $j \neq i$ (all observations other than the one from the same unit). In such case, the zero conditional mean assumption (Assumption I) may be conditioned on X_i only, i.e., $E\left(u_i \mid X_i\right) = 0$. That is why $E\left(u_i \mid X_i\right) = 0$ is sufficient for proving that the OLS estimators are unbiased, as shown above. For many time-series data, however, observations are correlated between time periods and violate the strict exogeneity assumption. In such cases, even when $E\left(u_t \mid X_t\right) = 0$, it is possible that $E\left(u_t \mid X_{t+1}\right) \neq 0$ and the OLS estimators are therefore biased; this topic is later explained in Chapter 10.

[Assumption II] Homoscedasticity: $Var\left(u_i \mid X_i\right) = \sigma^2$ for all i

This assumption of *homoscedasticity*, or equal variance, means that the dependent variable Y corresponding to various X values has the same variance (Figure 2.6). In other words, $Var\left(u_i \mid X_i\right) = \sigma^2$ implies $Var\left(Y_i \mid X_i\right) = \sigma^2$. If so, for all values of X, the Y observations are considered equally reliable because they are distributed around the conditional means with the same variance (i.e., with the same extent of being close to the means).

In contrast, the case of *heteroscedasticity*, or unequal variance, can be expressed as $Var\left(u_i \mid X_i\right) = \sigma_i^2$. Suppose that $Var\left(u_1 \mid X_1\right) < Var\left(u_2 \mid X_2\right) < \cdots < Var\left(u_n \mid X_n\right)$ as in Figure 2.7. If so, it is likely that the Y observations with $X = X_1$ tend to be closer to the population regression line than those with $X = X_2$, indicating that the Y observations with $X = X_1$ provide more reliable information on the population regression line than other observations with larger variances. Thus, when we extract information about the population regression line, it is desirable to apply higher weights to the observations with $X = X_1$ than to observations with larger variances.

The OLS method treats all observations equally by minimizing the *unweighted* sum of squared residuals. Therefore, only under the assumption of homoscedasticity, the OLS method will be valid; in other words, the OLS estimator is efficient. However, if the disturbance is heteroscedastic, then the OLS estimator is not efficient and we need to use other estimation methods which account for heteroscedastic disturbance; estimation methods for this case are explained in Chapter 5.

[Assumption III] No correlation between the disturbances:

$$Cov\left(u_i, u_j\right) = 0 \text{ for any } i \neq j$$

This assumption requires that the disturbances should not be correlated among them. If this assumption is violated, the OLS estimator is not efficient and can be biased for some cases.

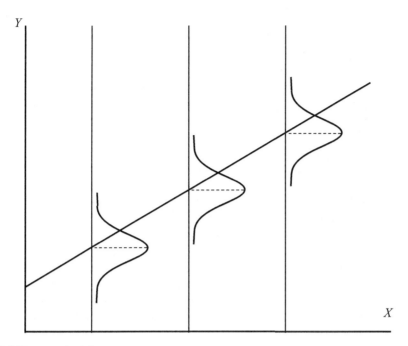

Figure 2.6 Homoscedasticity

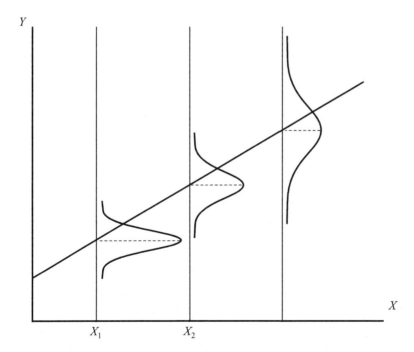

Figure 2.7 Heteroscedasticity

2.5.2 Gauss-Markov Theorem

When the above assumptions are satisfied, the OLS estimator is BLUE (Best Linear Unbiased Estimators). This means that the OLS estimator, which minimizes the unweighted sum of squared residuals, has the minimum variance among the linear unbiased estimators. On the other hand, it implies that if any one of the assumptions is not satisfied, the OLS estimator will be no longer BLUE. If so, we should look for better estimation methods. In the following chapters, we will introduce several cases where some of the assumptions are violated and suggest estimation methods appropriate for those cases. Now let us study about the BLUE in more detail.

i   *Linear*: The OLS estimator is linear functions of Y_i (or u_i), as shown in Eqs. (2.6)–(2.9). In other words, the OLS estimator is calculated by Y_i in a linear form.

ii   *Unbiased*: As shown above, $E\left(\hat{\beta}_0\right) = \beta_0$ and $E\left(\hat{\beta}_1\right) = \beta_1$. This unbiasedness requires Assumption I, i.e., the zero conditional mean assumption.

iii *Best*: It means that the OLS estimator $\hat{\beta}_1$ has the minimum variance among the linear unbiased estimators.[17] We know that the value of $\hat{\beta}_1$ can vary depending on which sample is selected. The variance of $\hat{\beta}_1$ measures the variability of its possible values around β_1. The smaller the variance of $\hat{\beta}_1$ is, the closer to β_1 the possible values of $\hat{\beta}_1$ are likely to be. Since we want to know the unknown β_1 value, we'd better use the estimator with the smallest sampling variance. It has been proven that if Assumptions II and III are satisfied, the OLS estimators $\hat{\beta}_0$ and $\hat{\beta}_1$ have the smallest variances among all of the linear unbiased estimators. Thus, Assumptions II and III are required for the efficiency of the OLS estimators.[18]

2.5.3 Consistency of the OLS estimators

In order to examine the unbiasedness of an estimator, we need to evaluate its expected value. In many cases, however, it is not possible to obtain the expected values of estimators for finite samples. The above linear regression model is one of relatively few settings in which the unbiasedness of the OLS estimator is well understood. For more general cases, we will examine the consistency rather than the unbiasedness.

The consistency is defined for sufficiently large samples as it checks whether an estimator converges to the true value of a parameter, in other words, whether it is *asymptotically unbiased*. In contrast, the unbiasedness is defined for any sample size and depends on whether the expected value of an estimator is equal to the true parameter value. If an estimator is unbiased and therefore consistent, it can be safely used for any sample size. If an estimator is biased but consistent, however, this estimator can be used safely for sufficiently large samples but with care for small-sized samples.

For the OLS estimator to be consistent, the following assumption needs to be satisfied.

[Assumption IV] No correlation between X_i and u_i

$$Cov\left(X_i, u_i\right) = 0 \text{ for all } i$$

This assumption of *no correlation* indicates that the explanatory variable X_i is linearly uncorrelated with the disturbance u_i. If this assumption is satisfied, the OLS estimator becomes consistent. Otherwise, X_i is endogenous and the OLS estimator is inconsistent; the proof will be given in Chapter 6.

For cross-sectional data whose observations are independently collected, this no-correlation within the same unit is sufficient for the consistency of the OLS estimator because $Cov(X_j, u_i) = 0$ for all $j \neq i$. For time-series data, this contemporaneous no-correlation, $Cov(X_t, u_t) = 0$, is also sufficient for the consistency of the OLS estimator if $\{X_t\}$ and $\{u_t\}$ are *asymptotically uncorrelated*, i.e., $Cov(X_{t+h}, u_t) \to 0$ and $Cov(X_{t-h}, u_t) \to 0$ as h increases to infinity; this is explained in Chapter 10. Therefore, in what follows, we will focus on Assumption IV to examine whether an estimator is consistent or not.

Assumption IV implies that X_i is *linearly* uncorrelated with u_i but Assumption I implies a stronger condition that *any function* of X_i is uncorrelated with u_i for all i.[19] Thus, this assumption of no correlation is weaker than the assumption of zero conditional mean (Assumption I); in other words, Assumption IV is always satisfied if Assumption I is satisfied, but not vice versa.[20] If an estimator is unbiased, it is always consistent. But, a consistent estimator could be biased for small-sized samples although it is asymptotically unbiased (that is, becomes unbiased as the sample size increases to infinity).

2.5.4 *Remarks on model specification*

When the above assumptions are satisfied, the OLS estimator is unbiased (thus consistent) and efficient. However, it does not imply that the given model itself is a good one. For example, certain regression models can satisfy the assumptions even when the models do not include some significant variables. If it is the case, the empirical results can be improved by including those omitted significant variables. Thus, the satisfaction of the assumptions is a necessary (but not sufficient) condition for a model to be good enough.

The question is how to find good models. An answer is that good models should include all variables which are suggested as important factors theoretically or empirically by previous studies. In this process, the selection of determining factors for a dependent variable can be quite subjective. A practical approach to model selection, called a "General-to-Simple" approach, is explained and illustrated in the next chapter.

2.6 Functional forms

Since we have estimated a regression line only, the linear regression model appears to be limited to linear relations. Even when it is not linear in variables, however, the linear regression model can be employed as long as the relation is *linear in parameters*. As an example, consider a model which includes the square of X_i as an independent variable:

$$Y_i = \beta_0 + \beta_1 X_i^2 + u_i$$

It is obviously nonlinear in X_i. However, if we treat X_i^2 as a new variable, say $Z_i = X_i^2$, then it becomes a linear regression:

$$Y_i = \beta_0 + \beta_1 Z_i + u_i$$

In general, by treating any variant of a variable as a new variable, we can estimate the relation using a regression line as long as it is linear in parameters.

Example 2.1 Do the following fit in the linear regression model?

---

a $Y_i = e^{\beta_0 + \beta_1 X_i + u_i}$

b $\ln Y_i = \gamma_0 + \gamma_1 \left(\dfrac{1}{X_i} \right) + u_i$

c $\ln Y_i = \beta_0 + \beta_1^{\beta_2} X_i + u_i$

d $Y_i = \beta_0 + (\beta_0 - 1) \beta_1 X_i + u_i$

[Answers]

a Taking the natural logarithm on both sides, we can obtain a simple linear (in parameters) model:
   $\ln Y_i = \beta_0 + \beta_1 X_i + u_i$

b $Y_i^* = \gamma_0 + \gamma_1 X_i^* + u_i$ This is linear in parameters.

c This is not linear in parameters because $\beta_1^{\beta_2}$ is not linear.

d This is not linear in parameters because of $(\beta_0 - 1) \beta_1$.

Some functional forms provide useful interpretation of their regression coefficients. Below are examples which are widely used in empirical studies.

2.6.1 Log-log linear models

Let us consider a demand function which relates the amount demanded (Q_i) of a good to its price (P_i). To measure the price elasticity of demand, the following log-log linear model is employed:

$$\ln Q_i = \beta_0 + \beta_1 \ln P_i + u_i \tag{2.13}$$

where ln denotes the natural logarithm, e.g., $\ln P_i = \log_e P_i$. The slope coefficient β_1 in Eq. (2.13) measures the change in the conditional average of $\ln Q$ per unit change in $\ln P$.

$$\beta_1 = \frac{\Delta \ln Q}{\Delta \ln P} \approx \frac{\dfrac{\Delta Q}{Q} \times 100}{\dfrac{\Delta P}{P} \times 100} = \frac{\% \text{ change in } Q}{\% \text{ change in } P}$$

Therefore, the slope coefficient β_1 measures the price elasticity of demand. In the above derivation, an approximate relation of $\Delta \ln Q \approx \Delta Q / Q$ is used, which is based on $\dfrac{d \ln Q}{dQ} = \dfrac{1}{Q}$. Notice that this approximation is valid only for a small change in Q; this approximation becomes more inaccurate as the change in Q becomes larger.

The logarithmic transformation cannot be used if a variable takes on zero or negative values. In cases where a variable x is non-negative but takes on the value of zero for a few observations, $\ln(1 + x)$ is sometimes used.[21] As $\Delta \ln(1 + x) = \Delta(1 + x) / (1 + x) = \Delta x / (1 + x) \approx \Delta x / x$, the interpretation as a percentage change is acceptable for large values of x. In cases where a variable can be negative, the following symmetric transformation would work: $\ln(1 + x)$ for $x \geq 0$ and $\ln(1 - x)$ for $x < 0$ (Michaud and van Soest, 2008).

Example 2.2 An Excel file '2-demand.xls' contains 10 observations about price (P) and demand (Q).

	A	B	C
1	No.	P	Q
2	1	100	73
3	2	105	71
4	3	106	70
5	4	109	62
6	5	110	59
7	6	115	67
8	7	117	59
9	8	119	65
10	9	120	63
11	10	122	61

In *EViews* we import this Excel file by choosing File/Open/Foreign Data as Workfile. . . . Once you follow the steps, the variable names will be shown in the Workfile window. To create new variables for their logarithmic values, press the Genr button on the workfile toolbar and enter "LNQ=LOG(Q)." The logarithmic values of the Q observations will be saved under a new name of "LNQ." Do the same for the observations on P. In order to estimate the demand function Eq. (2.13), click on Object/New Object/Equation and type "LNQ C LNP" in the Equation specification.

The OLS results in Output 2.2 show that the price elasticity of demand is $\hat{\beta}_1 = -0.783282$, implying that the demand decreases by 0.783282% for a 1% increase in the price.

Output 2.2 OLS estimation results: 2-demand.xls

Dependent Variable: LNQ
Method: Least Squares
Sample: 1 10
Included observations: 10

Variable	Coefficient	Std. Error	t-Statistic	Prob.
C	7.868171	1.440553	5.461909	0.0006
LNP	−0.783282	0.305226	−2.566240	0.0333

R-squared	0.451513	Mean dependent var		4.171693
Adjusted R-squared	0.382952	S.D. dependent var		0.077179
S.E. of regression	0.060626	Akaike info criterion		−2.591330
Sum squared resid	0.029404	Schwarz criterion		−2.530813
Log likelihood	14.95665	F-statistic		6.585587
Durbin-Watson stat	2.180613	Prob(F-statistic)		0.033322

2.6.2 Log-linear models

For data collected over time t, i.e., time-series data, the natural logarithm of Y_t can be related to time period t:

$$\ln Y_t = \gamma_0 + \gamma_1 t + u_t \qquad (2.14)$$

Then, the slope coefficient γ_1 in Eq. (2.14) measures the change in the conditional average of $\ln Y_t$ per period:

$$\gamma_1 = \frac{\Delta \ln Y_t}{\Delta t} \approx \frac{\Delta Y_t / Y_{t-1}}{1} = \text{growth rate of } Y_t$$

Since the unit change of the denominator is 1, the slope coefficient γ_1 represents the growth rate of Y_t.

Again, this interpretation is based on the approximation of $\Delta \ln Y_t \approx \Delta Y_t / Y_{t-1}$, which is valid only for a small change in Y. For large changes, the following exact relation can be used to calculate accurate growth rates.

$$\gamma_1 \Delta t = \Delta \ln Y_t = \ln Y_t - \ln Y_{t-1} = \ln\left(\frac{Y_t}{Y_{t-1}}\right)$$

$$\Rightarrow \frac{Y_t}{Y_{t-1}} = \exp(\gamma_1 \Delta t)$$

$$\Rightarrow \frac{Y_t - Y_{t-1}}{Y_{t-1}} = \frac{Y_t}{Y_{t-1}} - 1 = \exp(\gamma_1 \Delta t) - 1$$

$$\Rightarrow \%\Delta Y = 100 \times \left[\exp(\gamma_1 \Delta t) - 1\right]$$

Example 2.3   Consider the following annual time series of Y_t (2-growth.xls)

	A	B
1	t	Y
2	1995	123
3	1996	145
4	1997	150
5	1998	144
6	1999	147
7	2000	158
8	2001	163
9	2002	165
10	2003	168
11	2004	173
12	2005	171

After importing the Excel file, we create a new variable for the logarithmic values. Press the Genr button on the Workfile toolbar and enter "LNY=LOG(Y)." Once we type "LNY C T" in the Equation specification window, we obtain the OLS results shown in Output 2.3. The estimate for the slope coefficient is 0.027902, implying that the value of Y has increased approximately at an average rate of 0.027902, i.e., 2.79% per year. The exact growth rate is $100 \times [\exp(0.027902) - 1] = 2.8293\%$.

Output 2.3   OLS estimation results: 2-growth.xls

Dependent Variable: LNY
Method: Least Squares
Sample: 1995 2005
Included observations: 11

Variable	Coefficient	Std. Error	t-Statistic	Prob.
C	−50.76346	8.160203	−6.220858	0.0002
T	0.027902	0.004080	6.838509	0.0001
R-squared	0.838609	Mean dependent var		5.040092
Adjusted R-squared	0.820677	S.D. dependent var		0.101053
S.E. of regression	0.042792	Akaike info criterion		−3.301946
Sum squared resid	0.016481	Schwarz criterion		−3.229602
Log likelihood	20.16070	F-statistic		46.76521
Durbin-Watson stat	1.660314	Prob(F-statistic)		0.000076

2.7 Effects of changing measurement units and levels

This section is to show that the significance of regression relation is not affected merely by changing measurement units. This is intuitively accepted; if the significance changes when different measurement units are used, we will not be able to arrive at any conclusion. Thus R^2, t-ratio and p-value are unchanged when we change the measurement units of variables. In contrast, coefficient estimates and their standard errors are affected in their decimal points only.[22] Often, we change the measurement units to improve the appearance of estimation results, for example, to reduce the number of zeros after a decimal point in coefficient estimates.

2.7.1 Changes of measurement units

Using the data measured in the \$1,000 unit (Table 2.2), we obtained the following results (Output 2.1):

OLS line $\hat{Y}_i = 0.460039 + 0.793372 X_i$
$R^2 = 0.975929$
For $H_0 : \beta_0 = 0$, the t-statistic = 0.180579 and the p-value = 0.8587
For $H_0 : \beta_1 = 0$, the t-statistic = 27.01486 and the p-value = 0.0000.

To see the effects of changing measurement units, let us estimate the model using the \$1 unit. Output 2.4 shows the OLS estimation results using new variables $X_i^* (= X_i \times 1000)$ and $Y_i^* (= Y_i \times 1000)$, measured in the \$1 unit.

Output 2.4   OLS estimation results when the $1 unit is used.

Dependent Variable: Y_STAR
Method: Least Squares
Sample: 1 20
Included observations: 20

Variable	Coefficient	Std. Error	t-Statistic	Prob.
C	460.0390	2547.578	0.180579	0.8587
X_STAR	0.793372	0.029368	27.01486	0.0000

R-squared	0.975929	Mean dependent var	67500.00
Adjusted R-squared	0.974592	S.D. dependent var	16162.01
S.E. of regression	2576.194	Akaike info criterion	18.64065
Sum squared resid	1.19E + 08	Schwarz criterion	18.74023
Log likelihood	−184.4065	F-statistic	729.8027
Durbin-Watson stat	2.541867	Prob(F-statistic)	0.000000

We can see that all quantities are not affected, except the intercept estimate and its standard error.[23] It is natural to have R^2, t-statistics and p-values unchanged because any changes in the measurement units do not alter the relation between the dependent and independent variables.

Let us use a general case to see the effects of changing measurement units. The OLS line in the original unit is

$$Y_i = \hat{\beta}_0 + \hat{\beta}_1 X_i + \hat{u}_i \tag{2.15}$$

When we change measurement units, the OLS line can be expressed in terms of new variables X_i^* and Y_i^*:

$$Y_i^* = \hat{\alpha}_0 + \hat{\alpha}_1 X_i^* + \hat{u}_i^* \tag{2.16}$$

where

$$X_i^* = c_x X_i \text{ and } Y_i^* = c_y Y_i \tag{2.17}$$

To see the relation between the regression coefficients, we plug Eq. (2.17) into Eq. (2.16) and obtain the following:

$$Y_i = \hat{\alpha}_0 \left(\frac{1}{c_y} \right) + \hat{\alpha}_1 \left(\frac{c_x}{c_y} \right) X_i + \hat{u}_i^* \left(\frac{1}{c_y} \right) \tag{2.18}$$

Comparing the coefficients in Eq. (2.18) with the ones in Eq. (2.15), we have

$$\hat{\beta}_0 = \hat{\alpha}_0 \cdot \left(\frac{1}{c_y} \right) \text{ and } \hat{\beta}_1 = \hat{\alpha}_1 \cdot \left(\frac{c_x}{c_y} \right)$$

Thus, the coefficients in the new measurement units will be

$$\hat{\alpha}_0 = \hat{\beta}_0 \cdot c_y \text{ and } \hat{\alpha}_1 = \hat{\beta}_1 \cdot \left(\frac{c_y}{c_x}\right)$$

In the above case of changing units from \$1,000 to \$1, the scaling factors c_x and c_y are 1,000. Now, we can see why the intercept estimate 460.039 in the new measurement units is equal to the estimate in the \$1,000 unit multiplied by 1,000, i.e., $0.460039 \times 1,000$. For the slope coefficient, the multiplying factor is 1 ($= c_y / c_x = 1000 / 1000$), leaving the estimate unchanged.

The coefficient of determination R^2 is the ratio of *RSS* and *TSS*. If we change the measurement unit of the dependent variable, it will affect *RSS* and *TSS* in the same way. For example, by changing the unit from \$1,000 to \$1, both *RSS* and *TSS* will be multiplied by 1000^2. Since the multiplying factor is canceled out, the value of R^2 will remain unchanged.

Concerning the effects on the *t*-statistic and the *p*-value, we can intuitively understand why they are not affected by any changes in the measurement units. Theoretically, the *t*-statistic is the ratio of a coefficient estimate and its standard error, $t = \hat{\beta} / s.e.$ Since $\hat{\beta}$ and *s.e.* are affected in the same way, the *t*-statistic is unchanged, thereby the *p*-value also being unchanged.

2.7.2 Changes in the levels

Suppose we change the levels of *Y* and *X* in Eq. (2.15) as follows:

$$Y_i^0 = \hat{\theta}_0 + \hat{\theta}_1 X_i^0 + \hat{u}_i^0 \tag{2.19}$$

where

$$X_i^0 = X_i + d_x \quad and \quad Y_i^0 = Y_i + d_y \tag{2.20}$$

Substituting Eq. (2.20) for Eq. (2.19), we obtain

$$Y_i = \left(\hat{\theta}_0 - d_y + \hat{\theta}_1 d_x\right) + \hat{\theta}_1 X_i + \hat{u}_i^0 \tag{2.21}$$

Comparison of Eq. (2.21) with Eq. (2.15) yields the following relations:

$$\hat{\beta}_0 = \hat{\theta}_0 - d_y + \hat{\theta}_1 d_x \text{ and } \hat{\beta}_1 = \hat{\theta}_1$$

Changes in the level affect intercept estimates, but not slope coefficients. Intuitively, we can understand that any changes in the levels of *Y* and *X* should not affect the R^2, *t*-statistic nor *p*-value.

2.8 Summary

1   A linear regression model is an approximation to the true relationship between variables. It is designed to identify the determinants of a (dependent) variable of our interest.
2   Parameters of a regression model are estimated by the ordinary least squares (OLS) method because the OLS estimator is unbiased, efficient and consistent under certain assumptions.

3   When we test hypotheses about a regression coefficient β_i, we need to consider the variability of a sample estimate $\hat{\beta}_i$ which is measured by its standard error, $se(\hat{\beta}_i)$. Following the Central Limit Theorem, we base the test on the t-statistic $[= \hat{\beta}_i / se(\hat{\beta}_i)]$ and the p-value.

4   The OLS estimation can be applied to any models which are linear in parameters. The variables in the models may be in any functional forms, such as logarithmic, quadratic, cross product, etc. In such cases, the regression coefficients need to be interpreted accordingly.

5   Changes of measurement units do not affect the fundamental relation between variables; R^2, t-ratio and p-value are unchanged. Thus, the significance of variables will remain unchanged.

Review questions

1   In estimating a simple linear regression relation $Y = \beta_0 + \beta_1 X + u$, we look for the line which is located closest to all points. Explain how to implement this idea.

2   According the Central Limit Theorem, the OLS estimator ($\hat{\beta}_1$) approximately follows a normal distribution for sufficiently large sample sizes, i.e., $\hat{\beta}_1 \sim N\left(\beta_1, \dfrac{\sigma^2}{\sum (X_i - \bar{X})^2}\right)$, given that Assumption I in the text is satisfied, i.e., $E(u_i | X_i) = 0$ for all i.

Explain whether $\hat{\beta}_1$ is unbiased and consistent.

3   Using the following simple regression model, we are going to show that X is a determining factor for Y.

$$Y_i = \beta_0 + \beta_1 X_i + u_i$$

(a)   Write the null and alternative hypotheses.

(b)   Explain the test procedures.

(c)   Instead of following the test procedures, we may use computer software to obtain statistics such as the p-value. Explain how we can conclude about the null hypothesis based on the p-value.

(d)   The coefficient of determination (R^2) measures the proportion of the total variation in Y explained by the model and thus a measure of the goodness of fit. However, this measure (R^2) is rarely used to test whether X is a significant factor for Y.

Explain why.

4   One widely used measure of *the stock price synchronicity* is the coefficient of determination (R^2) from the following simple linear regression.

$$RET_{jt} = \alpha_j + \beta_j RET_{mt} + u_{jt}$$

where RET_{jt} is stock j's return in period t, and RET_{mt} is a market index return.

(a)   Explain what R^2 measures.

(b)   Explain how the R^2 in the above regression can measure the stock price synchronicity.

5   A data file (2-insurance.xls) contains information about the amount insured and the family income for a sample of households. Answer the following questions using *EViews*.

Y (the amount insured, $1,000)	X (family income, $1,000)
10	43
20	74
50	80
90	95
125	110
135	130

(a) Find the ordinary least squares line $\hat{Y}_i = \hat{\beta}_0 + \hat{\beta}_1 X_i$ using *EViews*.

(b) What is the coefficient of determination (R^2) for the data? Interpret the calculated R^2.

(c) According to the ordinary least squares line, how much is the difference in the conditional average of Y when the independent variable X is different by one unit (i.e., $1,000)?

(d) Calculate the following (approximate) 95% confidence interval for the slope coefficient:

$$\left[\hat{\beta}_1 - 2 \times (standard\ error),\ \hat{\beta}_1 + 2 \times (standard\ error) \right]$$

This confidence interval allows for the uncertainty associated with the OLS estimate $\hat{\beta}_1$. Does the confidence interval include 0?

(e) Calculate the *t*-ratio, $t = \hat{\beta}_1 / s.e.$

(f) At the significance level of 0.05, test the following hypotheses using the *p*-value.

$H_0 : \beta_1 = 0 \qquad H_a : \beta_1 \neq 0$

(g) Is the OLS estimate of β_1 different from zero? If so, why do we bother to test whether $\beta_1 = 0$ or not?

6   We have data on the per capita income observed in year 1990 ($INC90_i$) and the per capita income observed in year 1980 ($INC80_i$) for state i in the US. The following shows a part of the observations.

State	INC90	INC80
AZ	25.2	20.1
IL	31.1	29.2
MA	39.2	34.1
NY	40.5	35.0

(unit: $1,000)

Suppose that the US government had implemented a policy to reduce the income gap between states over the 10-year period. To evaluate the effectiveness of the policy, we employ a regression model

$$INC90_i = \beta_0 + \beta_1 INC80_i + u_i$$

(a) Interpret the meaning of the slope coefficient β_1.

(b) What does $\beta_1 = 1$ imply?

(c) What does $\beta_1 > 1$ imply?

(d) What does $\beta_1 < 1$ imply?

(e) If we use the above model to evaluate the effectiveness of the policy, what are the null and alternative hypotheses?

7   Interpret what is measured by the regression coefficient β_1 in the following models.

(a) $\ln Y_i = \beta_0 + \beta_1 X_i + u_i$

(b) $Y_i = \beta_0 + \beta_1 \ln X_i + u_i$

(c) $\ln Y_i = \beta_0 + \beta_1 \ln X_i + u_i$

(d) $(Unemp_t) = \beta_0 + \beta_1 \ln(M_t) + u_t$

where $Unemp_t$ = unemployment rate, and M_t = money supply in period t.

(e) $\ln(Unemp_t) = \beta_0 + \beta_1 \ln(M_t) + \varepsilon_t$

8   The Gauss-Markov Theorem says that the OLS estimator is unbiased and efficient if the assumptions listed in text are satisfied.

(a)   Explain why we care about the unbiasedness and efficiency.

(b)   Explain when the OLS estimator becomes biased.

(c)   Explain when the OLS estimator becomes inefficient.

(d)   Explain when the OLS estimator becomes inconsistent.

9   Answer the following questions using the data file "2-cons-sample.xls" shown in Table 2.2. The observations are measured in the $1,000 unit.

(a)   Reestimate the model after changing the measurement unit to $1 for consumption ($Y$) only. Explain what happens to the coefficient estimates, the t-statistics, the p-values and R^2.

(b)   Reestimate the model after changing the measurement unit to $1 for income ($X$) only. Explain what happens to the coefficient estimates, the t-statistics, the p-values and R^2.

(c)   Reestimate the model after changing the measurement unit to $1 for consumption ($Y$) and income ($X$). Explain what happens to the coefficient estimates, the t-statistics, the p-values and R^2.

(d)   Suppose that the income data include a lump-sum tax of $2,000. The regression model should relate the consumption to the disposable income, X-2:

$$Y_i = \alpha_0 + \alpha_1(X_i - 2) + u_i$$

Estimate the above new model. What happens to the coefficient estimates, the t-statistics, the p-values and R^2 ?

Notes

1   The variable on the left-hand side is called a dependent or response variable. And the variables on the right-hand side are called independent, explanatory or regressor variables.

2   For certain types of data, such as time-series data, it is more appropriate to interpret the slope coefficient in terms of *change* rather than *difference*. In such applications we can say that β_1 measures the change in the conditional average of Y per unit change in X.

3   The intercept of the consumption function represents the subsistence level, the minimum consumption level needed to survive even when there is no income. Therefore, a positive intercept would make more sense. In this illustration, however, we intentionally set the intercept to zero for simplicity.

4   There are three types of data. (i) *Cross-sectional data* consist of a sample of households, firms, countries or other observational units which are taken during the same period of time. The stock returns of the companies listed in the NYSE during year 2018 are cross-sectional data. (ii) *Time-series data* are observations collected at a number of points in time from the same observational unit. An example is a set of observations on the annual stock return of Apple Inc. from year 1990 until 2018. (iii) *Cross-section and time-series data* have both cross-sectional and time-series features. An example is a set of observations on annual stock returns of the companies listed in the NYSE for the period from 1990 until 2018. To express these types of data, we usually use a subscript i for cross-sectional data, t for time-series data, and it for cross-sectional and time-series data.

5 We denote an estimator by putting a hat for its corresponding parameter. For example, estimators for β_0 and β_1 are denoted by $\hat{\beta}_0$ and $\hat{\beta}_1$, respectively. The OLS fitted (or predicted) values of the dependent variable are also denoted with a hat, $\hat{Y}_i = \hat{\beta}_0 + \hat{\beta}_1 X_i$; this equation is from the OLS regression line.

6 Appendix 2 in this chapter explains how to use *EViews*, *SAS* and *R* for the OLS estimation.

7 The third line in Eq. (2.10) holds because the cross product term $\sum_{i=1}^{n}(\hat{Y}_i - \bar{Y})\hat{u}_i$ is always equal to zero.

8 Another widely used measure of the total variation is the variance which is defined as $TSS/(n-1)$. The values of both measures will be larger when observed values of Y_i are more different. For example, *TSS* is 0 for observations $\{2, 2, 2\}$ since there is no variation in them. For observations $\{1, 2, 3\}$, *TSS* is $2 = (1-2)^2 + (2-2)^2 + (3-2)^2$, and for observations $\{0, 2, 4\}$, it increases to $8 = (0-2)^2 + (2-2)^2 + (4-2)^2$. Thus, *TSS* is proportional to the total variation in data and can be used as a measure of the variation.

9 The coefficient of determination R^2 is the ratio of *RSS* and *TSS*. If we change the measurement unit of the dependent variable, it will affect *RSS* and *TSS* in the same way. For example, by changing the measurement unit from \$1,000 to \$1, both *RSS* and *TSS* will be multiplied by 1000^2. Since the multiplying factors are canceled out, the value of R^2 remains unchanged.

10 When the null of $H_0: \beta_1 = 0$ is rejected at a significance level of $\alpha = 0.05$, we conclude that the coefficient for X_1 (β_1) is *significantly* (at $\alpha = 0.05$) different from zero. Since we never know the true value of β_1, we cannot make a strong statement that β_1 is different from zero. The significance level indicates that the conclusion could be wrong at the probability of $\alpha = 0.05$.

11 What is explained about the slope coefficient (β_1 and $\hat{\beta}_1$) in what follows can be applied to the intercept (β_0 and $\hat{\beta}_0$) in the same way. For simplicity, we will here discuss about the slope coefficient only.

12 The t distribution is bell-shaped and symmetric at zero (Figure 2.5). Roughly speaking, if the degree of freedom is large enough, only 5% of the possible t values are larger than 2 or smaller than -2. The degree of freedom comes from the sample estimate $\hat{\sigma} = \sqrt{\sum(Y_i - \hat{Y}_i)^2 / (n-2)}$. A general form of its denominator inside the square root is $(n - k)$, where n is the total number of observations and k is the number of coefficients to be estimated (β_0 and β_1, so $k = 2$). Thus, the degree of freedom for the t-statistic is $(n - 2)$ in this simple regression. The degree of freedom can be understood as the effective number of independent observations.

13 This standard error has a similarity to the one for the sample mean $\bar{X}$ in Chapter 1, which is $\hat{\sigma}/\sqrt{n}$. Thus, the standard error of $\hat{\beta}_1$ also converges to zero because the denominator $\sqrt{\sum_{i=1}^{n}(X_i - \bar{X})^2}$ increases to infinity as the sample size (n) increases to infinity. Since the standard error converges to zero, the OLS estimator is therefore consistent, i.e., *plim* $\hat{\beta}_1 \rightarrow \beta_1$.

14 For large degrees of freedom, the critical values for the 5% significance level are approximately 2 and -2. Since the observed t-statistic is 27.01486, much larger than the critical value, the null hypothesis $H_0: \beta_1 = 0$ is rejected.

15 If $E(u_i|X_i) \neq 0$ but is constant over i, then it does not violate Assumption I. When $E(u_i|X_i) = c$, the regression model can be rewritten as $Y_i = (\beta_0 + c) + \beta_1 X_i + (u_i - c) = \beta_0^* + \beta_1 X_i + u_i^*$. Then the nonzero mean is merged into the intercept and the new disturbance will satisfy the zero conditional mean assumption, i.e., $E(u_i^*|X_i) = 0$.

16 The terms "endogenous" and "exogenous" originated in economic modeling and simultaneous equation analysis. In econometrics, these terms are used to define whether an explanatory variable is correlated or uncorrelated with the disturbance.

17 If an unbiased estimator has the minimum variance among all possible unbiased estimators, we say that the estimator is *efficient* or *best*, as defined in Chapter 1.

18 If data are collected by random sampling, i.e., *independently and identically* from a population, they will satisfy Assumptions II and III.

19 It is possible that $Cov(X_i, u_i) = 0$ but X_i^2 is correlated with u_i, $Cov(X_i^2, u_i) \neq 0$.

20 Assumption IV does not mean that the explanatory variable is exogenous because Assumption IV is a weaker condition than Assumption I. If Assumption IV is violated, it indicates that the explanatory variable is endogenous.

21 The percentage change is not defined at 0. If there are many observations which take on 0, it is suggested to use different models such as the Tobit and censored regression models; these are explained in Chapter 12.

22 Since a coefficient estimate and its standard error are affected in the same way from using different measurement units, their ratio $t = \hat{\beta}/s.e.$, i.e., the t ratio remains unchanged.

23 Since the intercept estimate and its standard error are affected in the same way, i.e., multiplied by 1,000, its t- and p-values are unchanged.

References

Dechow, P.M. (1994), "Accounting Earnings and Cash Flows as Measures of Firm Performance: The Role of Accounting Accruals," *Journal of Accounting and Economics*, 18, 3–42.

Jin, L., and S.C. Myers (2006), "R^2 Around the World: New Theory and New Tests," *Journal of Financial Economics*, 79, 257–292.

Michaud, P. and A. van Soest (2008), "Health and Wealth of Elderly Couples: Causality Tests Using Dynamic Panel Data Models," *Journal of Health Economics*, 27, 1312–1325.

Morck, R., B. Yeung and W. Yu (2000), "The Information Content of Stock Markets: Why Do Emerging Markets Have Synchronous Stock Price Movements?" *Journal of Financial Economics*, 58, 215–260.

Appendix 2 How to use *EViews, SAS* and *R*

In this illustration we import the following Excel file (2-cons-sample.xls) which contains 20 observations on consumption (Y) and income (X).

	A	B	C
1	No	Y (consumption)	X (income)
2	1	39	50
3	2	42	50
4	3	47	60
5	4	53	70
6	5	55	70
7	6	56	70
8	7	61	70
9	8	61	80
10	9	64	80
11	10	68	80
12	11	67	90
13	12	70	90
14	13	72	90
15	14	75	90
16	15	78	100
17	16	81	100
18	17	87	110
19	18	88	110
20	19	91	110
21	20	95	120

Using *EViews*[1]

To import this Excel file, use File/Open/Foreign Data as Workfile . . . and locate the Excel file. Once you follow the steps, the variable names will be shown in the Workfile window; refer to the *EViews* manuals for detailed explanation.

To estimate a regression model, $Y = \beta_0 + \beta_1 X + u$ where Y = consumption and X = income, you need to specify the model. Choose Objects/New Object. . . /Equation. In the Equation specification, enter the dependent variable followed by an intercept and independent variables, i.e., "Y C X." The intercept (β_0) is entered as C between the dependent and independent variables. Click OK and you will obtain the OLS estimation results as in Output 2.5.

Output 2.5   OLS estimation results: 2-cons-sample.xls

Dependent Variable: Y
Method: Least Squares
Sample: 1 20
Included observations: 20

Variable	Coefficient	Std. Error	t-Statistic	Prob.
C	0.460039	2.547578	0.180579	0.8587
X	0.793372	0.029368	27.01486	0.0000

R-squared	0.975929	Mean dependent var	67.50000
Adjusted R-squared	0.974592	S.D. dependent var	16.16201
S.E. of regression	2.576194	Akaike info criterion	4.825143
Sum squared resid	119.4620	Schwarz criterion	4.924716
Log likelihood	−46.25143	F-statistic	729.8027
Durbin-Watson stat	2.541867	Prob(F-statistic)	0.000000

To test a null hypothesis $H_0 : \beta_1 = 1$, choose View/Coefficient Diagnostics/Wald Test-Coefficient Restrictions. . . . After then, type in the null hypothesis "C(2)=1" in the given space. Note that the intercept β_0 is denoted by C(1) and the second parameter β_1 is by C(2) in *EViews*. As shown in Output 2.6, the *p*-value for the null hypothesis $H_0 : \beta_1 = 1$ is 0.000000.[2] Therefore, we can reject H_0 and conclude that β_1 is significantly different from 1.

Output 2.6　Test results

Wald Test:
Equation: Untitled

Test Statistic	Value	df	Probability
F-statistic	49.50264	(1, 18)	0.0000
Chi-square	49.50264	1	0.0000

Using *SAS*[3]

In order to read in an Excel file, you need to keep the Excel file open and run the following *SAS* code.

```
FILENAME f1 DDE 'EXCEL|[2-cons-sample.XLS]sample!R2C2:R21C3';
TITLE '< EXAMPLE 2-cons-sample.xls >';
DATA cons; INFILE f1;      INPUT consumption income;
TITLE2 '===== SIMPLE REGRESSION =====';
PROC REG DATA=cons;
    MODEL consumption = income;
    TEST income =1; /***** To test if its coefficient =1 *****/
RUN;
```

Below is the *SAS* Output.

< EXAMPLE 2-cons-sample.xls >　　　　　　　　1
===== SIMPLE REGRESSION =====

The REG Procedure
Model: MODEL1
Dependent Variable: consumption

Number of Observations Read	20
Number of Observations Used	20

Analysis of Variance

Source	DF	Sum of Squares	Mean Square	F Value	Pr > F
Model	1	4843.53801	4843.53801	729.80	<.0001

Error	18	119.46199	6.63678	
Corrected Total	19	4963.00000		

Root MSE	2.57619	R-Square	0.9759
Dependent Mean	67.50000	Adj R-Sq	0.9746
Coeff Var	3.81658		

Parameter Estimates

Variable	DF	Parameter Estimate	Standard Error	t Value	Pr > |t|
Intercept	1	0.46004	2.54758	0.18	0.8587
income	1	0.79337	0.02937	27.01	<.0001

Test 1 Results for Dependent Variable consumption

Source	DF	Mean Square	F Value	Pr > F
Numerator	1	328.53801	49.50	<.0001
Denominator	18	6.63678		

Using R[4]

```
> dataset <- read.csv("d:/data/2-cons-sample.csv")
> fm <- lm(Consumption ~ Income, data=dataset)
> summary(fm)
Call:
lm(formula = Consumption ~ Income, data = dataset)

Residuals:
   Min      1Q   Median     3Q     Max
-4.8635 -1.2958 -0.3304 1.3699 5.0039

Coefficients:
            Estimate Std.   Error   t value   Pr(>|t|)
(Intercept)  0.46004       2.54758  0.181     0.859
Income       0.79337       0.02937  27.015    5.09e-16 ***
---
Signif. codes:  0 '***' 0.001 '**' 0.01 '*' 0.05 '.' 0.1 ' ' 1

Residual standard error: 2.576 on 18 degrees of freedom
Multiple R-squared: 0.9759,   Adjusted R-squared: 0.9746
F-statistic: 729.8 on 1 and 18 DF,  p-value: 5.086e-16
```

```
> confint(fm, level=0.95)
                   2.5 %       97.5 %
(Intercept)    -4.8922246    5.8123026
Income          0.7316725    0.8550722
```

Notes

1 IHS Global Inc. has kindly permitted me to use *EViews* output in this book. *EViews* Student Version Lite can be downloaded from the *EViews* website. Manuals are also available at the website.

2 Output 2.6 shows the *p*-values from two test methods which use *F*- and *Chi*-square statistics, respectively. You may use either one as they produce almost the same results.

3 BASE SAS 9.4 and SAS/STAT 13.1. SAS Institute Inc., Cary, NC.

4 *R* is a free language and environment for statistical computing by *R* Core Team, *R* Foundation for Statistical Computing, Vienna, Austria. *R* version 3.5.1 2018. *R* and its manuals can be downloaded from www.r-project.org. The illustrations of the use of *R* in the next chapters are available at the e-Resource Hub for this book.

3 Multiple linear regression models

Learning objectives

In this chapter, you should learn about:

- Differences between the multiple and the simple linear regression models;
- Net effects and confounding effects;
- Estimation bias due to correlated-omitted variables;
- Model selection by the General-to-Simple approach.

In the previous chapter we have learned what the simple linear regression model is, how the regression coefficients are estimated and under what assumptions the OLS estimator is BLUE (best linear unbiased estimator). In the consumption-income example in Chapter 2, consumption has been related only to income assuming that all other factors affecting consumption are held constant.

However, if other factors such as age, location and the number of household members are different between households, their consumption could differ even for the same income level. As consumption is influenced by many factors, it is not correct to relate all the difference in consumption to the difference in income only. Thus, although our interest is in the relation between consumption and income, we should also include other variables to control for their possible confounding effects with the income variable. In this chapter we study why the simple regression model might produce biased estimates and how the multiple regression model can correct the bias.

3.1 The basic model

The conditional average of the dependent variable Y is expressed as a linear function of several variables, $X_1, X_2, \cdots, X_k$:

$$E\left(Y \mid X_1, X_2, \cdots, X_k\right) = \beta_0 + \beta_1 X_1 + \beta_2 X_2 + \cdots + \beta_k X_k \tag{3.1}$$

This is called the **population regression function**.[1] Parameters $\left(\beta_0, \beta_1, \cdots, \beta_k\right)$ are called the **regression coefficients**.

Like the simple linear regression model, individual values of Y are not necessarily equal to their corresponding conditional averages. In order to model for possible differences in the dependent variable, we add an error term (or disturbance). For the i-th observation, the Y_i value is modeled as the sum of its conditional average and an error term.

$$Y_i = E\left(Y_i \mid X_{1i}, X_{2i}, \cdots, X_{ki} \right) + u_i$$
$$= \beta_0 + \beta_1 X_{1i} + \beta_2 X_{2i} + \cdots + \beta_k X_{ki} + u_i$$

The error term u_i is a proxy for the effects of all omitted variables that may determine Y_i but are not (or cannot be) included as explanatory variables.

For the above regression model to be good enough, its error term should not show any systematic pattern at the minimum. The following are the assumptions which the error term is required to satisfy. As shown in the previous chapter, the OLS estimator will be unbiased, consistent and efficient if these assumptions are satisfied.

[Assumption I] unbiasedness

$$E\left(u_i \mid X_{1i}, \cdots, X_{ki} \right) = 0 \text{ for all } i$$

This assumption, called the *zero conditional mean assumption*, requires that the conditional (on $X_{1i}, \cdots, X_{ki}$) average of each disturbance u_i be equal to zero, implying that the conditional expected value of u_i is not a function of the independent variables. In other words, the independent variables have no relation with u_i and are called *exogenous* explanatory variables. If this assumption is not satisfied, for example, $E\left(u_i \mid X_{1i}, \cdots, X_{ki} \right) = f\left(X_{1i} \right) \neq 0$, then X_{1i} is correlated with u_i and called an *endogenous* explanatory variable. As proven in Chapter 2, Assumption I guarantees that the OLS estimator is unbiased, i.e., $E\left(\hat{\beta}_j \mid X_1, \cdots, X_k \right) = \beta_j$ for $j = 1, \ldots, k$.

[Assumption II] efficiency

$$Var\left(u_i \mid X_{1i}, \cdots, X_{ki} \right) = \sigma^2 \text{ for all } i$$

This assumption of *homoscedasticity*, or equal variance, means that the dependent variable Y corresponding to various values of $X_{1i}, \cdots, X_{ki}$ has the same variance. In other words, $Var\left(u_i \mid X_{1i}, \cdots, X_{ki} \right) = \sigma^2$ implies $Var\left(Y_i \mid X_{1i}, \cdots, X_{ki} \right) = \sigma^2$. If so, for any values of $X_1, \cdots, X_k$, the Y observations are equally reliable because they are distributed around the conditional mean with the same variance (i.e., with the same extent of being close to the conditional mean).

In contrast, the case of *heteroscedasticity*, or unequal variance, can be expressed as $Var\left(u_i \mid X_{1i}, \cdots, X_{ki} \right) = \sigma_i^2$. As explained in Chapter 2, it is desirable to apply different weights to the observations according to their variances. As the OLS estimation is based on unweighted minimization, they are efficient only under the assumption of homoscedasticity. The issues related to heteroscedasticity will be discussed in Chapter 5.

[Assumption III] efficiency and unbiasedness

$$Cov\left(u_i, u_j \right) = 0 \text{ for any } i \neq j$$

This assumption requires that the disturbances should not be correlated among them. If this assumption is violated, the OLS estimator is not efficient. In some cases such as autocorrelated disturbances of a time-series regression model, the OLS estimator can be biased; this is explained in Chapter 10.

The Gauss-Markov Theorem in Chapter 2 proves that the OLS estimator is BLUE (best linear unbiased estimators) if the above assumptions are satisfied. For the OLS consistency, the regression model has to satisfy the following assumption which is weaker than Assumption I.

[Assumption IV] consistency

$$Cov\left(u_i, X_{pi} \right) = 0 \quad \text{for all } i \text{ and } p = 1, \cdots, k$$

This assumption of *no correlation* indicates that the explanatory variables $X_{1i}, \cdots, X_{ki}$ are *linearly* uncorrelated with the disturbance u_i. If this assumption is satisfied, the OLS estimator becomes consistent. Otherwise, X_{pi} is correlated with u_i and called an *endogenous* explanatory variable. The OLS estimator is inconsistent (also biased) if there exist at least one endogenous explanatory variables.

3.2 Ordinary least squares estimation

3.2.1 Obtaining the OLS estimates

The OLS estimation method finds $\hat{\beta}_0, \hat{\beta}_1, \cdots, \hat{\beta}_k$ which minimize the sum of squared residuals

$$\sum_{i=1}^{n} \hat{u}_i^2 = \sum_{i=1}^{n} \left(Y_i - \hat{Y}_i \right)^2$$
$$= \sum_{i=1}^{n} \left\{ Y_i - \left(\hat{\beta}_0 + \hat{\beta}_1 X_{1i} + \cdots + \hat{\beta}_k X_{ki} \right) \right\}^2$$

The solution for $\hat{\beta}$ can be derived by calculus, but it is not necessary to memorize the formula for $\hat{\beta}$ because we can obtain OLS estimates using econometrics computer packages including *EViews*, *SAS* and *R*.

Table 3.1 Excel data file: 3-consumption.xls (unit: $1,000)

	A	B	C	D	E
	No	Y	X1	X2	X3
1		(consumption)	(income)	(# of members)	(age)
2					
3	1	39	50	1	29
4	2	42	50	1	31
5	3	47	60	2	30
6	4	53	70	2	42
7	5	55	70	3	38
8	6	56	70	3	42
9	7	61	70	4	51
10	8	61	80	3	50
11	9	64	80	4	39
12	10	68	80	4	46
13	11	67	90	3	39
14	12	70	90	4	57
15	13	72	90	4	51
16	14	75	90	4	49
17	15	78	100	4	49
18	16	81	100	3	41
19	17	87	110	4	35
20	18	88	110	4	46
21	19	91	110	4	40
22	20	95	120	5	51

Let us revisit the consumption-income example in Chapter 2. To consider the effects of other variables, we now add information about the number of household members and the age of household head. Table 3.1 shows an Excel data file (3-consumption.xls).

Using *EViews*, we type "Y C X1 X2 X3" in the Equation specification window and can obtain the OLS estimation results as shown in Output 3.1. The OLS regression function is

$$\hat{Y}_i = 3.802 + 0.712X_{1i} + 2.289X_{2i} - 0.094X_{3i} \tag{3.2}$$

Output 3.1 OLS estimation results: 3-consumption.xls

Dependent Variable: Y
Method: Least Squares
Sample: 1 20
Included observations: 20

Variable	Coefficient	Std. Error	t-Statistic	Prob.
C	3.802054	3.915689	0.970980	0.3460
X1	0.711965	0.047973	14.84105	0.0000
X2	2.289399	1.128464	2.028775	0.0595
X3	-0.093881	0.105058	-0.893611	0.3848

R-squared	0.981115	Mean dependent var	67.50000
Adjusted R-squared	0.977574	S.D. dependent var	16.16201
S.E. of regression	2.420325	Akaike info criterion	4.782537
Sum squared resid	93.72757	Schwarz criterion	4.981684
Log likelihood	-43.82537	F-statistic	277.0738
Durbin-Watson stat	2.473608	Prob(F-statistic)	0.000000

3.2.2 Interpretation of regression coefficients

The simple linear regression model considered in Chapter 2 relates consumption (Y) to income (X_1) only, thereby attributing the entire difference in Y to the difference in X_1. It is because this simple regression model ignores other factors including the number of household members (X_2) and age (X_3). However, a part of the difference in Y might have been caused by the difference in X_2 and X_3. As an example, consider the second and third households in Table 3.1. The simple regression model estimates that their consumption difference of $5,000 has been caused entirely by their income difference of $10,000. However, this is not correct because the two households are different in the number of household members (1 vs. 2) and the age (31 vs. 30).

In order to correctly estimate the *net* effect of X_1 on Y, we need to hold the other factors of X_2 and X_3 constant. Since the other factors are not under our control in most cases, it is not possible to hold their values constant. Fortunately, the net effect of X_1 on Y can be estimated using a multiple linear regression model which includes X_2 and X_3 as explanatory variables.

The regression coefficients in multiple regression models are often called *partial* regression coefficients. The meaning of partial regression coefficients is: β_1 measures the *difference (or change)* in the conditional mean of Y per one unit difference (or change) in X_1, holding the values of the other variables $X_2, \cdots, X_k$ constant.[2] Put differently, it gives the *net* effect of a unit difference in X_1 on the conditional mean of Y, net of any effects that $X_2, \cdots, X_k$ may have on Y. In general, $\beta_p \left(p = 1, \cdots, k \right)$ measures the difference in the conditional mean of Y per one unit difference in X_p, holding the others constant.[3]

In Eq. (3.2), the coefficient estimate for X_1 is 0.712, meaning that the average consumption increases by \$712 when income increases by \$1,000, holding X_2 and X_3 constant. The coefficient estimate for X_2 is 2.289, indicating that each addition of one more household member is, on average, associated with a higher consumption of \$2,289, holding X_1 and X_3 constant.

3.3 Estimation bias due to correlated-omitted variables

Suppose that X_2 is a significant determinant for Y (therefore, $\beta_2 \neq 0$) and that the following regression is considered as the true model. Then, β_1 measures the net effect of X_1, controlling for the confounding effect of X_2.

$$Y = \beta_0 + \beta_1 X_1 + \beta_2 X_2 + u \qquad \text{(true model)} \qquad (3.3)$$

Now, we estimate the coefficient for X_1 with omitting X_2.

$$Y = \alpha_0 + \alpha_1 X_1 + \varepsilon \qquad \text{(estimation model)} \qquad (3.4)$$

The error term ε in the estimation model Eq. (3.4) includes the omitted variable component $\beta_2 X_2$. If X_2 is correlated with the independent variable X_1, then the estimation model violates Assumption IV of no correlation between the error term and the independent variables. Consequently, the OLS estimator for α_1 is inconsistent (and of course biased) and does not correctly measure the net effect of X_1. This is known as the *correlated-omitted-variable bias*.[4]

To help you understand why the correlated omitted variable causes a bias in the OLS estimation, use the following diagram.

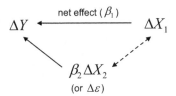

Since X_2 is correlated with X_1, X_2 will change when X_1 changes. According to the true model Eq. (3.3), this change in X_2 leads to a change in Y through its nonzero coefficient β_2. Thus, there are two channels by which a change in X_1 affects Y, its net effect and a confounding effect through X_2. Therefore, if we relate ΔY to ΔX_1 without netting out the confounding effect by ΔX_2, our estimate of the X_1 net effect will be biased as much as the confounding effect.

Using calculus, the two channels of relation can be expressed as follows.

$$\alpha_1 = \frac{dY}{dX_1} = \frac{\partial Y}{\partial X_1} + \frac{\partial Y}{\partial X_2} \times \frac{dX_2}{dX_1} = \beta_1 + \beta_2 \times \frac{dX_2}{dX_1} \qquad (3.5)$$

What we need to estimate is the net effect of X_1, $\beta_1 = \partial Y / \partial X_1$. However, if we use the estimation model Eq. (3.4) with X_2 omitted, the estimated response of Y to a unit change in X_1 will be the sum of its net effect (β_1) and a confounding effect of X_2 (i.e., $\beta_2 \times dX_2 / dX_1$), thereby the OLS estimator for the X_1 net effect being biased.

In contrast, if the omitted variable X_2 is uncorrelated with a regressor X_1, i.e., $dX_2 / dX_1 = 0$, the second term in Eq. (3.5) becomes zero, thereby the OLS estimator being consistent even though X_2 is omitted. That is why we use the expression of the *correlated*-omitted-variable problem.[5]

Kennedy (1992, p. 135) succinctly explains about the correlated-omitted-variable bias as follows:

> This is because the OLS procedure, in assigning "credit" to regressors for explaining variation in the dependent variable, assigns, in error, some of the disturbance-generated variation of the dependent variable to the regressor with which that disturbance is contemporaneously correlated. Consider as an example the case in which the correlation between the regressor and the disturbance is positive. When the disturbance is higher, the dependent variable is higher. And owing to the correlation between the disturbance and the regressor, the regressor is likely to be higher, implying that too much credit for making the dependent variable higher is likely to be assigned to the regressor.

3.4 R^2 and the adjusted R^2

3.4.1 Definition and interpretation of R^2

The definition and the interpretation of R^2 are the same as for the simple linear regression models in Chapter 2.

$$R^2 = \frac{RSS}{TSS}$$

where *TSS* (total sum of squares) measures the total variation in Y_i; *RSS* (regression sum of squares) measures how much of *TSS* is explained by the least squares function; and *ESS* (error sum of squares) represents the unexplained portion in *TSS*. The R^2 represents the proportion of the total variation in Y explained by the OLS line and thus measures the goodness of fit.

3.4.2 Adjusted R^2

When any variables are added to a regression model whether or not they make sense in the context, the corresponding R^2 cannot decrease, but is likely to increase. Thus, one is always tempted to add new variables in order just to increase R^2, regardless of the importance of the variables to the problem at hand. However, if more explanatory variables are added to a regression model, they will use up the degree of freedom $(n-k-1)$, where n is the number of observations and k is the number of slope coefficients. Since there are more coefficients (k) to estimate for a given number of observations (n), in other words, since the effective number of independent observations $(n-k-1)$ becomes smaller, the estimation will become less precise.[6] Thus, the best model is not necessarily the one which maximizes R^2.

To penalize for adding variables of little help, a different measure of goodness of fit has been suggested. This measure is called the adjusted R^2 and denoted by $\bar{R}^2$.

$$\bar{R}^2 = 1 - \left(1 - R^2\right)\frac{n-1}{n-k-1}$$

This $\bar{R}^2$ can be understood as the proportion of the total variation in Y explained by the model, with adjusting for the degree of freedom. Now, $\bar{R}^2$ can increase or decrease when a new variable is added to a regression model, depending on the relative size of its improvement in the fit and its damage to the degree of freedom.

Since $\bar{R}^2$ has been constructed using the original R^2, both measures share the following properties:

a $\bar{R}^2$ and R^2 are not used for testing hypotheses because their sampling distributions do not follow standard distributions.

b When the dependent variables of two regression models are different, it is improper to compare their $\bar{R}^2\left(R^2\right)$ values. It is because the denominators in the $\bar{R}^2\left(R^2\right)$ calculation are the total variations of two different dependent variables.

3.5 Hypothesis test

This section explains how to test hypotheses about the coefficients in a multiple regression model, $Y = \beta_0 + \beta_1 X_1 + \cdots + \beta_k X_k + u$. For $j = 1, \ldots, k$

$$H_0 : \beta_j = 0 \quad vs. \quad H_1 : \beta_j \neq 0$$

The null hypothesis $H_0 : \beta_j = 0$ implies that X_j has no net effect on Y. In other words, given the other variables, X_j does not provide any information useful for explaining the variation in Y because X_j is not related with Y. Thus, X_j can be dropped when the other variables are included in a regression model. In contrast, the alternative hypothesis $H_1 : \beta_j \neq 0$ implies that the coefficient for X_j is different from zero, indicating that there exists the net effect of X_j. In other words, X_j provides an incremental information for explaining the Y variation even when the other variables are already present in the regression model. Therefore, X_j should be kept in the regression model.

For testing purposes, use of the p-value is sufficient. The p-value is the smallest significance level at which H_0 can be rejected. Thus, H_0 is rejected at any significance level greater than the p-value. The p-value could also be interpreted as the extent to which observations are against H_0 or as the probability of making a Type I error when we reject H_0. The smaller the p-value is, the stronger the evidence is against H_0. A detailed explanation about the use of p-values is given in Chapter 1.

Using the OLS estimation results produced by computer packages, we can easily obtain a p-value for testing whether a regression coefficient is significantly different from zero. However, for various types of hypotheses such as $H_0 : \beta_j = 1$ and $H_0 : \beta_1 = \beta_2 = 0$, we need to follow one more step in the computer packages. See "Appendix 2 How to Use *Eviews*, *SAS* and *R*" and "Appendix 3A Hypothesis Test Using *EViews* and *SAS*."

Example 3.1   Based on the following computer output, researcher A concluded that independent variables $X1$, $X5$, $X6$, $X7$ and $X8$ are not useful for explaining the variation in the dependent variable because their p-values are greater than a significance level of 0.05. Therefore, the researcher recommended that only $X2$, $X3$ and $X4$ are used. Is it correct?

Variable	Coefficient	Std. Error	t-Statistic	Prob
C	−1507.8	778.6	−1.94	0.071
X1	2.010	1.931	1.04	0.313
X2	0.037	0.008	4.54	0.000
X3	0.151	0.047	3.21	0.006
X4	199.1	67.03	2.97	0.009
X5	290.9	186.8	1.56	0.139
X6	5.549	4.775	1.16	0.262
X7	19.79	33.68	0.59	0.565
X8	8.2	128.5	0.06	0.950

This recommendation is not correct. It should be based on a joint null hypothesis $H_0 : \beta_1 = \beta_5 = \beta_6 = \beta_7 = \beta_8 = 0$. However, the above computer output does not give a p-value for the joint hypothesis. Each p-value in the output is the smallest significance level at which a simple null hypothesis of $H_0 : \beta_p = 0$ is rejected, indicating how significant the net effect of each variable is. For example, since the p-value for $X8$ is 0.950 and greater than the significance level of 0.05, we can conclude that $X8$ does not provide any incremental information useful for explaining the Y variation, given that the other variables $X1, \cdots, X7$ are already included. The other insignificant coefficients can be interpreted in the same way. Therefore, we may delete only one of the variables whose p-value is greater than the significance level of 0.05. After we delete one variable, e.g., $X8$, we again estimate the resulting model to see if any variable in a new model is insignificant.

3.6 Model selection

Although R^2 and $\bar{R}^2$ are useful measures of the goodness of fit, they should be carefully used for model selection. It is possible that one model gives larger values of R^2 and $\bar{R}^2$ than others while its coefficient estimates do not conform to the researchers' expectations and previous results. The fit of a regression model is only a supplementary criterion in selecting a good model. A more useful and important criterion is whether the model estimates are economically meaningful.

3.6.1 General-to-simple approach

One of the most widely employed approach to model selection is known as the "General-to-Simple Approach." The idea of this approach is to find a simple model which does not omit any significant variables. Remember that any omission of significant variables will cause an estimation bias. However, it is not desirable to include too many factors in a model specification because the purpose of modeling is not to mimic the reality but is to capture the essential forces affecting the outcome. It is typical to leave out those factors that are believed to have insignificant impacts or are peculiar to certain individuals.

In implementing this approach, we select as many relevant variables as possible, based on economic, accounting and finance theories. After we estimate an unrestricted model which include all of the selected variables, we reduce it by eliminating one variable at a time whose coefficient is not significant.

Example 3.2 In order to set the profit-maximizing price, a company needs to know how sensitive its customers are to price changes. The company asked a researcher to analyze data and to find a good demand function. Based on economic theory, the researcher considers the following variables for possible factors which influence the demand for the company's product. Below are shown several estimation results.

LOGY = dependent variable, (logarithmic) amount of demand;
LOGX = average (logarithmic) income of the consumers;
LOGP = (logarithm) price of the product;
LOGS1, LOGS2, LOGS3 = (logarithmic) prices of three substitute goods of the product.

<Model 1> $R^2 = 0.37$, $\bar{R}^2 = 0.32$

Variable	Coefficient	Std. Error	t-Statistic	Prob.
C	−6.369	1.877	−3.393	0.000
LOGX	0.998	0.115	8.678	0.000
LOGP	−2.522	0.594	−4.246	0.000
LOGS1	0.487	1.023	0.476	0.481
LOGS2	−0.653	1.007	−0.648	0.517
LOGS3	0.593	1.078	0.550	0.683

<Model 2> $R^2 = 0.37$, $\bar{R}^2 = 0.34$

Variable	Coefficient	Std. Error	t-Statistic	Prob.
C	−6.095	1.807	−3.373	0.001
LOGX	0.986	0.116	8.500	0.000
LOGP	−2.529	0.595	−4.250	0.000
LOGS1	0.988	1.008	0.980	0.231
LOGS2	0.703	1.089	0.646	0.383

<Model 3> $R^2 = 0.36$, $\bar{R}^2 = 0.35$

Variable	Coefficient	Std. Error	t-Statistic	Prob.
C	−6.112	1.809	−3.379	0.001
LOGX	0.980	0.121	8.099	0.000
LOGP	−2.498	0.599	−4.170	0.000
LOGS1	0.105	0.024	4.375	0.000

Following the General-to-Simple approach, we first estimate a model including all factors. Three variables in Model 1 have larger *p*-values than a usual significance level of 0.05. So, we can delete only one of them. When we reestimate Model 2 after dropping LOGS3, we still have large *p*-values for LOGS1 and LOGS2. After deleting one of them (here LOGS2), we arrive at Model 3 whose variables are all significant. Therefore, we conclude that Model 3 is the best because it includes all significant variables and is the simplest model.[7]

However, if our interest is in LOGX and LOGP but not in LOGS1, LOGS2 and LOGS3, Models 1 and 2 could also be good enough even though these models are not so simple as Model 3. In these models, the variables LOGS1, LOGS2 and LOGS3 are included only to control for confounding effects.

Notice that the coefficient estimates for LOGX and LOGP are very similar across the three models. Therefore, we can argue that the estimates for LOGX and LOGP are reliable as they are not sensitive to model specification.

<Model 4> $R^2 = 0.31$, $\bar{R}^2 = 0.30$

Variable	Coefficient	Std. Error	t-Statistic	Prob.
C	−7.112	1.901	−3.741	0.000
LOGX	1.380	0.125	11.040	0.000
LOGP	−3.587	0.612	−5.861	0.000

Consider Model 4 which omits a significant variable (LOGS1) from Model 3. The coefficient estimates for LOGX and LOGP in Model 4 are very different from the ones in the above three models. It is because the indirect effect through LOGS1 are confounded in the coefficient estimates in Model 4. This is a case of the bias caused by correlated omitted variables.

This bias can be illustrated using the following diagrams. In Model 3, LOGY receives significant effects from LOGS1 as well as LOGX and LOGP. When LOGS1 is omitted as in Model 4, its influencing route will be added to the ones of the other variables, proportionally to its correlations with LOGX and LOGP. These added routes, represented by dotted lines, are the bias due to the omission of a significant variable LOGS1.

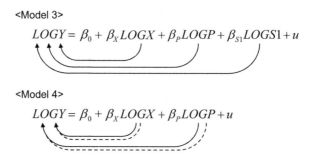

One interesting question is why LOGS1 is insignificant when it is included together with LOGS2 and LOGS3 in Models 1 and 2, but it becomes very significant when LOGS2 and LOGS3 are not included in Model 3. The reason is because the three variables are very similar, in other words, highly correlated with each other. Remember that each regression coefficient measures the *net* effect of a variable after controlling for the effects of the other variables in a multiple regression model. If LOGS1 is similar to LOGS2 and LOGS3, the *net* effect of LOGS1 will be insignificant because little is left after the effects of similar variables LOGS2 and LOGS3 are netted out. In other words, in the presence of LOGS2 and LOG3, the variable LOGS1 does not have an incremental contribution to the understanding of the dependent variable because the information in LOGS1 is similar to the one in LOGS2 and LOGS3. This is a case of **multicollinearity**, to be explained in Chapter 5.

3.6.2 A comment on hypothesis testing

The statistical significance is a *continuous* measure of the extent to which the evidence rejects (or supports) hypotheses. For example, a *p*-value of 0.003 rejects the null hypothesis more strongly than a *p*-value of 0.04 does, although both of them can reject the null hypothesis at a usual significance level of 0.05. Thus, they are not equal in terms of the extent to which they reject the null hypothesis. For another example, a p-value of 0.051 is little different from a p-value of 0.049. However, with a significance level of 0.05, the former cannot reject the null hypothesis while the latter does. Being statistically significant or insignificant depends on the significance level chosen by an analyst. It implies that the statistical significance should be interpreted in a continuous way, but not in a discrete way (i.e., reject or accept) with an arbitrarily chosen significance level.

If a certain variable is supported by economic theory and previous studies, we had better keep the variable in our regression models although its statistical significance is relatively weak. On the other hand, if you find a statistically significant variable but cannot explain why the variable is related to the dependent variable, your regression model does not make sense. Thus, no matter how high the statistical significance is, we should not include variables which cannot be justified by economic reasoning.

In addition, McCloskey and Zeliak (1996) argue that many economists fail to see the way in which the economy really works because they interpret the statistical significance in a discrete way and rely too much on the results of hypothesis tests. A large effect may not be statistically significant at a given significance level.[8] McCloskey and Zeliak (1996) emphasize that analysis should be focused on *economic* significance, not *statistical* significance.

3.6.3 Guidelines for model selection

1   The correlated-omitted-variable problem indicates that important (strongly significant and economically meaningful) factors should not be omitted from a model. Any models which have omitted such significant variables could produce biased results.
2   We had better include weakly significant variables if they are of our interest and justified by theoretical and empirical results.[9]
3   We had better delete weakly significant variables if they are not of our interest and get little support from theory and previous studies. Following the "General-to-Simple approach," we are looking for simpler models which include fewer parameters to be estimated.[10]
4   We should not include variables which cannot be justified by economic reasoning, no matter how high their statistical significance levels are.

3.7 Applications

3.7.1 Mitton (2002)

Weak corporate governance has frequently been cited as one of the causes of the East Asian financial crisis of 1997–1998. While weak corporate governance may not have triggered the East Asian crisis, the corporate governance practices in East Asia could have made countries more vulnerable to a financial crisis and could have exacerbated the crisis once it began.

If corporate governance was a significant factor in the crisis, then corporate governance should explain not just cross-country differences in performance during the crisis, but also cross-firm differences in performance within countries. This paper uses firm-level data from the five East Asian crisis economies of Indonesia, Korea, Malaysia, the Philippines and Thailand to study the impact of corporate governance on firm performance during the crisis.

(i) Variables and models

To measure firm performance during the crisis, Mitton uses stock returns over the crisis period, from July 1997 through August 1998. The returns are dividend inclusive and are expressed in local currencies adjusted for local price index changes. Mitton does not calculate abnormal returns because of data limitations. As an alternative, Mitton uses measures of leverage and size, industry dummies and country dummies in the regressions to control for factors that could affect expected returns.[11]

To assess the impact of corporate governance variables on firm stock price performance during the crisis (*Crisis Period RET*), Mitton estimates the following model:

$$Crisis\ Period\ RET = \beta_0 + \beta_1$$
$$+ \beta_2(Size) + \beta_3(Leverage)$$
$$+ \beta_4(Country\ Dummies) + \beta_5(Industry\ Dummies) + u$$

This study uses three aspects of corporate governance: disclosure quality, ownership structure and corporate diversification. The results using ownership concentration are reported in this chapter. As a measure of ownership concentration, Mitton uses data reported by Worldscope, which identifies all parties that own 5% or more of each firm. The ownership data Mitton uses are pre-crisis data, which means the last reported data from each firm prior to July 1997. Mitton considers two measures of ownership concentration. The first is the ownership percentage (in terms of cash flow rights) of the largest shareholder in the firm, which Mitton refers to as "largest blockholder concentration." The second is the total holding of all shareholders that own 5% or more of the stock, which Mitton refers to as "summed ownership concentration."

Mitton uses other variables to control for factors that could affect firm performance. The first is firm size, measured by the logarithm of total assets. An additional control variable is the firm's debt ratio, measured as the book value of total debt divided by the book value of total capital. These data are reported by Worldscope. Mitton includes dummy variables for four of the five countries included in the regressions to control for country fixed effects. Mitton also includes 10 dummy variables for the 11 industries.

(ii) Results

Table 3.2 presents the results of regressions of crisis-period stock returns on ownership structure variables. The first two columns analyze the largest blockholder concentration. With all control variables included, the coefficient on the largest blockholder concentration is 0.261. This indicates that each increase of 10% in ownership concentration is associated with a higher return of 2.6% during the crisis.[12] The coefficient on the largest blockholder concentration is significant at the 1% level. The second two columns analyze summed ownership concentration. With all control variables included, the coefficient on summed ownership concentration is 0.174, indicating a higher return of 1.7% for each increase of 10% in ownership concentration. This coefficient is significant at the 5% level. These results indicate that the presence of a strong blockholder was beneficial during the crisis, consistent with the hypothesis that a strong blockholder has the incentive and power to prevent expropriation.

Note 1: In regression (ii), the firm size and the debt ratio are shown to be significant factors at the 1% level. Thus, the estimates in regression (i) are biased because these significant variables are omitted. For the same reason, the author interprets regression (iv) but not regression (iii).

Note 2: A certain variable is included as a control variable when it has a significant net effect on the dependent variable. The firm size and the debt ratio can be such control variables as they are significant at the 1% level.

Table 3.2 Crisis-period stock returns and ownership structure

	(i)	*(ii)*	*(iii)*	*(iv)*
Constant	−0.649***	−1.257***	−0.737***	−1.266***
	(−8.24)	(−5.52)	(−7.77)	(−5.47)
Largest blockholder concentration	0.327***	0.261***		
	(4.36)	(3.42)		
Summed ownership concentration			0.275***	0.174**
			(3.76)	(2.41)
Firm size		0.083***		0.080***
		(3.42)		(3.14)
Debt ratio		−0.0027***		−0.0027***
		(−4.64)		(−4.66)
Country dummies	Included	Included	Included	Included
Industry dummies	Included	Included	Included	Included
No of observations	301	394	301	294
R^2	0.218	0.307	0.214	0.296

Source: Mitton (2002, Table 3 Panel A on page 230).
Note: Heteroscedasticity-consistent *t*-statistics are given in brackets and asterisks denote significance levels:
* = 10%, ** = 5%, and *** = 1%.

3.7.2 McAlister, Srinivasan and Kim (2007)

Most senior management and finance executives focus on maximizing shareholder value and do not value marketing performance metrics (e.g., awareness, sales growth, loyalty, customer satisfaction, repeat purchase), because they do not understand how or even whether these metrics are of interest to the firm's shareholders. Consequently, marketing executives are urged to "speak in the language of finance" to gain internal support for marketing initiatives.

To address this gap, the authors examine whether a firm's advertising and R&D expenditures affect the firm's systematic risk (measured by the market *Beta* in the Capital Asset Pricing Model), which is a metric of interest to both finance executives and senior management. The following two hypotheses, in alternative form, are tested:

H_{1a}: (Advertising) The higher a firm's advertising, the lower is its systematic risk.
H_{1b}: (R&D) The higher a firm's R&D, the lower is its systematic risk.

The data for this study included all firms listed on the New York Stock Exchange (NYSE) during the period between 1979 and 2001. The authors obtained accounting, financial, advertising and R&D data from COMPUSTAT, and obtained the stock prices for the computation of systematic risk from CRSP.
The main regression model is

$$Beta_{it} = \alpha_0 + \alpha_1 \left(\frac{adv}{sales} \right)_{i,t-1} + \alpha_2 \left(\frac{R \& D}{sales} \right)_{i,t-1}$$
$$+ \alpha_3 Growth_{it} + \alpha_4 Leverage_{it} + \alpha_5 Liquidity_{it} + \alpha_6 \log Size_{it}$$
$$+ \alpha_7 Earnings_{it} + \alpha_8 Dividend_{it} + \alpha_9 Age_{it} + \alpha_{10} Comp_{it}$$
$$+ v_i + \delta_t + \varepsilon_{it}$$

Table 3.3 shows a part of their estimation results supporting the two hypotheses; higher lagged advertising/sales ($\hat{\alpha}_1 = -3.187$) and higher lagged R&D/sales ($\hat{\alpha}_2 = -0.501$) lower the firm's systematic risk. These negative net effects are significant at the 1% level.

Table 3.3 Estimation results

Variable	Coefficient estimate (standard error)
Lagged advertising/sales	−3.187 (0.754)***
Lagged R&D/sales	−0.501 (0.180)***
Growth	0.359 (0.084)***
Leverage	0.515 (0.124)***
Liquidity	0.001 (0.010)
logSize	−0.091 (0.032)***
Earnings variability	−0.018 (0.032)
Dividend payout	0.000 (0.000)
Age	−0.022 (0.006)***
Competitive Intensity	−0.885 (0.335)***
other control variables	Included
R^2	0.161
Number of firms (observations)	644 (3198)

Source: Adapted from McAlister et al. (2007, Table 2 on page 42).
Note: Asterisks denote significance levels: * = 10%, ** = 5%, and *** = 1%

3.7.3 *Collins, Pincus and Xie (1999)*

This paper points out that the following simple regression suffers from the correlated-omitted variable problem because it does not control for the confounding effects of other variables such as the book value of equity.

$$P_{it} = \beta_0 + \beta_1 X_{it} + u_{it}$$

where P_{it} is the ex-dividend share price and X_{it} is earnings per share.

Equity valuation models have been used extensively in accounting research to examine the value relevance of accounting data. One such valuation model is the above simple earnings capitalization model. In this model, stock price is expressed as a function of earnings or the components of earnings under the assumption that earnings reflect information about expected future cash flows. Typically, researchers pool earnings observations cross-sectionally to estimate the earnings capitalization model. In so doing, they assume (implicitly or explicitly) that the security price-earnings relation is both *positive* and *homogeneous* over the entire range of earnings realizations; that is, β_1 is positive and the same for all observations.

Evidence in recent studies raises questions about the assumption of a positive and homogeneous relation between price and earnings across profits and losses. Hayn (1995) separates firms into those reporting losses and those reporting profits. Hayn finds that the cross-sectional return-earnings relation for loss firms is much weaker than that for profit firms, suggesting that the price-earnings relation may not be homogeneous across profit and loss firms. Jan and Ou (1995) also document a nonhomogeneous price-earnings relation; more strikingly, the relation is *negative* for loss firms.

The primary purpose of this paper is to investigate and provide an explanation for the anomalous negative coefficient on earnings in the simple earnings capitalization model for loss firms. The authors postulate that the anomalous negative price-earnings relation for loss firms is caused by a *correlated omitted variable problem*. More specifically, they hypothesize that the simple earnings capitalization model is misspecified due to the omission of book value of equity. This hypothesis is based on several competing arguments in the literature about the role that book value of equity plays in a price-earnings specification.

One possible role is that book value of equity is an economically meaningful value-relevant factor in its own right. There appear to be two distinct views in the literature on the nature or source of book value of equity's value relevance. Ohlson (1995) and Penman (1992) argue that the book value proxies for expected future normal earnings, consistent with viewing the firm as a going concern. The other view is that the value relevance of the book value stems from its role as a proxy for adaptation or abandonment value.[13] Omission of the book value of equity in the simple earnings capitalization model will induce a negative bias in the coefficient on earnings if the book value is positively correlated with stock price but negatively correlated with earnings for loss firms.

The authors find that when stock price is regressed on earnings for loss firms, the coefficient on earnings is reliably negative in 16 of the 18 years in this study. This is consistent with the findings reported by Jan and Ou (1995). When they augment the simple earnings capitalization model with book value of equity, the coefficient on earnings becomes either positive (often significantly) or insignificantly different from zero for each year in their 18-year sample period. The average of the coefficients on earnings over 18 sample years is also significantly positive. This provides strong evidence that the simple earnings capitalization model is misspecified due to the omission of book value, and the omission induces a negative bias in the coefficient on earnings for loss firms.

3.7.4 Angrist and Pischke (2009, pp. 64–68)

Bad controls are variables that are themselves outcome variables in the notional experiment at hand. Good controls are variables that we can think of as having been fixed at the time the regressor of interest was determined.

Suppose we are estimating the effects on earnings (E) of employees' schooling (S) and innate ability (A) when the three variables are related as follows:

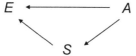

1   Estimating the effects of S on E

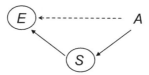

(i)   If A is observed by researchers, A can be included as a control variable. Then β_1 correctly measures the net effects of S on E after controlling for the confounding effects of A.

$$E = \beta_0 + \beta_1 S + \beta_2 A + u \tag{3.6}$$

(ii) In most cases, however, A is not observed by researchers. If the unobserved variable A is omitted from a regression model, the OLS estimation is biased due to the correlated-omitted variable.

$$E = \alpha_0 + \alpha_1 S + v$$

In addition to the net effects of S on E, α_1 also includes a part of the A effects on E whose magnitude depends on the correlation between A and S; $\alpha_1 = \beta_1 + \beta_2(dA / dS)$.

(iii) If the unobserved variable A is proxied by AM, an ability measure collected after schooling is completed (say, the score on a test used to screen job applicants), AM is a bad control because it is an outcome from S. In general, schooling increases AM ($\pi_1 > 0$).

$$AM = \pi_0 + \pi_1 S + \pi_2 A$$

Using $A = (AM - \pi_0 - \pi_1 S) / \pi_2$, we express the regression of E, Eq. (3.6), in terms of S and AM.

$$E = \left(\beta_0 - \beta_2 \frac{\pi_0}{\pi_2}\right) + \left(\beta_1 - \beta_2 \frac{\pi_1}{\pi_2}\right)S + \left(\frac{\beta_2}{\pi_2}\right)AM + u$$

Use of AM reduces the measured net effects of S on E. In the following diagram, the reduced net effects are represented by the route from S to AM to E. Therefore, we should not use AM to proxy for A.

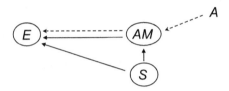

In contrast, think of an IQ score that measures innate ability in eighth grade, before any relevant schooling choices are made. This is a good control because IQ is measured before schooling is determined. Note that there is no influencing route from S to IQ and thus no reduction in the net effects of S.

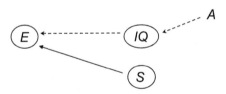

2   Estimating the effects of A on E

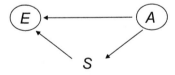

Since S is an outcome from A, S is a bad control. Thus, we should not include S for estimating the net effects of A on E.

One moral of the bad control stories is that when thinking about controls, timing matters. Variables measured before the variable of interest was determined are generally good controls; they cannot themselves be outcomes in the causal nexus.

3.8 Summary

1   Each regression coefficient in multiple regression models measures the net effect of its explanatory variable, that is, the difference in the conditional mean of the dependent variable for one unit difference in its explanatory variable when the other variables are held constant.

2   In order to correctly estimate the net effect of a variable, we have to include other variables which are significantly correlated with the dependent variable. Otherwise, the confounding effects of the omitted variables will bias the estimation of the net effect; this is called the correlated-omitted-variable problem.

3   Statistical significance should be interpreted in a continuous way, not in a discrete way of rejecting or accepting a null hypothesis. Since any null hypothesis can be rejected for an arbitrarily chosen significance level, it is not very meaningful to say that we reject or accept a null hypothesis. Thus, if a certain explanatory variable is of our interest and justified by theoretical and empirical results, we had better include the variable even though it is weakly significant.

4   At the same time, we have to worry about possible over-parameterization. If some explanatory variables are weakly significant and get little support from theory and previous studies, we had better delete them to save the degree of freedom; this is an application of the General-to-Simple approach to model selection.

Review questions

1   Let $CONS_i$ denote the consumption of household i and INC_i denote its income during the last period. A simple regression of $CONS_i$ on INC_i is

$$CONS_i = \beta_0 + \beta_1 INC_i + u_i$$

(a)   Explain why we need the disturbance u_i.
(b)   What factors could be contained in the disturbance? List at least two possible factors.
(c)   Are these factors likely to be correlated with the income variable INC_i? If they are correlated, what problem does the OLS estimation of the above simple regression have?
(d)   Explain how to correct the estimation problem in (c).

2   To examine the determinants of stock returns, we regress stock returns (R) on profitability (*profit*) and debt ratio (*debt*). Below are the OLS estimation results.

Dependent variable: R

Variable	Coefficient	Std. Error	t-Statistic	Prob.
Intercept	3.01	0.61	4.93	0.000
profit	1.79	0.23	7.78	0.000
debt	−0.52	0.17	−3.06	0.002
$R^2 = 0.64$	No. of observations = 255			

(a)   Write the fitted regression equation.
(b)   To see whether *profit* is a significant factor for the stock returns, we test $H_0 : \beta_{profit} = 0$ against $H_1 : \beta_{profit} > 0$. The above table shows that its estimate is 1.79 and obviously different from zero. Why do we bother to test the hypothesis?
(c)   What is your conclusion of the hypothesis test? Explain.

    (d)   Interpret the meaning of $R^2 = 0.64$.

    (e)   If the debt ratio (*debt*) increases by 1 unit while *profit* is held constant, by how much is R estimated to fall?

    (f)   If *profit* = 0.1 and *debt* = 0.1, what is your predicted value of R?

3   Suppose that the true model is $Y = \beta_0 + \beta_1 X_1 + \beta_2 X_2 + u$, where $\beta_2 \neq 0$. If we use a simple regression model $Y = \alpha_0 + \alpha_1 X_1 + \varepsilon$ with X_2 omitted, then the OLS estimator for the coefficient of X_1 ($\hat{\alpha}_1$) might provide biased information about the true net effect of X_1 on Y. In other words, $E(\hat{\alpha}_1) = \alpha_1$ is different from β_1, the true net effect.

    (a)   Explain why the estimator $\hat{\alpha}_1$ is biased.

    (b)   Explain when the estimator $\hat{\alpha}_1$ can still be unbiased even when X_2 is omitted.

    (c)   If the omission of X_2 does not cause a bias as in (b), is it better to omit X_2?

4   Interpret what is measured by a regression coefficient β_1 in the following multiple regression models.

    (a) $Y_i = \beta_0 + \beta_1 X_i + \beta_2 Z_i + u_i$

    (b) $\log Y_i = \beta_0 + \beta_1 \log X_i + \beta_2 \log Z_i + u_i$

5   To understand the factors of production, we estimate the following Cobb-Douglas production function using data saved in "3-production.xls."

$$\log Q_i = \beta_0 + \beta_1 \log K_i + \beta_2 \log L_i + u_i$$

Below is a part of data collected from 33 sampled firms. They show how much of input they used (capital K and labor L) and how much of output they produced (Q) in year 2004.

A	B	C	D
Firm ID	Output (Q)	Capital (K)	Labor (L)
ABS	1385	1850	951
ABT	2893	3544	1289
ACK	1209	1548	783
ACY	1715	3568	948

    (a)   Estimate the Cobb-Douglas production function.

    (b)   Interpret the coefficient estimates $\hat{\beta}_1$ and $\hat{\beta}_2$.

    (c)   Are the inputs (K and L) significant factors of production?

    (d)   Test whether the production function is homogeneous of degree one, in other words, constant returns-to-scale. That is, test the null hypothesis $H_0 : \beta_1 + \beta_2 = 1$ against $H_1 : \beta_1 + \beta_2 \neq 1$.

6   In order for the OLS estimator to be unbiased, consistent and efficient, the error term in the following multiple regression model should satisfy several assumptions.

$$Y_i = \beta_0 + \beta_1 X_{1i} + \beta_2 X_{2i} + \cdots + \beta_k X_{ki} + u_i$$

    (a)   Explain what are meant by "best" and "unbiased" in BLUE.

    (b)   One of the assumptions is that the variance of the error term is constant. If this assumption is violated, what problem does the OLS estimator have?

    (c)   One of the assumptions is that the error term is not correlated with the independent variables. If this assumption is violated, what problem does the OLS estimator have?

7   To examine the determinants of a variable (Y), we have estimated the following regression models. Answer the questions based on the OLS estimation results shown below.

<Model 1> $R^2 = 0.86$, $\bar{R}^2 = 0.77$

Variable	Coefficient	Std. Error	t-Statistic	Prob.
C	2.88	0.63	4.57	0.000
X1	1.78	0.25	7.12	0.000
X2	−0.50	0.20	(a)	0.007
X3	3.10	2.89	1.07	0.160
X4	2.10	1.53	1.37	0.132
X5	0.13	0.06	2.33	0.009

<Model 2> $R^2 = 0.85$, $\bar{R}^2 = 0.78$

Variable	Coefficient	Std. Error	t-Statistic	Prob.
C	2.98	0.62	4.81	0.000
X1	1.79	0.26	7.46	0.000
X2	−0.53	0.21	−2.79	0.005
X4	2.01	1.54	1.54	0.150
X5	0.14	0.06	2.33	0.009

<Model 3> $R^2 = 0.83$, $\bar{R}^2 = 0.77$

Variable	Coefficient	Std. Error	t-Statistic	Prob.
C	3.01	0.64	4.70	0.000
X1	1.79	0.27	6.63	0.000
X2	−0.52	0.21	−2.48	0.010
X5	0.16	0.07	2.29	0.012

<Model 4> $R^2 = 0.61$, $\bar{R}^2 = 0.59$

Variable	Coefficient	Std. Error	t-Statistic	Prob.
C	4.20	0.82	5.12	0.000
X1	2.10	0.36	5.83	0.000
X2	−0.67	0.26	−2.58	0.010

(a) Calculate the *t*-statistic value for X2 in Model 1.

(b) Compare Model 1 and Model 2. We omitted X3 which is not significant at a usual significance level of 10%, Nonetheless, the coefficient estimates after the omission slightly changed. Explain why the estimates can change when an insignificant variable is omitted.

(c) Compare Model 3 and Model 4. The coefficient estimates in Model 3 are consistent with our predicted values. However, when we omitted X5, the estimates of the coefficients of X1 and X2 have changed substantially to 2.10 and −0.67, respectively, and these values are too large (in absolute) with respect to our predictions. Explain why this can happen.

(d) After an omission of X5 in Model 3, the standard errors have substantially increased in Model 4. Explain why.

(e) Which regression model among the above four would you choose and why?

8   A researcher would like to estimate the rate of returns to schooling, denoted by β_1, using the following regression:

$$\log(wage) = \beta_0 + \beta_1 S + \theta A + u \tag{Q3.1}$$

where S is the years of schooling completed, A is a measure of ability and the disturbance u is not correlated with S and A. Since the ability variable A is not observable (to the analyst), he or she will have to estimate the following regression model and interpret an estimate of α_1 as a measure of the rate of schooling returns.

$$\log(wage) = \alpha_0 + \alpha_1 S + w \tag{Q3.2}$$

Because of the omitted variable A, the OLS estimator for α_1 in Eq. (Q3.2) could be biased. To understand this bias, suppose that the ability A is related to the schooling S as follows.

$$A = \delta_0 + \delta_1 S + \varepsilon \tag{Q3.3}$$

(a) Express how α_1 is related with β_1. What is the correlated-omitted-variable bias in this expression?

(b) People with higher ability tend to have more schooling; $\delta_1 > 0$ as A and S are positively correlated. Does α_1 over- or under-estimate β_1, the true rate of returns to schooling?

(c) If δ_1 is equal to zero, does the bias still exist? Explain why.

9   McAlister et al. (2007) examine whether the firm's advertising and R&D expenditures affect the firm's systematic risk (measured by the market *Beta* in the CAPM). They used the following regression model.

$$\begin{aligned}
Beta_{it} = \alpha_0 &+ \alpha_1 \left(\frac{adv}{sales}\right)_{i,t-1} + \alpha_2 \left(\frac{R\&D}{sales}\right)_{i,t-1} \\
&+ \alpha_3 (Growth)_{it} + \alpha_4 (Leverage)_{it} + \alpha_5 (Liquidity)_{it} + \alpha_6 (\log Size)_{it} \\
&+ \alpha_7 (Earnings)_{it} + \alpha_8 (Dividend)_{it} + \alpha_9 (Age)_{it} + \alpha_{10} (Comp)_{it} \\
&+ v_i + \delta_t + \varepsilon_{it}
\end{aligned}$$

Variable	Coefficient estimates		
	(i)	(ii)	(iii)
Lagged advertising/sales (α_1)	−3.187***	−5.587***	−4.125***
Lagged R&D/sales (α_2)	−0.501***	−2.154***	−0.109*
Growth	0.359***		0.124***
Leverage	0.515***		0.113**
Liquidity	0.001		0.145**
(log) Size	−0.091***		
Earnings variability	−0.018		
Dividend payout	0.000		
Age	−0.022***		
Competitive Intensity	−0.885***		
Other control variables	Included	Included	Included

Asterisks denote significance levels: * = 10%, ** = 5%, and *** = 1%

(a) Using a coefficient in the regression model, write the null and alternative hypotheses which can examine the effect of advertising expenditures, that is, whether the systematic risk is lower with higher advertising expenditures.

(b) The coefficient estimates are very different between regressions (i), (ii) and (iii). Explain why.

(c) What is your conclusion about the effect of advertising expenditures?

Notes

1 When there is more than one independent variable, the regression relation is no longer a line and cannot be graphically displayed in a two-dimensional plane.

2 From Eq. (3.1), we can derive a difference equation $\Delta E(Y \mid all\ Xs) = \beta_1 \Delta X_1 + \beta_2 \Delta X_2 + \cdots + \beta_k \Delta X_k$. When $X_2, \cdots, X_k$ are held constant, i.e., $\Delta X_2 = \cdots = \Delta X_k = 0$, it becomes $\Delta E(Y \mid all\ Xs) = \beta_1 \Delta X_1$. Thus, β_1 represents the net effect of X_1 on Y. Using calculus, we can express each regression coefficient as a partial derivative, e.g., $\beta_1 = \partial Y / \partial X_1$.

3 The terms *holding constant, controlling for* and *netting out* are synonymous and used interchangeably.

4 If an OLS estimator is not consistent, it is always biased for finite samples; remember that Assumption IV for the consistency is weaker than Assumption I for the unbiasedness.

5 Another possible case is that X_2 is correlated with X_1 but not a significant factor for Y (i.e., $\beta_2 = 0$). If so, the omitted component $\beta_2 X_2$ will be equal to zero. Since nothing is omitted, the OLS estimator is still consistent. Intuitively, this makes sense because the omission of an insignificant variable will not damage estimation at all.

6 As explained in Chapter 2, the standard error of an OLS estimator is proportional to $1/(n-k-1)$.

7 Regarding which variable to delete among insignificant variables, you may choose a variable which is least justified by theory and previous studies. Or, you may choose the variable whose *p*-value is the largest. As long as those insignificant variables are not of your interest, it does not matter which variable to delete. In order to avoid an estimation bias due to correlated-omitted variables, we should keep all significant variables.

8 The following example is from the article "Economics focus: Signifying nothing?" published in *The Economist* on January 31, 2004. In the 1980s, the State of Illinois launched a program to keep people off the dole. Economists asked whether its costs outweighed its benefits. One study estimated that the program produced benefits that were more than four times as large as the costs. Although this seemed a good deal for taxpayers, the authors of the study rejected such a finding because their estimate of the difference between the benefits and the costs was not statistically significant at the 10% level.

9 We intentionally use the term "weakly significant" instead of "insignificant." Being insignificant means that the *p*-value is larger than an arbitrarily chosen significance level, e.g., 10%, 5% or 1%. However, there is no reason why such significance levels should be used. This guideline suggests that even though a *p*-value is greater than a chosen significance level (e.g., $\alpha = 10\%$), we had better include the variable if it is supported by theoretical results and previous empirical studies. That is because a *p*-value of 0.32, for example, does not mean that the variable is surely unrelated. In other words, although a large *p*-value cannot strongly reject a null hypothesis of no relation, it does not indicate that the null hypothesis is true. Instead, a correct interpretation is that there exists some extent of evidence against the null hypothesis but the evidence is not so strong as the 10% significance level.

10 If we include too many weakly significant explanatory variables, there will be too many parameters to be estimated for a given sample size (n). Then the degree of freedom ($n-k-1$), or the effective number of independent observations, will be smaller, where k is the number of independent variables (i.e., slope coefficients). The resulting loss of degree of freedom will increase standard errors and thereby decrease the significance of estimation results. Notice that the standard error is proportional to $\hat{\sigma} = \sqrt{ESS/(n-k-1)}$.

11 Use of dummies to control for country and industry factors is explained in Chapter 7.

12 It should be "each increase of 10% *points* in ownership concentration is associated with a higher return of 2.6% *points* during the crisis."

13 Abandonment value is akin to the value from liquidating the entity, while adaptation value reflects the value of a firm's net resources in their next best alternative use.

References

Angrist, J.D. and J.S. Pischke (2009), *Mostly Harmless Econometrics: An Empiricist's Companion*, Princeton, NJ: Princeton University Press.

Collins, D.W., M. Pincus and H. Xie (1999), "Equity Valuation and Negative Earnings: The Role of Book Value of Equity," *The Accounting Review*, 74, 29–61.

Hayn, C. (1995), "The Information Content of Losses," *Journal of Accounting and Economics*, 20, 125–153.

Jan, C.L., and J. Ou (1995), "The Role of Negative Earnings in the Valuation of Equity Stocks," Working paper, New York University and Santa Clara University.

Kennedy, P. (1992), *A Guide to Econometrics*, Cambridge: MIT Press.

Lewis, M. (2003), *Moneyball: The Art of Winning an Unfair Game*, New York: Norton.

McAlister, L., R. Srinivasan and M.C. Kim (2007), "Advertising, Research and Development, and Systematic Risk of the Firm," *Journal of Marketing*, 71, 35–48.

McCloskey, D. and S. Zeliak (1996), "The Standard Error of Regression," *Journal of Economic Literature*, 34, 97–114.

Mitton, T. (2002), "A Cross-Firm Analysis of the Impact of Corporate Governance on the East Asian Financial Crisis," *Journal of Financial Economics*, 64, 215–241.

Ohlson, J.A. (1995), "Earnings, Book Values, and Dividends in Security Valuation," *Contemporary Accounting Research*, 11, 661–687.

Penman, S. (1992), "Return to Fundamentals," *Journal of Accounting, Auditing and Finance*, 7, 465–483.

The Economist (2004), "Signifying nothing?" January 31, 2004, 70.

Appendix 3A Hypothesis test using *EViews* and *SAS*

Using *EViews*

We estimate a consumption function using three independent variables:

$$Y_i = \beta_0 + \beta_1 X_{1i} + \beta_2 X_{2i} + \beta_3 X_{3i} + u_i$$

After importing an Excel file (3-consumption.xls) which contains 20 observations, we estimate the regression model by clicking Objects/New Object . . . /Equation. The estimation results are shown in Output 3.1 in Section 3.2.

Suppose that we want to test a joint null hypothesis, $H_0 : \beta_2 = \beta_3 = 0$. After obtaining the OLS estimation results, choose View/Coefficient Diagnostics/Wald Test-Coefficient Restrictions . . . and type the null hypothesis "C(3)=0, C(4)=0." In *EViews*, the coefficients are automatically named as C(.), the number in parenthesis indicating the order in the equation specification: C(1) is the intercept β_0, C(2) is β_1 and so on.

Output 3.2   Test results for $H_0 : \beta_2 = \beta_3 = 0$

Wald Test:
Equation: Untitled

Test Statistic	Value	df	Probability
F-statistic	2.196529	(2, 16)	0.1436
Chi-square	4.393058	2	0.1112

According to the test results in Output 3.2, the *p*-value for the null hypothesis is 0.1436 (using *F*-statistic) or 0.1112 (using *Chi*-square), thereby failing to reject the null hypothesis at a significance level of 0.1.

Now we test a linear function of the regression coefficients, $H_0 : \beta_1 = 3\beta_2 + \beta_3$. After obtaining the OLS estimation results as above, choose View/Coefficient Diagnostics/Wald Test-Coefficient Restrictions . . . and type the null hypothesis "C(2)=3*C(3)+C(4)."

Output 3.3   Test results for $H_0 : \beta_2 = \beta_3 = 0$

Wald Test:
Equation: Untitled

Test Statistic	Value	df	Probability
F-statistic	3.263478	(1, 16)	0.0897
Chi-square	3.263478	1	0.0708

The test results in Output 3.3 show that the p-values are smaller than a significance level of 0.1 for the F-statistic and *Chi*-square, thereby rejecting the null hypothesis at the 10% level.

Using *SAS*[1]

```
FILENAME f1 DDE 'EXCEL|[3-consumption.xls]sample!R2C2:R21C5';
TITLE '< HYPOTHESIS TESTING >';
DATA dat1; INFILE f1;   INPUT cons income num age;
PROC REG;
    MODEL cons = income num age;
    TEST num=0, age=0;
    TEST income=3*num+age;
RUN;
```

$\leftarrow H_0 : \beta_2 = \beta_3 = 0$

$\leftarrow H_0 : \beta_1 = 3\beta_2 + \beta_3$

Appendix 3B Geometric interpretation of the OLS regression equation

The OLS regression equation decomposes each Y value into two components, the fitted value $\hat{Y} = \hat{\beta}_0 + \hat{\beta}_1 X_1 + \cdots + \hat{\beta}_k X_k$ and the residual $\hat{u}$, i.e., $Y = \hat{Y} + \hat{u}$. Geometrically, the OLS method can be interpreted as projecting the dependent variable onto the space formed by the independent variables $X_1, \cdots, X_k$. Then, the projected value of Y on the space, which is equal to the fitted value, represents the component in Y correlated with the independent variables. The residual $\hat{u} = Y - \hat{Y}$ is orthogonal to the space (also $\hat{Y}$) because the component correlated with the independent variables has been separated into $\hat{Y}$. Thus, the projection decomposes the dependent variable into two mutually orthogonal components: the projected component which is correlated with the independent variables and the residual component which is not correlated with them.

This geometric interpretation helps us understand the meaning of "controlling for," "netting out" or "removing" the confounding effects of other factors. As explained above, each regression coefficient in multiple regression models represents its net effect on the dependent variable. For example, β_1 in the following multiple regression measures the net effect of X_1 on Y after controlling for the confounding effects of $X_2, \cdots, X_k$.

$$Y = \beta_0 + \beta_1 X_1 + \beta_2 X_2 + \cdots + \beta_k X_k + u \tag{A3.1}$$

Now, we estimate β_1 by following the definition of net effect. In order to estimate the net effect of X_1, we should change X_1 only while holding $X_2, \cdots, X_k$ constant. To do it, we remove from X_1 the component correlated with $X_2, \cdots, X_k$. As explained above, the projection of X_1 onto the space formed by $X_2, \cdots, X_k$ decomposes X_1 into two components, the projected and residual components.

$$\begin{aligned} X_1 &= \left(\hat{d}_0 + \hat{d}_2 X_2 + \cdots + \hat{d}_k X_k \right) + \left(residual \right) \\ &= \hat{X}_1 + X_1^0 \end{aligned} \tag{A3.2}$$

The projected value $\hat{X}_1$ represents the component correlated with, $X_2, \cdots, X_k$ but the residual component X_1^0 is uncorrelated with them.

Consider the following simple regression which includes X_1^0 instead of X_1.

$$Y = \beta_0^* + \beta_1 X_1^0 + u^* \tag{A3.3}$$

Since the new independent variable X_1^0 is, by construction, uncorrelated with the other explanatory variables $X_2, \cdots, X_k$, this simple regression can measure a change in Y due to a change in X_1 with holding the other variables $X_2, \cdots, X_k$ constant. Thus, the coefficient β_1 in Eq. (A3.3) has the same interpretation as β_1 in the above multiple regression Eq. (A3.1). Both measure the net effect of X_1 on Y with holding $X_2, \cdots, X_k$ constant.

This explanation of two-step regressions, Eq. (A3.2) and Eq. (A3.3), is only to illustrate the interpretation of the partial regression coefficients in multiple regression models. In fact, we don't need to follow these two steps to estimate the net effect of explanatory variables. Instead, by estimating a multiple regression model Eq. (A3.1), we can obtain estimates of the regression coefficients which represent the net effects of corresponding explanatory variables.

However, use of the original variable X_1 in a simple regression produces a biased estimate. Consider the following simple regression which relates a change in X_1 to a change in Y.

$$Y = \alpha_0 + \alpha_1 X_1 + u^0 \tag{A3.4}$$

Since the independent variable X_1 contains not only the orthogonal component X_1^0 but also the component ($\hat{X}_1$) correlated with $X_2, \cdots, X_k$, any change in X_1 will also involve changes in $X_2, \cdots, X_k$. These changes in $X_2, \cdots, X_k$ will also affect the dependent variable Y.

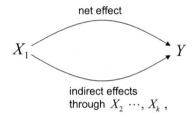

net effect

X_1 Y

indirect effects
through $X_2 \cdots, X_k$,

Thus, the coefficient α_1 in the simple regression Eq. (A3.4) represents not only the net effect but also the indirect effects (or confounding effects) through $X_2, \cdots, X_k$. In contrast, β_1 in Eq. (A3.3) represents the net effect of X_1 because the residual component X_1^0 is uncorrelated with $X_2, \cdots, X_k$.

In a special case in which X_1 is not correlated with $X_2, \cdots, X_k$ (i.e., $\hat{X}_1 = 0$), however, the OLS estimate of α_1 in Eq. (A3.4) is the same as the OLS estimates of β_1 in the other regressions, Eq. (A3.1) and Eq. (A3.3). When X_1 is projected onto $X_2, \cdots, X_k$, nothing will be extracted because they are not correlated at all, thereby $X_1 = X_1^0$. Then, Eq. (A3.4) is identical to Eq. (A3.3).

Note

1 BASE SAS 9.4 and SAS/STAT 13.1. SAS Institute Inc., Cary, NC.

4 Dummy explanatory variables

Learning objectives

In this chapter, you should learn about:

- Use of dummy variables to examine the differences between groups;
- Interpretation of the coefficients for dummy variables;
- Use and interpretation of the product of a dummy variable and a quantitative variable.

Until now, we have been using quantitative variables whose values themselves have meaning and can be used for calculation of OLS estimates. However, qualitative variables are observed not by numbers, but by an indication of the presence or absence of an attribute. Examples of observed values of qualitative variables are "male or female," "spring, summer, fall or winter," etc. These qualitative variables cannot be used for calculation of OLS estimates.

When a qualitative variable is to be included in a regression model, it first needs to be transformed into a quantitative variable. One way of quantifying the attributes is by constructing artificial (dummy) variables that take on values of 0 or 1, 0 indicating the absence of an attribute and 1 indicating the presence of that attribute.[1] These dummy variables can be used in regression analysis just as readily as quantitative variables.

4.1 Dummy variables for different intercepts

4.1.1 When there are two categories

Using a dummy variable, we can differentiate one group from the other. Consider a regression model which includes a dummy and a quantitative variable.

$$Y_i = \beta_0 + \beta_1 D_i + \beta_2 X_i + u_i \tag{4.1}$$

where D_i is 0 for group 0 and 1 for group 1. For an interpretation of the dummy coefficient in Eq. (4.1), it is recommended to write the conditional expected values of the dependent variable for all possible dummy values.

$$E(Y_i \mid X_i, D_i = 0) = \beta_0 + \beta_2 X_i$$

$$E(Y_i \mid X_i, D_i = 1) = \beta_0 + \beta_1 + \beta_2 X_i$$

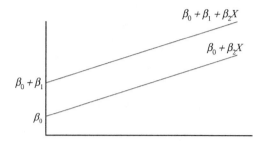

The coefficient of the dummy variable, β_1, represents the difference in the conditional mean of Y between the two groups, when the same value for X is used for both groups. More specifically, β_1 measures how much the average Y value of group 1 is larger than the average Y value of group 0, when their X values are the same. In this comparison, group 0 ($D = 0$) is treated as the reference group. The null hypothesis of $\beta_1 = 0$ implies that there is no difference in the intercept (or the level of the dependent variable) between the two groups.

Example 4.1   An economic research institute collected 20 observations to examine what determines households' consumption; below is a part of the Excel data file (4-dummy.xls). The variables are the monthly consumption (Y), the monthly income (X) and a dummy variable ($MALE$) taking on 1 if the household's head is male and 0 otherwise.[2]

	A	*B*	*C*	*D*
1	Consumption	Income	Dummy for Male	Gender
2	Y	X	MALE	
3	1280	1800	1	male
4	1380	1950	1	male
5	1260	1790	0	female
6	1090	1660	0	female
7	1120	1520	0	female
8	1460	2090	1	male
9	1330	1390	0	female
10	1460	2180	0	female

A   Consider the following simple regression.

$$Y = \alpha_0 + \alpha_1 MALE + u$$

(a) Interpret the coefficients α_0 and α_1.

(b) Estimate the coefficients α_0 and α_1 using the ordinary least squares (OLS) method.

(c) Test a hypothesis $H_0 : \alpha_1 = 0$ at a significance level of 0.05. Interpret the test results.

B   Consider the following regression which includes a dummy variable *MALE* and a quantitative variable *X*.

$$Y = \beta_0 + \beta_1 MALE + \beta_2 X + u$$

(d) Interpret coefficients β_1 and β_2.
(e) Estimate the coefficients β_1 and β_2 using the OLS method.
(f) Test a hypothesis $H_0 : \beta_1 = 0$ at a significance level of 0.05. Interpret the test results.
(g) What is your conclusion about the difference in consumption between the male-head and the female-head households?

[Answers]

(a) $E(Y \mid MALE = 0) = \alpha_0$ and $E(Y \mid MALE = 1) = \alpha_0 + \alpha_1$
   α_0 is the average consumption of the female-head households.
   α_1 measures how much the average consumption of the male-head households is greater than the one of the female-head households.
(b) $\hat{\alpha}_0 = 1190$, $\hat{\alpha}_1 = 279.0909$.

Variable	Coefficient	Std. Error	t-Statistic	Prob.
C	1190.000	55.00230	21.63546	0.0000
MALE	279.0909	74.16508	3.763104	0.0014

(c) The coefficient for *MALE* (α_1) is significant at a usual level of 5% because the *p*-value is 0.0014 (< 0.05). It indicates that the average consumption of the male-head households is significantly greater than the one of the female-head households. However, we are not sure whether the difference is entirely due to the gender of the household heads because it does not control for the effects of other possible factors including their income (*X*).
(d) $E(Y \mid MALE = 0, X) = \beta_0 + \beta_2 X$
   $E(Y \mid MALE = 1, X) = (\beta_0 + \beta_1) + \beta_2 X$
   β_1 measures how much the average consumption of the male-head households is higher than the one of the female-head households, when they have the same level of income. β_2 measures the marginal propensity to consume, i.e., how much the average consumption increases when the income increases by one unit, other things being equal. This marginal propensity to consume is assumed the same for both the female-head and male-head households.
(e) $\hat{\beta}_1 = 15.89432$, $\hat{\beta}_2 = 0.45866$.

Variable	Coefficient	Std. Error	t-Statistic	Prob.
C	419.9612	168.7268	2.489001	0.0235
MALE	15.89432	75.54592	0.210393	0.8359
X	0.458660	0.097997	4.680323	0.0002

(f) The coefficient for *MALE* (β_1) is not significant because the *p*-value is 0.8359 (> 0.05). It indicates that there is no significant difference in consumption between the male-head and the female-head households if they have the same level of income.
(g) Following the results in (f), I would conclude that there is no significant difference. The conflicting result in (c) is due to the confounding effects of income. In other words, the significant difference in (c) has arisen because the male-head households had, on average, higher income than the female-head households. Thus, the estimates in (c) are biased due to the omission of a significant variable *X*; this belongs to the correlated-omitted-variable problem.

4.1.2 When there are more than two categories

Since there are more than two categories, one dummy variable taking on 0 and 1 cannot differentiate all of the categories. Treating any one category as the reference group, we need to measure the differences between the reference group and the other categories. Thus, we need as many dummy variables as the number of categories minus one. For an example, consider the following model which includes quarter dummies to control for quarterly (or seasonal) effects. Treating quarter 4 as the reference group, we use three dummy variables representing the differences between quarter 4 and the other three quarters.

$$Y = \beta_0 + \beta_1 D1 + \beta_2 D2 + \beta_3 D3 + \gamma X + u$$

where $D1 = 1$ if quarter 1, 0 otherwise; $D2 = 1$ if quarter 2, 0 otherwise; and $D3 = 1$ if quarter 3, 0 otherwise. Then, the model implies:

Quarter 1, $E(Y \mid D1 = 1, D2 = 0, D3 = 0, X) = \beta_0 + \beta_1 + \gamma X$

Quarter 2, $E(Y \mid D1 = 0, D2 = 1, D3 = 0, X) = \beta_0 + \beta_2 + \gamma X$

Quarter 3, $E(Y \mid D1 = 0, D2 = 0, D3 = 1, X) = \beta_0 + \beta_3 + \gamma X$

Quarter 4, $E(Y \mid D1 = 0, D2 = 0, D3 = 0, X) = \beta_0 \quad\ + \gamma X$

The coefficient β_1 represents the effect of quarter 1, measuring how much the values during quarter 1 are on average larger than the values during quarter 4, when the other independent variables (X) have the same values. Similarly, β_2 and β_3 represent the effects of quarters 2 and 3, respectively.

4.1.3 Interpretation when the dependent variable is in logarithm

$$\ln Y = \alpha_0 + \alpha_1 D + \alpha_2 X + u$$

The above model implies

$$E(\ln Y \mid X, D = 0) = \alpha_0 + \alpha_2 X \qquad \Rightarrow \qquad E(Y \mid X, D = 0) = e^{\alpha_0 + \alpha_2 X}$$

$$E(\ln Y \mid X, D = 1) = \alpha_0 + \alpha_1 + \alpha_2 X \qquad \Rightarrow \qquad E(Y \mid X, D = 1) = e^{\alpha_0 + \alpha_1 + \alpha_2 X}$$

The percentage difference in Y between $D = 1$ and $D = 0$ is calculated as follows.

$$\frac{E(Y \mid X, D = 1) - E(Y \mid X, D = 0)}{E(Y \mid X, D = 0)} = \frac{e^{\alpha_0 + \alpha_1 + \alpha_2 X} - e^{\alpha_0 + \alpha_2 X}}{e^{\alpha_0 + \alpha_2 X}} = e^{\alpha_1} - 1 \cong \alpha_1.$$

The last approximation holds when α_1 is small enough. Thus, the dummy coefficient ($\times 100$) measures the percentage difference in Y between the two groups.

Example 4.2   Suppose we obtained the following estimated equation.

$$\ln \hat{Y} = 1.5 + 0.053D + 2.8X$$

It shows that, for a given value of X, the difference in $\ln Y$ between $D = 1$ and $D = 0$ is 0.053. This implies that the value of Y for the $D = 1$ group is 5.4% $= (e^{0.053} - 1) \times 100$ higher than the one for the $D = 0$ group, after controlling for the effect of X. The calculated percentage difference is approximately equal to the coefficient estimate for D times 100, i.e., 5.3%.

4.1.4 Application: Mitton (2002)

This paper was cited in Chapter 3 to illustrate multiple regression models. Remember that Mitton uses three aspects of corporate governance: disclosure quality, ownership structure and corporate diversification. In Chapter 3, we have looked at the analysis which uses the ownership structure for a measure of corporate governance. Here, we look at the analysis which uses dummy variables about the disclosure quality.

To measure disclosure quality, Mitton uses two dummy variables. The first dummy variable is set to one if the firm had an ADR listed in the US at the beginning of the crisis, and zero otherwise. The second dummy variable is set to one if the firm is audited by one of the Big Six international accounting firms, and zero otherwise.

Table 4.1 presents the results of regressions of crisis-period stock returns on measures of disclosure quality. The first two columns include the *ADR* indicator (with and without controls for size and leverage), the second two columns include the *Big Six auditor* indicator and the final two columns include both dummy variables. All columns include country and industry fixed effects. The final column of Table 4.1 shows that the coefficient on ADR is 0.108 after all controls are included. The magnitude of the coefficient indicates that firms with ADRs had, on average, a higher return of 10.8% over the crisis period.[3] The coefficient on *ADR* is significant at the 5% level. The coefficient on *Big Six auditor* is 0.081 with all controls included. The magnitude of the coefficient indicates that firms with *Big Six auditors* had, on average, an additional higher return of 8.1% over the crisis period. The coefficient on *Big Six auditor* is also significant at the 5% level.

Note: Regressions (i)–(v) suffer from the correlated-omitted-variable bias because some of the significant variables are not included. Therefore, the author interprets the results of regression (vi) only.

Table 4.1 Crisis-period stock returns and disclosure quality

	(i)	(ii)	(iii)	(iv)	(v)	(vi)
Constant	−0.468***	−0.550**	−0.481***	−0.776***	−0.509***	−0.596**
	(−5.56)	(−2.15)	(−5.29)	(−3.20)	(−5.61)	(−2.34)
ADR	0.123**	0.114**			0.117**	0.108**
	(2.56)	(2.27)			(2.55)	(2.30)
Big Six Auditor			0.098**	0.087**	0.092**	0.081**
			(2.26)	(2.09)	(2.18)	(2.01)
Firm size		0.025		0.050**		0.026
		(0.96)		(2.09)		(1.00)
Debt ratio		−0.0033***		−0.0033***		−0.0032***
		(−6.02)		(−6.04)		(−5.93)
Country dummies	Included	Included	Included	Included	Included	Included
Industry dummies	Included	Included	Included	Included	Included	Included
No of observations	398	384	398	384	398	384
R^2	0.204	0.265	0.199	0.262	0.214	0.273

Source: Mitton (2002, Table 2 on page 228).

Note: Heteroscedasticity-consistent *t*-statistics are given in brackets and asterisks denote significance levels: * = 10%, ** = 5%, and *** = 1%.

4.1.5 Application: Hakes and Sauer (2006)[4]

In his 2003 book *Moneyball*, financial reporter Michael Lewis made a striking claim: the valuation of skills in the market for baseball players was grossly inefficient. The discrepancy was so large that when the Oakland Athletics hired an unlikely management group consisting of Billy Beane, a former player with mediocre talent, and two quantitative analysts, the team was able to exploit this inefficiency and outproduce most of the competition, while operating on a shoestring budget.

In this paper, the authors test the central portion of Lewis's (2003) argument with elementary econometric tools and confirm his claims. In particular, they find that hitters' salaries during this period did not accurately reflect the contribution of various batting skills to winning games. This inefficiency was sufficiently large that knowledge of its existence, and the ability to exploit it, enabled the Oakland Athletics to gain a substantial advantage over their competition. Further, they find that market adjustments were in motion. These adjustments took place around the time Lewis's book was published, and with sufficient force that baseball's labor market no longer exhibits the *Moneyball* anomaly.

Measures of batting skill

The most common measure of batting skill is the *batting average*, which is the ratio of hits to total at-bats. The batting average is a crude index. By weighting singles and home runs the same, it ignores the added productivity from hits of more than a single base. Much better is the *slugging percentage*, which is total bases divided by at-bats, so that doubles count twice as much as singles, and home runs twice as much as doubles. Since a fundamental element of batting skill is the ability to avoid making an out, the failure to account for walks is a serious omission. Hitting a single leads to a higher batting average, and receiving a walk doesn't show up in batting average, but in both cases the batter ends up at first base. The statistic that takes walks into account is called *on-base percentage*, which is defined as the fraction of plate appearances (including both official at-bats as well as walks) in which the player reached base successfully through either a hit or a walk.

Members of the Society for American Baseball Research (SABR) have studied a variety of combinations of on-base percentage and slugging percentage in the hope of generating a single statistic that will capture a batter's contribution. It has long been known among this group, dubbed "sabermetricians," that linear combinations of these two percentages are very highly correlated with runs scored, the primary objective of an offense.

The essence of the *Moneyball* hypothesis is that "the ability to get on base was undervalued in the baseball labor market."

Contribution to winning

In Table 4.2, the dependent variable in the regression is the team's winning percentage. Column 1 of Table 4.2 shows that looking only at a team's own on-base percentage and the on-base percentage of its opponent can explain 82.5% of the variation in winning percentage. Column 2 shows that looking only at a team's own slugging percentage and the opponent's slugging percentage can explain 78.7% of the variation in winning percentage. Column 3 incorporates both measures of batting skill, which improves the explanatory power of the regression to 88.5% of variance. The coefficients on skills for a team and its opponents are quite close to each other, as would be expected in a two-sided symmetric game.

The final column of Table 4.2 is used to assess *Moneyball*'s claim (Lewis, 2003, p. 128) that, contrary to then-conventional wisdom, on-base percentage makes a more important contribution to winning

Table 4.2 The impact of on-base and slugging percentage on winning

	Model			
	1	*2*	*3*	*4*
Constant	0.508	0.612	0.502	0.500
	(0.114)	(0.073)	(0.099)	(0.005)
On-Base	3.294		2.141	2.032
	(0.221)		(0.296)	(0.183)
On-Base against	−3.317		−1.892	−2.032[R]
	(0.196)		(0.291)	
Slugging		1.731	0.802	0.900
		(0.122)	(0.149)	(0.106)
Slugging against		−1.999	−1.005	−0.900[R]
		(0.112)	(0.152)	
Number of observations	150	150	150	150
R^2 (%)	82.5	78.7	88.5	88.4

Hypothesis test of model 4, H_0: On-Base = Slugging
$F(1, 147) = 16.74$, *p*-value = 0.0001

Source: Hakes and Sauer (2006, Table 1 on page 176).

Notes: Data are aggregate statistics for all 30 teams from 1999 to 2003. Coefficient estimates were obtained using the OLS. Intercepts and the coefficients for annual 0/1 dummy variables are suppressed. Standard errors are in parentheses. Superscript "R" indicates that the coefficient was restricted to equal its counterpart in the regression. The *p*-value for the null hypothesis that restrictions are valid is 0.406 ($F = 0.52$).

games than slugging percentage. To facilitate the comparison, the "on-base" and "on-base against" coefficients are restricted to be the same, as are the "slugging" and "slugging against" coefficients. The coefficients in this regression for on-base percentage are more than twice as large as the coefficients for slugging, which supports Lewis's claim. A one-point change in a team's on-base percentage makes a significantly larger contribution to team winning percentage than a one-point change in team slugging percentage.

Valuation of batting skill in baseball

An efficient labor market for baseball players would, all other factors held constant, reward on-base percentage and slugging percentage in the same proportion that those statistics contribute to winning. The authors assess this proposition by estimating earnings equations for position players (excluding pitchers) for the 2000–2004 seasons. The dependent variable is the logarithm of annual salary. All productivity variables are calculated based on performance in the prior year, because salary is generally determined prior to performance, and based on expected productivity given observed performance in previous years.

The regression specification holds a number of other factors constant. The base category is for younger players who have limited power to negotiate for higher salaries under the collective bargaining agreement that governs baseball, and effectively face a monopsony employer of their labor. Players with more experience become eligible for salary arbitration, in which the team and player each propose a salary and the arbitrator must choose one of the positions, without splitting the difference. Players also eventually become eligible for free agency, which allows them to offer their services to all teams. The regression also includes a variable for playing time, as measured by plate appearances. It also adjusts for the fact that defensive skills are more important at certain positions by including indicator variables for players at the more demanding defensive positions of catcher and infielder (including second base, third base and shortstop).

The first column of results in Table 4.3 reports coefficient estimates from the log salary regression when all five years of data are pooled. All significant coefficients have the expected signs. Relative to younger players who have limited ability to negotiate their pay, players who are eligible for arbitration earn more, with an additional increment for players eligible to become free agents. There also exist positive and statistically significant returns to expected playing time.

The returns to on-base percentage and slugging are both positive, as expected. However, the coefficient for slugging on the income of a player is considerably larger than the coefficient for on-base percentage, which is the reverse of their importance to team success. This is consistent with *Moneyball's* claim that on-base percentage is undervalued in the labor market.

Column 3 through column 7 of Table 4.3 display parameter estimates for the same equation for each individual season. These results indicate that pooling is inappropriate, as labor market returns to player attributes differ across seasons. In the first four years of data (i.e., 2000–2003), the slugging coefficients are all statistically significant and of similar magnitude, ranging between 2.047 and 3.102. In contrast, the on-base percentage coefficients are smaller than their slugging counterparts in each of these years, ranging between - 0.132 and 1.351, and are not statistically significant.

This finding contrasts with the evidence from Table 4.2, which indicates that swapping a small increment of slugging percentage in return for a small increment of on-base percentage would increase a team's winning percentage. The lack of a market premium for hitters with superior skill at the patient art of reaching base through walks validates the systematic approach taken by the Oakland Athletics in identifying such players, and thereby winning games at a discount relative to their competition.

The relative valuation of on-base and slugging percentage is abruptly reversed for the year 2004. The salary returns to slugging are similar in 2004 to prior years, but 2004 is the first year in which

Table 4.3 The baseball labor market's valuation of on-base and slugging percentage

	All Years	2000–2003	2000	2001	2002	2003	2004
On-Base	1.360	0.842	1.334	−1.132	0.965	1.351	3.681
	(0.625)	(0.678)	(1.237)	(1.230)	(1.489)	(1.596)	(1.598)
Slugging	2.392	2.453	2.754	3.102	2.080	2.047	2.175
	(0.311)	(0.338)	(0.628)	(0.613)	(0.686)	(0.850)	(0.788)
Plate appearances	0.003	0.003	0.003	0.003	0.003	0.003	0.003
	(0.000)	(0.000)	(0.000)	(0.000)	(0.000)	(0.000)	(0.000)
Arbitration eligible	1.255	1.242	1.293	1.106	1.323	1.249	1.323
	(0.047)	(0.048)	(0.102)	(0.100)	(0.100)	(0.111)	(0.115)
Free agency	1.683	1.711	1.764	1.684	1.729	1.663	1.575
	(0.044)	(0.185)	(0.096)	(0.092)	(0.097)	(0.107)	(0.105)
Catcher dummy	0.152	0.185	0.137	0.065	0.208	0.343	0.059
	(0.056)	(0.061)	(0.124)	(0.116)	(0.122)	(0.134)	(0.133)
Infielder dummy	−0.029	−0.007	0.060	0.069	−0.087	−0.054	−0.100
	(0.040)	(0.044)	(0.087)	(0.083)	(0.086)	(0.095)	(0.098)
Observations	1,736	1,402	353	357	344	342	340
R^2 (%)	67.5	68.7	67.6	72.8	69.5	65.5	63.5

Source: Hakes and Sauer (2006, Table 3 on page 179).

Notes: The dependent variable is ln(Salary) for year t, and performance variables are from t–1. Intercepts are included but not reported. 0/1 dummies for each year are included in the pooled regressions. Standard errors are in parentheses. The sample includes all players with at least 130 plate appearances during the relevant season.

on-base percentage becomes statistically significant. The labor market in 2004 appears to have substantially corrected the apparent inefficiency in prior years, as the coefficient of on-base percentage jumps to 3.68, and the ratio of the monetary returns to reaching base and slugging is very close to the ratio of the statistics' contributions to team win percentage.

This diffusion of statistical knowledge across a handful of decision-making units in baseball was apparently sufficient to correct the mispricing of skill. The underpayment of the ability to get on base was substantially, if not completely, eroded within a year of *Moneyball*'s publication.

4.2 Dummy variables for different slopes

4.2.1 Use of a cross product with a dummy variable

A cross product of a dummy and a quantitative variable may be included in a regression:

$$Y_i = \beta_0 + \beta_1 D_i + \beta_2 X_i + \beta_3 (D_i \times X_i) + u_i \tag{4.2}$$

The conditional expected values of Y_i are

$$E(Y_i \mid X_i, D_i = 0) = \beta_0 + \beta_2 X_i$$

$$E(Y_i \mid X_i, D_i = 1) = (\beta_0 + \beta_1) + (\beta_2 + \beta_3) X_i$$

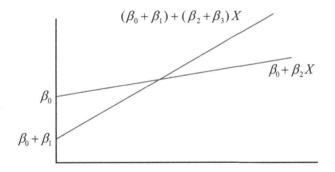

A null hypothesis of $\beta_3 = 0$ implies that there is no difference in the slope (or the net effect of the explanatory variable) between the two categories. Similarly, a null hypothesis of $\beta_1 = 0$ implies that there is no difference in the intercept between the two categories.[5] Together, a null hypothesis of $\beta_1 = \beta_3 = 0$ implies that there is no difference in the relation of Y and X between the two categories.

Example 4.3   (continued from Example 4.1)

Consider the following regression which includes a dummy variable and a product of the dummy and X.

$$Y = \gamma_0 + \gamma_1 MALE + \gamma_2 X + \gamma_3 (X \times MALE) + u$$

(h) Interpret the coefficients γ_1, γ_2 and γ_3.
(i) Estimate the coefficients γ_1, γ_2 and γ_3 using the OLS method.
(j) Test a hypothesis $H_0 : \gamma_3 = 0$ at a significance level of 0.05. Interpret the test results.
(k) Test a hypothesis $H_0 : \gamma_1 = \gamma_3 = 0$ at a significance level of 0.05. Interpret the test results.

[Answers]

(h) $E(Y \mid MALE = 0, X) = \gamma_0 + \gamma_2 X$

  $E(Y \mid MALE = 1, X) = (\gamma_0 + \gamma_1) + (\gamma_2 + \gamma_3) X$

  γ_1 measures how much the average consumption of the male-head households is higher than the one of the female-head households, when their income level is zero. Since our interest is not limited to the case of zero income, this coefficient does not have much meaning.

  γ_2 is the marginal propensity to consume (MPC) of the female-head households.

  γ_3 measures how much the MPC of the male-head households is larger than the one of the female-head households.

(i) Before estimating the model, we need to generate a new variable for $X \times MALE$, a cross product of X and $MALE$. Click the Genr button in the *EViews* Workfile menu and type an expression, "$X\_MALE = X \times MALE$." The calculated values are saved in a new variable name X_MALE:

obs	MALE	X	X_MALE	Y
1	1	1800	1800	1280
2	1	1950	1950	1380
3	0	1790	0	1260
4	0	1660	0	1090
5	0	1520	0	1120
6	1	2090	2090	1460

The OLS estimates are $\hat{\gamma}_1 = -396.161$, $\hat{\gamma}_2 = 0.311257$, $\hat{\gamma}_3 = 0.220462$, according to the following *EViews* output.

Variable	Coefficient	Std. Error	t-Statistic	Prob.
C	667.4339	287.1453	2.324377	0.0336
MALE	−396.1610	394.8762	−1.003254	0.3307
X	0.311257	0.169586	1.835392	0.0851
X_MALE	0.220462	0.207398	1.062990	0.3036

(j) The coefficient for the interaction term (γ_3) is not significant because the *p*-value (0.3036) is larger than the 5% significance level. It indicates that there is no significant difference in MPC between the male-head and the female-head households.

(k) Following the instructions given in Appendix 3A, we can obtain the following Wald-test results. Since the *p*-value is 0.5558 (or 0.5674), we do not reject H_0.

Wald Test:			
Equation: Untitled			

Test Statistic	Value	df	Probability
F-statistic	0.587275	(2, 16)	0.5674
Chi-square	1.174551	2	0.5558

FYI: For models which include many dummy variables and their cross products, it is recommended that you express the conditional expected values of the dependent variable for all possible cases of dummy values. By comparing the conditional expected values, you will be able to interpret the regression coefficients. A good example is in DeFond and Subramanyam (1998, p. 53).

4.2.2 Application: Basu (1997)

This study interprets accounting conservatism as capturing accountants' tendency to require a higher degree of verification for recognizing "good news" than "bad news" in financial statements. Under this interpretation of conservatism, earnings reflect bad news more quickly than good news. Using firms' stock returns as a proxy variable for good and bad news, Basu predicts that the contemporaneous sensitivity of earnings to negative returns is higher than that of earnings to positive returns, that is, an asymmetric response of earnings.

Basu regresses annual earnings on current stock returns.

$$X_{it} / P_{i,t-1} = \alpha_0 + \alpha_1 DR_{it} + \beta_0 R_{it} + \beta_1 (R_{it} \times DR_{it}) + u_{it} \tag{4.3}$$

where X_{it} is the earnings per share for firm i in fiscal year t, $P_{i,t-1}$ is the price per share at the beginning of the fiscal year, and R_{it} is the return on firm i from nine months before fiscal year-end t to three months after fiscal year-end t. And, a dummy variable DR_{it} is set to 1 if $R_{it} < 0$, i.e., bad news, and 0 otherwise. The conditional expected values of $X_{it} / P_{i,t-1}$ in Eq. (4.3) are

$$E(X_{it} / P_{i,t-1} | DR_{it} = 0, R_{it}) = \alpha_0 + \beta_0 R_{it}$$

$$E(X_{it} / P_{i,t-1} | DR_{it} = 1, R_{it}) = (\alpha_0 + \alpha_1) + (\beta_0 + \beta_1) R_{it}$$

According to the accounting conservatism, the dependent variable (earnings) is believed to contain more timely information for "bad news" firms. Thus, the slope coefficient for stock returns is predicted to be greater for the "bad news" sample, i.e., $\beta_1 > 0$, because earnings are more sensitive to negative returns.

Table 4.4 presents pooled cross-sectional regression results for price deflated earnings on inter-announcement period returns. The above regression divides firm-year observations into "good news" and "bad news" samples based on whether the return was greater than or less than zero. Dummy variables capture the intercept and slope effects for the negative return sample. The interactive slope coefficient, β_1, which measures the difference in sensitivity of earnings to negative and positive returns, is significant, and implies that earnings is about four and a half times, $4.66 = (0.216 + 0.059)/0.059$, as sensitive to negative returns as it is to positive returns.

Table 4.4 Coefficients and adjusted R^2s from pooled cross-sectional regressions, excluding outliers, of price deflated earnings on inter-announcement period returns

α_0	α_1	β_0	β_1	Adj. R^2
0.090***	0.002	0.059***	**0.216*****	10.09
(68.03)	(0.86)	(18.34)	**(20.66)**	

Source: Adapted from Basu (1997, Table 1 on page 13).

Notes: White (1980) heteroscedasticity-consistent t-statistics are given in parentheses and asterisks (***) denote a 1% significance level. Statistics that test the hypotheses are indicated in bold typeface.

4.3 Structural stability of regression models

4.3.1 Test by splitting the sample (Chow test)

The following *full model* allows a possibility for different coefficients between two periods:

$$Y_t = \alpha_0 + \alpha_1 X_t + \alpha_2 Z_t + u_{1t}, \quad \text{for} \quad t \leq t_0$$
$$Y_t = \beta_0 + \beta_1 X_t + \beta_2 Z_t + u_{2t}, \quad \text{for} \quad t > t_0$$

The null hypothesis of no structural change is expressed as $\alpha_0 = \beta_0$, $\alpha_1 = \beta_1$ and $\alpha_2 = \beta_2$. Then, the *reduced model*, i.e., the model under the null hypothesis, will be

$$Y_t = \alpha_0 + \alpha_1 X_t + \alpha_2 Z_t + u_t, \quad \text{for all} \quad t$$

The test statistic of the following form is known to follow an F distribution:

$$F = \frac{(ESS_R - ESS_F)/k}{ESS_F/(n-2k)} \sim F(k, n-2k)$$

where ESS_R is the error sum of squares for the reduced model and ESS_F is the error sum of squares for the full model. The numerator measures how restrictive the null hypothesis is, in other words, how much we can reduce the error sum of squares by eliminating the restriction of the null hypothesis. If the null hypothesis is supported by the data, the F value will be small because the null hypothesis is not restrictive. In contrast, if the null hypothesis is not consistent with the data, the F value will be large, rejecting the null hypothesis.

4.3.2 Test using dummy variables

Instead of applying the above Chow test, the structural stability can also be tested using dummy variables as follows.

$$Y_t = \gamma_0 + \gamma_1 D_t + \gamma_2 X_t + \gamma_3 (D_t \times X_t) + \gamma_4 Z_t + \gamma_5 (D_t \times Z_t) + u_t$$

where $D_t = 0$ for $t \leq t_0$ and 1 for $t > t_0$. Then the conditional expected values are

$$E(Y_t \mid X_t, D_t = 0) = \gamma_0 + \gamma_2 X_t + \gamma_4 Z_t$$
$$E(Y_t \mid X_t, D_t = 1) = (\gamma_0 + \gamma_1) + (\gamma_2 + \gamma_3)X_t + (\gamma_4 + \gamma_5)Z_t$$

The coefficients for the interaction terms $(\gamma_1, \gamma_3, \gamma_5)$ represent the differences in their corresponding coefficients. Therefore, the null hypothesis of $\gamma_1 = \gamma_3 = \gamma_5 = 0$ implies that there is no change in the coefficients between the two periods.

The dummy-variable approach has an advantage over the sample division as in the Chow test. Using the dummy variables, we can test just a few of the regression coefficients for structural change; for example, $H_0 : \gamma_3 = \gamma_5 = 0$.

4.4 Piecewise linear regression models

The slope of a piecewise regression model can vary as an explanatory variable changes, but this piecewise regression has only one slope for each value of the explanatory variable. In contrast, a regression model with an interaction of a dummy (D) and an explanatory variable has two slopes for the same value of the explanatory variable; one slope for $D = 0$ and the other for $D = 1$.

4.4.1 Using dummy variables

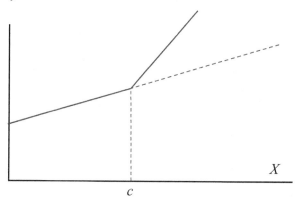

The above piecewise regression can be modeled using a dummy variable as follows.

$$Y_i = \beta_0 + \beta_1 X_i + \beta_2 (X_i - c) \times D_i + u_i \qquad (4.4)$$

where $D_i = 0$ if $X_i < c$ and 1 otherwise.

This model implies

$$
\begin{aligned}
E(Y_i \mid X_i, D_i = 0) &= \beta_0 + \beta_1 X_i \\
E(Y_i \mid X_i, D_i = 1) &= \beta_0 + \beta_1 X_i + \beta_2 (X_i - c) = \beta_0 - \beta_2 c + (\beta_1 + \beta_2) X_i
\end{aligned}
\qquad (4.5)
$$

When $D_i = 0$, the piecewise regression describes the Y-X relation for the range of X less than c. And $D_i = 1$ expresses the relation for the X range greater than or equal to c. Thus, the coefficient for the cross-product term, β_2, measures the change in the slope coefficient as X exceeds c. The null hypothesis of $H_0 : \beta_2 = 0$ implies that the slope is constant for the entire range of X.

4.4.2 Using quantitative variables only

Instead of using the dummy variable, we can express the above model using new variables of Z_{1i} and Z_{2i}

$$Y_i = \gamma_0 + \gamma_1 Z_{1i} + \gamma_2 Z_{2i} + u_i$$

where $Z_{1i} = X_i$ and $Z_{2i} = 0$ if $X_i < c$; $Z_{1i} = c$ and $Z_{2i} = X_i - c$ if $X_i \geq c$. Then the conditional expected values are

$$E(Y_i \mid X_i < c) = \gamma_0 + \gamma_1 X_i \qquad\qquad (4.6)$$
$$E(Y_i \mid X_i \geq c) = \gamma_0 + \gamma_1 c + \gamma_2 (X_i - c)$$

From Eq. (4.5) and Eq. (4.6), we obtain the following relations between the two different expressions of the piecewise regression.

$$\gamma_0 = \beta_0, \quad \gamma_1 = \beta_1, \quad \gamma_2 = \beta_1 + \beta_2$$

Coefficients β_1 and γ_1 have the same meaning, i.e., the response of Y to a unit change in X. But, the meaning of β_2 is different from the one of γ_2. As X exceeds c, the response of Y can be decomposed into two components: one is the same response (β_1) as when X is less than c, and the other is an *incremental* response (β_2) to a unit change in X exceeding c. In contrast, γ_2 is the *total* response of Y to a unit change in X exceeding c, i.e., $\gamma_2 = \beta_1 + \beta_2$. Thus, a null hypothesis of $H_0 : \gamma_1 = \gamma_2$ implies that the slope coefficient is constant for all values of X, equivalent to $H_0 : \beta_2 = 0$ in Eq. (4.4).

4.4.3 Morck, Shleifer and Vishny (1988)

The authors investigate the relationship between management ownership and market valuation of the firm, as measured by Tobin's Q. In a 1980 cross-section of 371 Fortune 500 firms, they find evidence of a significant nonmonotonic relationship. As shown in Figure 4.1, Tobin's Q first increases, then declines, and finally increases slightly as ownership by the board of directors increases.

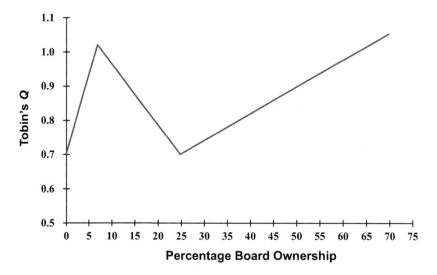

Figure 4.1 The relationship between board ownership and Tobin's Q

Source: Morck et al. (1988, Figure 1 on page 301).

To estimate the nonmonotonic relationship, the authors define three new variables (Z_1, Z_2, Z_3) according to the management ownership X.

$$
\begin{aligned}
Z_{1i} &= X_i & \text{if } X_i < 0.05 \\
&= 0.05 & \text{if } X_i \geq 0.05
\end{aligned}
$$

$$
\begin{aligned}
Z_{2i} &= 0 & \text{if } X_i < 0.05 \\
&= X_i - 0.05 & \text{if } 0.05 \leq X_i < 0.25 \\
&= 0.20 & \text{if } X_i \geq 0.25
\end{aligned}
$$

$$
\begin{aligned}
Z_{3i} &= 0 & \text{if } X_i < 0.25 \\
&= X_i - 0.25 & \text{if } X_i \geq 0.25
\end{aligned}
$$

Below is the regression model.

$$Tobin\ Q_i = \beta_0 + \beta_1 Z_{1i} + \beta_2 Z_{2i} + \beta_3 Z_{3i} + (controls) + u_i$$

where the control variables include R&D expenditure, advertising expenditures, long-term debt, replacement cost and industry dummies. Figure 4.1 shows the estimated piecewise regression line.

4.5 Summary

1   When qualitative variables are included in regression models, they need first be transformed into quantitative variables; for an easy interpretation of the dummy coefficients, we define dummy variables to take on values of 0 or 1. Regression models which include dummy variables can be estimated by the OLS method in the same way.

2   The coefficient of a dummy variable D measures the difference in the conditional mean of the dependent variable between the reference group ($D = 0$) and the comparison group represented by the dummy variable ($D = 1$).

3   If there are $G(\geq 2)$ groups to compare, we need to include $(G - 1)$ dummy variables; one group is used as the reference group.

4   By including the product of a dummy variable (D) and a quantitative variable, we can allow the regression coefficient for the quantitative variable to vary between the two groups of $D = 0$ and $D = 1$.

Review questions

1   To examine the determinants of households' consumption, a research institute used the following variables: monthly consumption (Y), monthly income (X_1), number of household's members (X_2) and a dummy variable ($RURAL$) taking on 1 if the household lives in a rural area and 0 otherwise. Consider the following regression model

$$Y_i = \beta_0 + \beta_1 X_{1i} + \beta_2 X_{2i} + \beta_3 RURAL_i + u_i$$

(a)   What is the expression of the average consumption for the households living in rural areas, i.e., $E(Y_i \mid X_{1i}, X_{2i}, RURAL_i = 1)$?

(b)   What is the expression of the average consumption for the households living in urban areas, i.e., $E(Y_i \mid X_{1i}, X_{2i}, RURAL_i = 0)$?

(c)   What is the meaning of β_1, β_2 and β_3?

2   Consider the following multiple regression model.

$$E_i = \beta_0 + \beta_1 P_i + \beta_2 \log BV_i + \beta_3 BIG5_i + u_i$$

where E_i is the annual earnings per share for firm i; P_i is the stock price of the firm; $\log BV_i$ is the logarithm of the book value of equity per share; and $BIG5_i$ is a dummy variable that takes the value of 1 if the auditor is a Big Five and 0 otherwise.

(a)   Explain what β_1 measures.

(b)   If a null hypothesis $H_0 : \beta_1 = 0$ is rejected, what does it imply?

(c)   Explain what β_2 measures. (Notice that the variable is in the logarithm of BV.)

(d)   If a null hypothesis $H_0 : \beta_2 = 0$ is rejected, what does it imply?

(e)   Explain what β_3 measures.

(f)   If a null hypothesis $H_0 : \beta_3 = 0$ is rejected, what does it imply?

3   When we analyze quarterly data, we need to account for the quarterly (or seasonal) effects. To do it, we include quarterly dummies as follows.

$$Y_{it} = \beta_0 + \beta_1 D1_{it} + \beta_2 D2_{it} + \beta_3 D3_{it} + \gamma X_{it} + u_{it}$$

where $D1_{it} = 1$ if quarter 1, 0 otherwise; $D2_{it} = 1$ if quarter 2, 0 otherwise; and $D3_{it} = 1$ if quarter 3, 0 otherwise.

(a)   If the dummy coefficients $(\beta_1, \beta_2, \beta_3)$ are known, how can we eliminate the quarterly effects from the dependent variable?

(b)   If the dummy coefficients are not known, how can we eliminate the quarterly effects from the dependent variable?

4   Consider the following models.

(1) $Y = \alpha_0 + \alpha_1 MALE + \theta X + u_1$

(2) $Y = \beta_0 + \beta_1 FEMALE + \theta X + u_2$

(3) $Y = \gamma_1 MALE + \gamma_2 FEMALE + \theta X + u_3$

(4) $Y = \delta_0 + \delta_1 MALE + \delta_2 FEMALE + \theta X + u_4$

where $MALE = 1$ if male, 0 otherwise; $FEMALE = 1$ if female, 0 otherwise; Y and X are quantitative variables.

(a)   Interpret the coefficients α_0 and α_1 in Eq. (1).

Using the coefficients, express the difference in Y between the $MALE$ and $FEMALE$ groups, for the same value of X.

(b)   Interpret the coefficients β_0 and β_1 in Eq. (2).

Using the coefficients, express the difference in Y between the two groups, for the same value of X.

(c)   Interpret the coefficients γ_1 and γ_2 in Eq. (3).

Using the coefficients, express the difference in Y between the two groups, for the same value of X.

(d) Show that Eqs. (1), (2) and (3) are equivalent in the estimation of the difference in Y between the *MALE* and *FEMALE* groups.

(e) Explain why Eq. (4) cannot be estimated.

5   Consider the following regression where the intercept and the coefficient for *ASIAN* are known.

$$Y_i = 1 + 2 \times ASIAN_i + \beta X_i + u_i$$

Two dummy variables are defined:

$ASIAN_i = 1$ if a subject is an Asian, 0 otherwise;

$NonASIAN_i = 1$ if a subject is not an Asian, 0 otherwise;

(a) Given the same value of the quantitative variable X, what is the expected difference of Y between the Asian and the non-Asian subjects?

(b) If we use a different dummy variable *NonASIAN*, what are the values of α_0 and α_1 in the following regression?

$$Y_i = \alpha_0 + \alpha_1 NonASIAN_i + \beta X_i + u_i$$

(c) If we include both dummy variables without an intercept, what are the values of γ_1 and γ_2?

$$Y_i = \gamma_1 ASIAN_i + \gamma_2 NonASIAN_i + \beta X_i + u_i$$

(d) If we include the two dummy variables and also an intercept, what are the values of δ_0, δ_1 and δ_2?

$$Y_i = \delta_0 + \delta_1 ASIAN_i + \delta_2 NonASIAN_i + \beta X_i + u_i$$

6   Consider the following two regressions which include dummy variables.

(A) $Y_i = \alpha_0 + \alpha_1 LARGE_i + \alpha_2 FINANCE_i + \delta X_i + v_i$

(B) $Y_i = \beta_0 + \beta_1 LARGE_i + \beta_2 FINANCE_i + \beta_3 (LARGE_i \times FINANCE_i) + \gamma X_i + u_i$

where Y and X are quantitative variables; $LARGE = 1$ if a firm's size is bigger than the median of the sample, 0 otherwise; and $FINANCE = 1$ if a firm belongs to the finance industry, 0 otherwise.

(a) Interpret the dummy coefficients (α_1, α_2) in Eq. (A).

(b) Interpret the dummy coefficients $(\beta_1, \beta_2, \beta_3)$ in Eq. (B).

(c) What is the difference between the two regressions?

7   To examine the differences between four quarters, we defined the following four dummies.

$D1_t = 1$ if quarter 1, 0 otherwise; $D2_t = 1$ if quarter 2, 0 otherwise;

$D3_t = 1$ if quarter 3, 0 otherwise; $D4_t = 1$ if quarter 4, 0 otherwise.

Using three dummies, we obtained the following estimates.

$$\hat{Y}_t = 2 + 1.5 D1_t + 3 D2_t - 0.5 D3_t$$

(a)   What is the expected value of Y for each quarter?

(b)   What is the difference in the expected value of Y between quarters 2 and 3?

(c)   Now we are using quarter 1 as the reference group. Calculate the estimates for $(\alpha_0, \alpha_2, \alpha_3, \alpha_4)$ in the following model.

$$Y_t = \alpha_0 + \alpha_2 D2_t + \alpha_3 D3_t + \alpha_4 D4_t + u_t$$

Notes

1   You may use dummy variables which take on any other values, e.g., 5 or -10. However, it will be very difficult (even impossible) to interpret their regression coefficients if other values than 0 and 1 are assigned to dummy variables.

2   When we name a dummy variable, it is recommended to use a name which describes the group taking on value 1. If so, the coefficient on the dummy variable measures how much the average Y value of this group (described by the dummy name) is larger than the one of the reference group.

3   It should be "a higher return of 10.8% *point.*"

4   Copyright American Economic Association; reproduced with permission of the *Journal of Economic Perspectives*.

5   If $\beta_3 \neq 0$, this null hypothesis of $\beta_1 = 0$ has no meaning because β_1 measures the Y difference only at $X = 0$. In contrast, if $\beta_3 = 0$, then the two lines are parallel and thus measures the difference in Y for all levels of the explanatory variable, as explained in the previous section.

References

Basu, S. (1997), "The Conservatism Principle and the Asymmetric Timeliness of Earnings," *Journal of Accounting and Economics*, 24, 3–37.

DeFond, M.L. and K.R. Subramanyam (1998), "Auditor Changes and Discretionary Accruals," *Journal of Accounting and Economics*, 25, 35–67.

Hakes, J.K. and R.D. Sauer (2006), "An Economic Evaluation of the *Moneyball* Hypothesis," *Journal of Economic Perspectives*, 20(3), 173–185.

Lewis, M. (2003), *Moneyball: The Art of Winning an Unfair Game*, Notron: New York.

Mitton, T. (2002), "A Cross-Firm Analysis of the Impact of Corporate Governance on the East Asian Financial Crisis," *Journal of Financial Economics*, 64, 215–241.

Morck, R., A. Shleifer and R.W. Vishny (1988), "Management Ownership and Market Valuation: An Empirical Analysis," *Journal of Financial Economics*, 20, 293–315.

White, H. (1980), "A Heteroscedasticity Consistent Covariance Matrix Estimator and A Direct Test for Heteroscedasticity," *Econometrica*, 48, 817–838.

Appendix 4 Dummy variables in *EViews* and *SAS*

An Excel file "4-dummy-quarter.xls" contains quarterly time-series data on the growth rate of real GDP (*RGDP*), interest rate (*INTEREST*) and the growth rate of real government expenditures (*RGEXP*), from 2001Q1 until 2006Q4.

	A	B	C	D	E
1	Year	QT	RGDP	INTEREST	RGEXP
2	2001	1	2.3	4.3	3.2
3	2001	2	1.2	4.6	2.4
4	2001	3	2.5	4.2	3.0
5	2001	4	3.2	3.9	3.5
6	2002	1	2.1	4.2	2.9
7	2002	2	1.5	4.6	2.1
8	2002	3	2.1	4.3	3.1

Using *EViews*

After importing this Excel file, we need to generate dummy variables using the quarter variable QT. Having the fourth quarter as the reference group, we generate three dummies which represent quarters 1, 2 and 3. Click the Genr button and enter a logical expression "D1 = QT=1" for the quarter 1 dummy. The logical expression is evaluated for each observation, assigning 1 to a dummy variable D1 if QT = 1 and 0 otherwise. Repeat the same procedures for two more dummies using their logical expressions, "D2 = QT=2" and "D3 = QT=3."

To estimate a regression model, click Objects/New Object/Equation in the Workfile menu and type the equation "RGDP C INTEREST RGEXP D1 D2 D3." The OLS estimation results are shown in Output 4.1

Output 4.1   OLS estimation results: 4-dummy-quarter.xls

Dependent Variable: RGDP
Method: Least Squares
Sample: 2001Q1 2006Q4
Included observations: 24

Variable	Coefficient	Std. Error	t-Statistic	Prob.
C	3.071983	2.772472	1.108030	0.2824
INTEREST	−0.407702	0.562639	−0.724624	0.4780
RGEXP	0.528081	0.256475	2.059000	0.0543
D1	−0.558301	0.255113	−2.188447	0.0421
D2	−0.845654	0.419342	−2.016624	0.0589
D3	−0.470310	0.204282	−2.302262	0.0335

Using *SAS*[1]

```
FILENAME F1 DDE 'EXCEL|[4-dummy-quarter.XLS]DUMMY!R2C1:R25C5';
DATA DAT1; INFILE F1; INPUT YEAR QT RGDP INTEREST RGEXP;
    IF QT=1 THEN D1=1; ELSE D1=0;
    IF QT=2 THEN D2=1; ELSE D2=0;
    IF QT=3 THEN D3=1; ELSE D3=0;
PROC REG ;
    MODEL RGDP=INTEREST RGEXP D1 D2 D3;
RUN;
```

Notes

1 BASE SAS 9.4 and SAS/STAT 13.1. SAS Institute Inc., Cary, NC.

5 More on multiple regression analysis

Learning objectives

In this chapter, you should learn about:

- Consequences and solutions of multicollinearity;
- Heteroscedastic vs. homoscedastic disturbances;
- Use and interpretation of squared variables;
- Use and interpretation of the product of two quantitative variables.

5.1 Multicollinearity

The multicollinearity arises when explanatory variables are highly correlated. To see why high correlation among explanatory variables causes a problem, consider an extreme case. As shown in Table 5.1, the values of $X1$ are exactly the same as the ones of $X3$ although they are named differently.

When we regress Y on $X1$ only, the OLS estimates are shown in Output 5.1, that is,

$$\hat{Y} = \hat{\beta}_0 + \hat{\beta}_1 X1 = 11.46667 + 0.860606 \times X1 \tag{5.1}$$

Table 5.1 An example of multicollinearity

obs	Y	X1	X2	X3
1	10	1	1	1
2	13	2	2	2
3	15	3	3.5	3
4	16	4	4	4
5	18	5	5	5
6	17	6	6	6
7	18	7	7	7
8	16	8	8	8
9	19	9	9	9
10	20	10	10	10

Output 5.1   Regression of Y on X1

Dependent Variable: Y
Method: Least Squares
Sample: 1 10
Included observations: 10

Variable	Coefficient	Std. Error	t-Statistic	Prob.
C	11.46667	1.038744	11.03897	0.0000
X1	0.860606	0.167409	5.140745	0.0009
R-squared	0.767626	Mean dependent var		16.20000
Adjusted R-squared	0.738579	S.D. dependent var		2.973961

Since $X1$ and $X3$ are perfectly correlated, however, all of the following regression lines are identical to Eq. (5.1).

$$
\begin{aligned}
\hat{Y} &= 11.46667 + 0.860606 \times X1 + 0 \times X3 \\
&= 11.46667 + 0 \times X1 + 0.860606 \times X3 \\
&= 11.46667 + 100.860606 \times X1 - 100 \times X3
\end{aligned}
\tag{5.2}
$$

That is, estimates of the coefficients for $X1$ and $X3$ can be any values as long as the sum of their estimates is equal to 0.860606. Therefore, it is impossible to determine estimates for their coefficients.[1]

From this extreme example, we can infer that if explanatory variables are highly correlated, e.g., $X1$ and $X2$ in Table 5.1, there are many possible values which can be assigned to their coefficient estimates.[2] In other words, their coefficients cannot be estimated precisely, thereby their standard errors being large.

A comparison of Output 5.1 and Output 5.2 shows that the standard error of the $X1$ coefficient estimate increases from 0.167409 to 3.424819 when $X2$ is added to the regression model. As a result, the absolute t-ratio drops to -0.412645 from 5.140745, thereby the coefficient of $X1$ being not significantly different from zero.[3]

Output 5.2   Regression of Y on $X1$ and $X2$

Dependent Variable: Y
Method: Least Squares
Sample: 1 10
Included observations: 10

Variable	Coefficient	Std. Error	t-Statistic	Prob.
C	11.15882	1.172321	9.518570	0.0000
X1	−1.413235	3.424819	−0.412645	0.6922
X2	2.308824	3.473040	0.664785	0.5275
R-squared	0.781426	Mean dependent var		16.20000
Adjusted R-squared	0.718976	S.D. dependent var		2.973961

5.1.1 Consequences of multicollinearity

A high correlation among explanatory variables does not violate any of the four assumptions listed in Chapters 2 and 3. Therefore, the OLS estimators are still BLUE; that is, they are unbiased and efficient. Therefore, it is still valid to test hypotheses on coefficients using the t-statistics and the p-values derived by the OLS method.

If so, why do we care about multicollinearity? Although the OLS estimators are unbiased and efficient, their standard errors become large, thereby t-statistics being small (thus p-values being large). As a result, the coefficients tend to be insignificant. A main objective of employing regression analysis is to show that certain independent variables are significant factors for the dependent variable. However, large standard errors caused by multicollinearity would reduce the significance of possible factors.

The estimation results in Output 5.1 show that $X1$ is significantly correlated with the dependent variable Y with the t-statistic of 5.14 and the p-value of 0.0009. However, when we include highly correlated variables $X1$ and $X2$ together, their coefficients become insignificant with small t-statistics due to large standard errors. It implies that $X1$ can be excluded when $X2$ is present or that $X2$ can be excluded when $X1$ is present. This conclusion indicates that either $X1$ or $X2$ does not make any incremental contribution to the understanding of the Y variation because they contain similar information about Y.

In addition, multicollinearity makes it difficult to interpret individual coefficient estimates in many cases. In Output 5.2, the coefficient estimate of $X1$ is negative (-1.413235) when $X1$ is positively correlated with Y. It is because the multicollinearity increases the standard error and does not allow precise estimation.

Now, we discuss ways of detecting multicollinearity. First, by calculating pair-wise correlations among independent variables, we can confirm how highly they are correlated.

Second, when there exists multicollinearity, the overall R^2 is high, but individual coefficients are insignificant with small t-statistics (or large p-values). Output 5.2 shows that the R^2 is high (0.781426) while the coefficients for $X1$ and $X2$ are insignificant with large p-values of 0.6922 and 0.5275, respectively. As explained above, both $X1$ and $X2$ share similar information and can explain a large portion of the variation in Y. However, each variable does not contain any incremental information, thereby each coefficient being insignificant.

Third, multicollinearity makes coefficient estimates sensitive to model specification. That is, regression coefficient estimates are drastically altered when variables are added or dropped. The coefficient estimate for $X1$ is 0.860606 when it is included alone (Output 5.1), but it has drastically changed to -1.413235 when $X2$ is added (Output 5.2).

Concerning the identification of multicollinearity it is important to understand multicollinearity in a *continuous* way.[4] Multicollinearity is the extent to which an independent variable is correlated with other independent variables. In fact, all observed variables are correlated with each other to some extent. Thus, it is not correct to conclude whether there exists multicollinearity. Instead, our concern is whether a correlation among independent variables prevents us from obtaining significant results. If we obtain the significant results we want, we don't need to worry about, if any, multicollinearity. This reasoning helps us find solutions for multicollinearity.

5.1.2 Solutions

1   Even with a high correlation among independent variables, if their regression coefficients are significant and have meaningful signs and magnitudes, we need not be too concerned about multicollinearity. If a coefficient is significant even in the presence of multicollinearity, it is clearly a strong result.

2   The surest way to eliminate or reduce an effect of multicollinearity is to drop one or more of the variables from a model. One way is to apply the General-to-Simple approach explained in Chapter 3.

3   If a variable is included in a model for a theoretical reason and is strongly supported by previous studies, it would be safe to keep the variable no matter how insignificant its coefficient is. You may reduce an effect of multicollinearity by eliminating other insignificant variables which are weakly supported by theory and previous studies.

4   If an analyst is less interested in interpreting individual coefficients but more interested in obtaining fitted values of the dependent variable, multicollinearity may not be a serious concern. One can simply ignore it without any dire consequences. It is because a fitted value is a linear combination of the independent variables. In Eq. (5.2), all expressions yield the same value of $\hat{Y}$ although each expression has very different coefficient estimates for $X1$ and $X3$ from the others.

5.2 Heteroscedasticity

Remember that the OLS estimator is the best linear unbiased estimator (BLUE) if regression models satisfy the four assumptions listed in Chapter 2. One of the assumptions is that the variance of the error term is constant over observations. In this section, we consider a case in which the assumption of equal variance is violated. That is, the variance of the error term varies over observations. This heteroscedasticity can be expressed with a subscript i added.

$$Var(u_i \mid X_{2i}, \cdots, X_{ki}) = \sigma_i^2$$

5.2.1 Consequences of heteroscedasticity

Even though the error term is heteroscedastic, the OLS estimator for β is still unbiased and consistent.[5] However, the OLS estimator becomes inefficient: in other words, its variance is not the smallest among the unbiased estimators.[6] Therefore, it is possible to find another unbiased estimator which has a smaller variance than the OLS estimator.

When the error term is heteroscedastic, the estimated variance (and the standard error) of the OLS estimator is not correct because the OLS ignores the differences in the variances in the error term, thereby yielding an incorrect t-value and p-value. As a result, test of hypotheses (e.g., $H_0 : \beta = 0$) based on the OLS estimation is no longer valid.

5.2.2 Testing for heteroscedasticity

(i) Visual inspection

This is just a preliminary procedure. We can graph the squared residuals against a variable that is suspected to be a cause of heteroscedasticity. If the model has several explanatory variables, one might want to graph $\hat{u}_i^2$ against each of these variables or graph it against $\hat{Y}_i$, the OLS fitted value of the dependent variable. It should be pointed out, however, that this graphing technique is subjective and only suggestive of heteroscedasticity and is not a substitute for formal tests.

(ii) White (1980) test

This White test has been developed mainly to test for heteroscedasticity. But, the White procedure in fact tests a *joint* null hypothesis that a regression model is homoscedastic and the disturbances are independent of the explanatory variables (or no specification error in a sense).[7] Thus, a rejection of the joint null hypothesis indicates that the regression disturbances are heteroscedastic or/and the disturbances are correlated with the explanatory variables. Therefore, when the White test rejects the null hypothesis, it is recommended to use the White's heteroscedasticity-consistent standard errors *only if* the model is believed well specified (no correlation between the disturbance and explanatory variables).

When the null hypothesis is rejected, a more thorough investigation of the model's specification is recommended. If the investigator is unsure about the correctness of the regression model, the rejection of the test indicates only that something is wrong, but not what. One practical way of proceeding in this case would be to apply the tests proposed by Hausman (1978) and Ramsey (1969), which are explained in Chapter 6. The null hypothesis for these tests is that the disturbances are not correlated with the explanatory variables. Accepting the null hypothesis of no correlation by such tests would indicate that the rejection by the White test is indeed due to heteroscedasticity.

The White test is often employed to check the robustness of results. If the White test cannot reject the joint null hypothesis, it indicates that the model (thus the results therefrom) has passed a robustness check.

The White (1980) test is implemented by following two steps[8]: (1) obtain the residuals ($\hat{u}_i$) from the OLS estimation of Y on independent variables Xs; (2) regress the squared residuals ($\hat{u}_i^2$) on the explanatory variables, their squared values and their cross products.[9] For a case of three independent variables and an intercept, the regression in the second step is

$$\begin{aligned}
\hat{u}_i^2 &= \alpha_0 + \alpha_1 X_{i2} + \alpha_2 X_{i3} + \alpha_3 X_{i4} \\
&+ \alpha_4 X_{i2}^2 + \alpha_5 X_{i3}^2 + \alpha_6 X_{i4}^2 \\
&+ \alpha_7 X_{i2} X_{i3} + \alpha_8 X_{i2} X_{i4} + \alpha_9 X_{i3} X_{i4} + (error\ term)
\end{aligned} \tag{5.3}$$

If the joint null hypothesis is correct, the second-stage regression of Eq. (5.3) should have little explaining power and give a low R^2. For a test statistic, we use nR^2 which follows a *Chi*-square distribution, $nR^2 \sim \chi^2_{k(k+1)/2-1}$ where R^2 is the (constant-adjusted) coefficient of determination.[10] This *Chi*-square test is asymptotically equivalent to testing the joint hypothesis $\alpha_1 = \alpha_2 = \cdots = \alpha_{k(k+1)/2-1} = 0$. Appendix 5 explains how to apply the White test using *EViews* and *SAS*.

(iii) Estimation of correct standard errors

If we conclude that the error term is heteroscedastic after applying the White test, we should not use the standard errors from the OLS estimation. It is because the OLS estimators are not efficient in the presence of heteroscedasticity.

When the functional form of heteroscedasticity is known, we can use a weighted least squares method. However, in most cases the functional form of σ_i^2 is not known. Therefore, it is recommended to use the *White (1980)'s method* to calculate standard errors robust to heteroscedasticity. Appendix 5 demonstrates how to obtain the White's heteroscedasticity-consistent standard errors using *EViews* and *SAS*.

5.2.3 Application: Mitton (2002, p. 225)

The author discusses econometric issues by stating that:

> A number of econometric issues in the regression analysis need to be addressed. Multicollinearity does not appear to be a problem in the model. With all key variables included in the model, the

average variance inflation factor is 2.6 (with a maximum of 5.8), which is not unreasonably high. I correct for heteroscedasticity using robust standard errors.

1   Regardless of whether the explanatory variables are highly correlated or not, this study reports significant results about the corporate governance variables, as shown in Chapters 2 and 3. Thus, the results are strong and robust to, if any, muliticollinearity. The variance inflation factor (VIF) measures the inflation in the variances of the parameter estimates due to multicollinearity that exist among the explanatory variables. There are no formal criteria for deciding whether a VIF is large enough to affect the predicted values. It means that the VIF values are just used as a reference only. A common rule of thumb is that if VIF > 5, then multicollinearity is high. And 10 has been proposed as a cut-off value by some studies.

2   In the tables shown in Chapters 3 and 4, it is noted that "heteroscedasticity-consistent *t*-statistics are given in brackets." It means that the White test has concluded that the disturbance of the regression model is heteroscedastic. Therefore, the author reports the standard errors which account for the heteroscedasticity.

5.3 More on functional form

5.3.1 Quadratic function

In some applications, quadratic functions are often used to examine a possibility of decreasing and increasing marginal effects. The following includes a quadratic term of X.

$$Y = \beta_0 + \beta_1 X + \beta_2 X^2 + \beta_3 Z + u$$

The net effect of X on Y is derived as

$$\frac{\partial Y}{\partial X} = \beta_1 + 2\beta_2 X$$

Thus, the net effect of X on Y depends on the value of X. In many applications, β_2 is negative, implying a decreasing marginal effect. Examples are the diminishing marginal utility and the diminishing marginal products of labor and capital. Education investment is also often estimated as having a diminishing effect on wage.

5.3.2 Interaction terms

For some cases, the net effect of an explanatory variable depends on the magnitude of other explanatory variables. In this section we introduce models which include an interaction term of two quantitative variables.

One such model is to allow a coefficient to vary in a continuous way according to values of a quantitative variable. In the following simple regression model, suppose that the coefficient for X_i, β_i, varies proportionally to values of a certain variable (e.g., Z_i).

$$Y_i = \alpha + \beta_i X_i + u_i$$
$$\beta_i = \delta_0 + \delta_1 Z_i$$

Then this model includes the variable X_i and its interaction term with Z_i

$$
\begin{aligned}
Y_i &= \alpha + \left(\delta_0 + \delta_1 Z_i\right) \times X_i + u_i \\
&= \alpha + \delta_0 X_i + \delta_1 \left(Z_i \times X_i\right) + u_i
\end{aligned}
$$

A more general model is to include both variables and their interaction term.

$$
Y_i = \beta_0 + \beta_1 X_i + \beta_2 Z_i + \beta_3 \left(X_i \times Z_i\right) + u_i
$$

The net effects are measured as

$$
\frac{\partial Y_i}{\partial X_i} = \beta_1 + \beta_3 Z_i, \quad \frac{\partial Y_i}{\partial Z_i} = \beta_2 + \beta_3 X_i \tag{5.4}
$$

Each net effect depends on values of the other variable. If $\beta_3 > 0$, each effect becomes larger as the other variable increases. In other words, there is a positive *interaction effect* (or a *synergy effect*) between two explanatory variables X and Z. Thus, this model can be applied to examine whether there exist interaction effects between variables.

Care must be exercised when interpreting the coefficients in the presence of interaction terms. The coefficients do not have an immediate interpretation of net effects. Since the net effects are not constant, we have to evaluate them at selected values of other variables.

Example 5.1   Consider the following estimated regression of wage (W) on education (ED) and experience (EX).

$$
\log(\hat{W}) = 0.5 - 0.7 ED - 3.5 EX + 0.5(ED \times EX)
$$

Although the coefficients for ED and EX are negative, they do not mean that their net effects on wage are negative. For example, the net effect of EX is $\dfrac{\partial \log(W)}{\partial EX} = -3.5 + 0.5\,ED$. If the values of ED range from 8 to 16 years, the net effect of EX is between 0.5 and 4.5.

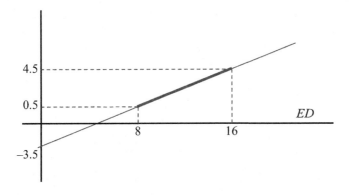

When reporting the net effects, we often evaluate Eq. (5.4) at interesting values of X and Z, such as their means in the sample. To do it, we can apply the *centering* to the regression model. The centering refers to the practice of subtracting the sample mean from each variable in a regression model.

Suppose that the sample means of ED and EX are 12 and 5, respectively. The above estimated regression can be rewritten in terms of the centered variables.[11]

$$\log(\hat{W}) = -4.1 + 1.8(ED - 12) + 2.5(EX - 5) + 0.5(ED - 12) \times (EX - 5)$$
$$= -4.1 + 1.8ED^{dev} + 2.5EX^{dev} + 0.5(ED^{dev} \times EX^{dev})$$

where $ED^{dev} = ED - 12$ and $EX^{dev} = EX - 5$. The net effect of EX evaluated at the sample mean 12 of ED is 2.5, which is simply the coefficient estimate for EX^{dev} because the sample mean of ED^{dev} is equal to zero.

$$\frac{\partial \log(W)}{\partial EX^{dev}} = 2.5 + 0.5ED^{dev} = 2.5$$

In the same way, the net effect of ED evaluated at the sample mean 5 of EX is 1.8. Thus, the coefficients of the centered model have an immediate meaning of the net effects of their corresponding variables, evaluated at the sample mean of the other variable.

5.4 Applications

5.4.1 Bharadwaj, Tuli and Bonfrer (2011)

This study examines the impact of brand quality on three components of shareholder wealth: stock returns, systematic risk and idiosyncratic risk. In this section, only the analysis related to stock returns is included; see the paper for the analysis about the other two components.

(a) Hypotheses

Stock returns represent investors' expectations about a firm's future cash flows. Prior research identified three key reasons for an unanticipated increase (decrease) in brand quality to be a signal of higher (lower) future cash flows. First, as quality increases, brands have a greater likelihood of being purchased and repurchased because it signals an increase in brand's credibility and reduces customers' perceived risk and information costs. In turn, this impact on purchase and repurchase leads to greater future cash flows. Second, cash flows also increase because consumers are willing to pay premium prices for higher-quality brands. Third, marketing actions such as promotions and advertising are more effective for higher-quality brands. As a result, an increase in brand quality signals potential cost savings, leading to higher future cash flows. Thus, a hypothesis in an alternative form is

H_1 : Unanticipated changes in brand quality are positively related to stock returns.

MODERATING ROLE OF UNANTICIPATED CHANGES IN CURRENT-PERIOD EARNINGS

An unanticipated increase in current-period earnings is a signal that the future performance of a firm is likely to be better than current expectations. Consequently, in general, investors react positively to unanticipated increases in current-period earnings.

Payoffs from intangible assets such as brand quality are considered uncertain because their benefits generally accrue in the future. Therefore, if an unanticipated increase in brand quality is accompanied by an unanticipated increase in current-period earnings, it is a signal to investors that the firm is able to build brand quality without sacrificing its current and future performance. Unanticipated increases in earnings also suggest that a firm is likely to invest in resources required to maintain and strengthen its brand quality.

H_4 : The effect of unanticipated changes in brand quality on stock returns is more (less) positive when there is an unanticipated increase (decrease) in current-period earnings.

MODERATING ROLE OF UNANTICIPATED CHANGES IN INDUSTRY CONCENTRATION

An unanticipated increase in brand quality raises the probability of customers choosing a brand and paying a higher price for it, thereby increasing future cash flows. Investors are likely to appreciate unanticipated increases in brand quality more for firms in industries in which there is an unanticipated decrease in concentration. This is because an unanticipated decrease in industry concentration indicates that firms are likely to face higher competition and, thus, greater difficulty in increasing cash flows.

H_5 : The effect of unanticipated changes in brand quality on stock returns is more (less) positive when there is an unanticipated decrease (increase) in industry concentration.

(b) Models

Building on the benchmark three-factor model of Fama and French (1993, 2004), this study uses the following regression which is augmented with the variables for the main and moderating effects, also with another control variable, $U\Delta TS$. For firm i in industry j for year t,

$$
\begin{aligned}
(R_{ijt} - R_{ft}) = \alpha &+ \beta(R_{mt} - R_{ft}) + s(SMB_t) + h(HML_t) \\
&+ \gamma_1(U\Delta BQ_{ijt}) + \gamma_2(U\Delta E_{ijt}) + \gamma_3(U\Delta IC_{jt}) + \gamma_4(U\Delta TS_{ijt}) \\
&+ \gamma_5(U\Delta BQ_{ijt} \times U\Delta E_{ijt}) + \gamma_6(U\Delta BQ_{ijt} \times U\Delta IC_{jt}) + \varepsilon_{ijt}
\end{aligned}
$$

where
R_{ijt} = compounded monthly stock returns,
R_{ft} = risk-free rate of returns calculated using US Treasury bonds,
R_{mt} = stock market returns,
SMB_t = Fama and French size portfolio returns,
HML_t = Fama and French book-to-market value portfolio returns,
$U\Delta BQ_{ijt}$ = unanticipated changes in brand quality,
$U\Delta E_{ijt}$ = unanticipated changes in current-period earnings,
$U\Delta IC_{jt}$ = unanticipated changes in industry concentration,
$U\Delta TS_{ijt}$ = unanticipated changes in total sales,
$\varepsilon_{ijt} = \delta_i + \theta_j + u_{ijt}$, which accounts for the firm- and industry-specific effects.

(c) Data

The panel data contain 519 observations from 132 firms, covering a period of six years from 2000 to 2005. See the paper for the data sources and a more detailed description of the data.

(d) Results

Model fit diagnostics support the full model (including the moderating effects) over the main-effects-only model; the likelihood ratio test yields a small p-value (< 0.01) for the null hypothesis $H_0 : \gamma_5 = \gamma_6 = 0$. Table 5.2 also shows that the interaction terms in the full model are significant at the 1% level.

The estimation results of the full model support H_1 because $\hat{\gamma}_1 = 0.48$ ($p < 0.01$).[12] The interaction of $U\Delta BQ$ and $U\Delta E$ has a positive effect on stock returns ($\hat{\gamma}_5 = 8.18$, $p < 0.01$), supporting H_4. The interaction of $U\Delta BQ$ and $U\Delta IC$ has a negative effect on stock returns ($\hat{\gamma}_6 = -13.65, p < 0.01$), supporting H_7.

To illustrate the impact of these interactions, this study calculates the marginal effect of $U\Delta BQ$ on stock returns and plots it against $U\Delta E$ and $U\Delta IC$.[13] Panel A in Figure 5.1 shows that the positive effect of $U\Delta BQ$ on stock returns becomes stronger when there is an unanticipated increase in current-period earnings ($U\Delta E > 0$). In contrast, Panel B shows that the positive effects of $U\Delta BQ$ decrease when there is an unanticipated increase in industry concentration ($U\Delta IC > 0$).[14]

5.4.2 Ghosh and Moon (2005)

This study analyzes how investors perceive auditor tenure. It tests whether reported earnings are perceived as being more reliable (of higher quality) as auditor tenure increases. They use earnings

Table 5.2 Changes in brand quality impact on stock returns

	Main-effects model	Full model
$U\Delta BQ_{ijt}$ (γ_1)	0.47^{***}	0.48^{***}
$U\Delta BQ_{ijt} \times U\Delta E_{ijt}$ (γ_5)		8.18^{***}
$U\Delta BQ_{ijt} \times U\Delta IC_{jt}$ (γ_6)		-13.65^{***}
Control variables	Included	Included
No of observations	519	519
R^2	0.38	0.41

Source: Adapted from Bharadwaj et al. (2011, Table 5 on page 97).
*** denotes $p < 0.01$ (one-sided).

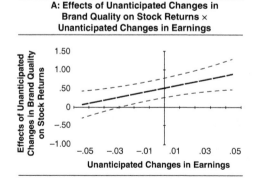
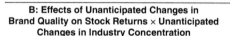
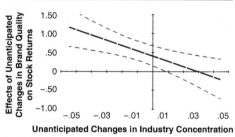

Figure 5.1 The moderating impact of unanticipated changes in earnings and industry concentration

Source: Bharadwaj, Tuli and Bonfrer (2011, Figure 1 on page 98).

Note: The dotted lines indicate the 95% confidence interval bands.

response coefficients (ERCs) from contemporaneous returns-earnings regressions to measure investor perceptions of earnings quality.[15]

$$CAR_{it} = \alpha + \theta_{it}E_{it} + u_{it}$$

where CAR_{it} is the cumulative market-adjusted 12-month stock returns in year t for firm i, the market-adjusted returns being the difference between raw returns and value-weighted CRSP market returns. E_{it} is reported earnings and its coefficient θ_{it} is the ERC for firm i.[16]

Now, the question is whether θ_{it} (ERC) is a function of auditor tenure ($TENURE_{it}$). Including various control variables for ERC as well, they have derived the following regression model.

$$\theta_{it} = \beta_1 + \beta_2 TENURE_{it} + (control\ variables)$$

$$CAR_{it} = \alpha + \beta_1 E_{it} + \beta_2(E_{it} \times TENURE_{it}) + (control\ variables) + u_{it}$$

This study has rejected a null hypothesis $H_0 : \beta_2 = 0$ against $H_1 : \beta_2 > 0$, concluding that reported earnings are perceived as being of higher quality as auditor tenure increases.

Related study: Using the same interaction terms, Fan and Wong (2002) examine the relations between earnings informativeness, measured by the above ERC, and the ownership structure of 977 companies in seven East Asian economies during the period of 1991–1995.

5.4.3 Arora and Vamvakidis (2005)

South Africa is often described as an engine of growth in Africa, in the sense that South African economic growth is believed to have a substantial impact on growth in other African countries. This paper measures the extent to which South African economic growth is an engine of growth in sub-Saharan Africa during the last four decades of the 20th century, 1960–1999.

Several growth regressions are estimated for the 47 countries in sub-Saharan Africa. Among them, the following regression includes two interaction terms, $(SAF_t)(TRADE_{it})$ and $(SAF_t)(DIST_{it})$. For country i (= 1, . . ., 47) in year t (= 1960 ~ 1999)

$$\%\Delta GDP_{it} = \beta_0 + \beta_1 SAF_t + \beta_2(SAF_t)(TRADE_{it}) + \beta_3(SAF_t)(DIST_{it})$$
$$+ \beta_4 X_{4,it} + \cdots + \beta_k X_{k,it} + (country\ dummies) + u_{it}$$

where $\%\Delta GDP_{it}$ is the per capita real GDP growth rate in country i in year t, SAF_t the per capita real GDP growth rate in South Africa in year t, $TRADE_{it}$ the share of exports to South Africa in country i's total exports in year t and $DIST_{it}$ the distance of country i from South Africa. $X_{4,it},...,X_{k,it}$ represent other factors from the economic growth literature, including the logarithm of per capita real GDP in the initial year of the period under consideration, investment/GDP, trade/GDP, primary school enrollment, age dependency ratio and inflation rate.

The results in Table 5.3 suggest that growth in South Africa and in the rest of sub-Saharan Africa are closely correlated. The coefficient estimate for SAF_t is 0.55 with the t-statistic of 4.04, being significantly different from zero at a significance level less than 1%. However, the coefficients for the interaction terms are statistically insignificant, indicating that the significant impact of the South African economy on the rest of Africa does not seem to depend on the size of countries' bilateral trade with South Africa ($TRADE_{it}$), or their distance from South Africa ($DIST_{it}$). These results are not surprising given the relatively small trade flows between South Africa and other African countries.

Table 5.3 Impact of growth in South Africa on growth in rest of sub-Saharan Africa: importance of trade shares and distance from South Africa

Independent variables	(i)	(ii)	(iii)
SAF	0.55***	0.62***	0.53*
	(4.04)	(4.34)	(1.78)
(SAF)(TRADE)		0.21	
		(0.20)	
(SAF)(DIST)			−4.88
			(−0.40)
Other factors/country dummies	included	included	included
Adjusted R^2	0.48	0.54	0.53

Source: Adapted from Arora and Vamvakidis (2005, Tables 8 and 10).
Notes: Heteroscedasticity-consistent *t*-statistics are in parentheses. The country differences are captured by dummy variables, the fixed effects model explained in Chapter 7.
Asterisks denote significance levels: * = 10%, ** = 5% and *** = 1%.

5.5 Summary

1　Even with multicollinearity among independent variables, the OLS estimator is still unbiased and efficient. However, the multicollinearity could reduce the significance of possible factors because of large standard errors of OLS estimators, thereby preventing us from showing that certain independent variables are significant factors for the dependent variable.

2　We can eliminate or reduce the effect of multicollinearity by deleting one or more of the highly correlated variables from a model; this is an application of the General-to-Simple approach.

3　If the error term is heteroscedastic, the OLS estimator is inefficient although it can be unbiased. Therefore, we need to correct the standard errors of OLS estimators.

4　The White method tests a *joint* null hypothesis that a regression model is homoscedastic *and* the errors are independent of the explanatory variables (or no specification error in a sense). If the White test rejects the joint null hypothesis, it is recommended to first check whether the model is correctly specified. After we confirm that the model is correctly specified, we use the White's heteroscedasticity-consistent standard errors.

5　By including a quadratic term, we can examine whether net effect is diminishing or increasing.

6　By including the product of two quantitative variables, we can estimate their interaction effect.

Review questions

1　Explain how the following affect the unbiasedness and the efficiency of the OLS estimators.

(a)　The variance of the disturbance is not constant.
(b)　A significant variable has been omitted from the regression model.
(c)　Two independent variables are highly correlated. (Their sample correlation coefficient is over 0.95.)

2　We estimate the following linear regression to understand why the output level varies across firms.

$$Q_i = \alpha_0 + \alpha_1 K_i + \alpha_2 L_i + u_i$$

Below is a part of data collected from 33 sampled firms. They show how much of input they used (capital K and labor L) and how much of output they produced (Q) in year 2018.

< Datafile: 3-production.xls >

	A	B	C	D
1	Firm ID	Output (Q)	Capital (K)	Labor (L)
2	ABS	1385	1850	951
3	ABT	2893	3544	1289
4	ACK	1209	1548	783
5	ACY	1715	3568	948

(a) Estimate the above linear production function by the OLS method.

(b) Interpret the coefficient estimates $\hat{\alpha}_1$ and $\hat{\alpha}_2$.

(c) Test whether the error term is homoscedastic. (Assume that there is no specification error in the production model.)

(d) If the error term is not homoscedastic, find the heteroscedasticity-consistent estimates by applying the White method.

(e) Is the capital (K) a significant factor? Is the labor (L) is a significant factor?

3 If your regression model includes several independent variables which are highly correlated with each other, then you might have some problems. Now answer the following questions which are about the consequences of multicollinearity.

(a) Is the ordinary least squares estimator biased? Why?

(b) Explain the effects of multicollinearity on the significance of their coefficients. (Your explanation should include standard error, t-ratio and p-value.)

4 Suppose that X_1 and X_2 are highly correlated in the following multiple regression.

$$Y_i = \alpha_0 + \alpha_1 X_{1i} + \alpha_2 X_{2i} + u_i$$

Due to the multicollinearity, we cannot reject $H_0 : \alpha_1 = 0$ nor $H_0 : \alpha_2 = 0$. If we omit one of the variables, e.g., X_2, from the regression model, do you think the omission will cause a bias?

5 To examine the effect of industry composition on employment growth, we estimate the following regression using the observations in an Excel file '5-share.xls.'

$$Y_t = \alpha_0 + \alpha_1 P1_t + \alpha_2 P2_t + \theta X_t + u_t \tag{Q5.1}$$

where Y_t is annual growth rate of employment in year t ; $P1_t$ is the share of service industry in the total output; $P2_t$ is the share of manufacturing industry in the total output; and X_t is the interest rate. Letting $P3_t$ denote the share of the rest, we have a perfect collinear relation of $P1_t + P2_t + P3_t = 1$. Below is a part of the annual data from 1990 until 2006.

< Datafile: 5-share.xls >

	A	B	C	D	E	F
1	Year	Y	P1	P2	P3	X
2	1990	3.4	0.36	0.34	0.30	2.1
3	1991	2.9	0.38	0.33	0.29	2.6
4	1992	1.5	0.36	0.34	0.30	2.9

(a) To see why we should not include all share variables, estimate the following regression.

$$Y_t = \alpha_0 + \alpha_1 P1_t + \alpha_2 P2_t + \alpha_3 P3_t + \theta\, X_t + u_t \qquad\qquad (Q5.2)$$

(b) Estimate (Q5.1). And estimate two more regressions by omitting one of the share variables at each time.

$$Y_t = \beta_0 + \beta_1 P1_t + \beta_3 P3_t + \theta\, X_t + u_t \qquad\qquad (Q5.3)$$

$$Y_t = \gamma_0 + \gamma_2 P2_t + \gamma_3 P3_t + \theta\, X_t + u_t \qquad\qquad (Q5.4)$$

(i) In the three regressions, do the coefficient estimate and its standard error for X_t vary? Explain why.

(ii) Using the coefficient estimates for $P1_t$ and $P2_t$ in (Q.5.1), we can calculate the coefficient estimates in (Q5.3) and (Q5.4). Explain what relations exist between the estimates. Also, explain the relation of their standard errors.

6 Suppose we are interested in estimating returns to education. We begin with a wage equation which recognizes that ability (*ABIL*) affects wage.

$$\log(WAGE) = \beta_0 + \beta_1 ED + \beta_2 \left(ED\right)^2 + \beta_3 EXP + \beta_4 MARRIED$$
$$+ \beta_5 ABIL + u$$

where $\log(WAGE)$ is the logarithm of annual wage; *ED* is the number of education years; *EXP* is the number of years with the current job; and *MARRIED* is a dummy variable set to 1 if married, 0 otherwise. $\left(ED\right)^2$, the square of *ED*, is included to study the nature of returns to education.

The above model indicates that we need to hold ability (*ABIL*) constant when measuring the returns to education. Since *ABIL* is not observed, we may alternatively use a proxy variable. One possible proxy variable is the intelligence quotient (*IQ*).

$$\log(WAGE) = \beta_0 + \beta_1 ED + \beta_2 \left(ED\right)^2 + \beta_3 EXP + \beta_4 MARRIED$$
$$+ \beta_5 IQ + u$$

In order to examine possible synergy effects on wage of ability (*IQ*) and experience (*EXP*), we extend the above regression to include an interaction term of *IQ* and *EXP*.

$$\log(WAGE) = \beta_0 + \beta_1 ED + \beta_2 \left(ED\right)^2 + \beta_3 EXP + \beta_4 MARRIED$$
$$+ \beta_5 IQ + \beta_6 (IQ \times EXP) + u$$

The estimation results are summarized in the following table. (Note: In answering the questions, if you need to test hypotheses, use a 5% significance level.)

(a) It is stated above that our interest is in the returns to education, but not in the returns to ability. Why do we need to hold ability (*ABIL*) constant when measuring the returns to education only? What will happen if we simply omit the unobserved variable *ABIL*? Explain.

(b) To test about the synergy effects, we set up a null and an alternative hypothesis as $H_0 : \beta_6 = 0$ vs. $H_1 : \beta_6 > 0$. Explain the meaning of $\beta_6 > 0$.

Explanatory variables	(i)	(ii)	(iii)	(iv)
constant	5.321	4.552	4.101	3.153
	(0.000)	(0.000)	(0.000)	(0.000)
ED	0.075	0.013	0.041	0.042
	(0.001)	(0.001)	(0.000)	(0.000)
ED²	−0.002	−0.001	−0.007	−0.007
	(0.003)	(0.003)	(0.002)	(0.003)
EXP	0.012	−	0.021	0.023
	(0.008)	−	(0.007)	(0.008)
MARRIED	0.154	0.121	0.132	0.131
	(0.012)	(0.013)	(0.014)	(0.012)
IQ	−	0.015	0.018	0.019
		(0.005)	(0.003)	(0.004)
IQ×EXP	−	−	−	0.001
				(0.232)
R² (%)	20.1	29.3	35.1	35.2

The number in each parenthesis is the *p*-value for testing the significance of each coefficient.

(c) The coefficient estimates for *ED* and $(ED)^2$ in models (iii) and (iv) are very different from the ones in models (i) and (ii). Explain why they are so different and which ones are wrong.

(d) Which model do you think is the best among the four estimated models shown in the table? Explain.

(e) To examine the nature of returns to education, we include $(ED)^2$, the square of *ED*. We test $H_0 : \beta_2 = 0$ against $H_0 : \beta_2 < 0$. Interpret what the alternative hypothesis $\beta_2 < 0$ implies about the returns to education.

(f) Based on the model you selected in (d), what is your conclusion about the nature of returns to education?

7   Consider the following regression which includes an interaction term.

$$\log(Wage) = \beta_0 + \beta_1(Education) + \beta_2(Experience) + \beta_3(Education) \times (Experience) + u$$

(a) Express the net effect of *Education* on log(*Wage*).

(b) Express the net effect of *Experience* on log(*Wage*).

(c) Write the null hypothesis that the return to education (i.e., the net effect of *Education*) does not depend on the level of *Experience*.

(d) If $\beta_3 > 0$, what does it imply about the net effect of *Education* on log(*Wage*)? What does it also imply about the net effect of *Experience* on log(*Wage*)?

8   Consider the following regression which includes a quadratic term.

$$Y = \beta_0 + \beta_1 X + \beta_2 X^2 + \beta_3 Z_3 + \beta_4 Z_4 + u$$

(a) Interpret the meaning of β_3. In other words, what does β_3 represent?

(b) Express the net effect of *X* on *Y*.

(c) If β_2 is significantly negative, what does it imply about the net effect of *X* on *Y*?

9   Mitton (2002) examines whether the disclosure quality, measured by two dummies of *ADR* and *BIG6*, is a significant factor for firm performance, measured by stock returns.

$$StockReturns = \beta_0 + \beta_1 ADR + \beta_2 BIG6 + (controls) + u$$

where *ADR* is set to one if the firm had an ADR listed in the US at the beginning of the crisis, and zero otherwise; *BIG6* is set to one if the firm was audited by one of the Big Six international accounting firms, and zero otherwise.

(a)   Interpret the dummy coefficients, β_1 and β_2.

(b)   If a firm had an ADR listed and was audited by one of the Big Six international accounting firms, what is an expected effect on the stock return as compared to the reference group ($ADR = 0$ and $BIG6 = 0$)?

(c)   We also want to test whether there exists any interaction effect of *ADR* and *BIG6*. Modify the above regression model for the test. Also, write a null and an alternative hypothesis.

Notes

1   When two identical variables are included together, OLS estimates cannot be calculated because the denominator of the OLS estimator becomes zero, called a singularity problem. In general, if there exists a perfect correlation between independent variables, it is impossible to obtain OLS estimates for the same singularity problem. For example, let P1, P2 and P3 denote the shares such that $P1 + P2 + P3 = 1$. Due to the perfect correlation, the OLS estimation cannot be conducted when all three share variables are included as regressors. An example is given as a review question (#5) in this chapter. Another example of the singularity problem is review question #4 in Chapter 4.

2   To avoid the singularity problem, i.e., a perfect correlation, our estimation uses X2, instead of X3, which is slightly different from X1.

3   Remember that under the null hypothesis of $H_0 : \beta_1 = 0$, the t-statistic is calculated as $t = \hat{\beta}_1 / (s.e.)$.

4   Similarly, the statistical significance is also a *continuous* measure of the extent to which evidence rejects a null hypothesis, as explained in Chapter 3.

5   The OLS estimator becomes inconsistent (also biased) when the error term is correlated with the independent variables, as explained in Chapters 2 and 3.

6   Strictly speaking, this expression is not correct because there is more than one regression coefficient. Theoretically, we compare covariance matrices which consisted of variances and covariances of estimators $\hat{\beta}_1, \cdots, \hat{\beta}_k$. In case of heteroscedasticity, the covariance matrices of OLS estimators are not the smallest in the following sense: we say that one covariance matrix (*A*) is smaller than the other (*B*) if the difference matrix $A - B$ is negative definite.

7   White (1980) conjectures that when the model is misspecified, the disturbance will contain the specification error. If so, it is impossible for the regressors to be independent of the disturbance term.

8   Since most econometrics computer packages can perform the White test and produce *p*-values, you don't need to follow the two steps. This explanation is only for your information.

9   We need to test whether the error variance depends on the regressors. Since $E(u|X) = 0$, $Var(u|X) = E(u^2|X)$, that is, the error variance is equal to the expected value of the squared error term. Thus, we test whether $\hat{u}^2$ depends on the regressors by regressing $\hat{u}^2$ on the regressors, their squared values and their cross products.

10   *k* is the number of independent variables plus one (intercept). Since the intercept causes a redundancy in Eq. (5.3), we subtract one from $k(k+1)/2$ to obtain the total number of all distinct terms in the product of column vectors $\begin{bmatrix} 1 & X_{i2} & X_{i3} & X_{i4} \end{bmatrix}' \begin{bmatrix} 1 & X_{i2} & X_{i3} & X_{i4} \end{bmatrix}$. For the above case of $k = 4$, there are 9 terms in Eq. (5.3) excluding the intercept. Therefore, the degree of freedom is $9 \ (= 4 \times 5 / 2 - 1)$.

11   An alternative but better way is to use computer software and directly obtain the OLS estimates for the centered variables. We first generate centered variables, $ED^{dev} (=ED - 12)$ and $EX^{dev} (=EX - 5)$. Applying the OLS method to the regression of the centered variables, we can obtain the estimates.

12   This interpretation is valid only when the net effect of $U\Delta BQ$ on stock returns is evaluated at $U\Delta E = 0$ and $U\Delta IC = 0$. However, the net effect is not constant at γ_1 because $\partial \left(R_{i\,jt} - R_{ft} \right) / \partial U\Delta BQ_{i\,jt} = \gamma_1 + \gamma_5 U\Delta E_{i\,jt} + \gamma_6 U\Delta IC_{jt}$. A correct approach is to evaluate the net effect for the sample ranges of $U\Delta E$ and $U\Delta IC$.

13 The graph shows that the marginal (net) effect of $U\Delta BQ$ on stock returns is significantly positive for the ranges of $-0.04 < U\Delta E < 0.04$ and $-0.04 < U\Delta IC < 0.04$, supporting H_1. Descriptive statistics of the data show that both $U\Delta E$ and $U\Delta IC$ have a sample mean of 0 and a standard deviation of 0.04.

14 A correct interpretation is as follows: "Panel A in Figure 5.1 shows that the positive effect of $U\Delta BQ$ on stock returns becomes stronger when $U\Delta E$ increases. In contrast, Panel B shows that the positive effect of $U\Delta BQ$ decreases when $U\Delta IC$ increases."

15 The higher the ERC is, the more responsive the stock returns are to earnings. Thus, high values of ERC are interpreted as implying that earnings are of higher quality (or more informative).

16 In Ghosh and Moon (2005), ERCs are estimated from regressions of stock returns (CAR) on both earnings (E) and changes in earnings (ΔE). For simplicity, a regression model with E only is presented here. See Ali and Zarowin (1992) and Easton and Harris (1991) for explanations about why E and ΔE together can produce better estimates of ERC.

References

Ali, A. and P. Zarowin (1992), "The Role of Earnings Levels in Annual Earnings-Returns Studies," *Journal of Accounting Research*, 20, 286–296.

Arora, V. and A. Vamvakidis (2005), "The Implications of South African Economic Growth for the Rest of Africa," IMF Working Paper.

Bharadwaj, S.G., K.R. Tuli and A. Bonfrer (2011), "The Impact of Brand Quality on Shareholder Wealth," *Journal of Marketing*, 75, Sept, 88–104.

Davidson, R. and J.G. MacKinnon (1993), *Estimation and Inference in Econometrics*, New York: Oxford University Press.

Easton, P.D. and T.S. Harris (1991), "Earnings as an Explanatory Variable for Returns," *Journal of Accounting Research*, 29, 19–36.

Fama, E.F. and K.R. French (1993), "Common Risk Factors in the Returns on Stocks and Bonds," *Journal of Financial Economics*, 33, 3–56.

Fama, E.F. and K.R. French (2004), "The Capital Asset Pricing Model: Theory and Evidence," *Journal of Economic Perspectives*, 18, 25–46.

Fan, J.P.H. and T.J. Wong (2002), "Corporate Ownership Structure and the Informativeness of Accounting Earnings," *Journal of Accounting and Economics*, 33, 401–425.

Ghosh, A. and D. Moon (2005), "Auditor Tenure and Perceptions of Audit Quality," *The Accounting Review*, 80, 585–612.

Hausman, J.A. (1978), "Specification Tests in Econometrics," *Econometrica*, 46, 1251–1272.

Mitton, T. (2002), "A Cross-Firm Analysis of the Impact of Corporate Governance on the East Asian Financial Crisis," *Journal of Financial Economics*, 64, 215–241.

Ramsey, J.B. (1969), "Tests for Specification Errors in Classical Linear Least Squares Regression Analysis," *Journal of the Royal Statistical Society: Series B*, 31, 350–371.

White, H. (1980), "A Heteroscedasticity Consistent Covariance Matrix Estimator and A Direct Test for Heteroscedasticity," *Econometrica*, 48, 817–838.

Appendix 5 Testing and correcting for heteroscedasticity

We estimate the following model using an Excel file "5-housing.xls" which contains 20 observations on annual housing expenditures (*HEXP*) and annual income (*INC*).

$$HEXP_i = \beta_0 + \beta_1 INC_i + u_i$$

Using *EViews*

After importing the Excel file, we estimate the regression model by clicking Objects/New Object. . . / Equation. The OLS estimation results are shown in Output 5.3.

Output 5.3   OLS estimation results: 5-housing.xls

Dependent Variable: HEXP
Method: Least Squares
Sample: 1 20
Included observations: 20

Variable	Coefficient	Std. Error	t-Statistic	Prob.
C	0.890000	0.204312	4.356086	0.0004
INC	0.237200	0.014921	15.89724	0.0000
R-squared	0.933511	Mean dependent var		3.855000
Adjusted R-squared	0.929817	S.D. dependent var		1.408050

In order to apply the White test for heteroscedasticity, click Views/Residual Diagnostics/Heteroskedasticity Tests . . . and select White for Test type. You can include White cross terms in the test equation. For models with many independent variables, it may not be practical to include their cross-product terms because there are too many of them. In that case, you do not check the Include White cross terms box.

Output 5.4   White's heteroscedasticity test

White Heteroskedasticity Test:

F-statistic	5.979575	Probability	0.010805
Obs*R-squared	8.259324	Probability	0.016088

Test Equation:
Dependent Variable: RESID^2
Method: Least Squares
Sample: 1 20
Included observations: 20

Variable	Coefficient	Std. Error	t-Statistic	Prob.
C	0.092180	0.178932	0.515169	0.6131
INC	−0.021234	0.032647	−0.650395	0.5241
INC^2	0.001592	0.001285	1.238321	0.2324
R-squared	0.412966	Mean dependent var		0.125230
Adjusted R-squared	0.343903	S.D. dependent var		0.177434
S.E. of regression	0.143721	Akaike info criterion		−0.904400
Sum squared resid	0.351149	Schwarz criterion		−0.755040
Log likelihood	12.04400	F-statistic		5.979575
Durbin-Watson stat	1.235556	Prob(F-statistic)		0.010805

The Obs*R-squared is the White's test statistic which is, under H_0, asymptotically distributed as a χ^2 with degrees of freedom explained in footnote 10. In this example, the observed value of the White's test statistic is 8.259324 and the p-value is 0.016088. Therefore, the null hypothesis of homoscedasticity is rejected at a significance level of 0.05.[1]

We now need to correct for heteroscedasticity. By following the procedures explained here, we can obtain correct standard errors. First, return to the Equation specification dialog by pressing the Estimate button. Then press the Options button and pull down the menu for Covariance method. Select Huber-White, HC (various) and HAC (Newey-West). The Huber-White option is the basic estimator consisting of White (1980). The HC (various) option accounts for finite samples by adjusting the weights given to residuals. The **Newey-West** option can be used when both heteroscedasticity and autocorrelation of unknown form are present. The White's corrected estimates in Output 5.5 are from selecting Huber-White. Notice the change of the standard errors from the OLS.

Output 5.5 White's corrected estimates

Dependent Variable: HEXP
Method: Least Squares
Sample: 1 20
Included observations: 20
White Heteroskedasticity-Consistent Standard Errors & Covariance

Variable	Coefficient	Std. Error	t-Statistic	Prob.
C	0.890000	0.157499	5.650847	0.0000
INC	0.237200	0.016710	14.19495	0.0000
R-squared	0.933511	Mean dependent var		3.855000
Adjusted R-squared	0.929817	S.D. dependent var		1.408050
S.E. of regression	0.373021	Akaike info criterion		0.960274
Sum squared resid	2.504600	Schwarz criterion		1.059847
Log likelihood	−7.602738	F-statistic		252.7223
Durbin-Watson stat	1.363966	Prob(F-statistic)		0.000000

Using *SAS*[2]

```
FILENAME F1 DDE 'EXCEL|[5-HOUSING.XLS]housing!R2C1:R21C2';
TITLE '< TESTING FOR HETEROSCEDASTICITY: 5-HOUSING.xls >';
DATA D1;
    INFILE F1; INPUT HEXP INC; WEIGHT=1/INC; WT2=WEIGHT**2; NO= _N_;
```

```
TITLE2 '< OLS and White test >';
PROC MODEL;
    PARMS B1 B2;
    HEXP= B1+B2*INC;
    FIT HEXP/OLS WHITE;  RUN;
```

*===;

```
TITLE2 '< Correcting for the Heteroscedasticity using PROC MODEL and HCCME=1 >';
PROC MODEL;
    PARMS B1 B2;
    HEXP= B1+B2*INC;
    FIT HEXP/ OLS HCCME=1;  RUN;
```

```
TITLE2 '< Correcting for the Heteroscedasticity using PROC REG and and HCCMETHOD=1 >';
PROC REG;
    MODEL HEXP = INC/HCC HCC HCCMETHOD=1;  RUN;
```

```
TITLE2 '< Correcting for the Heteroscedasticity using GMM function >';
PROC MODEL;
    PARMS B1 B2;
    HEXP= B1+B2*INC;
    FIT HEXP/ GMM KERNEL=(PARZEN,0,0);
    INSTRUMENTS INC;  RUN;
```

Note: The HCCME option specifies the type of heteroscedasticity-consistent covariance matrix estimator. To make estimates more reliable for small samples, *SAS* uses three different modifications following Davidson and MacKinnon (1993).

HCCME = 0 : $\hat{u}_i^2$ (no correction)

HCCME = 1 : $\dfrac{n}{n-k}\hat{u}_i^2$ (n = number of observations, k = number of coefficients)

HCCME = 2 : $\hat{u}_i^2 / (1 - \hat{h}_i)$ ($\hat{h}_i$ = i th diagonal element of $X(X'X)^{-1}X'$

HCCME = 3 : $\hat{u}_i^2 / (1 - \hat{h}_i)^2$

Davidson and MacKinnon (1993) conclude that HCCME = 1 should always be preferred to HCCME = 0. While generally HCCME = 3 is preferred to 2 and HCCME = 2 is preferred to 1, the calculation of HCCME = 2 and 3 is difficult in some cases. If so, HCCME = 1 may be used.

When the PROC REG procedure is used, the HCC option requests heteroscedasticity-consistent standard errors of the parameter estimates. The values for the "HCCMETHOD =" option are the same as for the HCCME option.

Notes

1 Here, we assume that there is no specification error in the model. Therefore, the rejection of the null hypothesis concludes that the disturbance is heteroscedastic.
2 BASE SAS 9.4, SAS/ETS 13.1 and SAS/STAT 13.1. SAS Institute Inc., Cary, NC.

6 Endogeneity and two-stage least squares estimation

> **Learning objectives**
>
> In this chapter, you should learn about:
> - Consequences and solutions of measurement errors;
> - Causes and solutions of the endogeneity problem;
> - Two-stage least squares estimation method;
> - Conditions required for the instrumental variables.

In order to examine the unbiasedness of an estimator, we need to derive its expected value. In many cases, however, it is not possible to obtain the expected values of estimators for finite samples. The OLS estimator for linear regression models is one of relatively few settings in which its finite-sample properties of unbiasedness are well understood. Thus, for a more general discussion in this chapter, we will examine the consistency of the OLS estimator rather than the unbiasedness.

The consistency is defined for sufficiently large samples as it checks whether an estimator converges to the true value of a parameter. In contrast, the unbiasedness is defined for any sample size and checks whether the expected value of an estimator is equal to the true parameter value. If an estimator is unbiased and therefore consistent, it can be used for any sample size without a bias. If an estimator is biased but consistent, this estimator can be used only for sufficiently large samples. Obviously, if an estimator is neither unbiased nor consistent, it should not be used for any cases.

For a regression model of $Y_i = \beta_0 + \beta_1 X_{1i} + u_i$, the OLS estimator for β_1 is[1]

$$
\begin{aligned}
\hat{\beta}_1 &= \frac{\sum_{i=1}^{n}\left(X_{1i} - \bar{X}_1\right)\left(Y_i - \bar{Y}\right)/n}{\sum_{i=1}^{n}\left(X_{1i} - \bar{X}_1\right)^2/n} \\
&= \beta_1 + \frac{\sum_{i=1}^{n}\left(X_{1i} - \bar{X}_1\right)\left(u_i - \bar{u}\right)/n}{\sum_{i=1}^{n}\left(X_{1i} - \bar{X}_1\right)^2/n}
\end{aligned}
\tag{6.1}
$$

In order to check its consistency, we first examine the probability limit of the OLS estimator. It can be shown that the numerator and the denominator in Eq. (6.1) converge in probability as follows:

$$plim \sum_{i=1}^{n} (X_{1i} - \bar{X}_1)(Y_i - \bar{Y})/n = Cov(X_1, Y)$$

$$plim \sum_{i=1}^{n} (X_{1i} - \bar{X}_1)(u_i - \bar{u})/n = Cov(X_1, u)$$

$$plim \sum_{i=1}^{n} (X_{1i} - \bar{X}_1)^2/n = Var(X_1)$$

Thus, the OLS estimator $\hat{\beta}_1$ in Eq. (6.1) converges to

$$
\begin{aligned}
plim \, \hat{\beta}_1 &= \frac{plim \sum_{i=1}^{n} (X_{1i} - \bar{X}_1)(Y_i - \bar{Y})/n}{plim \sum_{i=1}^{n} (X_{1i} - \bar{X}_1)^2/n} \\
&= \frac{Cov(X_1, Y)}{Var(X_1)} \\
&= \frac{Cov(X_1, \beta_0 + \beta_1 X_1 + u)}{Var(X_1)} \\
&= \frac{Cov(X_1, \beta_0)}{Var(X_1)} + \frac{Cov(X_1, \beta_1 X_1)}{Var(X_1)} + \frac{Cov(X_1, u)}{Var(X_1)} \\
&= \beta_1 + \frac{Cov(X_1, u)}{Var(X_1)}
\end{aligned}
\tag{6.2}
$$

where $Cov(X_1, \beta_0) = 0$ because the parameter β_0 is constant and thus does not covary with X_1. If the explanatory variable is not correlated with the error term, i.e., $Cov(X_1, u) = 0$, $\hat{\beta}_1$ converges in probability to β_1, indicating that the OLS estimator $\hat{\beta}_1$ is consistent.

$$plim \, \hat{\beta}_1 = \beta_1$$

If an explanatory variable is not correlated with the error term, it is called an *exogenous* explanatory variable. In contrast, an explanatory variable correlated with the error term is called an *endogenous* explanatory variable.[2] If at least one explanatory variable is endogenous, the OLS estimator will be inconsistent because $Cov(X_1, u) \neq 0$ in Eq. (6.2). In what follows, we will explain several cases in which such endogeneity problem arises.

6.1 Measurement errors

In some economic applications, we cannot collect data on certain variables which are defined in economic theory. A good example is the permanent income of a household, which consists of current income, future income, wealth, etc. Our limited observation does not allow us to calculate the permanent income. Instead, we might have to use current income for estimating economic models. As the current income is obviously different from the permanent income, the estimation models would contain measurement errors. In this section, we examine the consequence of measurement errors for ordinary least squares (OLS) estimation.

6.1.1 Measurement errors in the dependent variable

Suppose that the dependent variable Y is not observable, but observed only with a measurement error v.

$$Y^0 = Y + v$$

Where $Y^0 = $ observed value and $v = $ measurement error. It is assumed that $E(v) = 0$, $Cov(v, Y) = 0$ and $Cov(v, X_1) = 0$. Then the *estimation* model needs to be expressed by observable variables Y^* and X_1:

$$Y = \beta_0 + \beta_1 X_1 + u \quad \Rightarrow \quad Y^0 - v = \beta_0 + \beta_1 X_1 + u$$
$$\Rightarrow \quad Y^0 = \beta_0 + \beta_1 X_1 + (u + v)$$

The error term in the estimation model now has changed to $(u + v)$. The OLS estimator for this estimation model is still consistent because $Cov(X_1, u) = 0$ and $Cov(X_1, v) = 0$.

$$
\begin{aligned}
plim\ \hat{\beta}_1 &= \frac{Cov\left(X_1, Y^0\right)}{Var\left(X_1\right)} \\
&= \frac{Cov\left(X_1, \beta_0 + \beta_1 X_1 + u + v\right)}{Var\left(X_1\right)} \\
&= \frac{Cov\left(X_1, \beta_0\right)}{Var\left(X_1\right)} + \frac{Cov\left(X_1, \beta_1 X_1\right)}{Var\left(X_1\right)} + \frac{Cov\left(X_1, u + v\right)}{Var\left(X_1\right)} \\
&= 0 + \beta_1 + \frac{Cov\left(X_1, u + v\right)}{Var\left(X_1\right)} \\
&= \beta_1
\end{aligned}
$$

However, the variance of the error term $(u + v)$ in the estimation model is larger than the one without the measurement error, i.e., $Var(u + v) > Var(u)$. The variance of $\hat{\beta}_1$ (also its standard error) becomes larger than when there is no such measurement error in Y.[3]

$$Var\left(\hat{\beta}_1\right) = \frac{Var(u + v)}{\sum\left(X_1 - \bar{X}_1\right)^2} > \frac{Var(u)}{\sum\left(X_1 - \bar{X}_1\right)^2}$$

Therefore, the increased variance of the error term due to the Y-measurement error inflates the standard errors of *all* coefficients' estimates, thereby making their t-statistics smaller and lowering the significance of the coefficients.

The Y-measurement error decreases the R^2 value. Since $Var(Y^0) = Var(Y + v) = Var(Y) + Var(v) > Var(Y)$, the total variation in Y^0 is larger than the one in Y. Therefore, the R^2 for Y^0 (with measurement error) will be smaller than the R^2 for Y (no measurement error).

$$\frac{variation\ explained\ by\ X_1}{total\ variation\ in\ Y^0} < \frac{variation\ explained\ by\ X_1}{total\ variation\ in\ Y}$$

6.1.2 Measurement errors in an explanatory variable

Suppose that the independent variable X_1 is not observable, but observed only with a measurement error η.

$$X_1^0 = X_1 + \eta$$

where X_1^0 = observed value and η = measurement error. It is assumed that $E(\eta) = 0$ and $Cov(\eta, X_1) = 0$. Then the *estimation* model needs to be expressed in observable variables Y and X_1^* as follows:

$$Y = \beta_0 + \beta_1 X_1 + u \implies Y = \beta_0 + \beta_1 (X_1^0 - \eta) + u$$

$$\implies Y = \beta_0 + \beta_1 X_1^0 + (u - \beta_1 \eta)$$

The error term in the estimation model has changed to $(u - \beta_1 \eta)$. The measurement error η is included both in the independent variable (X_1^0) and in the error term $(u - \beta_1 \eta)$, thereby causing the independent variable to be correlated with the error term. As a result, the OLS estimator is inconsistent and biased toward zero as shown below.

$$plim\ \hat{\beta}_1 = \frac{Cov\ (X_1^0, Y)}{Var\ (X_1^0)}$$

$$= \frac{Cov\ (X_1^0, \beta_0 + \beta_1 X_1^0 + u - \beta_1 \eta)}{Var\ (X_2^0)}$$

$$= \frac{Cov\ (X_1^0, \beta_0)}{Var\ (X_1^0)} + \frac{Cov\ (X_1^0, \beta_1 X_1^0)}{Var\ (X_1^0)} + \frac{Cov\ (X_1^0, u - \beta_1 \eta)}{Var\ (X_1^0)}$$

$$= 0 + \beta_1 + \frac{Cov\ (X_1 + \eta, u - \beta_1 \eta)}{Var\ (X_1^0)}$$

$$= \beta_1 + \frac{-\beta_1 Var\ (\eta)}{Var\ (X_1^0)}$$

$$= \beta_1 \left[1 - \frac{Var\ (\eta)}{Var\ (X_1) + Var\ (\eta)} \right]$$

$$< \beta_1$$

Example 6.1   Permanent income hypothesis

The permanent income hypothesis can be estimated and tested by a simple regression model:

$$CONS_i = \beta_1 + \beta_2 PI_i + u_i$$

where $CONS_i$ is the consumption expenditure and PI_i is the permanent income of household i. The permanent income is defined as a "normal" level of income determined by current income and expected future income over a person's lifetime. Since the permanent income (PI_i) is not observed, researchers have to use only observable measures of income, such as current income (CI_i).

$$CONS_i = \alpha_0 + \alpha_1 CI_i + u_i \tag{6.3}$$

However, the current income does not include the expected future income and is therefore not equal to the permanent income. We can treat the difference between the permanent and the current income as a measurement error (η_i).

$$CI_i = PI_i + \eta_i$$

The above analysis indicates that the OLS estimator for Eq. (6.3), $\hat{\alpha}_1$, is biased toward zero because the measurement error is included in the explanatory variable.

$$E(\hat{\alpha}_1) < \beta_1 \quad \text{and} \quad plim \; \hat{\alpha}_1 < \beta_1$$

Therefore, when we estimate the consumption function using current income, the estimated propensity to consume ($\hat{\alpha}_1$) is smaller than the one predicted by the permanent income hypothesis.

6.2 Specification errors

6.2.1 Omitted variables

Suppose that the *true* model includes two independent variables X_1 and X_2.

$$Y = \beta_0 + \beta_1 X_1 + \beta_2 X_2 + u$$

where $\beta_1 \neq 0, \beta_2 \neq 0$ and $Cov(X_1, u) = Cov(X_2, u) = 0$. Now let's consider what will happen if we estimate β_1 with omitting a significant variable X_2. That is, we use the following *estimation* model.

$$Y = \alpha_0 + \alpha_1 X_1 + e \tag{6.4}$$

The probability limit of the OLS estimator $\hat{\alpha}_1$ for Eq. (6.4) is:

$$
\begin{aligned}
plim \; \hat{\alpha}_1 &= \frac{Cov(X_1, Y)}{Var(X_1)} \\
&= \frac{Cov(X_1, \beta_0 + \beta_1 X_1 + \beta_2 X_2 + u)}{Var(X_1)} \\
&= \frac{Cov(X_1, \beta_0)}{Var(X_1)} + \frac{Cov(X_1, \beta_1 X_1)}{Var(X_1)} + \frac{Cov(X_1, \beta_2 X_2)}{Var(X_1)} + \frac{Cov(X_1, u)}{Var(X_1)} \\
&= \beta_1 + \frac{Cov(X_1, \beta_2 X_2)}{Var(X_1)}
\end{aligned}
\tag{6.5}
$$

Correlated omitted variable

The OLS estimator $\hat{\alpha}_1$ from the under-specified model is inconsistent if X_1 is correlated with the omitted variable X_2, i.e., $Cov(X_1, \beta_2 X_2) = \beta_2 Cov(X_1, X_2) \neq 0$; the asymptotic bias is the second term in the final equation of Eq. (6.5). The sign and magnitude of the bias depend on $Cov(X_1, \beta_2 X_2)$. If $Cov(X_1, \beta_2 X_2) > 0$, the bias will be in the positive direction, and vice versa.

Uncorrelated omitted variable

If the omitted variable X_2 is uncorrelated with X_1, the OLS estimator $\hat{\alpha}_1$ is still consistent because $Cov(X_1, X_2) = 0$ in Eq. (6.5). Since X_2 is omitted, however, the variation explained by the estimation model will be smaller than the one by the true model which includes X_2 as well. As a result, the variance of the error term (e) in the estimation model will be larger than the one in the true model. This increased variance will blow up the variances of *all* coefficients' estimates, thereby making their

t-statistics smaller and p-values larger. Therefore, it is suggested that you include explanatory variables which are supported by theory and accepted in the literature, although they are uncorrelated with other explanatory variables and not of your interest.[4]

6.2.2 Inclusion of irrelevant variables

Suppose that the *true* model includes only one independent variable X_1.

$$Y = \beta_0 + \beta_1 X_1 + u$$

where $Cov(X_1, u) = 0$. Now let's consider what will happen to the OLS estimator if we include an irrelevant variable W. That is, we use the following estimation model.

$$Y = \alpha_0 + \alpha_1 X_1 + \alpha_2 W + e \tag{6.6}$$

where $Cov(W, Y) = Cov(W, e) = 0$ because W is irrelevant to Y. Since all of the independent variables in Eq. (6.6) are not correlated with the error term e, the OLS estimators $\hat{\alpha}_1$ and $\hat{\alpha}_2$ are consistent; that is, $plim\ \hat{\alpha}_1 = \beta_1$ and $plim\ \hat{\alpha}_2 = 0$.

This result, coupled with the earlier result regarding the bias caused by omission of relevant variables, might lead us to believe that it is better to include variables (when in doubt) rather than exclude them. However, this is not always so, because although the inclusion of irrelevant variables has no damage to the consistency of OLS estimators, it uses up the degree of freedom and increases the standard errors of coefficient estimates, particularly for small-sized samples. Therefore, it is recommended to delete variables whose coefficients are not significant nor of your interest.

6.2.3 A guideline for model selection

The correlated-omitted-variable problem indicates that important (strongly significant and economically meaningful) factors should not be omitted from a model. It is because any models which omit significant variables would produce biased results.

If a significant variable is not correlated with the explanatory variables in a model, omission of the significant variable will not affect the consistency of the OLS estimator. However, by including the significant variable in the model, we can reduce the ESS (error sum of squares) and the standard errors of coefficient estimates, thereby making the t-statistics bigger and increasing the significance of regression coefficients. Remember that the t-statistic is the ratio of a coefficient estimate and its standard error, $t = \dfrac{\hat{\beta}}{s.e.}$ where $s.e. = \hat{\sigma} \Big/ \sqrt{\sum\limits_{i=1}^{n}\left(X_{2i} - \bar{X}\right)^2}$ with $\hat{\sigma} = \sqrt{\dfrac{ESS}{(n-k-1)}} = \sqrt{\sum\limits_{i=1}^{n}(Y_i - \hat{Y}_i)^2 \Big/ (n-k-1)}$.

Therefore, it is recommended to include all of the strongly significant variables.

At the same time, we also have to worry about possible over-parameterization. That is, if we include too many weakly significant explanatory variables, there will be too many parameters to be estimated for a given size of sample (n).[5] Then, the degree of freedom $(n-k-1)$, or the effective number of independent observations, will be smaller. The resulting loss of degree of freedom will also increase standard errors and therefore decrease the significance of estimation results, *particularly for small-sized samples*. Therefore, it is recommended to delete weakly significant variables which are not of our interest and get little support from theory and previous studies.

In sum, we can suggest the following guideline regarding variable selection:

i   We should include all strongly significant and economically meaningful variables;
ii   We should include weakly significant variables if they are of our interest and justified by theoretical and empirical results;
iii We delete weakly significant variables if they are not of our interest and get little support from theory and previous studies.

6.3 Two-stage least squares estimation

This two-stage least squares (2SLS) estimation method is designed to solve the endogeneity problem. The idea is that we create a new variable which is not correlated with the disturbance but is similar to the endogenous explanatory variable. In creating such new variable, we need the help of additional variables, called **instrumental variables** (IVs). As these IVs are supposed to solve the endogeneity problem, they have to be uncorrelated with the disturbance. In the first stage, we use the IVs to create the OLS fitted variable of the endogenous explanatory variable. In the second stage, after having the fitted variable replace its corresponding endogenous variable, we can apply the OLS estimation. In practice, we don't need to follow these two stages of estimation because most econometrics computer packages have functions for the 2SLS estimation. The following explanation is only to help you understand the idea of the 2SLS estimation.

Consider the following regression in which X is endogenous, i.e., $Cov(X,u) \neq 0$, thereby the OLS estimator being inconsistent and biased.

$$Y = \beta_0 + \beta_1 X + \beta_2 Z_1 + u \tag{6.7}$$

where the other exogenous explanatory variable is denoted by Z_1 and $Cov(Z_1,u) = 0$. In order to cut the correlation between the endogenous regressor (here X) and the error term (u), we regress X on IVs and calculate its fitted value using the OLS estimates.[6]

$$\begin{aligned} X &= d_0 + d_1 Z_1 + d_2 Z_2 + \cdots + d_s Z_s + v \\ &= (\hat{d}_0 + \hat{d}_1 Z_1 + \hat{d}_2 Z_2 + \cdots + \hat{d}_s Z_s) + \hat{v} \\ &= \hat{X} + \hat{v} \end{aligned} \tag{6.8}$$

where the exogenous regressor Z_1 and additional exogenous variables $Z_2, \cdots, Z_s$ are used as IVs for X. In fact, with the help of the IVs, this first-stage regression decomposes the endogenous explanatory variable (X) into two components: one is the exogenous component ($\hat{X}$) which is a linear combination of the IVs and the other is the endogenous component ($\hat{v}$) which consists of the residuals in this first-stage regression.

When there is more than one IV for an endogenous explanatory variable, we need to summarize them into one fitted variable ($\hat{X}$). It is known that the OLS fitted variable $\hat{X}$ is more similar to the original X variable than any other possible linear combination for a given set of IVs. That is why we use the OLS method in obtaining a fitted variable in this first stage.[7]

In the second stage, we substitute the fitted variable $\hat{X}$ for X in the original regression, Eq. (6.7).

$$Y = \beta_0 + \beta_1 \hat{X} + \beta_2 Z_1 + u \tag{6.9}$$

As the fitted variable $\hat{X}$ is uncorrelated with the disturbance u, we can apply the OLS method and obtain consistent estimates for the coefficients (β_0, β_1, β_2). An illustration of using *EViews* and *SAS* is presented in Appendix 6A to this chapter.

When there is one endogenous explanatory variable (here X), it is required to have at least one new instrumental variable which is significantly correlated with the endogenous variable (X) but is not included in the main regression, Eq. (6.7). Consider an extreme case where all of the newly added instrumental variables $Z_2, \cdots, Z_S$ in Eq. (6.7) have no significant relation with X. Then their coefficients will be zero and the fitted variable in the first stage becomes $\hat{X} = \hat{d}_0 + \hat{d}_1 Z_1$, a function of Z_1 only. As a result, the second-stage regression Eq. (6.9) cannot be estimated because of the perfect multicollinearity between $\hat{X}$ and Z_1. Similarly, if too few significant exogenous variables are newly added in the first-stage regression, the fitted variable could be highly correlated with the existing exogenous variable (here Z_1) in the second-stage regression, causing a multicollinearity problem. If so, the second-stage estimates will not be accurate with large standard errors.[8] Therefore, researchers are required to identify exogenous (instrumental) variables which are significant in the first stage but are excluded from the main regression; this is the *exclusion restriction*.[9]

Larcker and Rusticus (2010) advise that researchers report the explanatory power of the newly added instrumental variables in the first-stage regression. However, many empirical studies report the first-stage estimation results not in sufficient detail. The first-stage R^2 (coefficient of determination) reported in those studies is the explanatory power of the *total* first-stage model, but not the *partial* explanatory power of the instruments which are unique to the first-stage regression. The proper measure of the strength of the newly added instruments is the *partial* R^2, which can be easily computed by

$$
\begin{aligned}
partial\ R^2 &= \frac{R^2_{X,Z} - R^2_{X,Z_1}}{1 - R^2_{X,Z_1}} \\[2mm]
&= \frac{explained\ X\ variation\ by\ Z_2, \cdots, Z_S}{unexplained\ X\ variation\ by\ Z_1} \\[2mm]
&= \frac{(explained\ X\ variation\ by\ Z) - (explained\ X\ variation\ by\ Z_1)}{unexplained\ X\ variation\ by\ Z_1}
\end{aligned}
$$

where $Z = \{Z_1, Z_2, \cdots, Z_S\}$ is the combined set of the preexisting and newly added exogenous instrumental variables; and $R^2_{X,Z}$ (R^2_{X,Z_1}) is the R^2 from a regression of X on Z (Z_1). The numerator measures the increase in the X-variation explained by the addition of new exogenous variables $\{Z_2, \cdots, Z_S\}$ in the first-stage regression. Thus, the partial R^2 can measure the incremental explanatory power of the newly added instruments.

An alternative approach to assess the quality of newly added instruments is to test their significance in the first-stage regression. For example, in Eq. (6.8) we conduct a partial F-test for $H_0 : d_2 = \cdots = d_S = 0$ in the first stage, a significance test of the newly added instrumental variables. If this partial F-statistic is low and thus yields a large p-value, this indicates that the selected instruments are too weak to be used as instruments. Stock et al. (2002) present critical values of the F-statistic; when the number of instruments is 1, 2, 3, 5, 10, 15, their suggested critical F-values are 8.96, 11.59, 12.83, 15.09, 20.88 and 26.80, respectively. If the first-stage partial F-statistic falls below the critical values, the instruments are considered to be weak. In such cases of weak instruments, it is necessary to examine the costs and benefits from using the 2SLS estimator. For detailed discussions about the issues of weak instruments, refer to Larcker and Rusticus (2010), Stock et al. (2002), and the references therein.

Based on the above explanation, we summarize that the 2SLS can perform well only when the IVs satisfy the following three conditions:

Condition 1: *Exogeneity*

The 2SLS method is designed to solve the endogeneity problem with the help of IVs. Therefore, the IVs have to be uncorrelated with the disturbance of the main regression.

Condition 2: *Relevance*

In the second-stage regression, the endogenous explanatory variable (X) is replaced by the fitted variable ($\hat{X}$) from the first stage. Thus, the 2SLS can perform well only when $\hat{X}$ is similar to X. If IVs are not significantly correlated with X, $\hat{X}$ will be substantially different from X. With such weak IVs, the 2SLS method would perform poorly.

Condition 3: *Exclusion restriction*

In order to reduce the effect of multicollinearity in the second-stage regression, the fitted variable ($\hat{X}$) should not be highly correlated with the exogenous variables already included in the main regression (here Z_1). Therefore, we need enough numbers of newly added instrumental variables which are significant in the first stage but are excluded from the second-stage regression.

6.4 Generalized method of moments (GMM)

For an easy understanding, let us use the following multiple regression where Z_1 is exogenous but X is endogenous.

$$Y_i = \beta_0 + \beta_1 X_i + \beta_2 Z_{1i} + u_i$$

Using instrumental variables Z_2 and Z_3, we have four orthogonality (uncorrelatedness) conditions.

$$E[u_i] = 0, \qquad E[Z_{1i} u_i] = 0$$
$$E[Z_{2i} u_i] = 0, \qquad E[Z_{3i} u_i] = 0$$

The intuition for this method is that parameter estimators must have sample properties that mimic the properties in the population. Thus, the sample means corresponding to the orthogonality conditions are

$$E[u_i] = 0 \quad \Rightarrow \quad \frac{1}{n}\sum_{i=1}^{n} \hat{u}_i \quad = \frac{1}{n}\sum_{i=1}^{n}\left(Y_i - \hat{\beta}_0 - \hat{\beta}_1 X_i - \hat{\beta}_2 Z_{1i}\right) = 0$$

$$E[Z_{1i} u_i] = 0 \quad \Rightarrow \quad \frac{1}{n}\sum_{i=1}^{n} Z_{1i}\hat{u}_i \quad = \frac{1}{n}\sum_{i=1}^{n} Z_{1i}\left(Y_i - \hat{\beta}_0 - \hat{\beta}_1 X_i - \hat{\beta}_2 Z_{1i}\right) = 0$$

$$E[Z_{2i} u_i] = 0 \quad \Rightarrow \quad \frac{1}{n}\sum_{i=1}^{n} Z_{2i}\hat{u}_i \quad = \frac{1}{n}\sum_{i=1}^{n} Z_{2i}\left(Y_i - \hat{\beta}_0 - \hat{\beta}_1 X_i - \hat{\beta}_2 Z_{1i}\right) = 0$$

$$E[Z_{3i} u_i] = 0 \quad \Rightarrow \quad \frac{1}{n}\sum_{i=1}^{n} Z_{3i}\hat{u}_i \quad = \frac{1}{n}\sum_{i=1}^{n} Z_{3i}\left(Y_i - \hat{\beta}_0 - \hat{\beta}_1 X_i - \hat{\beta}_2 Z_{1i}\right) = 0$$

Since there are four moment equations for three parameters $(\hat{\beta}_0, \hat{\beta}_1, \hat{\beta}_2)$, more than one solution is possible depending on which moment equation is used. The GMM estimation finds values for $(\hat{\beta}_0, \hat{\beta}_1, \hat{\beta}_2)$ which make all of the moment equations hold as close as possible. The moment equations might be different in their importance which could be measured by their variances. Thus, it would be more efficient if we use a weighted criterion in which the weights are inversely proportional to the variances of the moment equations. In constructing the weighting matrix, we incorporate the heteroscedasticity and autocorrelation of disturbances.[10] The GMM estimators will then minimize the weighted sum of squared values of the moment equations.

6.4.1 GMM vs. 2SLS

The 2SLS uses the OLS method both in the first and in the second stage. For efficiency, it requires the disturbances to be homoscedastic and uncorrelated between them. In contrast, the GMM incorporates heteroscedasticity and serial correlation in estimating the parameters and their standard errors. Thus, unless the disturbances are independently and identically distributed, the GMM is expected to perform better than the 2SLS.

As most cross-sectional observations are collected independently from observational units, the 2SLS method is often employed in addressing the endogeneity problem for cross-sectional data. However, the GMM method is more often used for time-series data because time-series data show serial correlation and/or time-varying (heteroscedastic) variance of the disturbances (Wooldridge, 2001).

6.5 Tests for endogeneity

6.5.1 Ramsey (1969) test

This is a general test for two types of specification errors: (i) correlation between the explanatory variables and the disturbance (endogeneity), and (ii) incorrect functional form. This test uses a regression augmented with extra variables W_j s and tests a null hypothesis $H_0 : \delta_1 = \cdots = \delta_m = 0$.

$$Y = \beta_0 + \beta_1 X + \beta_2 Z_1 + \sum_{j=1}^{m} \delta_j W_j + u$$

The extra variables W_js are powers of the fitted values ($\hat{Y}^2, \hat{Y}^3, \hat{Y}^4, \cdots$). As the fitted values are linear combinations of explanatory variables (here X and Z_1), inclusion of their powers is equivalent to including the powers and cross products of the explanatory variables. If the model is correctly specified (under the null hypothesis), then the extra variables should become insignificant.

6.5.2 Hausman (1978) test

The Hausman test is designed to detect an endogeneity, i.e., a correlation between the disturbance and explanatory variables. Thus, this is a general test for the following cases: (i) correlated omitted variables (Chapter 3); (ii) endogeneity caused by measurement errors in explanatory variables (this chapter); (iii) fixed vs. random effects for panel data models (Chapter 7); and (iv) simultaneity (Chapter 8). All of these cases result in inconsistent and biased estimates due to the endogeneity.

The idea of this test is as follows. Suppose that there are two estimators, say $\hat{\beta}^0$ and $\hat{\beta}^*$. Under the null hypothesis of { H_0 : No endogeneity}, both $\hat{\beta}^0$ and $\hat{\beta}^*$ are consistent and $\hat{\beta}^*$ is asymptotically efficient. Under the alternative of endogeneity, $\hat{\beta}^0$ is consistent, but $\hat{\beta}^*$ is inconsistent because it requires the assumption of no correlation between the disturbance and explanatory variables. For example, $\hat{\beta}^0$ is an 2SLS estimator using instrumental variables and $\hat{\beta}^*$ is the OLS estimator. Noticing that the two estimators are affected differently by the failure of no endogeneity, Hausman has developed a test statistic which is based on the difference of the two estimators, $\hat{\beta}^0 - \hat{\beta}^*$.

Alternatively, the Hausman test can be conducted in a simpler way. As an example, let us test the endogeneity of X.

$$Y = \beta_0 + \beta_1 X + \beta_2 Z_1 + u \tag{6.10}$$

First, we estimate an OLS regression of X on a set of instrumental variables and calculate its fitted values; this is the first-stage regression of the 2SLS.

$$\hat{X}_i = \hat{d}_0 + \hat{d}_1 Z_{1i} + \hat{d}_2 Z_{2i} + \cdots + \hat{d}_S Z_{Si}$$

Since $X_i = \hat{X}_i + \hat{v}_i$ where $\hat{v}_i$ is the residual, we obtain the following expression by substituting $\hat{X}_i + \hat{v}_i$ for X_i in Eq. (6.10).

$$Y_i = \beta_0 + \beta_1 \hat{X}_i + \theta \hat{v}_i + \beta_2 Z_{1i} + u_i \tag{6.11}$$

$\hat{X}_i$ is a linear combination of instrumental variables only and is orthogonal to the disturbance. However, $\hat{v}_i$ is uncorrelated with the disturbance if X is exogenous, but correlated otherwise. Under the null hypothesis that X is exogenous, there is no endogeneity problem in Eq. (6.11). Therefore, the OLS estimator for θ is consistent and supports $\theta = \beta_1$. In contrast, under the alternative of endogeneity, the OLS estimator for θ is inconsistent and thus rejects $\theta = \beta_1$. For an easy implementation, we rewrite Eq. (6.11) by substituting $\hat{X}_i = X_i - \hat{v}_i$:

$$Y_i = \beta_0 + \beta_1 X_i + (\theta - \beta_1) \hat{v}_i + \beta_2 Z_{1i} + u_i \tag{6.12}$$

Since the coefficient for $\hat{v}_i$ is equal to 0 under the null hypothesis of no endogeneity, the Hausman test performs a t-test on the coefficient for $\hat{v}_i$ in Eq. (6.12). An illustration of the Hausman test using *EViews* and *SAS* is given in Appendix 6B.

6.6 Applications

6.6.1 Dechow, Sloan and Sweeney (1995)

This study evaluates alternative accrual-based models for detecting earnings management. As many studies of earnings management focus on management's use of discretionary accruals, their evaluation is conducted in the following regression framework:

$$DA_{it} = \alpha + \beta \times PART_{it} + \sum_{k=1}^{K} \gamma_k X_{k,it} + \varepsilon_{it}$$

where DA is discretionary accruals; X_k s are other relevant variables influencing discretionary accruals; and ε is an error term. *PART* is a dummy variable which is set equal to one if systematic earnings management is hypothesized in response to the stimulus identified by the researcher and zero if no systematic earnings management is hypothesized. The null hypothesis of no earnings management in response to the stimulus will be rejected if the coefficient for *PART* (β) has the expected sign and is statistically significant at conventional levels.

Unfortunately, researchers cannot readily identify the other relevant variables (X_k s) and so excluded them from the model. Similarly, the researchers do not observe *DA* and are forced to use a proxy (*DAP*) that measures *DA* with a measurement error (v):

$$DAP_{it} = DA_{it} + v_{it}$$

Thus, the correctly specified model can be expressed in terms of the researchers' proxy for discretionary accruals as

$$DAP_{it} = \alpha + \beta \times PART_{it} + \left(\sum_{k=1}^{K} \gamma_k X_{k,it} + v_{it} \right) + \varepsilon_{it}$$

This model can be summarized as

$$DAP_{it} = \alpha + \beta \times PART_{it} + \mu_{it} + \varepsilon_{it}$$

where μ_{it} captures the sum of the effects of the omitted relevant variables on discretionary accruals and the measurement error in the researchers' proxy for discretionary accruals.

The model of earnings management typically estimated by the researchers can be represented as

$$DAP_{it} = \hat{\alpha} + \hat{b} \times PART_{it} + \hat{e}_{it} \tag{6.13}$$

The researchers' model is misspecified by the omission of μ. Recall that the μ represents omitted relevant variables influencing *DA* and a measurement error in *DAP*. Eq. (6.13), estimated by the OLS, has two undesirable consequences:

i $\hat{b}$ is a biased estimator of β, with the direction of the bias being of the same sign as the correlation between *PART* and μ; and

ii   The standard error $SE(\hat{b})$ in Eq. (6.13) is a biased estimator for $SE(\hat{\beta})$, the standard error in the correctly specified model. In particular, if *PART* and μ are uncorrelated, $SE(\hat{b})$ will provide an upwardly biased estimate of $SE(\hat{\beta})$ because the omitted variables will make the error sum of squares (*ESS*) bigger.[11]

These consequences lead to the following three possible problems for statistical inference in tests for earnings management:

Problem 1: *Bias away from zero*

If the earnings management that is hypothesized to be caused by *PART* does not take place (i.e., the true coefficient on *PART* is zero) and μ is correlated with *PART*, then the estimated coefficient on *PART* will be biased away from zero, increasing the probability of the Type I error.

Problem 2: *Bias toward zero*

If the earnings management that is hypothesized to be caused by *PART* does take place (i.e., the true coefficient on *PART* is different from zero) and the correlation between μ and *PART* is opposite in sign to the true coefficient on *PART*, then the estimated coefficient on *PART* will be biased toward zero. This will increase the probability of making an error that the null hypothesis is not rejected when it is not correct; this is the Type II error.

Problem 3: *Low power test*

Low power means that the test is more likely to accept the null when it is incorrect and should be rejected.[12] If μ is not correlated with *PART*, then the estimated coefficient on *PART* will not be biased. However, the exclusion of relevant variables leads to an inflated standard error of the coefficient estimate for *PART* because the omitted variables will make the error sum of squares (*ESS*) bigger. This increase in standard errors thus lowers the power of a test, in other words, increases the probability of accepting the null when it is not correct.[13]

6.6.2 Beaver, Lambert and Ryan (1987)

"*Conventional*" *regression*: Regression of a percentage change (%Δ) in security price (G_{it}) on a %Δ in earnings (g_{it})

$$G_{it} = \beta + \gamma g_{it} + u_{it} \tag{6.14}$$

"*Reverse*" *regression*: Regression of g_{it} on G_{it}

$$g_{it} = \alpha + \delta G_{it} + e_{it} \tag{6.15}$$

where $G_{it} = 100 \times \Delta P_{i,t} / P_{i,t-1}$, $g_{it} = 100 \times \Delta X_{i,t} / X_{i,t-1}$ with $P_{i,t}$ and $X_{i,t}$ denoting the security price and observed annual earnings, respectively, for firm i and year t.

The conventional regression Eq. (6.14) suffers from a bias due to measurement errors in g (earnings).[14] However, the reverse regression Eq. (6.15) places the measurement error associated with g in the disturbance term. As a result, the estimate of the slope coefficient is not biased. (It is based on an assumption that security prices contain no measurement error, or at a minimum much less than earnings.)

In addition to the econometric issues explained above, there is another advantage of employing the reverse regression. The notion of the information content of prices is that they may reflect information on a more timely basis than do earnings. The reverse regression Eq. (6.15) provides a way to examine the incremental explanatory power of lagged values of G (security price) with respect to g (earnings) via a multiple regression of the following form:

$$g_{it} = \alpha + \delta_1 G_{it} + \delta_2 G_{i,t-1} + e_{it} \tag{6.16}$$

In Beaver et al. (1987), the coefficient on $G_{i,t-1}$, δ_2, has been found statistically significant, which is consistent with the information content of prices with respect to future earnings. Such incremental explanatory power indicates the extent to which information is reflected in prices on a more timely basis than it is in earnings. The reverse regression also provides a basis for forecasting earnings based upon current and past values of price changes.

One remark related to the issues of specification error is in order. In a previous study of Beaver et al. (1980), the contemporaneous variable $G_{i,t}$ is omitted, that is,

$$g_{it} = \alpha + \delta_2 G_{i,t-1} + e_{it} \tag{6.17}$$

However, regression Eq. (6.16) possesses some potentially desirable properties relative to regression Eq. (6.17). If $G_{i,t}$ and $G_{i,t-1}$ are correlated, regression Eq. (6.16) provides a consistent test of the incremental explanatory power of $G_{i,t-1}$, because $G_{i,t}$ would constitute a *correlated omitted variable* in Eq. (6.17). In addition, if $G_{i,t}$ and $G_{i,t-1}$ are uncorrelated, regression Eq. (6.16) provides a more powerful test and a more efficient estimate of δ_2, because the standard error is reduced by the inclusion of $G_{i,t}$; a case of *uncorrelated omitted variable*.

Note: Which regression model we choose depends on which regression model satisfies the assumption of no correlation between the explanatory variables and the disturbance.

6.6.3 Himmelberg and Petersen (1994)

This study empirically examines an argument that because of capital market imperfection, internal finance is an important determinant of R&D investment, particularly for small and high-tech firms. This argument is based on the existence of information asymmetries between suppliers of external finance and such firms. Since the adjustment costs for R&D are high, firms set the level of R&D investment in accordance with the "permanent" level of internal finance. When a firm believes that a change in the flow of internal funds is "transitory," it attempts to maintain the planned level of R&D investment by adjusting physical investment or others.

In their econometric specification, the authors decompose current cash flow (a measure of internal fund) into a permanent component and a transitory component. Since R&D is relatively unresponsive to transitory movements due to high adjustment costs, the correct empirical model should be between R&D investment and permanent movements in cash flow. Thus, after decomposing observed cash flow (CF) into a permanent component (CF^*) and a transitory component (w), they estimate the effect of the permanent component on R&D investment using the following regression: for firm i in year t,

$$RD_{it} = \beta_0 + \beta_1 CF_{it}^* + e_{it}$$

This can be rewritten in terms of observable cash flows, $CF_{it} = CF_{it}^* + w_{it}$, as

$$RD_{it} = \beta_0 + \beta_1 CF_{it} + (e_{it} - \beta_1 w_{it})$$

Since the w_{it} component in the composite error term is negatively correlated with CF_{it}, the OLS estimate of β_1 is downward biased. This is identical to the errors-in-variables problem; w_{it} corresponds to the measurement error.

To solve this bias problem, the authors employ an instrumental-variables estimation method. Assuming that the transitory component w_{it} is independent between time periods, the natural instruments are lags of cash flows $(CF_{i,t-1}, CF_{i,t-2}, \ldots)$, which are believed highly correlated with CF_{it} and also CF_{it}^*.

6.7 Summary

1   Measurement errors in dependent variables do not affect the consistency of the OLS estimator but reduce the significance of regression coefficients because they inflate the standard errors.
2   Measurement errors in explanatory variables cause the OLS estimators to be inconsistent and biased; a case of the endogeneity problem. The ideal solution is to measure the variables without an error.
3   If significant variables correlated with the existing explanatory variables are omitted, the OLS estimators will be inconsistent and biased; another case of the endogeneity problem. The ideal solution is not to omit any significant variables.

4   If the above ideal solutions are not practically possible, then we can use alternative estimation methods instead of the OLS. With the help of instrumental variables (IVs), the 2SLS and GMM methods can produce consistent estimators.

5   For the IV estimation methods to perform well, the IVs need to be exogenous and relevant. And there have to be enough numbers of newly added instrumental variables which are significantly correlated with the endogenous explanatory variable.

6   The Ramsey and Hausman tests examine whether the error term is correlated with explanatory variables, i.e., the endogeneity problem.

Review questions

1   Consider the following *true* model which includes only one significant factor X_1.

$$Y = \beta_0 + \beta_1 X_1 + u$$

(a)   If we add an irrelevant (insignificant) variable X_2 to the regression, what will happen to the consistency of the OLS estimator? Explain.

(b)   It is known that omission of variables could bias the OLS estimator. This correlated-omitted-variable problem, coupled with the answer to (a), might suggest that it is always better to include variables (although not of our interest) rather than exclude them. Do you think this suggestion is correct? Explain.

(c)   Explain whether the following statement is True or False.
    "Under any circumstances, we have to omit variables which are not significant at a 5% significance level."

2   A main purpose of applying the multiple regression analysis is to show that certain variables are significant factors for the dependent variable of our interest. With a given dataset, however, we sometimes obtain an insignificant estimate for an explanatory variable. Below is one possible comment on such insignificant estimation results.

"It is expected that a more sophisticated model with more observations in the sample could produce more significant results."

(a)   A more sophisticated model would be an extended one which includes more relevant variables. Explain why such an extended model could yield significant results.

(b)   A more sophisticated model could also be obtained by deleting irrelevant variables. Explain why it is better to delete weakly significant variables which are not of our interest and get little support from theory and previous studies.

(c)   Explain why more observations would increase the significance.

3   The OLS estimator $\hat{\beta}_1$ for a simple linear regression, $Y_i = \beta_0 + \beta_1 X_i + u_i$, converges to the following.

$$plim\ \hat{\beta}_1 = \frac{plim \sum_{i=1}^{n}(X_i - \bar{X})(Y_i - \bar{Y})/n}{plim \sum_{i=1}^{n}(X_i - \bar{X})^2/n} = \frac{Cov(X,Y)}{Var(X)} = \beta_1 + \frac{Cov(X,u)}{Var(X)}$$

(a)   What condition is required for the OLS estimator $\hat{\beta}_1$ to be consistent?

(b)   If the condition is not satisfied, what is the direction (sign) of the bias?

4   A researcher would like to estimate the rate of returns to schooling, denoted by β_1, using the following regression:

$$\log(wage) = \beta_0 + \beta_1 S + \theta A + u \tag{Q6.1}$$

where S is the years of schooling completed, A is a measure of ability and the disturbance u is not correlated with S and A. Since the ability variable A is not observable (to the analyst), he or she will have to estimate a regression that omits A and interpret an estimate of α_1 as the rate of schooling returns.

$$\log(wage) = \alpha_0 + \alpha_1 S + w \tag{Q6.2}$$

Because of the omitted variable A, the OLS estimator for α_1 in Eq. (Q6.2) could be biased. To understand this bias, suppose that the ability A is related to the schooling S as follows.

$$A = \delta_0 + \delta_1 S + \varepsilon \tag{Q6.3}$$

(a) Express how α_1 is related with β_1. What is the correlated-omitted-variable bias in this expression?

(b) People with higher ability tend to have more schooling, $\delta_1 > 0$. Does α_1 over- or under-estimate β_1, the true rate of returns to schooling?

(c) If δ_1 is equal to zero, does the bias still exist? Explain why.

5   Consider the following regression model where $\beta_1 \neq 0$ and $\beta_2 \neq 0$.

$$Y = \beta_0 + \beta_1 X_1 + \beta_2 X_2 + u$$

(a) Since Y is unobservable, we are going to use a proxy variable Y^* which contains a measurement error (η), i.e., $Y^* = Y + \eta$. This means that we are estimating the following regression model, where $Cov(\eta, X_1) = 0$ and $Cov(\eta, X_2) = 0$.

$$Y^* = \beta_0 + \beta_1 X_1 + \beta_2 X_2 + u^*, \qquad (u^* = u + \eta)$$

Explain what happens to the consistency of the OLS estimators in this regression. Does the measurement error increase/decrease the standard errors of the OLS estimators?

(b) Suppose X_1 is observed only with a measurement error (δ). That is, X_1 is unobservable but $X_1^* (= X_1 + \delta)$ is observed. Now we have to estimate the following regression, where $Cov(\delta, X_1) = 0$ and $Cov(\delta, X_2) = 0$.

$$Y^* = \beta_0 + \beta_1 X_1^* + \beta_2 X_2 + u^0, \qquad (u^0 = u - \beta_1 \delta)$$

Explain what happens to the consistency of the OLS estimators in this regression.

(c) If we do not have any information about a significant variable X_2, we will have to omit X_2 and estimate the following regression.

$$Y = \beta_0 + \beta_1 X_1 + w, \qquad (w = u + \beta_2 X_2)$$

What does happen to the consistency and the standard errors of the OLS estimators due to the omission? Explain for each case of $Cov(X_1, X_2) = 0$ and $Cov(X_1, X_2) \neq 0$.

6   To show that X_1 is significantly related with Y, we estimate the following regression using the 2SLS method because X_1 is endogenous.

$$Y = \beta_0 + \beta_1 X_1 + \beta_2 X_2 + \beta_3 X_3 + u$$

Below are shown the estimates in the first and second stages.

< First-stage regressions: dependent variable = X1 >

– Regression 1 –

Variable	Coefficient	Std. Error	t-Statistic	Prob.
C	0.526	0.214	2.36	0.01
X2	0.539	0.321	1.54	0.19
X3	−0.121	0.372	−0.31	0.65
Z1	0.212	0.222	0.99	0.43
Z2	−1.121	0.909	−1.21	0.36
Z3	0.890	1.011	0.88	0.51
Z4	0.892	2.121	0.48	0.60
R-squared	0.95			

– Regression 2 –

Variable	Coefficient	Std. Error	t-Statistic	Prob.
C	0.621	0.210	2.96	0.00
X2	0.630	0.311	2.03	0.02
X3	−0.225	0.352	−0.64	0.55
R-squared	0.75			

< Second-stage regression: dependent variable = Y >

Variable	Coefficient	Std. Error	t-Statistic	Prob.
C	1.222	0.314	3.36	0.00
X1hat*	0.590	0.211	2.86	0.01
X2	−0.321	0.112	−2.34	0.01
X3	−0.987	0.232	3.24	0.00
R-squared	0.61			

*X1hat is the fitted variable of X1 from the first-stage regression (Regression 1).

(a) Explain how the first- and the second-stage estimation are conducted.

(b) In the first stage, all variables are insignificant but the R^2 is quite high. How can this happen? Explain.

(c) Explain whether the following statement is True, False or Uncertain.
   "The first-stage estimates show that all variables are insignificant. Therefore, we should not use these 2SLS estimation results for testing $H_0 : \beta_1 = 0$."

(d) Evaluate the quality (partial explanatory power) of the newly added instrumental variables (Z_1, Z_2, Z_3, Z_4).

7   The following questions are about the two-stage-least-squares (2SLS) method.

(a) Explain why the multicollinearity is not our concern in the first-stage regression.

(b) Explain why we need to care about multicollinearity in the second-stage regression.

(c)   To avoid the multicollinearity problem in the second-stage regression, what do we need?

(d)   Explain how we can confirm whether the newly added instrumental variables significantly contribute in reducing the multicollinearity in the second-stage regression.

8   Consider the following regression where X_1 and X_2 are exogenous but S is endogenous.

$$Y = \beta_0 + \beta_1 X_1 + \beta_2 X_2 + \gamma S + u$$

To address the endogeneity of S, we are going to employ the 2SLS method using instrumental variables of Z_1 and Z_2. If we use the following regression in the first stage, can we obtain consistent estimates in the second stage? Notice that an exogenous variable X_2 in the main regression is not used in the first stage.

$$Y = \delta_0 + \delta_1 X_1 + \delta_2 Z_1 + \delta_3 Z_2 + \eta$$

9   [2SLS for a nonlinear regression of an endogenous variable, (Angrist and Pischke, 2009, p. 192)]

Consider the following model which is nonlinear in an endogenous variable S.

$$Y_i = \alpha_0 + \alpha_1 X_i + \beta_1 S_i + \beta_2 S_i^2 + u_i$$

where X_i is exogenous and a set of instrumental variables $\{Z_{1i}, \cdots, Z_{Si}\}$ is available.

(a)   To obtain 2SLS estimates, you might want to work with a single first stage. That is, you obtain the first-stage fitted values $\hat{S}_i = \hat{d}_0 + \hat{d}_1 Z_{1i} + \cdots + \hat{d}_S Z_{Si}$ and estimate the following second-stage regression with also using their squares $\hat{S}_i^2$.

$$Y_i = \alpha_0 + \alpha_1 X_i + \beta_1 \hat{S}_i + \beta_2 \hat{S}_i^2 + u_i$$

Explain whether this produces consistent 2SLS estimates.

(b)   Alternatively, you can treat S_i and S_i^2 as separate endogenous variables. Given at least two instruments, you work with two first-stage equations, one for S_i and the other for S_i^2. In doing so, you can use not only the original instruments but also their squares. Explain whether this produces consistent 2SLS estimates.

Notes

1   For simplicity, we focus only on the slope coefficient β_1 in a simple regression. The results can be applied to all coefficients in multiple regressions in the same way, only with unnecessary complexity. In Eq. (6.1), a relation of $Y_i - \bar{Y} = (\beta_0 + \beta_1 X_{1i} + u_i) - (\beta_0 + \beta_1 \bar{X}_1 + \bar{u}) = \beta_1 (X_{1i} - \bar{X}_1) + (u_i - \bar{u})$ has been utilized.

2   The term "endogenous" and "exogenous" originated in economic modeling and simultaneous equation analysis. In econometrics, these terms are used to define whether an explanatory variable is correlated or uncorrelated with the disturbance.

3   Remember from Chapter 2 that the variance of the OLS estimator in a simple regression is $Var(\hat{\beta}_1) = Var(error\ term)/\sum(X_1 - \bar{X}_1)^2 = Var(u + v)/\sum(X_1 - \bar{X}_1)^2$.

4   When the four assumptions introduced in Chapter 2 are satisfied, the OLS estimator is unbiased (thus consistent) and efficient. However, it does not imply that the given model itself is a good one. For example, a certain regression model can satisfy the assumptions even when the model omits a significant variable which is not correlated with the included explanatory variables. If it is the case, the empirical results can be improved by including the omitted variable. Thus, the satisfaction of the assumptions is a necessary (but not sufficient) condition for a model to be good enough.

5 The significance is a continuous measure of the extent to which the evidence rejects the hypotheses. Here, we intentionally use a term "weakly significant" instead of "insignificant." Being insignificant means that the p-value is larger than an arbitrarily chosen significance level, e.g., 10%, 5% or 1%. However, there is no reason why such significance levels should be used. This guideline suggests that even though a p-value is greater than 0.1, we had better include the variable if it is supported by theoretical results and previous empirical studies. That is because a p-value of 0.32, for example, does not mean that the variable is surely insignificant. In other words, although a large p-value cannot strongly reject a null hypothesis $H_0 : \beta_1 = 0$, it does not indicate that the null hypothesis is true. Instead, a correct interpretation would be that there exists some extent of evidence against the null hypothesis but the evidence is not so strong as the 10% significance level.

6 In the first stage, all we need are the fitted values ($\hat{X}$) which are used in the second stage. As we are not interested in the accuracy of coefficient estimates, we don't need to worry about possible multicollinearity although many instrumental variables are used in the first stage.

7 Notice that since the OLS method minimizes the sum of squared residuals, it makes the fitted variable as similar to X as possible *for a given set of* IVs. It implies that the similarity of $\hat{X}$ to X depends on IVs. If IVs are not significantly correlated with X, the fitted variable $\hat{X}$ will be substantially different from X even though the OLS estimation is used. This is a case of *weak* IVs. With such weak IVs, the 2SLS method would perform poorly because $\hat{X}$ replaces X in the second stage when $\hat{X}$ is substantially different from X. Thus, the success of the 2SLS method depends on how significantly the IVs are correlated with their corresponding endogenous variable X. If *strong* IVs which are significantly correlated with X are used, then the fitted variable $\hat{X}$ from the first-stage regression will be similar to X, yielding satisfactory 2SLS estimates.

8 In the first-stage regression we are not concerned about multicollinearity as we need only a fitted variable for the endogenous regressor. In contrast, in the second-stage regression (or the main regression), we need to estimate the coefficients efficiently, i.e., having the smallest possible standard errors. Thus, we have to minimize the effect of possible multicollinearity by making $\hat{X}$ (from the first-stage regression) different from the exogenous variables included in the main regression, Z_1 in Eq. (6.9), as much as possible.

9 It is important to provide a clear and sensible argument for why certain instrumental variables affect outcomes (Y) only through the endogenous variable (X) but not directly in the main regression; this is not an easy task, though.

10 The 2SLS estimator is a GMM estimator that uses a weighting matrix constructed under homoscedasticity and no autocorrelation.

11 Remember from Chapter 2 that for a simple regression the OLS standard error is $\hat{\sigma} / \sqrt{\sum (X_i - \bar{X})^2}$ where $\hat{\sigma} = \sqrt{ESS/(n-2)}$ and ESS is the error sum of squares.

12 A hypothesis test is said to be *powerful* if at a chosen level of significance, it has the largest probability of rejecting the null when it is not correct. Thus, the power of a test indicates the extent to which an incorrect null hypothesis is rejected; in other words, an alternative hypothesis is concluded when it is correct.

13 The power of a test is determined by the standard error of an estimator. If the standard error is large, then its sampling distribution is widely distributed, making the rejection region appear far left and far right. It means that the acceptance region will cover a wide range of estimated values. Therefore, it is more likely to accept the null hypothesis, yielding low power.

14 The measurement errors are the effects on earnings of events that have no effect on security prices. Examples of such events include a change in the mandatory treatment of deferred taxes and a year-end adjustment for earnings smoothing. Another example is the stale component that market had anticipated before it was reflected in earnings; this is resulted from the price-lead-earnings relation (Kothari and Zimmerman, 1995). The information in $g_{i,t}$ has already been reflected in earlier periods' security prices, e.g., $G_{i,t-1}$, but not in $G_{i,t}$.

References

Angrist, J.D. and J.S. Pischke (2009), *Mostly Harmless Econometrics: An Empiricist's Companion*, Princeton, NJ: Princeton University Press.

Beaver, W.H., R.A. Lambert and D. Morse (1980), "The Information Content of Security Prices," *Journal of Accounting and Econometrics*, 2, 3–28.

Beaver, W.H., R.A. Lambert and S.G. Ryan (1987), "The Information Content of Security Prices: a second look," *Journal of Accounting and Economics*, 9, 139–157.

Dechow, P.M, R.G. Sloan and A.P. Sweeney (1995), "Detecting Earnings Management," *The Accounting Review*, 70, 193–225.

Hausman, J.A. (1978), "Specification Tests in Econometrics," *Econometrica*, 46, 1251–1272.

Himmelberg, C.P. and B.C. Petersen (1994), "R&D and Internal Finance: A Panel Study of Small Firms in High-Tech Industries," *The Review of Economics and Statistics*, 76(1), 38–51.

Kothari, S.P. and J.L. Zimmerman (1995), "Price and Return Models," *Journal of Accounting and Economics*, 20, 155–192.

Larcker, D.F. and T.O. Rusticus (2010), "On the Use of Instrumental Variables in Accounting Research," *Journal of Accounting and Economics*, 49, 186–205.

Ramsey, J.B. (1969), "Tests for Specification Errors in Classical Linear Least Squares Regression Analysis," *Journal of the Royal Statistical Society: Series B*, 31, 350–371.

Stock, J.H., J.H. Wright and M. Yogo (2002), "A Survey of Weak Instruments and Weak Identification in Generalized Method of Moments," *Journal of Business and Economics Statistics*, 20, 518–529.

Wooldridge, J.M. (2001), "Applications of Generalized Method of Moments Estimation," *Journal of Economic Perspectives*, 15(4), 87–100.

Appendix 6A Estimation of 2SLS and GMM using *EViews* and *SAS*

An Excel file "8-sem.xls" contains observations with variable names "YEAR GDP I GOV M TB." They are annual time-series data on national income (*GDP*), gross private investment (*I*), government expenditure (*GOV*), money supply (*M*) and an interest rate (*TB*) for the period from 1970 to 1994. Consider the following GDP function.

$$GDP_t = \alpha_0 + \alpha_1 M_t + \alpha_2 I_t + \alpha_3 GOV_t + u_t \qquad (A6.1)$$

The Hausman test in Appendix 6B shows that M_t is endogenous. This appendix now illustrates how this *GDP* equation is estimated by the 2SLS and the GMM method. It is assumed that I_t, GOV_t and TB_t are exogenous and therefore uncorrelated with the disturbance u_t. So, these variables are used as instrumental variables. In addition, the lagged variables (GDP_{t-1}, M_{t-1}, I_{t-1}, GOV_{t-1}, TB_{t-1}) can also be used as instrumentals. It is because they had been *predetermined* in an earlier period *t*-1 and thus are uncorrelated with the unexpected change in period *t* (u_t).

Using *EViews*

After importing the Excel file (8-sem.xls), we generate the lagged variables (GDP_{t-1}, M_{t-1}, I_{t-1}, GOV_{t-1}, TB_{t-1}) by pressing the Genr button and entering "L_GDP=GDP(−1)," where (−1) is a lag operator. We apply this lag operator to the other variables. We now create a system object and specify the system of equations by choosing Objects/New Object. . . /System. In the System window, enter the equation and list the instrumental variables following a command INST:

GDP = C(1) + C(2)*M + C(3)*I + C(4)*GOV
INST I GOV TB L_GDP L_M L_I L_GOV L_TB

Once we have created the system, we press the Estimate button on the toolbar. From the System Estimation dialog, we choose Two-Stage Least Squares for the estimation method. The estimation results are shown in Output 6.1.

Output 6.1   2SLS estimation results

System: UNTITLED
Estimation Method: Two-Stage Least Squares
Sample: 1971 1994
Included observations: 24
Total system (balanced) observations 24

	Coefficient	Std. Error	t-Statistic	Prob.
C(1)	-209.0064	101.6771	-2.055589	0.0531
C(2)	3.453374	0.525349	6.573483	0.0000
C(3)	0.310709	0.687259	0.452098	0.6561
C(4)	-11.60862	3.249930	-3.571958	0.0019
Determinant residual covariance		31014.95		

Equation: GDP = C(1) + C(2)*M + C(3)*I + C(4)*GOV			
Instruments: I GOV TB L_GDP L_M L_I L_GOV L_TB C			
Observations: 24			
R-squared	0.990567	Mean dependent var	3637.363
Adjusted R-squared	0.989152	S.D. dependent var	1852.258
S.E. of regression	192.9195	Sum squared resid	744358.8
Durbin-Watson stat	0.621280		

For GMM estimation, you can choose one from the list of two estimation methods:

1   GMM-Cross section (White cov) uses a weighting matrix that is robust to heteroscedasticity and contemporaneous correlation of unknown form.
2   GMM-Time series (HAC) extends this robustness to autocorrelation of unknown form.

Using *SAS*[1]

```
FILENAME F1 DDE 'EXCEL|[9-SEM.XLS]SEM!R2C1:R26C6';
DATA K; INFILE F1 LRECL=1000;
    INPUT YEAR GDP I GOV M TB;
    LGDP=LAG(GDP); LM=LAG(M); LI=LAG(I); LGOV=LAG(GOV); LTB=LAG(TB);

TITLE '======= OLS, PROC REG =======';
PROC REG DATA=K ;
    MODEL GDP = M I GOV; RUN;
TITLE '======= OLS, PROC MODEL =======';
PROC MODEL DATA=K ;
    PARMS B0 B1 B2 B3;
    GDP = B0 +B1*M +B2*I +B3*GOV;
    FIT GDP; RUN;

TITLE '======= 2SLS, PROC SYSLIN =========';
PROC SYSLIN DATA=K 2SLS FIRST;
    ENDOGENOUS GDP M;
    INSTRUMENTS TB I GOV LGDP LM LI LGOV LTB;
    MODEL GDP = M I GOV; RUN;
TITLE '======= 2SLS, PROC MODEL =========';
PROC MODEL DATA=K ;
    ENDOGENOUS GDP M;
    EXOGENOUS I GOV ;
    PARAMETERS B0 B1 B2 B3;
    GDP = B0 +B1*M +B2*I +B3*GOV;
```

```
    FIT GDP/IT2SLS FSRSQ ;
    INSTRUMENTS TB I GOV LGDP LM LI LGOV LTB; RUN;

TITLE '========= GMM: serially uncorrelated (White correction) =========';
PROC MODEL DATA=K ;
    ENDOGENOUS GDP M;
    EXOGENOUS I GOV ;
    PARMS BO B1 B2;
    GDP = BO +B1*M +B2*I +B3*GOV;
    FIT GDP/ITGMM KERNEL=(PARZEN, O, 0);
    INSTRUMENTS TB I GOV LGDP LM LI LGOV LTB; RUN;
TITLE '========= GMM: serially correlated =========';
PROC MODEL DATA=K ;
    ENDOGENOUS GDP M;
    EXOGENOUS I GOV ;
    PARMS BO B1 B2;
    GDP = BO +B1*M +B2*I +B3*GOV;
    FIT GDP/ITGMM KERNEL=(BART, 0.5, 0.333);
    INSTRUMENTS TB I GOV LGDP LM LI LGOV LTB; RUN;
TITLE '========= GMM: serially correlated =========';
PROC MODEL DATA=K ;
    ENDOGENOUS GDP M;
    EXOGENOUS I GOV ;
    PARMS BO B1 B2;
    GDP = BO +B1*M +B2*I +B3*GOV;
    FIT GDP/ITGMM KERNEL=(PARZEN, 1, 0.2);
    INSTRUMENTS TB I GOV LGDP LM LI LGOV LTB; RUN;
```

Note: If the disturbances are serially uncorrelated, set c to 0 in KERNEL=(PARZEN, c, e) or KERNEL = (BART, c, e). If they are serially correlated, you can choose values for c and e with considering how many lags have nonzero serial correlations. Their default values are KERNEL = (PARZEN, 1, 0.2) or KERNEL = (BART, 0.5, 1/3). For more details about the KERNEL options, refer to the SAS manual (PROC MODEL/Estimation Methods).

Appendix 6B Hausman test for endogeneity using *EViews* and *SAS*

Consider the GDP function, Eq. (A6.1) from Appendix 6A.

$$GDP_t = \alpha_0 + \alpha_1 M_t + \alpha_2 I_t + \alpha_3 GOV_t + u_t \qquad (A6.1)$$

where I_t, GOV_t and TB_t are assumed exogenous and therefore uncorrelated with the disturbance u_t. However, we are not sure whether M_t is exogenous or endogenous. If M_t is correlated with the disturbance u_t, the OLS estimator will be inconsistent and also biased. To test for its endogeneity, we can apply the specification test devised by Hausman (1978). The null hypothesis of this Hausman test is that M_t is exogenous.

First, we estimate an OLS regression of M_t on a set of instrumental variables and obtain its fitted values

$$\hat{M}_t = \hat{d}_0 + \hat{d}_1 I_t + \hat{d}_2 GOV_t + \hat{d}_3 TB_t$$
$$+ \hat{d}_4 GDP_{t-1} + \hat{d}_5 M_{t-1} + \hat{d}_6 I_{t-1} + \hat{d}_7 GOV_{t-1} + \hat{d}_8 TB_{t-1} \qquad (A6.2)$$

where all exogenous variables (I_t, GOV_t, TB_t) are used as instrumental variables. Since the predetermined variables (GDP_{t-1}, M_{t-1}, I_{t-1}, GOV_{t-1}, TB_{t-1}) are not correlated with the disturbance u_t, they can also be used as instrumental variables.

M_t can be decomposed into the fitted values and the residuals by the OLS estimation; $M_t = \hat{M}_t + \hat{v}_t$ where $\hat{v}_t$ s are the residuals from the regression of Eq. (A6.2). By substituting $\hat{M}_t + \hat{v}_t$ for M_t in Eq. (A6.1), we obtain the following expression:

$$GDP_t = \alpha_0 + \alpha_1 \hat{M}_t + \theta \hat{v}_t + \alpha_2 I_t + \alpha_3 GOV_t + u_t \qquad (A6.3)$$

Since the fitted variable M_t is a linear combination of instrumental variables only, it is uncorrelated with u_t. Under the null hypothesis that M_t is uncorrelated with u_t, the residuals $\hat{v}_t$ must be uncorrelated with u_t. If so, the OLS estimator of θ is consistent and equal to α_1, thereby supporting $H_0 : \theta = \alpha_1$. In contrast, if M_t is correlated with u_t, the correlated component in M_t is included in $\hat{v}_t$ because $\hat{M}_t$ is by construction uncorrelated with u_t. Then the correlation between $\hat{v}_t$ and u_t causes the estimator for θ to be inconsistent, leading to a rejection of $H_0 : \theta = \alpha_1$.

It is more convenient to test whether a certain coefficient is significantly different from zero, rather than to test if $\theta = \alpha_1$. To do it, rewrite Eq. (A6.3) using $\hat{M}_t = M_t - \hat{v}_t$:

$$GDP_t = \alpha_0 + \alpha_1 M_t + (\theta - \alpha_1)\hat{v}_t + \alpha_2 I_t + \alpha_3 GOV_t + u_{1t} \qquad (A6.4)$$

Under the null hypothesis of no endogeneity, it holds that $\theta = \alpha_1$ and also that the coefficient for $\hat{v}_t$ is equal to 0. Thus, we regress GDP_t on M_t, $\hat{v}_t$, I_t and perform a t-test on the coefficient for $\hat{v}_t$. If its coefficient is significantly different from zero, we reject the null of no endogeneity and conclude that M_t is endogenous.

Using *EViews*

Using the Excel data file (8-sem.xls), we test whether M_t is endogenous in the above GDP regression model, Eq. (A6.1).

i   We first regress M_t on the instrumental variables by choosing Objects/New Object. . . /Equation and entering a regression model "M C I GOV TB L_GDP L_M L_I L_GOV L_TB." We will get the OLS estimation results as shown in Output 6.2.

Output 6.2   OLS estimation of *M* on the instrumental variables

Dependent Variable: M
Method: Least Squares
Sample (adjusted): 1971 1994
Included observations: 24 after adjustments

Variable	Coefficient	Std. Error	t-Statistic	Prob.
C	22.44292	42.09946	0.533093	0.6018
I	0.444789	0.188623	2.358088	0.0324
GOV	1.113713	1.478137	0.753457	0.4628
TB	-11.77211	7.341038	-1.603603	0.1296
L_GDP	-0.103869	0.064038	-1.621973	0.1256
L_M	0.986535	0.221765	4.448569	0.0005
L_I	-0.102647	0.209704	-0.489486	0.6316
L_GOV	-0.344690	1.269065	-0.271610	0.7896
L_TB	15.86158	10.41485	1.522977	0.1486
R-squared	0.999341	Mean dependent var		2156.796
Adjusted R-squared	0.998989	S.D. dependent var		1023.438

---

ii   You will also get a residual series named "resid" in the Workfile window. To use the residual series in the next stage of the Hausman test, we need to save it using a different name. In the Workfile menu, press Genr and enter "RESID_M = resid."

iii   Regress *GDP* on *M*, *I*, *GOV*, and the residuals (RESID_M). To do it, choose Objects/New Object. . . /Equation and enter a regression model "GDP C M I GOV RESID_M" to obtain the following Hausman test results in Output 6.3. The coefficient of RESID_M is significantly different from zero at the 5% (*p*-value = 0.0474 < 0.05). Therefore, we reject the null hypothesis of no endogeneity.

Output 6.3   Hausman test results

Dependent Variable: GDP
Method: Least Squares
Sample (adjusted): 1971 1994
Included observations: 24 after adjustments

Variable	Coefficient	Std. Error	t-Statistic	Prob.
C	-209.0064	92.77734	-2.252774	0.0363
M	3.453374	0.479365	7.204053	0.0000
I	0.310709	0.627104	0.495466	0.6260
GOV	-11.60862	2.965464	-3.914603	0.0009
RESID_M	-3.129745	1.476694	-2.119427	0.0474

Using *SAS*[2]

```
FILENAME F1 DDE 'EXCEL|[8-SEM.XLS]SEM!R2C1:R26C6';
DATA K; INFILE F1 LRECL=1000;
      INPUT YEAR GDP I GOV M TB;
      LGDP=LAG(GDP); LM=LAG(M); LI=LAG(I); LGOV=LAG(GOV); LTB=LAG(TB);

TITLE '======= To obtain residuals by OLS =======';
PROC REG;
      MODEL M = I GOV TB LGDP LM LI LGOV LTB;
      Output OUT=RES R= M_RESIDUAL; RUN;
TITLE '======= Regression of the original with the Residuals ======';
PROC REG DATA=RES;
      MODEL GDP = M I GOV M_RESIDUAL;
RUN;
```

Notes

1 BASE SAS 9.4, SAS/ETS 13.1 and SAS/STAT 13.1. SAS Institute Inc., Cary, NC.
2 BASE SAS 9.4 and SAS/STAT 13.1. SAS Institute Inc., Cary, NC.

7 Models for panel data

Learning objectives

In this chapter, you should learn about:
- Consequences and solutions of unit- and time-specific effects in panel data models;
- Model transformation to eliminate the unit-specific effects;
- Dynamic panel data models and unit-specific effects;
- Fixed effects models vs. random effects models.

If observations are collected both from cross-sectional units and over time, they are called *panel data* or *cross-section* and *time-series data*. In a special case where the entire cross-sectional units are observed over all time periods (i.e., no missing observations), these panel data are said to be *balanced*. In contrast, if cross-sectional units are not observed for certain time periods, these panel data are *unbalanced*. Although there might be subtle differences, we will treat them in the same way in this chapter.

7.1 One big regression

In the following regression model, the relation between the dependent and the explanatory variables is governed by the same regression coefficients for all cross-sectional units $i \, (=1,\cdots,N)$ and time periods $t \, (=1,\cdots,T)$.

$$Y_{it} = \beta_0 + \beta_1 X_{1,it} + \cdots + \beta_k X_{k,it} + u_{it} \tag{7.1}$$

This model assumes that the disturbance u_{it} has zero mean and constant variance and is uncorrelated across cross-sectional units and between time periods. That is, for $i, j = 1,\cdots,N$ and $s,t = 1,\cdots,T$

$$E(u_{it}|X) = 0., \quad Var(u_{it}|X) = \sigma^2 \text{ and } Cov(u_{is},u_{jt}) = 0.$$

Thus, this model is called *one big regression*. For the consistency of the OLS estimation, it is also assumed that the disturbance is not correlated with the independent variables. Since no distinction is made between cross-sectional units and time periods, we can simply pool all of the observations and apply the OLS estimation method; the one-big regression is also called a *pooled regression*.

However, the constraint that one regression equation can fit all of the observations is likely to be violated in practice. Consider an example of production function which relates output to inputs used (capital, labor, etc.). Although the same amount of inputs is used, the output level might be different between firms depending on their managers' and workers' ability, location, industry, etc. These differences across cross-sectional units are called *unit-specific effects* caused by cross-sectional heterogeneity. As a result, some firms have produced a higher level of output in the past than other firms, even when they employed the same amount of inputs. Also, each year we experience many changes which are unique for the year, including technological changes, bad weather, economic crisis and avian flu. In addition to the inputs employed, these year-specific changes would also determine the output of production. These resulting differences between time periods are called *time-specific effects*.

These unit- and time-specific effects are often correlated with the independent variables and therefore need to be accounted for. If these effects are ignored, the OLS estimator will be inconsistent and biased due to the correlated omitted effects. It is always better to account for unit and time differences by including all theoretical variables which represent the causes of the unit- and time-specific effects. In the above example of production function, a better approach to account for firm heterogeneity is to include firm-specific variables such as managers' and workers' ability, location, industry, etc. However, since the complete coverage of firm-specific factors is not possible in many cases, there would exist omitted variables. Therefore, we need to develop estimation methods which can control for unit- and time-specific differences without requiring us to completely explain the causes of the differences.

To do this, it is desirable to relax the restriction of having an error term with zero mean and constant variance for all i and t. One way to relax the restriction is to model the unit- and time-specific effects to be translated into unit-specific and time-specific intercepts, respectively.[1] This approach is called a *fixed effects* model. Another approach to control for the unit- and time-specific effects is to treat them as random variables, thus called a *random effects* model. These models are explained in what follows.

7.2 Fixed effects model

Let a_i represent the unit-specific effects and b_t the time-specific effects. Then the regression model Eq. (7.1) is expanded to account for the effects as follows:

$$Y_{it} = \beta_1 X_{1,it} + \cdots + \beta_k X_{k,it} + a_i + b_t + \varepsilon_{it} \tag{7.2}$$

where a_i and b_t are unknown (fixed) parameters. If a_i and b_t are not correlated with the independent variables X, the OLS estimation can still produce consistent estimates even though a_i and b_t are ignored as in the one big regression, Eq. (7.1). Notice that the unit-specific effects bias the OLS estimation only when they are significant factors for the dependent variable (i.e., $a_i \neq 0$ for at least one i) and are also correlated with the explanatory variables; the same is for the time-specific effects. However, in many cases, the unit- and time-specific effects are correlated with independent variables. Thus, if these effects are not taken care of, the OLS estimator would be inconsistent and biased. This occurrence of a bias belongs to the correlated-omitted-variable problem; that is, some causes of the unit- and time-specific effects are omitted. Below are explained several approaches to control for the fixed effects of unit- and time-specific heterogeneities.

7.2.1 Using time dummies (for b_t)

In many cases, panel data have a relatively small number of time-series observations in each unit, although they have a large number of cross-sectional units. Therefore, $(T-1)$ dummy variables are often used to control for time-specific effects. When $T = 3$, for example, using two time dummies we can rewrite Eq. (7.2) as

$$Y_{it} = \beta_1 X_{1,it} + \cdots + \beta_k X_{k,it} + a_i + \gamma_2 D2_t + \gamma_3 D3_t + \varepsilon_{it}$$

where a dummy variable $D2_t = 1$ if $t = 2$ and 0 otherwise for all i, and $D3_t = 1$ if $t = 3$ and 0 otherwise. A dummy coefficient γ_2 (γ_3) represents how much the average Y value in $t = 2$ ($t = 3$) is larger than the average Y value in $t = 1$ when the values of the other independent variables are the same. In this comparison, time period 1 ($t = 1$) is treated as the reference time period.

7.2.2 Using cross-section dummies (for a_i)

If the number of cross-sectional units N is small enough, then the model can be estimated by the OLS method with $(N-1)$ cross-section dummies. However, N is hundreds or thousands in many cases. If so, use of cross-section dummies is likely to exceed the storage capacity of the computer. Alternatively, we can control for unit-specific effects by applying the following transformations: the within-transformation and the first-differencing approach.

7.2.3 Applying transformations

Within-transformation

For simplicity, let us focus on the unit-specific effects only. In many cases the time-specific effects (b_t) can easily be controlled for by time dummies because the number of time periods is relatively small. The following is a simple case of one independent variable.

$$Y_{it} = \beta_1 X_{it} + a_i + \varepsilon_{it} \tag{7.3}$$

We can remove the unit-specific effects a_i by subtracting the within-unit averages. Taking the sum of Eq. (7.3) over t for each i, we obtain

$$\sum_{t=1}^{T} Y_{it} = \sum_{t=1}^{T} \beta_1 X_{it} + \sum_{t=1}^{T} a_i + \sum_{t=1}^{T} \varepsilon_{it} = \beta_1 \sum_{t=1}^{T} X_{it} + Ta_i + \sum_{t=1}^{T} \varepsilon_{it}$$

Dividing both sides by T, we obtain the following equation in terms of the averages within each unit i.

$$\bar{Y}_i = \beta_1 \bar{X}_i + a_i + \bar{\varepsilon}_i \tag{7.4}$$

where the bar over a variable denotes an average taken over the entire period for each i, e.g., $\bar{Y}_i = \sum_{t=1}^{T} Y_{it}/T$. Subtracting Eq. (7.4) from Eq. (7.3) term-by-term, we can eliminate the unit-specific effects a_i because they are common in both equations.

$$(Y_{it} - \bar{Y}_i) = \beta_1 (X_{it} - \bar{X}_i) + (\varepsilon_{it} - \bar{\varepsilon}_i) \tag{7.5}$$

Now, we can apply the OLS method to estimate the regression coefficient β_1 because Eq. (7.5) is free from the unit-specific effects a_i and the new independent variable $(X_{it} - \bar{X}_i)$ is uncorrelated with the new error term $(\varepsilon_{it} - \bar{\varepsilon}_i)$. This is called the *within-transformation* approach.[2]

When we apply this within-transformation, we need to use an appropriate degree of freedom. It loses one observation for each i because the error term in Eq. (7.5) adds up to zero when summed over t and thus one observation in each i is redundant. Therefore, the degree of freedom for Eq. (7.5) becomes $N(T-1)-k$ where k is the number of slope coefficients ($k=1$ here).[3] The dummy-variable approach also has the same degree of freedom. When we use ($N-1$) cross-section dummies along with one intercept and k independent variables, the number of coefficients to estimate is $(N-1)+(1+k)$. Thus, the degree of freedom is $NT-\{(N-1)+(1+k)\} = N(T-1)-k$.[4]

First-differencing approach

Alternatively, we can remove the unit-specific effects a_i by taking first differences of the regression equation. The *first-difference specification* of Eq. (7.3) is

$$(Y_{i,t} - Y_{i,t-1}) = \beta_1(X_{i,t} - X_{i,t-1}) + (\varepsilon_{i,t} - \varepsilon_{i,t-1}) \tag{7.6}$$

Since the unit-specific effects a_i do not vary over time, the first-difference specification becomes free from a_i. Therefore, we can apply the OLS method to estimate the regression coefficient β_1 in Eq. (7.6).

Since the first-difference specification uses the differenced equation between two adjacent periods, there is no differenced equation for $t=1$. Thus, its resulting regression Eq. (7.6) has $(T-1)$ observations for each unit i and $N(T-1)$ observations in total. Therefore, the degree of freedom for Eq. (7.6) becomes $N(T-1)-k$ where k is the number of slope coefficients ($k=1$ here). Note that the first-difference specification does not include an intercept.

Within-transformation or first-differencing?

For balanced panel data with $T=2$, these two methods produce identical coefficient estimates, standard errors, t-ratios and p-values. For balanced panel data with $T\geq3$, they could produce different estimates. So, the choice should be based on the efficiency. It is shown that if the disturbance ε_{it} is serially uncorrelated, the within-transformation is more efficient than the first-differencing.[5] When the disturbance is highly serially correlated, the first-differencing becomes more efficient. For an extreme example, if the disturbance follows a random walk, i.e., $\varepsilon_{i,t} = \varepsilon_{i,t-1} + \eta_{i,t}$, the new disturbance in the first-differenced equation Eq. (7.6) will be serially uncorrelated. If you are not sure about the serial correlation, it would be a good idea to apply both methods and to see how sensitive the results are.

For unbalanced panel data, we cannot calculate first-differences for time periods in which first-lagged observation is missing. In contrast, the within-transformation can still be applied to all observed periods as long as there are at least two observations within each cross-sectional unit.

Dynamic panel data models: first-differencing approach

If lagged dependent variables are included on the right-hand side of a regression equation, we cannot apply the OLS method to the regressions derived by the within-transformation or the first-differencing approach. Consider the following dynamic panel data model which includes a lagged dependent variable as a regressor.[6]

$$Y_{i,t} = \beta_1 X_{i,t} + \beta_2 Y_{i,t-1} + a_i + \varepsilon_{i,t} \tag{7.7}$$

The first-differencing yields

$$(Y_{i,t} - Y_{i,t-1}) = \beta_1(X_{i,t} - X_{i,t-1}) + \beta_2(Y_{i,t-1} - Y_{i,t-2}) + (\varepsilon_{i,t} - \varepsilon_{i,t-1}) \qquad (7.8)$$

Since $Y_{i,t-1}$ includes $\varepsilon_{i,t-1}$, the first-differenced variable $(Y_{i,t-1} - Y_{i,t-2})$ on the right-hand side is correlated with the new error term $(\varepsilon_{i,t} - \varepsilon_{i,t-1})$. As a result, the first-difference specification will cause the OLS estimation to be inconsistent and biased.

Arellano and Bond (1991) develop a GMM estimator for the first-differenced models, such as Eq. (7.8), thus called a GMM-DIFF method as it applies the GMM after taking the first difference of a dynamic panel data model. Since Eq. (7.8) is free from the unit-specific effects a_i, it is relatively easy to find instrumental variables. For instrumental variables for the endogenous explanatory variable $(Y_{i,t-1} - Y_{i,t-2})$, we can use lagged differences, $(Y_{i,t-2} - Y_{i,t-3})$ and more lagged differences), and lagged levels $(Y_{i,t-2}, Y_{i,t-3}, \cdots)$. Examples of this GMM-DIFF method are included in the next section.

Dynamic panel data models: within-transformation approach

If we eliminate the unit-specific fixed effects by applying the within-transformation, the OLS estimator is biased but can be consistent with time period (T) increasing to infinity. After the within-transformation, the above dynamic model, Eq. (7.7), is expressed as

$$(Y_{i,t} - \bar{Y}_i) = \beta_1(X_{i,t} - \bar{X}_i) + \beta_2(Y_{i,t-1} - \bar{Y}_i) + (\varepsilon_{i,t} - \bar{\varepsilon}_i)$$

where $\bar{X}_i = (X_{i1} + \cdots + X_{iT})/T$, $\bar{Y}_i = (Y_{i1} + \cdots + Y_{iT})/T$, and $\bar{\varepsilon}_i = (\varepsilon_{i1} + \cdots + \varepsilon_{iT})/T$. Since all $\varepsilon_{i,t}$s are included in the disturbance, this within-transformed regression violates the strict exogeneity; $E(\varepsilon_{i,t} - \bar{\varepsilon}_i | Y_{i1}, \cdots, Y_{iT}) \neq 0$. Therefore, the OLS estimator is biased.

The contemporaneous covariance between $(Y_{i,t-1} - \bar{Y}_i)$ and $(\varepsilon_{i,t} - \bar{\varepsilon}_i)$ includes

$$Cov(\bar{Y}_i, \bar{\varepsilon}_i) = (1/T^2) \times Cov(Y_{i1} + \cdots + Y_{iT}, \varepsilon_{i1} + \cdots + \varepsilon_{iT}) < \left(\frac{1}{T^2}\right)\left(T \times \frac{\sigma_\varepsilon^2}{1-\beta_2}\right) = \left(\frac{1}{T}\right)\left(\frac{\sigma_\varepsilon^2}{1-\beta_2}\right).$$ See Nick-

ell (1981) and Bruno (2005) for complete derivations of the covariance and thus the bias. The above covariance, $Cov(\bar{Y}_i, \bar{\varepsilon}_i)$, is nonzero but converges to zero as T increases to infinity. Therefore, the OLS estimator is consistent in T. However, since most panel data have relatively short time periods although the number of cross-sectional units is large, the OLS estimator could be far from consistency when T is small. Alternatively, the dynamic panel data model can be consistently estimated by the GMM-DIFF method with good instrumental variables.

In her Granger-causality test, Lundberg (1985) took deviations from means to account for the presence of individual effects, i.e., the within-transformation, when lagged dependent variables are included as explanatory variables. Because of the endogeneity explained above, her test results by the OLS method are biased and inconsistent. Although the OLS estimator can be consistent with infinitely long periods, it is far from the consistency for a short time period (i.e., a small T). Holtz-Eakin et al. (1988) employed an instrumental-variable estimation to solve this estimation problem.[7]

7.3 Applications

7.3.1 Cornwell and Trumbull (1994)

This paper points out that previous attempts at estimating the economic model of crime with aggregate data (aggregated over time, so one observation for each unit) relied heavily on cross-section econometric techniques, and therefore do not control for unobserved unit-specific heterogeneity. Using panel data, this study controls for unobservable unit-specific characteristics that may be correlated with explanatory variables in the regression model. The following crime model is applied to 90 counties in North Carolina for a period from 1981 to 1989.

$$R_{it} = \beta_1 P_{it}^A + \beta_2 P_{it}^C + \beta_3 P_{it}^P + \beta_4 S_{it} + X_{it}'\gamma + a_i + b_t + \varepsilon_{it} \tag{7.9}$$

where R_{it} is the crime rate in county i during period t, P_{it}^A the probability of arrest, P_{it}^C the probability of conviction (conditional on arrest), P_{it}^P the probability of imprisonment (conditional on conviction), S_{it} the severity of punishment and X_{it} represents other control variables including average weekly wages by industry. The a_i s are fixed effects which reflect unobservable county-specific characteristics that may be correlated with P_{it}^A, P_{it}^C, P_{it}^P, S_{it} and X_{it}. The b_t s are time-specific fixed effects which control for time variations in the crime rate common to all counties. The aggregate models used in previous studies are of the type as

$$R_{i.} = \beta_0^* + \beta_1 P_{i.}^A + \beta_2 P_{i.}^C + \beta_3 P_{i.}^P + \beta_4 S_{i.} + X_{i.}'\gamma + Ta_i + \varepsilon_{i.} \tag{7.10}$$

where the dot in each subscript denotes aggregation over time, e.g., $R_{i.} = \sum_{t=1}^{T} R_{it}$ and a new intercept becomes $\beta_0^* = \sum_{t=1}^{T} b_t$. As the time-specific effects are merged into the new intercept, they are automatically taken care of. However, the unobservable county-specific effects (a_i) still remain as a separate term and cannot be controlled for by the cross-sectional regression.

In general, failure to control for the unobserved effects (a_i) will result in biased estimates of the coefficients because a_i is often correlated with explanatory variables. As an example of how correlation between the independent variables and county-specific effects (a_i) might arise, consider two identical jurisdictions (or counties), except that the police in jurisdiction 1 record half the crimes reported to them and the police in jurisdiction 2 record all crimes reported. Jurisdiction 1 will appear to have a lower crime rate and a higher probability of arrest than jurisdiction 2. So, a_i and P_{it}^A are correlated because $a_1 < a_2$ and $P_{1t}^A > P_{2t}^A$. If this pattern of under-reporting exists, then the estimated deterrent effect of raising the probability of arrest will be overstated; that is, the OLS estimate $\hat{\beta}_1$ will be larger (in absolute) than the true value β_1 in Eq. (7.9).[8]

Thus, ignoring a_i in estimation will cause a correlated-omitted-variable bias. To control for the county-specific heterogeneity, we may use the following within-transformed regression.

$$\tilde{R}_{it} = \beta_1 \tilde{P}_{it}^A + \beta_2 \tilde{P}_{it}^C + \beta_3 \tilde{P}_{it}^P + \beta_4 \tilde{S}_{it} + \tilde{X}_{it}'\gamma + \delta_1 \tilde{D}81_t + \ldots + \delta_8 \tilde{D}88_t + \tilde{\varepsilon}_{it} \tag{7.11}$$

where the tilde ($\sim$) over each variable denotes a deviation from the mean within each county (i), e.g., $\tilde{R}_{it} = R_{it} - R_{i.}/T$. The year-specific effects (b_t) are controlled for by eight dummy variables; year 1989 is used as the reference year.

The "Between" in Table 7.1 is the OLS estimator applied to Eq. (7.10), a cross-sectional regression using aggregate data. This Between estimator is consistent *only if* all of the regressors are orthogonal to the county-specific effects. Since it is not the case as explained above, however, the Between estimator is likely to be biased. In contrast, the "Within" estimator uses the within-transformed model Eq. (7.11), which is free from the county-specific effects, and is therefore unbiased. As shown in Table 7.1, the difference in the Within and Between estimates is striking. Conditioning on the county-specific effects causes the (absolute value of the) coefficient estimates for P_A and P_C to decrease by approximately 45%,

Table 7.1 Estimation results for the crime model

	Between	Within	2SLS (fixed effects)	2SLS (no fixed effects)
Constant	−2.097)			−3.179
	(2.822)			(8.189)
P^A	−0.648	−0.355	−0.455	−0.507
	(0.088)	(0.032)	(0.618)	(0.251)
P^C	−0.528	−0.282	−0.336	−0.530
	(0.067)	(0.021)	(0.371)	(0.110)
P^P	0.297	−0.173	−0.196	0.200
	(0.231)	(0.032)	(0.200)	(0.343)
S	−0.236	−0.00245	−0.0298	−0.218
	(0.174)	(0.026)	(0.030)	(0.185)
Control variables	Included	Included	Included	Included

Source: Adapted from Cornwell and Trumbull (1994, Table 3 on page 365).

Note: Standard errors are given in parentheses.

from −0.648 to −0.355 and −0.528 to −0.282, respectively. The 2SLS estimation addresses possible endogeneity (caused by simultaneity) using instrumental variables, which is explained in Chapter 8.

In sum, Cornwell and Trumbull (1994) emphasize the importance of controlling for county-specific effects in panel data because differences across counties could be correlated with explanatory variables. Therefore, they employed a fixed effects model. As there are too many cross-sectional units, use of dummy variables is practically inappropriate. Instead, they applied the within-transformation approach to control for the county heterogeneity.

7.3.2 Blackburn and Neumark (1992)

This study examines several explanations of the persistent wage differentials between industries. One competitive-market explanation is that the inter-industry wage differentials are due to differences across workers in "unobserved" ability (unobserved to the researchers). To test the competitive-market explanation, they employed the following wage equation. For employee i and time period t,

$$w_{it} = \beta_0 + \sum_j \beta_j X_{j,it} + \sum_k \gamma_k D_{k,it} + \theta A_i + u_{it}$$

where w is the logarithm of the wage, X_j s are human capital variables or other observable measures of labor quality, D_k s are industry dummy variables, A is unobserved ability, u is a randomly distributed error and (β_j, γ_k, θ) are coefficients. The null hypothesis for the competitive-market explanation is that there exists no wage difference between industries given the other factors held constant: i.e., $H_0 : \gamma_k = 0$ for all k.

The unobserved ability (A) is believed to be correlated with explanatory variables (X_j) such as schooling, occupation, etc. Then, without controlling for the unobserved ability, the OLS estimation will be biased because of the correlated-omitted variable. Researchers supporting the competitive-market hypothesis argue that the persistent wage differentials between industries were resulted because the unobserved ability had not been controlled for.

Previous research has removed the unobserved ability by taking the first-difference of the wage equation, which differences out A_i (Gibbons and Katz, 1992). Alternatively, this study uses proxy measures (e.g., IQ test score) as indicators of ability. The following is a case of using the IQ test score as a measure of ability.

$$w_{it} = \beta_0 + \sum_j \beta_j X_{j,it} + \sum_k \gamma_k D_{k,it} + \theta\, IQ_i + u_{it}$$

where IQ_i is the IQ test score which can be observed and is assumed to be related to the ability (A_i). Their estimation results show that the coefficients for the industry dummies are still significant when several proxy measures for ability are included. Thus, these results do not support the competitive-market hypothesis about the industry wage differentials.

7.3.3 Garin-Munoz (2006)

This study examines the international tourism demand to the Canary Islands by estimating a dynamic panel data model. The model is a form of log-linear function and its coefficients measure the demand elasticities.

$$\ln Q_{it} = \beta_1 \ln Q_{i,t-1} + \beta_2 \ln PT_{it} + \beta_3 \ln PCO_{it} + \beta_4 \ln GDP_{it} + \lambda_t + \mu_i + \varepsilon_{it}$$

where Q_{it} is measured by tourist arrivals per capita to the Canary Islands from country i in year t; PT_{it} is an index expressing the cost of living of tourists in the Islands (TPI) relative to the cost of living in their respective origin countries (CPI) adjusted by the exchange rate (ER), i.e., $PT = TPI_{Canary} / (CPI_{Origin} \times ER_{Canary/Origin})$; PCO_{it} is the price of crude oil as a proxy for traveling cost; GDP_{it} is the per capita GDP of each of the countries of origin; λ_t is the year-specific effects[9]; μ_i is the country-specific effects; and the disturbance ε_{it} is assumed to be serially uncorrelated and cross-sectionally independent with zero mean but possibly heteroscedastic variance.

By taking the first differences, we can eliminate the unit-specific effects.[10]

$$\Delta \ln Q_{it} = \beta_1 \Delta \ln Q_{i,t-1} + \beta_2 \Delta \ln PT_{it} + \beta_3 \Delta \ln PCO_{it} + \beta_4 \Delta \ln GDP_{it} + \Delta \lambda_t + \Delta \varepsilon_{it}$$

Following Arellano and Bond (1991), this study employs the GMM to estimate the first-differenced equation, not the OLS because of the endogeneity between $\Delta \ln Q_{i,t-1}$ and $\Delta \varepsilon_{it}$. For instrumental variables, the authors use values of the dependent variable lagged two periods or more.

The results in Table 7.2 show that the lagged dependent variable has a significant effect on the demand of inbound tourism. It is also shown that the tourism demand significantly depends on price ($\ln PT$), cost of travel ($\ln PCO$) and the economic conditions of the origin markets ($\ln GDP$).

The coefficient estimates in the upper panel in Table 7.2 are short-run demand elasticities. If the long-run equilibrium is assumed, we have a relation of $\ln Q_{it} = \ln Q_{i,t-1}$. Using this equality, we can calculate the long-run elasticities by dividing each of the coefficient estimates by $(1 - \beta_1)$ or $(1-0.6) = 0.4$; the long-run elasticities are shown in the lower panel.

7.3.4 Tuli, Bharadwaj, and Kohli (2010)

It is increasingly common for suppliers in business-to-business (B2B) settings to build multiple types of ties with their customers. The "relationship multiplexity" refers to the number of diverse types of ties between two firms. Beyond selling goods/services, suppliers may have other ties, such as marketing alliances, R&D alliances, equity ownerships and board memberships with customers. However, a

Table 7.2 Estimation results

Variable	Arellano-Bond one-step estimates	
	Coefficient	Robust t-statistic
$\ln Q_{i,t-1}(\beta_1)$	0.60	6.78
$\ln PT_{it}(\beta_2)$	−0.74	−2.69
$\ln PCO_{it}(\beta_3)$	−0.13	−3.40
$\ln GDP_{it}(\beta_4)$	1.17	4.25
long-run parameters		
$\ln PT$	−1.85 (= −0.74/0.4)	
$\ln PCO$	−0.22 (= −0.13/0.4)	
$\ln GDP$	2.92 (= 1.17/0.4)	

Source: Adapted from Garin-Munoz (2006, Table 2 on page 289).

Note: The robust *t*-statistic uses the variance-covariance matrix calculated by the residuals. The other variables and an intercept are included in the estimation but their coefficient estimates are not reported in this table.

supplier that simply sells multiple offerings to a customer is not considered to have a multiplex relationship with it. This is because different offerings sold to a customer pertain to a single type of tie, that of a supplier-customer. In contrast, a supplier that sells goods/services to a customer and has an equity stake in it is considered to have a multiplex relationship with the customer. This is because the supplier has two distinct roles, that of a seller and an investor.

The purpose of this study is to investigate the effects of changes in the number of different types of ties on changes in supplier performance with an individual customer. We draw on the resource-based view (RBV) of a firm to argue that presence of multiple types of ties (i.e., relationship multiplexity) is a valuable resource for a supplier that is rare and difficult to imitate and/or substitute. It can be argued that by increasing the number of different types of ties with a customer, a supplier can obtain useful private information about a customer and build a long-term focus, or solidarity, with a customer.

Hypothesis: main effects of relationship multiplexity

Relationship multiplexity is a valuable resource that is rare and difficult for competitors to imitate or substitute. As multiplexity increases, it increases the benefits available to a supplier and a customer. The supplier is able to develop superior offerings and collaborate with a customer to identify and develop new offerings required by the customer. Therefore, a customer is likely to increase its purchases from a supplier as its relationship multiplexity with the supplier increases. Formally, the hypothesis this study tries to support is

H_1: A positive change in relationship multiplexity with a customer results in a positive change in sales to that customer.

Hypothesis: moderating effects of competitive intensity in customer industry

An increase in relationship multiplexity increases the probability of a supplier offering superior products/services, thus providing greater economic incentives to buy from the supplier. These incentives are expected to be more valuable for a customer as competitive intensity in its industry increases. This is because increases in competitive intensity put greater pressure on customers to procure superior offerings and lower their procurement costs. Therefore, as the competitive intensity in a customer's industry increases, it is likely to purchase more from a supplier with which it has a multiplex relationship. As such, we expect the following:

H$_3$: The association between a change in relationship multiplexity with a customer and the change in sales to that customer is more positive when the competitive intensity in the customer's industry increases.

Hypothesis: moderating effects of intangibles intensity in customer industry

Firms in industries with high-intangibles intensity find it relatively difficult to identify inputs that lead to the creation of intangible assets. Indeed, suppliers view customers in a high-intangibles intensity industry as belonging to an "opaque industry." Therefore, as intangibles intensity in a customer's industry increases, it becomes more difficult for the customer to accurately predict the goods/services it will need and to articulate the same to a supplier. Relationship multiplexity with a customer engenders solidarity and helps a supplier obtain private information about the customer. In turn, these enable the supplier to collaborate closely with the customer and complement the customer's knowledge of its business with the supplier's experience and knowledge. Such pooling of knowledge afforded by relationship multiplexity is more important for serving customers as the intangibles intensity in its industry increases. This is because it helps a supplier better anticipate the goods/services likely to be needed by customers and plan ahead to deliver the same and thus realize higher sales. In contrast, such close collaboration with a customer is less valuable when the intangibles intensity in a customer's industry decreases because these customers can now more readily articulate their needs to a supplier. Thus, a change in relationship multiplexity is likely to have a stronger positive effect on the change in supplier sales to customers as the intangibles intensity in a customer's industry increases. Formally,

H$_5$: The association between a change in relationship multiplexity with a customer and the change in sales to that customer is more positive when the intangibles intensity in the customer's industry increases.

Model: Sales growth

The following regression, called a level-level model, uses the level of sales as the dependent variable and the levels of relationship multiplexity and other variables as explanatory variables.[11] For relationship i at time t,

$$S_{it} = \beta_1 S_{i,t-1} + \beta_2 M_{it} + \beta_3 CI_{it} + \beta_4 (M_{it} \times CI_{it}) + \beta_5 \Pi_{it} + \beta_6 (M_{it} \times \Pi_{it}) \quad (7.12)$$
$$+ (controls) + (YearDummies) + \eta_i + \varepsilon_{it}$$

where S_{it} = log of sales to a customer; M_{it} = log of relationship multiplexity; CI_{it} = log of customer industry competitive intensity; Π_{it} = log of customer industry intangibles intensity; η_i = time-invariant unobservable factors; and ε_{it} = random error. (See the original paper for control variables.)

Since the time-invariant relationship-specific factor η_i is correlated with $S_{i,t-1}$, it has to be eliminated. The first-differencing approach can eliminate η_i from the regression and result in the following growth-growth model, in which a change in the log sales (i.e., sales growth) is the dependent variable and changes in the relationship multiplexity and control variables are explanatory variables: with/ denoting a change, e.g., $\Delta S_{it} = S_{it} - S_{i,t-1}$,

$$\Delta S_{it} = \beta_1 \Delta S_{i,t-1} + \beta_2 \Delta M_{it} + \beta_3 \Delta CI_{it}$$ (7.13)
$$+ \beta_4 \Delta (M_{it} \times CI_{it}) + \beta_5 \Delta \Pi_{it} + \beta_6 \Delta (M_{it} \times \Pi_{it})$$
$$+ (controls) + (YearDummies) + \Delta \varepsilon_{it}$$

Addressing endogeneity

The lagged dependent variable in Eq. (7.13) is correlated with the error term $\Delta \varepsilon_{it} = \varepsilon_{it} - \varepsilon_{i,t-1}$ because $\Delta S_{i,t-1} = S_{i,t-1} - S_{i,t-2}$ includes $\varepsilon_{i,t-1}$ in $S_{i,t-1}$. The relationship multiplexity and its interaction terms could also be endogenous. Other factors not included in Eq. (7.13), such as trust and relationship duration, are known to affect relationship performance (ΔS_{it} through $\Delta \varepsilon_{it}$) and are also potentially correlated with relationship multiplexity (ΔM_{it}). If so, ΔM_{it} is correlated with $\Delta \varepsilon_{it}$ and thus becomes endogenous.

The general method of moments (GMM) takes into account the endogeneity and produces consistent estimates. The instrumental variables used include lagged variables; for example, $S_{i,t-2}$ and $S_{i,t-3}$ can serve as instruments for $\Delta S_{i,t-1}$. The GMM can also account for possible heteroscedaticity and serial correlation of the error term.

Estimation results

As shown in Table 7.3, parameter estimates for the sales growth model support H_1; $\hat{\beta}_2 = 0.48$ with $p < 0.05$.[12] The interaction term of relationship multiplexity and customer industry competitive intensity has a negative and significant estimate ($\hat{\beta}_4 = -0.73$, $p < 0.05$).

The authors calculate the marginal effect of the relationship multiplexity on the sales and plot it across the customer industry competitive intensity.[13] Figure 7.1 shows that the positive effect of the relationship multiplexity on the sales becomes weaker as customer industry competitive intensity increases, thus contradicting H_3.

The results do not support H_5. As the plot shows, the effect of the relationship multiplexity on the sales remains constant as customer industry intangibles intensity increases. The coefficient estimate for the interaction term ($M_{it} \times \Pi_{it}$) in Eq. (7.12) is insignificant ($\beta_6 = -0.03$, $p \cong 0.8$).[14]

7.4 Random effects

Results from the fixed effects model would be applied only to the cross-sectional units included in the sample, but may not be extended to ones outside the sample. For example, analysis of stock

Table 7.3 Effects of changes in relationship multiplexity on sales growth

	Sales growth model
H_1 (β_2)	0.48*
H_3 (β_4)	−0.73*
H_5 (β_6)	−0.03
Control variables	Included

Source: Adapted from Tuli et al. (2010, Table 3 on page 44).
* denotes *p*-value < 0.05.

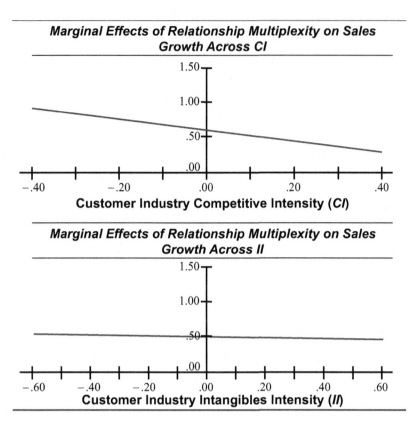

Figure 7.1 Marginal effects of changes in relationship multiplexity on sales growth across customer
        industry factors

Source: Tuli et al. (2010, Figure 2 on page 45).

market includes the full set of companies listed on a stock market and may use the fixed effects
models. However, if we believe that our data were drawn from a subpopulation and did not cover
all the cross-sectional units, it might be more appropriate to view unit-specific effects as randomly
distributed across cross-sectional units, thus using the random effects models. Survey data are a good
example. Specifically, we treat unit-specific effects (v_i) and time-specific effects (e_t) as random
variables:

$$Y_{it} = \beta_0 + \beta_1 X_{1,it} + \ldots + \beta_k X_{k,it} + v_i + e_t + \varepsilon_{it} \tag{7.14}$$

where $E(v_i) = 0$, $Var(v_i) = \sigma_v^2$, $E(e_t) = 0$ and $Var(e_t) = \sigma_e^2$.

However, the *key assumption* for the random effects models is that random effects v_i and e_t be uncorrelated with explanatory variables. This is somewhat restrictive and is not satisfied in many cases. (See
the applications in previous sections.) Obviously, if v_i and/or e_t are correlated with explanatory variables, the random effects models will produce biased results.

7.5 Fixed vs. random effects models

Hausman (1978) suggests that the choice of either fixed or random effects models be based on two considerations, one logical and the other statistical. The logical consideration, suggested by Chamberlain, is to decide whether the effects satisfy di Finnetti's exchangeability criterion which is both necessary and sufficient for random sampling. In other words, the criterion is to see whether we can exchange v_i and v_j between cross-sectional units i and j. If the cross-sectional heterogeneities are unique for each unit, they will not be exchangeable.

The other is a statistical consideration of orthogonality, i.e., no correlation between the random effects and the explanatory variables. This orthogonality condition can be tested by the Hausman (1978) specification test. Under the null hypothesis of no correlation between the random effects and the explanatory variables, the GLS estimator ($\hat{\beta}_{GLS}$) is consistent and efficient while the OLS estimator including dummy variables ($\hat{\beta}_{OLS}$) is consistent, but less efficient than $\hat{\beta}_{GLS}$. However, under the alternative hypothesis of correlation, $\hat{\beta}_{GLS}$ is inconsistent, but the dummy variable $\hat{\beta}_{OLS}$ is still consistent.[15] Noticing that the two estimators are affected differently by the failure of the orthogonality, Hausman has developed test statistics which are based on the difference of the two estimators, $\hat{\beta}_{OLS} - \hat{\beta}_{GLS}$. For more details, see Hausman (1978) and Hausman and Taylor (1981).

When he examines the determinants for the world volume of trade, Egger (2000) employs the following regression derived from the gravity models.

$$EX_{ijt} = \beta_0 + \beta_1 RLFAC_{ijt} + \beta_2 GDPT_{ijt} + \beta_3 SIMILAR_{ijt} + \beta_4 DIST_{ij}$$
$$+ a_i + \gamma_j + \delta_t + u_{ijt}$$

where EX_{ijt} is the log of country i's exports to country j in year t; $RLFAC_{ijt}$ measures the difference between the two countries in terms of relative factor endowments; $GDPT_{ijt}$ the overall economic space $GDPT_{ijt} = \ln(GDP_{it} + GDP_{jt})$ of the two countries; $SIMILAR_{ijt}$ the relative size of two countries in terms of GDP; and $DIST_{ij}$ the log of the distance variable which is a proxy for transportation costs. And a_i, γ_j reflect the country-specific effects and δ_t the time-specific effects.

Concerning the choice of a fixed or a random effects model, Egger considers some of the latent variables that would stand behind the country-specific and time-invariant export and import effects; they could be tariff policy measures (including tariffs, taxes, duties, etc.) and export driving or impeding environmental variables (including size of country, access to transnational infrastructure networks, geographical and historical determinants, etc.). As most of these effects are not random but deterministically associated with certain historical, political, geographical and other facts, Egger (2000) prefers a fixed effects model to a random effects model.

7.6 Summary

1   It is important to control for the unit- and time-specific effects because they are often correlated with the explanatory variables included in a regression model. Using panel data, we can control for the effects.

2   The fixed effects model assumes that the unit- and time-specific effects are unknown (fixed) parameters to be estimated. The fixed effects can be controlled for by dummy variables, by the within-transformation, or by the first-differencing approach.

3   For dynamic panel data models which include lagged dependent variables as regressors, we cannot apply the OLS to the first-differenced or within-transformed equations because there exists an

endogeneity problem. Instead, we may employ the GMM or the 2SLS with instrumental variables for the first-differenced equation.

4   The random effects model treats the unit- and time-specific effects as random variables and assumes that the random effects are not correlated with explanatory variables. This restrictive assumption limits the application of the random effects model.

Review questions

1   We need to estimate the following regression using balanced panel data. For $t = 1,2,3$ and $i = 1, 2, \ldots, 50000$,

$$Y_{it} = \beta_1 X_{it} + a_i + b_t + \varepsilon_{it}$$

where a_i and b_t denote unit- and time-specific fixed effects, respectively.

(a)   As the time period is short, we can use time-dummy variables. Using time dummies, rewrite the regression model.

(b)   To control for the unit-specific effects, we cannot use dummy variables since there are too many units. Instead, we may apply the first-differencing approach. Write down a first-differenced version of the dummy-variable regression equation in (a).

2   To examine the accounting conservatism, Basu (1997) regresses annual earnings on current stock returns using annual data from 1963 to 1990.

$$X_{it}/P_{i,t-1} = \alpha_1 DR_{it} + \beta_0 R_{it} + \beta_1 R_{it} \times DR_{it} + a_i + b_t + u_{it}$$

where X_{it} is the earnings per share for firm i in fiscal year t, $P_{i,t-1}$ is the price per share at the beginning of the fiscal year and R_{it} is the return on firm i from nine months before fiscal year-end t to three months after fiscal year-end t. And a dummy variable DR_{it} is set to 1 if $R_{it} < 0$, i.e., bad news, and 0 otherwise. a_i represents the unit- or firm-specific effects, and b_t represents the time-specific effects.

(a)   Explain why a_i representing the unit-specific (or firm-specific) effects do not have a time subscript 't.'

(b)   Explain why we need to include a_i and b_t when these are not observed.

(c)   Since the number of units is very large, it is not possible to use dummy variables to control for a_i. What is an alternative method to control for the unit-specific effects?

(d)   If we want to control for the time-specific (or year-specific) effects using dummy variables, how many dummies do we need to include?

3   Consider the following regression model for panel data $(i = 1, \cdots, 100;\ t = 2000, \cdots, 2006)$. We are interested only in β_1, the coefficient for an exogenous variable X_{it}.

$$Y_{it} = \beta_1 X_{it} + \beta_2 Y_{i,t-1} + a_i + \varepsilon_{it}$$

(a)   In many cases, there exist unit-specific differences whose effects on the dependent variable are represented by a_i in the above regression. If we ignore the unit-specific effects (a_i), the OLS estimation will be biased. Explain when and why a bias arises.

(b)   To control for the unit-specific effects, we consider applying the first-differencing approach. Do you think the OLS method can produce consistent estimates for the first-differenced regression? Explain why.

(c) What methods can produce a consistent estimator for β_1?

(d) We need instrumental variables to obtain a consistent estimator for β_1.

   ① Can $X_{i,t}$ be used as an instrumental variable? Explain.

   ② Can $Y_{i,t-1}$ be used as an instrumental variable? Explain.

   ③ Can $Y_{i,t-2}$ be used as an instrumental variable? Explain.

   ④ Can $(Y_{i,t-2} - Y_{i,t-3})$ be used as an instrumental variable? Explain.

(e) To eliminate the unit-specific effects, can we apply the within-transformation approach instead of the first-differencing one?

4   Garin-Munoz (2006) examines the tourism demand for the Canary Islands using the following dynamic panel data model. For $i = 1, \cdots, N$ and $t = 1992, \cdots, 2002,$

$$\ln Q_{i,t} = \beta_1 \ln Q_{i,t-1} + \beta_2 \ln PT_{i,t} + \beta_3 \ln PCO_{i,t} + \beta_4 \ln GDP_{i,t} + a_i + \lambda_t + \varepsilon_{i,t}$$

where $\ln Q$ denotes the natural logarithm of Q; a_i and λ_t represent unobservable unit- and time-specific fixed effects, respectively.

(a) If the number of cross-sectional units (N) is too large, it is practically difficult to use dummy variables in controlling for the unit-specific effects. As an alternative way, can we use the OLS method after we derive the first-differenced equation? Explain.

(b) The author of the paper employed the GMM-DIFF method developed in Arellano and Bond (1991); it applies the GMM method to the following first-differenced equation.

$$\Delta \ln Q_{i,t} = \beta_1 \Delta \ln Q_{i,t-1} + \beta_2 \Delta \ln PT_{i,t} + \beta_3 \Delta \ln PCO_{i,t} + \beta_4 \Delta \ln GDP_{i,t}$$
$$+ \Delta \lambda_t + \Delta \varepsilon_{i,t}$$

(i) Explain why the first-differencing (DIFF) approach is applied.

(ii) Explain why the GMM, instead of the OLS, was used in estimating the first-differenced equation.

(iii) The GMM method requires instrumental variables. Explain what properties the instrumental variables should have for good estimation results.

5   We want to examine the net effect of X on Y in terms of elasticity. Using annual panel data, we estimate the following log-log regression where α_i denotes the time-invariant unit-specific effect.

$$\log Y_{i,t} = \beta_1 \log Y_{i,t-1} + \beta_2 \log X_{i,t} + \beta_3 \log Z_{i,t}$$
$$+ (year\ dummies) + \alpha_i + u_{i,t} \tag{7Q.1}$$

Since there are too many cross-sectional units, we apply the first-differencing to remove α_i.

$$\Delta \log Y_{i,t} = \beta_1 \Delta \log Y_{i,t-1} + \beta_2 \Delta \log X_{i,t} + \beta_3 \Delta \log Z_{i,t}$$
$$+ (year\ dummies) + \Delta u_{i,t} \tag{7Q.2}$$

where Δ denotes a change, e.g., $100 \times \Delta \log Y_{i,t} = 100 \times (\log Y_{i,t} - \log Y_{i,t-1}) = \%\ change\ in\ Y_{it}$

(a) Explain why Eq. (7Q.1) cannot be estimated by the OLS method.

(b) Explain why the first-differenced equation, Eq. (7Q.2), cannot be estimated by the OLS method. What is an alternative estimation method to the OLS?

(c) Explain what β_2 measures in Eq. (7Q.1).

(d) Explain what β_2 measures in Eq. (7Q.2).

(e) We want to interpret the net effect of X on Y in terms of elasticity. Which equation is more appropriate?

(f) To examine moderating effects, we include an interaction term.

$$\log Y_{i,t} = \beta_1 \log Y_{i,t-1} + \beta_2 \log X_{i,t} + \beta_3 \log Z_{i,t}$$
$$+ \beta_4 (\log X_{i,t} \times \log Z_{i,t}) + (year\ dummies) + \alpha_i + u_{i,t} \quad (7Q.3)$$

We apply the first-differencing to remove α_i and obtain the following first-differenced equation.

$$\Delta \log Y_{i,t} = \beta_1 \Delta \log Y_{i,t-1} + \beta_2 \Delta \log X_{i,t} + \beta_3 \Delta \log Z_{i,t}$$
$$+ \beta_4 \Delta (\log X_{i,t} \times \log Z_{i,t}) + (year\ dummies) + \Delta u_{i,t} \quad (7Q.4)$$

To measure the net effect of X on Y with respect to X, Eq. (7Q.3) is appropriate, but Eq. (7Q.4) is not. Explain why.

6   Explain how to choose between a fixed effects model and a random effects model when we control for unit- and time-specific effects.

Notes

1 This approach is equivalent to the use of a dummy variable when we account for the difference between two groups, as explained in Chapter 4.

2 In fact, this within-transformation approach yields the same coefficient estimates as the dummy-variable approach. If appropriate degrees of freedom are used, the two approaches also yield the same standard errors and thus t-statistics. This can be understood by the Frisch-Waugh-Lovell Theorem. According to the theorem, the coefficient estimate for β_1 in a multiple regression with dummy variables is the same as its estimate from an orthogonal regression. The orthogonal regression uses the residuals from a regression of the explanatory variable X_{it} on the dummy variables representing the unit-specific effects a_i. Since the dummy variables cover all cross-sectional units, the residuals are just the deviations from the mean in each unit, $(X_{it} - \bar{X}_i)$. In the same way, the dependent variable in the orthogonal regression is $(Y_{it} - \bar{Y}_i)$. Therefore, the orthogonal regression is simply identical to the within-transformed regression, Eq. (7.5). See Appendix 3B in Chapter 3 for a geometric interpretation.

3 When we estimate this within-transformed regression using an econometrics computer software, the resulting standard errors need to be adjusted by the correct degree of freedom, $N(T-1)-k$. Note that Eq. (7.5) does not include an intercept. However, the computer software uses $NT-k$ for the degree of freedom. Thus, the standard errors produced by the software have to be multiplied by $\sqrt{\dfrac{NT-k}{N(T-1)-k}}$.

4 As explained in Chapter 2 the degree of freedom (df) is used in calculating a sample estimate of $\hat{\sigma} = \sqrt{\sum_i \sum_t (Y_{it} - \hat{Y}_{it})^2 / df} = \sqrt{ESS/df}$ where ESS is the error sum of squares. This estimate $\hat{\sigma}$ is the numerator of the $\hat{\beta}$ standard error; remember that for a case of simple regression $y_i = \beta_0 + \beta_1 X_i + u_i$, the $\hat{\beta}_1$ standard error is $\hat{\sigma} / \sqrt{\sum (X_i - \bar{X})^2}$.

5 The serial correlation is explained in Chapter 10.

6 There could exist omitted variables which are correlated with the included regressors. When we have no idea about how to obtain proxies for those omitted variables, we often use a lagged dependent variable as a control for them (Wooldridge, 2009, p. 310). In addition, the lagged dependent variable can also account for inertia and persistence in the dependent variable.

7 Estimation methods using instrumental variables are explained in Chapters 6 and 8.

8 Since a_i and P_{it}^A are negatively correlated, the OLS estimate $\hat{\beta}_1$ will be biased in a negative direction. It means that $\hat{\beta}_1$ will be more negative than β_1. Thus, the under-reporting pattern overstates the deterrent effect of raising P_{it}^A.

9 In the original paper, separate dummy variables for years 2001 and 2002 are included to capture the influence of the possible effects on tourism of the September 11th event. Since the model already includes the time-specific fixed effects λ_t for all years, the two dummies are redundant. The intercept α in the original paper is also redundant as λ_t and μ_i cover all time periods and units.

10 After the first-differencing approach is applied, the time-specific effects will remain as a first-differenced form, $\Delta\lambda_t = \lambda_t - \lambda_{t-1}$. Since the role of $\Delta\lambda_t$ is only to capture the differences between years, we may replace $\Delta\lambda_t$ with year dummies. The original paper includes first-differenced year dummies, incorrectly only for 2001 and 2002; the correct model should include the first-differenced time-specific effects $(\Delta\lambda_t)$ for all years and thus year dummies for all years except a reference year.

11 By including $S_{i,t-1}$, the logarithmic level of lagged sales, as a regressor, this model can have an effect of normalizing the level of sales of different firm size; $\log(sales_{i,t} / sales_{i,t-1})$ $= \log(sales_{i,t}) - \log(sales_{i,t-1}) = S_{it} - S_{i,t-1}$. When the lagged $S_{i,t-1}$ is moved to the right-hand side, its coefficient will be equal to one. But, because $S_{i,t-1}$ can also account for inertia, persistence in sales to a customer and the potential effects of omitted variables, its coefficient β_1 could be different from one and is estimated by data.

12 This interpretation is valid only when the net effect of M_{it} on S_{it} is evaluated at $CI_{it} = 0$ and $\Pi_{it} = 0$. However, the net effect is not constant because $\partial S_{it} / \partial M_{it} = \beta_2 + \beta_4 CI_{it} + \beta_6 \Pi_{it}$. A correct approach is to evaluate the net effect for the sample ranges of CI_{it} and Π_{it}, as displayed in Figure 7.1.

13 The marginal effect is expressed in terms of elasticity because the variables are in logarithm. In Eq. (7.12), $\partial S_{it} / \partial M_{it} = (\%\Delta sales / \%\Delta multiplexity) = \beta_2 + \beta_4 CI_{it} + \beta_6 \Pi_{it}$. Note that we are interested in Eq. (7.12) but use Eq. (7.13) for estimating the parameters because the relationship-specific factor η_i needs to be eliminated. So, our interpretation is based on Eq. (7.12).

14 Note that the coefficient for $(M_{it} \times \Pi_{it})$ in Eq. (7.12) is the same as the one for $\Delta(M_{it} \times \Pi_{it})$ in Eq. (7.13), whose estimate is reported in Table 7.3.

15 Assuming no correlation between the random effects and explanatory variables, $\hat{\beta}_{GLS}$ estimates the coefficients with incorporating the covariance structure of $v_i + e_t + \varepsilon_{it}$ in Eq. (7.14). It is therefore consistent and efficient only under the null hypothesis of no correlation. In contrast, the fixed effects model treats v_i and e_t as unknown parameters which could be correlated with the explanatory variables. The OLS estimator $\hat{\beta}_{OLS}$, which controls for the fixed effects using dummy variables, is consistent and efficient under the alternative hypothesis of correlation.

References

Arellano, M. and S. Bond (1991), "Some Tests of Specification for Panel Data: Monte Carlo Evidence and an Application to Employment Equations," *Review of Economic Studies*, 58, 277–297.

Basu, S. (1997), "The Conservatism Principle and the Asymmetric Timeliness of Earnings, " *Journal of Accounting and Economics*, 24, 3–37.

Blackburn, M. and D. Neumark (1992), "Unobserved Ability, Efficiency Wages, and Interindustry Wage Differentials," *The Quarterly Journal of Economics*, 107, November, 1421–1436.

Bruno, G.S.F. (2005), "Approximating the Bias of the LSDV Estimator for Dynamic Unbalanced Panel Data Models," *Economics Letters*, 87, 361–366.

Cornwell, C. and W.N. Trumbull (1994), "Estimating the Economic Model of Crime with Panel Data," *The Review of Economics and Statistics*, 76, 360–366.

Egger, P. (2000), "A Note on the Proper Econometric Specification of the Gravity Equation," *Economics Letters*, 66, 25–31.

Garin-Munoz, T. (2006), "Inbound International Tourism to Canary Islands: A Dynamic Panel Data Model," *Tourism Management*, 27, 281–291.

Gibbons, R. and L. Katz (1992), "Does Unmeasured Ability Explain Inter-Industry Wage Difference?" *Review of Economic Studies*, 59, 515–35.

Hausman, J.A. (1978), "Specification Tests in Econometrics," *Econometrica*, 46, 1251–1271.

Hausman, J.A. and W.E. Taylor (1981), "Panel Data and Unobservable Individual Effects," *Econometrica*, 49, 1377–1398.

Holtz-Eakin, D., W. Newey and H.S. Rosen (1988), "Estimating Vector Autoregressions with Panel Data," *Econometrica*, 56, 1371–1395.

Lundberg, S. (1985), "Tied Wage-Hours Offers and the Endogeneity of Wages," *Review of Economics and Statistics*, 67, 405–410.

McKinley, B and D. Neumark (1992), "Unobserved Ability, Efficiency Wages, and Interindustry Wage Differentials," *The Quarterly Journal of Economics*, 107, Nov, 1421–1436.

Nickell, S.J. (1981), "Biases in Dynamic Models with Fixed Effects," *Econometrica*, 49, 1417–1426.

Tuli, K.R., S.G. Bharadwaj and A.K. Kohli (2010), "Ties That Bind: The Impact of Multiple Types of Ties with a Customer on Sales Growth and Sales Volatility," *Journal of Marketing Research*, 47, 36–50.

Wooldridge, J.M. (2009), *Introductory Econometrics*, 4th ed., Mason, OH: South-Western, Cengage Learning.

Appendix 7A Controlling for fixed effects using *EViews* and *SAS*

For a firm-level analysis, we often use cross-section and time-series data. One easy approach to control for the effects of industry and time is to use dummy variables. This example explains how to create dummy variables and estimate regression models using *EViews*.

An Excel file "7-cobb.xls" contains 127 firm-year observations. The data period is 1990–1992 and observations are from three industries (industry code = 10, 20, 30). Shown below is a part of the data file.

	A	B	C	D	E	F	G
1	ID	Year	Industry	Output (Q)	non-IT (K)	Labor (L)	IT capital (IT)
2	ABS	1990	30	1385	1820	951	30
3	ABS	1991	30	1288	1958	1033	36
4	ABS	1992	30	1296	2109	1083	62
5	ABT	1990	10	2893	3250	1289	294
6	ABT	1991	10	3099	3605	1360	360
7	ABT	1992	10	3380	3962	1441	505
8	ACI	1991	30	116	306	17	118

Using the data, we will estimate the following Cobb-Douglas production function.

$$\log Q_{it} = \beta_1 \log K_{it} + \beta_2 \log L_{it} + \beta_3 \log IT_{it} + a_i + b_t + u_{it} \tag{A7.1}$$

Using *EViews*

After importing the Excel file, convert the variables into logarithmic values by pressing Genr and entering an equation for each variable: LOGQ = LOG(Q), LOGK = LOG(K), LOGL = LOG(L), and LOG_IT = LOG(IT).

Using dummy variables for the fixed effects of industry and time, the regression model Eq. (A7.1) can be written as follows:

$$\log Q_{it} = \beta_0 + \beta_1 \log K_{it} + \beta_2 \log L_{it} + \beta_3 \log IT_{it}$$
$$+ \gamma_{91} D91_t + \gamma_{92} D92_t + \gamma_2 IND2_i + \gamma_3 IND3_i + u_{it}$$

where $D91_t = 1$ if $t = 1991$, 0 otherwise for any i; $D92_t = 1$ if $t = 1992$, 0 otherwise for any i; $IND2_i = 1$ if a firm i belongs to industry 20, 0 otherwise; and $IND3_i = 1$ if a firm belongs to industry 30, 0 otherwise. In this illustration, the reference year is 1990 and the code of the reference industry is 10. To create dummy variables for industry and year, press the Genr button and enter the following equations one by one:

$$D91 = YEAR = 1991 \qquad D92 = YEAR = 1992$$
$$IND2 = INDUSTRY = 20 \qquad IND3 = INDUSTRY = 30$$

To estimate the Cobb-Douglas production function, choose Objects/New Object. . . /Equation and enter "LN_Q C LN_K LN_L LN_IT D91 D92 IND2 IND3" in the Equation Specification box. The estimation results are shown in Output 7.1.

Output 7.1   Estimation results for the panel data

Dependent Variable: LN_Q
Method: Least Squares
Sample: 1 127
Included observations: 127

Variable	Coefficient	Std. Error	t-Statistic	Prob.
C	0.400600	0.271926	1.473199	0.1433
LN_K	0.300197	0.049861	6.020659	0.0000
LN_L	0.544783	0.059393	9.172483	0.0000
LN_IT	0.217734	0.054996	3.959096	0.0001
D91	-0.069083	0.089926	-0.768226	0.4439
D92	-0.171053	0.089128	-1.919180	0.0574
IND2	-0.075055	0.085269	-0.880216	0.3805
IND3	-0.423196	0.089813	-4.711969	0.0000

R-squared	0.897954	Mean dependent var	7.400988
Adjusted R-squared	0.891952	S.D. dependent var	1.162398
S.E. of regression	0.382089	Akaike info criterion	0.974592
Sum squared resid	17.37301	Schwarz criterion	1.153753
Log likelihood	-53.88659	F-statistic	149.5921

Using *SAS*[1]

```
FILENAME F1 DDE 'EXCEL|[7-COBB.XLS]EX-DUMMY!R2C1:R128C7';
TITLE '< CONTROLLING FOR FIXED EFFECTS USING DUMMIES >';
DATA DAT1; INFILE F1; INPUT NAME $ YEAR INDUSTRY Q K L IT;
    LNQ=LOG(Q); LNK=LOG(K); LNL=LOG(L); LNIT=LOG(IT);
    IF YEAR=1991 THEN D91=1; ELSE D91=0;
    IF YEAR=1992 THEN D92=1; ELSE D92=0;
    IF INDUSTRY=20 THEN IND2=1; ELSE IND2=0;
    IF INDUSTRY=30 THEN IND3=1; ELSE IND3=0;
PROC REG;
    MODEL LOGQ=LOGK LOGL LOG_IT D91 D92 IND2 IND3; RUN;
```

Appendix 7B Is it always possible to control for unit-specific effects?

Hausman and Taylor (1981, p. 1377) state that "An important benefit from pooling time-series and cross-section data is the ability to control for individual-specific effects, possibly unobservable, which may be correlated with other included variables in a specification of an economic relationship. Analysis of cross-section data alone can neither identify nor control for such individual effects."

1. Cross-sectional Data

a   When all units have separate unit-specific effects:

$$Y_i = \beta X_i + a_i + \varepsilon_i$$

Observations have the following relations when there are five units $(i = 1, \cdots, 5)$:

$$Y_1 = \beta X_1 + a_1 + \varepsilon_1$$
$$Y_2 = \beta X_2 + a_2 + \varepsilon_2$$
$$Y_3 = \beta X_3 + a_3 + \varepsilon_3$$
$$Y_4 = \beta X_4 + a_4 + \varepsilon_4$$
$$Y_5 = \beta X_5 + a_5 + \varepsilon_5$$

# of coefficient parameters to be estimated = 6 ($\beta, a_1, \cdots, a_5$)
# of observations (or equations) = 5
The SIX parameters cannot be estimated by the FIVE equations only.
Therefore, the individual unit-specific effects cannot be controlled for.

b   When the cross-sectional units can be grouped (e.g., grouped by industry):

Suppose that there are two industries: Industry A includes units 1 and 2, and the other industry B includes units 3, 4 and 5. Denoting industry-specific effects by θ_A and θ_B, respectively, we have

$$Y_1 = \beta X_1 + \theta_A + \varepsilon_1$$
$$Y_2 = \beta X_2 + \theta_A + \varepsilon_2$$
$$Y_3 = \beta X_3 + \theta_B + \varepsilon_3$$
$$Y_4 = \beta X_4 + \theta_B + \varepsilon_4$$
$$Y_5 = \beta X_5 + \theta_B + \varepsilon_5$$

# of coefficient parameters to be estimated = 3 $(\beta, \theta_A, \theta_B)$
# of observations (or equations) = 5
The THREE parameters can be estimated using the FIVE equations. Since there are more equations than the number of parameters, there is no solution which satisfies all of the five equations. Instead, we choose estimates such that they make the disturbances (e.g., $\varepsilon_1 = Y_1 - \beta X_1 - \theta_A$) as small as possible; this is just the OLS estimation method.

Since each group has more than one observation, its group-specific effects can be estimated and thus controlled for. Assuming that the group-specific effects are the same for all units in each group, they are estimated as the average value in each corresponding group. For example, the estimates of θ_A and θ_B are $\hat{\theta}_A = \frac{1}{2}\sum_{i=1}^{2}(Y_i - \hat{\beta}X_i)$ and $\hat{\theta}_B = \frac{1}{3}\sum_{i=3}^{5}(Y_i - \hat{\beta}X_i)$, respectively. This indicates that in order to estimate the fixed group-specific effects θ_i, we need repeated observations on θ_i.

2. Panel data

$$Y_{it} = \beta X_{it} + a_i + b_t + \varepsilon_{it}$$

Observations have the following relations ($i = 1, \cdots, 5$ and $t = 1, 2$):

$$Y_{11} = \beta X_{11} + a_1 + b_1 + \varepsilon_{11}$$
$$Y_{12} = \beta X_{12} + a_1 + b_2 + \varepsilon_{12}$$

$$Y_{21} = \beta X_{21} + a_2 + b_1 + \varepsilon_{21}$$
$$Y_{22} = \beta X_{22} + a_2 + b_2 + \varepsilon_{22}$$

$$Y_{31} = \beta X_{31} + a_3 + b_1 + \varepsilon_{31}$$
$$Y_{32} = \beta X_{32} + a_3 + b_2 + \varepsilon_{32}$$

$$Y_{41} = \beta X_{41} + a_4 + b_1 + \varepsilon_{41}$$
$$Y_{42} = \beta X_{42} + a_4 + b_2 + \varepsilon_{42}$$

$$Y_{51} = \beta X_{51} + a_5 + b_1 + \varepsilon_{51}$$
$$Y_{52} = \beta X_{52} + a_5 + b_2 + \varepsilon_{52}$$

# of coefficient parameters to be estimated = 8 ($\beta, a_1, \cdots, a_5, b_1, b_2$)
# of observations (or equations) = 10
The OLS method can estimate the EIGHT parameters using the TEN equations. Since there is more than one observation for each unit (i) and also for each time period (t), the unit- and time-specific effects can be estimated and thus controlled for. Similarly to the above, the effects are estimated as the averages of appropriate quantities; for example, $\hat{a}_1 = \frac{1}{2}\sum_{t=1}^{2}(Y_{1t} - \hat{\beta}X_{1t} - \hat{b}_t)$ and $\hat{b}_1 = \frac{1}{5}\sum_{i=1}^{5}(Y_{i1} - \hat{\beta}X_{i1} - \hat{a}_i)$.

Note

1 BASE SAS 9.4 and SAS/STAT 13.1. SAS Institute Inc., Cary, NC.

8 Simultaneous equations models

Learning objectives

In this chapter, you should learn about:

- Simultaneous relations and the endogeneity problem;
- Estimation of simulation equations models;
- Identification problem in simultaneous relations.

8.1 Model description

If a right-hand-side regressor is simultaneously determined with the dependent variable, in other words, the two variables influence each other simultaneously, then the regressor will be correlated with the disturbance of the equation as explained below. If so, this *endogenous* explanatory variable will cause the OLS estimators to be biased. This is called the *simultaneity bias* as this endogeneity is due to the simultaneous relation.[1]

Below is a supply-and-demand model, a popular example of simultaneous equations models. For easy understanding of the simultaneity bias, we use quantity (Q_t) as the dependent variable in the supply function and price (P_t) as the dependent variable in the demand function.

$$Q_t = \alpha_0 + \alpha_1 P_t + \alpha_2 R_t + \varepsilon_t \qquad \text{(supply)} \qquad (8.1)$$

$$P_t = \beta_0 + \beta_1 Q_t + \beta_2 I_t + u_t \qquad \text{(demand)} \qquad (8.2)$$

where ε_t and u_t may be correlated but often assumed to be uncorrelated; and other factor variables I_t and R_t are assumed to be exogenous. The supply function posits that quantity supplied is determined by price and other factors (R_t, ε_t). And the demand function assumes that price is determined by quantity demanded and other factors (I_t, u_t). To estimate the equations, we use observations on equilibrium quantity and price which equalize quantity supplied and quantity demanded.[2] According to the supply-and-demand functions, Eqs. (8.1) and (8.2), price influences quantity while quantity also influences price in the same time period t. That is, quantity and price influence each other simultaneously.

To understand why the simultaneous relation makes P_t and Q_t endogenous, suppose that there is a positive shock ($\varepsilon_t \uparrow$) to the supply function. This positive shock then increases quantity ($Q_t \uparrow$). According to the demand function Eq. (8.2), the increase in quantity simultaneously decreases price ($P_t \downarrow$) as $\beta_1 < 0$. Therefore, in Eq. (8.1), P_t is negatively correlated with the disturbance ε_t, causing the OLS estimators to be biased.

Here is another simple example which demonstrates the simultaneity bias (Levitt, 2002). Hiring more police officers (X_t) should reduce crime (Y_t), predicting $\alpha_1 < 0$.

$$Y_t = \alpha_0 + \alpha_1 X_t + (controls) + \varepsilon_t$$
$$X_t = \beta_0 + \beta_1 Y_t + (controls) + u_t$$

However, it is also possible that when crime goes up, cities hire more police officers; this indicates a positive relation between X_t and Y_t, i.e., $\beta_1 > 0$ in the second equation. If we regress Y_t on X_t and other control variables as in the first equation, the OLS estimate of α_2 could be insignificant or even positive. Thus, the simultaneity can result in estimates which are opposite to theoretically predicted ones.

The above model specifies the interactions between the endogenous variables based on economic theory and is called a *structural model*. In contrast, we can transform the structural model so as to have only exogenous variables on the right-hand side. The resulting equation is called a *reduced-form model*.

$$Q_t = \pi_{11} + \pi_{12} I_t + \pi_{13} R_t + v_{1t}$$
$$P_t = \pi_{21} + \pi_{22} I_t + \pi_{23} R_t + v_{2t}$$

(8.3)

where $\pi_{11} = (\alpha_0 + \alpha_1 \beta_0)/(1 - \alpha_1 \beta_1)$, $\pi_{12} = \alpha_1 \beta_2/(1 - \alpha_1 \beta_1)$, $\pi_{13} = \alpha_2/(1 - \alpha_1 \beta_1)$, $\pi_{21} = (\beta_0 + \alpha_0 \beta_1)/(1 - \alpha_1 \beta_1)$, $\pi_{22} = \beta_2/(1 - \alpha_1 \beta_1)$ and $\pi_{23} = \alpha_2 \beta_1/(1 - \alpha_1 \beta_1)$. And v_{1t} and v_{2t} are correlated because $v_{1t} = (\varepsilon_t + \alpha_1 u_t)/(1 - \alpha_1 \beta_1)$ and $v_{2t} = (\beta_1 \varepsilon_t + u_t)/(1 - \alpha_1 \beta_1)$.

If the number of parameters in Eq. (8.3) is the same as the one in Eqs. (8.1) and (8.2), it is said to be just-identified and we can estimate the simultaneous equations model using the *indirect least squares method*. That is,

1   Estimate πs of the reduced-form model, Eq. (8.3), using the seemingly unrelated regression method.
2   From the estimates of πs, recover αs and βs of the structural model, Eqs. (8.1) and (8.2), using the above relations between π and (α, β).

In many cases, however, the indirect least squares method cannot be used because the number of parameters in reduced-form models is usually greater than the one in structural models; it is said to be over-identified. In some cases, we need to estimate only one equation in a structural model, not a whole system of equations. Below are explained the widely used estimation methods.

8.2 Estimation methods

8.2.1 Two-stage least squares (2SLS)

The 2SLS method is designed to estimate *only one equation* each time. Suppose that we are interested in estimating the supply function Eq. (8.1) only. As explained earlier, the OLS estimation is biased because an explanatory variable P_t is correlated with the disturbance ε_t. The 2SLS method follows two stages: (i) the first stage is to construct a variable which is similar to the endogenous variable P_t but is not correlated with the disturbance term ε_t; (ii) the second stage is to apply the OLS method after replacing the endogenous regressor with the variable constructed in the first stage.

(i) First stage

In the first stage, we eliminate the correlation between the disturbance and endogenous regressors. It involves regressing each endogenous regressor (here P_t) on a set of instrumental variables using the OLS method. **Instrumental variables** are ones that are correlated with the endogenous regressor but uncorrelated with the disturbance. All the exogenous explanatory variables in the whole model are good for instrumental variables. For time-series data, lagged dependent and independent variables are also used as instrumental variables.[3] Regressing the endogenous variable P_t on instrumental variables, we calculate the OLS fitted values for P_t.[4]

$$\hat{P}_t = \hat{d}_0 + \hat{d}_1 I_{t-1} + \hat{d}_2 R_t + \hat{d}_3 W_t + \hat{d}_4 Q_{t-1} + \hat{d}_5 P_{t-1} + \hat{d}_6 I_{t-1} + \hat{d}_7 R_{t-1}$$

where I_t and R_t are exogenous variables in the supply-and-demand equations; W_t represents additional instrumental variables not present in the supply-and-demand model; and Q_{t-1}, P_{t-1}, I_{t-1} and R_{t-1} are lagged values of the dependent and independent variables. In this first stage, all we need are the fitted values which will be used in the second stage. Thus, we are not interested in the accuracy of coefficient estimates and don't need to worry about any possible multicollinearity. Since the fitted variable $\hat{P}_t$ is a linear combination of instrumental variables, it is by construction uncorrelated with the disturbance ε_t.

(ii) Second stage

Substituting the fitted variable $\hat{P}_t$ for P_t in the supply function Eq. (8.1), we obtain

$$Q_t = \alpha_0 + \alpha_1 \hat{P}_t + \alpha_2 R_t + \varepsilon_t \tag{8.4}$$

Since $\hat{P}_t$ is uncorrelated with ε_t, the OLS estimation can now be applied to Eq. (8.4). It can theoretically be shown that the 2SLS estimator is consistent and thus works well for large samples, although the 2SLS estimator could be biased and suffer from finite-sample problems. See Chapter 6 for a detailed explanation about the 2SLS and the conditions for good instrumental variables.

8.2.2 Three-stage least squares (3SLS)

The 3SLS method adds one more stage to the 2SLS in order to estimate all equations in a structural model. It begins by applying the 2SLS method separately to each of all equations in the system. The estimates obtained from individual applications of the 2SLS are used to estimate the variance-covariance matrix of the disturbances, ε_t and u_t, in Eqs. (8.1) and (8.2). In the final stage, the estimate of the variance-covariance matrix is used to improve the estimation efficiency by exploiting the relative variances and correlations of the disturbances.

This full-information approach to estimation of all equations is in theory superior to the single-equation (or limited-information) approaches which estimate each equation separately, such as the 2SLS. However, the advantage comes with cost. If any one of the equations in a simultaneous model is misspecified, the error in one equation may contaminate estimates for the other equations in the simultaneous model. In contrast, if the single-equation approaches are used, only the misspecified equation will be poorly estimated.[5]

8.2.3 Generalized method of moments (GMM)

The GMM estimation is based on the orthogonality assumption that the disturbances in the equations are uncorrelated with a set of instrumental variables including exogenous explanatory variables. The GMM method selects parameter estimates so that the correlations between the instruments and disturbances are as close to zero as possible.[6] For the supply function Eq. (8.1), the selected instrumental variables should satisfy the following orthogonality conditions:

$$\sum \varepsilon_t = \sum (Q_t - \alpha_0 - \alpha_1 P_t - \alpha_2 R_t) = 0$$
$$\sum \varepsilon_t I_t = \sum (Q_t - \alpha_0 - \alpha_1 P_t - \alpha_2 R_t) \times I_t = 0$$
$$\sum \varepsilon_t R_t = \sum (Q_t - \alpha_0 - \alpha_1 P_t - \alpha_2 R_t) \times R_t = 0$$
$$\sum \varepsilon_t W_t = \sum (Q_t - \alpha_0 - \alpha_1 P_t - \alpha_2 R_t) \times W_t = 0$$
$$\sum \varepsilon_t Q_{t-1} = \sum (Q_t - \alpha_0 - \alpha_1 P_t - \alpha_2 R_t) \times Q_{t-1} = 0$$
$$\sum \varepsilon_t P_{t-1} = \sum (Q_t - \alpha_0 - \alpha_1 P_t - \alpha_2 R_t) \times P_{t-1} = 0$$
$$\sum \varepsilon_t I_{t-1} = \sum (Q_t - \alpha_0 - \alpha_1 P_t - \alpha_2 R_t) \times I_{t-1} = 0$$
$$\sum \varepsilon_t R_{t-1} = \sum (Q_t - \alpha_0 - \alpha_1 P_t - \alpha_2 R_t) \times R_{t-1} = 0$$

The first condition is when the constant (intercept) is used as an instrumental variable. The second and third equations are when the exogenous explanatory variables I_t and R_t are used and the fourth equation is when an additional instrumental variable W_t is used. The rest of the equations use lagged explanatory and dependent variables P_{t-1}, Q_{t-1}, I_{t-1} and R_{t-1}. This GMM method can be used for estimating some or all of the equations in a structural model. Since the GMM estimator is consistent but biased for small-sized samples, it performs well for large samples. See Chapter 6 for more explanation about the GMM estimation.

8.2.4 Full-information maximum likelihood (FIML)

The FIML method selects parameter estimates which maximize the likelihood function under the assumption that the contemporaneous disturbances, (ε_t, u_t) in Eqs. (8.1) and (8.2) above, have a joint normal distribution. Thus, it estimates all equations in the system together. The FILM is asymptotically efficient among estimators for the simultaneous-equations models if the distributional assumptions are correct.

8.3 Identification problem

To illustrate the identification problem, let us use the supply-and-demand model. The key feature of the problem is that it is not possible to specify a supply and a demand function based on equilibrium observations only. As in Figure 8.1(a), the observations are the equilibrium price and quantity in each period. The observed price and quantity in each period represent the intersection of a supply and a demand curve, as shown in Figure 8.1(b) and Figure 8.1(c), but do not show the curves themselves. As both cases are consistent with the observed data, they are said to be *observationally equivalent*. Unfortunately, there is no way of determining the supply-and-demand curves behind each observed equilibrium point.

However, if the supply curve shifts up and down while the demand curve remains constant as in Figure 8.1(d), the demand curve can be identified by connecting the observed points. It implies that for the demand curve to be identified, there should be exogenous variables which can shift the supply curve only. In the same way, the supply curve can be identified if only the demand curve shifts up and down while the supply curve remains unchanged, as in Figure 8.1(e). In general, for an equation to be identified, some exogenous variables should be included in the other equation only, thereby shifting the other equation. We can summarize this idea as the following order condition.

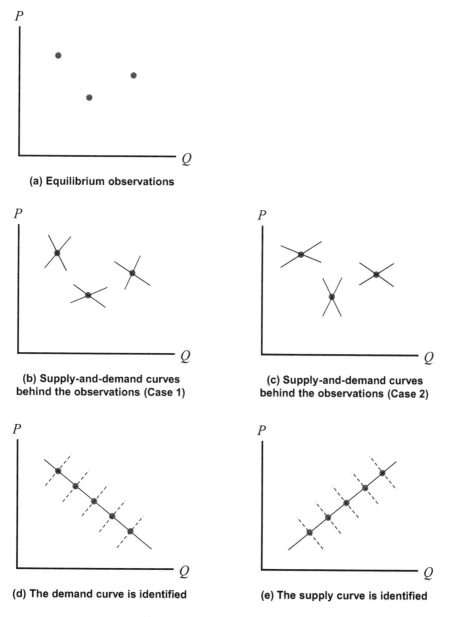

Figure 8.1 Identification problem

Order condition necessary for identification

In a simple case like the above supply-and-demand model, each equation includes one endogenous explanatory variable. The order condition for equation j ($= 1, 2$) to be identified in this simple case is that at least one exogenous or predetermined variable needs to be excluded from equation j; in other words, the other equation has to include at least one exogenous or predetermined variable which is not present in equation j.

For a general case in which there is more than one endogenous explanatory variable in equation j ($j = 1, \cdots, M$), the number of exogenous or predetermined variables excluded from equation j must be greater than or equal to the number of endogenous explanatory variables in that equation j.[7]

Example 8.1 We apply the order condition to the following simultaneous equations model, Eqs. (8.5) and (8.6).

$$GDP_t = \alpha_1 + \alpha_2 M_t + \alpha_3 I_t + \alpha_4 GOV_t + u_{1t} \tag{8.5}$$
$$M_t = \beta_0 + \beta_1 GDP_t + \beta_2 TB_t + u_{2t} \tag{8.6}$$

where I_t, GOV_t and TB_t are assumed exogenous and therefore uncorrelated with the disturbances, u_{1t} and u_{2t}, but GDP_t and M_t are treated as endogenous variables. The influence of M_t on GDP_t in Eq. (8.5) is based on the economic theory of monetary policy. At the same time, it is also likely that M_t is influenced by GDP_t because monetary policy makers consider the current economic situation (such as GDP_t) when they make a decision about money supply (M_t). Therefore, in the money-supply equation Eq. (8.6), GDP_t is included as an explanatory variable for M_t.

In Eq. (8.5),

> number of endogenous explanatory variables $= 1$ (M_t)
> number of exogenous variables excluded from Eq. (8.5) $= 1$ (TB_t)
> Therefore, the GDP equation is identified because $1 = 1$.

In Eq. (8.6),

> number of endogenous explanatory variables $= 1$ (GDP_t)
> number of exogenous variables excluded from Eq. (8.6) $= 2$ (I_t and GOV_t)
> Therefore, the M equation is identified because $2 > 1$.

8.4 Applications

8.4.1 Cornwell and Trumbull (1994)

This study estimates the following crime model using data from 90 counties in North Carolina for a period from 1981 to 1989; see 7.3.1 in Chapter 7 for an explanation of this model. Using panel

Table 8.1 Estimation results for the crime model

	Between	Within	2SLS (fixed effects)	2SLS (no fixed effects)
Constant	−2.097)			−3.179
	(2.822)			(8.189)
P^A	−0.648	−0.355	−0.455	−0.507
	(0.088)	(0.032)	(0.618)	(0.251)
P^C	−0.528	−0.282	−0.336	−0.530
	(0.067)	(0.021)	(0.371)	(0.110)
P^P	0.297	−0.173	−0.196	0.200
	(0.231)	(0.032)	(0.200)	(0.343)
S	−0.236	−0.00245	−0.0298	−0.218
	(0.174)	(0.026)	(0.030)	(0.185)
Control variables	Included	Included	Included	Included

Source: Adapted from Cornwell and Trumbull (1994, Table 3 on page 365).

Note: Standard errors are given in parentheses.

data, it controls for unobservable unit-specific characteristics that may be correlated with explanatory variables.

$$R_{it} = \beta_1 P_{it}^A + \beta_2 P_{it}^C + \beta_3 P_{it}^P + \beta_4 S_{it} + X_{it}{}'\gamma + a_i + b_t + \varepsilon_{it}$$

This study also addresses possible simultaneity using instrumental variables. One example of the simultaneity can arise from the dependency of the size of the police (one of the control variables in X) on the crime rate (R). The "fixed-effects 2SLS" applies the two-stage least squares method to the within-transformed model, thereby addressing both sources of endogeneity; that is, the county-specific effects are addressed by the within-transformation and the simultaneity is by the 2SLS method. In contrast, the "no-fixed-effects 2SLS" ignores the county-specific effects and would lead to biased estimates because the neglected county heterogeneity may be correlated with the instrumental variables used to compute the 2SLS estimates. Table 8.1 shows a large difference between the fixed-effects 2SLS and the no-fixed-effects 2SLS estimates.

In contrast, there is little difference between the Within estimates and the fixed-effects 2SLS estimates. It indicates that the simultaneity is not so significant, whereas the county-specific effects are significant and thus have to be controlled for, as explained in Chapter 7.

8.4.2 Beaver, McAnally and Stinson (1997)

This study views cross-sectional changes of security price (P) and earnings (E) as being jointly determined.

$$\frac{\Delta P_{it}}{P_{i,t-1}} = \alpha_0 + \alpha_1 \frac{\Delta E_{it}}{E_{i,t-1}} + \varepsilon_{it} \tag{8.7}$$

$$\frac{\Delta E_{it}}{E_{i,t-1}} = \beta_0 + \beta_1 \frac{\Delta P_{it}}{P_{i,t-1}} + u_{it} \tag{8.8}$$

where $Cov(\varepsilon_{it}, u_{it}) = 0$. This represents a new approach to understanding the bivariate price-earnings relation and econometrically captures two important features. First, price and earnings changes influence each other simultaneously. Second, price and earnings changes are also influenced by a set of informational variables that are difficult to specify explicitly. As a result, the traditional single-equation approaches potentially suffer from a simultaneity bias and a correlated-omitted-variable problem.

Hausman test

Empirical tests for endogeneity indicate that price changes and earnings changes act as if they are endogenously determined.

Identification

The above simultaneous equations (8.7) and (8.8) are not identified because they do not include exogenous variables and fail to satisfy the order condition. Therefore, coefficients estimated from a regression of either Eq. (8.7) or Eq. (8.8) in isolation are difficult to interpret. To solve the identification problem, they introduce two exogenous variables:

$$\frac{\Delta P_{it}}{P_{i,t-1}} = \alpha_0 + \alpha_1 \frac{\Delta E_{it}}{E_{i,t-1}} + \alpha_2 Beta_i + \varepsilon_{it}$$

$$\frac{\Delta E_{it}}{E_{i,t-1}} = \beta_0 + \beta_1 \frac{\Delta P_{it}}{P_{i,t-1}} + \beta_2 \frac{\Delta P_{i,t-1}}{P_{i,t-2}} + u_{it}$$

where $Beta_i$ (the sensitivity of percentage changes in price to percentage changes of the return on an economy-wide portfolio of securities) and $\Delta P_{i,t-1} / P_{i,t-2}$ (lagged price changes) are considered exogenous variables. The system is exactly identified because each equation has one exogenous variable which is not present in the other equation.

Estimation methods

The authors estimate the coefficients using the 2SLS and the 3SLS as well as the OLS. The OLS estimates provide a benchmark relative to prior studies and against which to assess the coefficient estimates obtained using the 2SLS and the 3SLS. A major challenge in applying the 2SLS and the 3SLS is the identification of a set of instrumental variables. The authors selected 19 instrumental variables based on prior research.

Empirical results

The results indicate that a portion of the single-equation bias can be mitigated by estimating the simultaneous equations. Although interpretation of the results is conditional upon the selection of instrumental variables, the approach adopted in this study has the potential advantage of recognizing simultaneity and identification issues.

8.4.3 Barton (2001)

This study estimates a set of simultaneous equations that captures managers' incentives to maintain a desired level of earnings volatility through hedging and accrual management, and presents evidence consistent with managers using derivatives and discretionary accruals as partial substitutes for smoothing earnings.

Barton develops a hypothesis that managers use these tools as substitute means of smoothing earnings. Managers presumably consider using derivatives and discretionary accruals jointly if the costs or effectiveness of these tools differ. In other words, the extent to which managers use derivatives (*DERIVATIVES*) vis-à-vis discretionary accruals (|*DAC*|) is likely endogenous. Assuming that managers use these tools to maintain an optimal level of earnings volatility, this study predicts and tests the following alternative hypothesis:

H$_a$: *DERIVATIVES* and |*DAC*| will be negatively associated, conditional on managers' maintaining a desired level of earnings volatility.

To test H$_a$, the author uses the following simultaneous equations:

$$DERIVATIVES_{it} = \alpha_0 + \alpha_1 \mid DAC \mid_{it} + (controls) + u_{it}$$
$$\mid DAC \mid_{it} = \beta_0 + \beta_1 DERIVATIVES_{it} + (controls) + v_{it}$$

H$_a$ predicts that the coefficients of *DERIVATIVES* and |*DAC*| will be negative. Because these coefficients are conditional on the firm's decision to use derivatives, they capture the ongoing relation between derivative use and accrual management once the firm has set up its risk management program.

The vector (*controls*) accounts for managers' incentives to use derivatives and manage accruals to maintain a desired level of earnings volatility. It includes two sets of variables, one common to all equations and the other intended to identify the simultaneous equations. There is one endogenous variable in each equation. To satisfy the order condition for identification, each equation should include one or more exogenous variables excluded from the other equation.

8.4.4 Datta and Agarwal (2004)

This study investigates the long-run relationship between telecommunications infrastructure and economic growth within a macroeconomic growth model, using data from 22 OECD countries for the period 1980–1992. Most previous studies that look at the determinants of growth have largely been conducted in a cross-section framework, which involves the estimation of single cross-country regressions. This typically requires the assumption of an identical production function for all countries. However, ignoring individual "country-specific effects" has been shown to lead to biased results (Islam, 1995). The following fixed effects panel model is employed to account for country effects.

$$GRTH_{it} = a_i + b_t + \beta_1 GRTH_{i,t-1} + \beta_2 GDP_{i,t-1} + \beta_3 POP_{it} + \beta_4 (G^c / Y)_{it}$$
$$+ \beta_5 (I / Y)_{it} + \beta_6 OPEN_{it} + \beta_7 TEL_{it} + \beta_8 TELSQ_{it} + u_{it}$$

where i indexes countries; t indexes time; a_i captures the unobserved country-specific effects; b_t, the unobserved time-effects and u_{it} is the transitory error term. *GRTH* is the rate of growth of real GDP per capita; GDP_{t-1} is lagged real GDP per capita measured in purchasing power parity (PPP).

The lagged growth rate $GRTH_{t-1}$ is included to account for the correlation between previous and subsequent values of growth, following Islam (1995)'s dynamic model. The lagged GDP variable is included to test for convergence.[8] A negative coefficient of GDP_{t-1} is expected to support the convergence, where a higher level of GDP_{t-1} leads to lower subsequent growth. *POP* is the rate of population growth, (G^c/Y) the share of government consumption in GDP and (I/Y) the share of fixed investment in GDP. *OPEN* measures the extent to which the country is integrated into the global economy; it is measured as the total of exports and imports for each country.

TEL is telecommunications infrastructure measured by access lines per 100 inhabitants. The expected sign for *TEL* is positive. The square of the telecom variable, *TELSQ*, is included to study the nature of returns to scale to telecom investment. For example, diminishing returns to telecommunications investment, captured by a negative coefficient of *TELSQ*, would indicate that as investment on telecommunications infrastructure increases, its incremental effect on growth diminishes. On the other hand, a positive sign would indicate increasing returns.

The estimation results, presented in Tables 8.2 and 8.3, show that the coefficient of lagged dependent variable, *GRTH*, is positive and significant. The coefficient of lagged *GDP*, which measures the effect of past levels of GDP on subsequent growth, is negative and significant at the 1% level. This result supports the convergence hypothesis that countries with higher levels of GDP per capita tend to grow at a slower rate.

The estimation results in Table 8.2 indicate a strong and positive relationship between telecommunications infrastructure and economic growth. The measure of telecom infrastructure used in this study, which is the stock of access lines per hundred, is an output measure and therefore the current value is expected to have the strongest association with that year's growth rate. However, previous studies have indicated a *two-way causation* (or *simultaneity*) between telecommunications investment and economic growth. In order to confirm that the results are not simply due to reverse causality, this relationship is tested using lagged values of *TEL* as well. The telecom variable is

Table 8.2 Determinants of growth

	(1)	(2)	(3)	(4)
GRTH(t−1)	0.254***	0.243***	0.258***	0.404***
GDP(t−1)	−0.0003***	−0.0003***	−0.00003***	−0.00003***
G^c/Y	−1.032***	−0.940***	−0.96***	−0.911***
I/Y	0.379***	0.401***	0.400***	0.369***
POP	−0.011***	−0.012***	−0.012***	−0.012***
TEL	0.004***	0.005***		
TEL(t−1)			0.003***	
TEL(t−2)				0.003***
OPEN		0.0007**	0.0006**	0.0005*
Fixed effects	Included	Included	Included	Included
R^2	0.60	0.62	0.62	0.62

Source: Adapted from Datta and Agarwal (2004, Table 2 on page 1653).
Asterisks denote significance levels: * = 10%, ** = 5% and *** = 1%.

Table 8.3 Returns to telecommunications investment

	(5)	(6)
GRTH(t−1)	0.183***	0.176***
GDP(t−1)	−0.0003***	−0.0002***
G^c/Y	−0.881***	−0.801***
I/Y	0.391***	0.411***
POP	−0.008***	−0.009***
OPEN	–	0.0006***
TEL	0.010***	0.010***
TELSQ	−0.0007***	−0.0007***
Fixed effects	Included	Included
R²	0.63	0.65

Source: Adapted from Datta and Agarwal (2004, Table 3 on page 1653).
Asterisks denote significance levels: * = 10%, ** = 5%, and *** = 1%.

positive and significant at the 1% level in all the various specifications of the model, suggesting that the results are robust.

Table 8.3 reports the results on "returns to telecom investment" by including a square term for telecommunications. The coefficient of *TELSQ* is significant and negative indicating diminishing returns, i.e., that the size of the effect of telecommunications investment is inversely related to its prior level. This implies that the positive effect of telecommunications on GDP growth is largest for countries with the smallest telecom infrastructure.

8.5 Summary

1   If a right-hand-side regressor is simultaneously determined with the dependent variable, in other words, the two variables influence each other simultaneously, then the regressor will be correlated with the disturbance of the equation; this belongs to the endogeneity problem.

2   The estimation methods which can solve the endogeneity problem for the simultaneous equations include the 2SLS, 3SLS and GMM which use instrumental variables.

3   A necessary condition for identification of simultaneous equations is the order condition: the number of exogenous variables excluded from an equation must be greater than or equal to the number of endogenous explanatory variables in that equation. The idea of the order condition is that for a certain equation to be identified, the other equation has to shift up and down while the equation of our interest remains unchanged.

Review questions

1   The following questions are about simultaneous equations models.

(a)   Explain why the OLS estimator has a simultaneity bias.
(b)   Explain what estimation methods should be used to avoid the simultaneity bias.

2   The following questions are about the simultaneous equations models.

(a)   The identification problem can exist for simultaneous equations models. Explain why it occurs.

    (b) Under what condition is the identification problem solved? Explain using an example.

    (c) In the following regression, $Y1$ and $Y2$ are endogenous. If we estimate this regression by the OLS method, what problem will there be?

$$Y1_t = \beta_0 + \beta_1 Y2_t + u_{1t}$$

    (d) Explain how we can estimate the above equation in (c). Suppose there are some exogenous variables ($X1$, $X2$, $X3$) which are relevant for the endogenous variables $Y1$ and $Y2$.

3   The following questions are about the endogeneity problem of the OLS estimation method.

    (a) Explain what the endogeneity problem is.

    (b) List four (4) cases where the endogeneity problem can occur.

    (c) For each case in (b), explain what the best solution is.

    If the best solution cannot be applied, explain how to estimate a model.

4   The following is a simultaneous equation model which explains the relation between the crime rate (Y) and the number of police officers (X).

$$Y_t = \alpha_0 + \alpha_1 X_t + \alpha_2 Y_{t-1} + \alpha_3 Z_{1t} + \varepsilon_t \qquad\qquad (Q8.1)$$

$$X_t = \beta_0 + \beta_1 Y_t + \beta_2 Y_{t-1} + \beta_3 Z_{1t} + \beta_4 Z_{2t} + \beta_5 Z_{3t} + u_t \qquad\qquad (Q8.2)$$

    (a) Explain why a simultaneous relation between Y and X causes an endogeneity problem.

    (b) Explain how we can obtain consistent estimates for Eq. (Q8.1).

    (c) Is Eq. (Q8.1) identified?

    (d) Is Eq. (Q8.2) identified? If not, explain how to revise the above model.

5   Abernethy, M.A., J. Bouwens, and L. van Lent (2004), "Determinants of Control System Design in Divisionalized Firms," *The Accounting Review*, 79, 545–570.

    (This paper has not been discussed in the text. However, the following questions can be answered without reading the paper.)

This study investigates the determinants of two choices in the control system of divisionalized firms, namely decentralization and use of performance measures. They treat decentralization and performance measurement choices as endogenous variables and examine the interrelation between these choices using the following simultaneous equations.

$$DSM_i = \alpha_0 + \alpha_1 DECEN_i + \alpha_2 INFORASYM_i + \alpha_3 IMPACT(THEM)_i$$
$$+\, \alpha_4 IMPACT(YOU)_i + \alpha_5 SENS_i + \alpha_6 PRECISION_i + \varepsilon_i^{DSM}$$

$$DECEN_i = \beta_0 + \beta_1 DSM_i + \beta_2 INFORASYM_i + \beta_3 IMPACT(THEM)_i$$
$$+\, \beta_4 IMPACT(YOU)_i + \beta_5 SIZE_i + \beta_6 GROWTH_i$$
$$+\, \beta_7 (SIZE_i \times INFORASYM_i) + \beta_8 EDUCATE_i$$
$$+\, \beta_9 EXPINPOS_i + \varepsilon_i^{DECEN}$$

where *DSM* = a measure of division performance (i.e., a divisional summary measure); *DECEN* = a measure of decentralization; *INFORASYM* = a measure of information asymmetries; *IMPACT(THEM)* = the extent to which their activities impact on other divisions' activities; *IMPACT(YOU)* = the extent to which their performance is affected by the activities carried out by other divisions; *SENS* = the sensitivity of performance measures; *PRECISION* = a measure of precision; *GROWTH* = a measure of growth opportunities; *SIZE* = the number of employees working in a division; *EDUCATE* = education level; and *EXPINPOS* = the number of years they were employed in their current position. Notice that *DSM* and *DECEN* are endogenous variables and the other variables are exogenous variables.

(a) Are the above simultaneous equations identified? Explain.
(b) To estimate the first equation (*DSM*), we can use the 2SLS (two-stage least squares) method. Explain how the 2SLS is conducted.

Notes

1 Until now, we have seen several cases in which the disturbances are correlated with independent variables. They are: (i) the correlated-omitted-variable problem as explained in Chapters 3 and 6; (ii) the errors-in-variable problem as explained in Chapter 6; (iii) the correlated unit- and time-specific effects as explained in Chapter 7; and (iv) the simultaneity bias in this chapter.
2 In what follows, we will simply say quantity without differentiating quantity supplied and quantity demanded because they are equal at equilibrium.
3 The lagged variables (e.g., P_{t-1} and Q_{t-1}) are said to be *predetermined* as they are independent of the current and subsequent disturbances u_{t+s} and ε_{t+s} ($s \geq 0$).
4 It is known that the OLS fitted variable $\hat{P}_t$ is more highly correlated with P_t than any other possible linear combinations of the instrumental variables.
5 Antonakis et al. (2010) suggest to test whether the full-information estimation yields different estimates from the limited-information estimation. If their estimates are significantly different, then the limited-information estimation must be used instead of the full-information estimation. This indicates that at least one equation in the simultaneous model is misspecified.
6 When there are more orthogonality conditions than the number of parameters, the GMM estimator is defined to minimize a *weighted* squared sum of the orthogonality conditions. Since the weights can account for heteroscedasticity and serial correlation of the disturbances, the GMM method can produce robust estimators. Therefore, the GMM is often applied to time-series data and panel data (Wooldridge, 2001). In contrast, the 2SLS method uses the OLS method both in the first and in the second stages without applying weights. Remember that the OLS estimator is efficient when the disturbances are homoscedastic and uncorrelated between them. So, the 2SLS is more often employed for cross-sectional data which are usually collected identically and independently. This is the key difference between the GMM and the 2SLS method.
7 Theoretically speaking, this order condition is a necessary but not sufficient condition for identification. It ensures that the simultaneous equations have at least one set of estimates for the parameters, but it does not ensure that it has only one. The sufficient condition for uniqueness, called the rank condition, ensures that there is exactly one set of estimates for the parameters. However, it is unusual for a model to pass the order but not the rank condition. Thus, only the order condition is verified in practice (Greene, 2003, pp. 393–394).
8 The convergence hypothesis of the neoclassical growth theory suggests that due to diminishing returns to capital, the growth rate of a country is inversely proportional to its initial level of income. This implies a tendency on the part of countries to converge to a steady-state rate of growth.

References

Antonakis, J., S. Bendahan, P. Jacquart and R. Lalive (2010), "On Making Causal Claims: A Review and Recommendations," *The Leadership Quarterly*, 21, 1086–1120.

Barton, J. (2001), "Does the Use of Financial Derivatives Affect Earnings Management Decisions?" *The Accounting Review*, 76, 1–26.

Beaver, W.H., M.L. McAnally and C.H. Stinson (1997), "The Information Content of Earnings and Prices: A Simultaneous Equations Approach," *Journal of Accounting and Economics*, 23, 53–81.

Cornwell, C. and W.N. Trumbull (1994), "Estimating the Economic Model of Crime with Panel Data," *The Review of Economics and Statistics*, 76, 360–366.

Datta, A. and S. Agarwal (2004), "Telecommunications and Economic Growth: A Panel Data Approach," *Applied Economics*, 36, 1649–1654.

Greene, W.H. (2003), *Econometric Analysis*, 5th ed., Upper Saddle River, NJ: Prentice Hall.

Islam, N. (1995), "Growth Empirics: A Panel Data Approach," *Quarterly Journal of Economics*, 110, 1127–1170.

Levitt, S.D. (2002), "Using Electoral Cycles in Police Hiring to Estimate the Effects of Police on Crime: Reply," *American Economic Review*, 92(4), 1244–1250.

Wooldridge, J.M. (2001), "Applications of Generalized Method of Moments Estimation," *Journal of Economic Perspectives*, 15(4), 87–100.

Appendix 8 Estimation of simultaneous equations models using *EViews* and *SAS*

An Excel file "8-sem.xls" contains observations with the variable names "YEAR GDP I GOV M TB." They are annual time-series data on national income (*GDP*), gross private investment (*I*), government expenditure (*GOV*), money supply (*M*) and an interest rate (*TB*) for the period from 1970 to 1994. We estimate the following simultaneous equations:

$$GDP_t = \alpha_1 + \alpha_2 M_t + \alpha_3 I_t + \alpha_4 GOV_t + u_{1t} \tag{8.5}$$

$$M_t = \beta_0 + \beta_1 GDP_t + \beta_2 TB_t + u_{2t} \tag{8.6}$$

where I_t, GOV_t and TB_t are assumed exogenous, and GDP_t and M_t are treated as endogenous variables.

Using *EViews*

After importing the Excel file (8-sem.xls), we generate the lagged variables GDP_{t-1}, M_{t-1}, I_{t-1}, GOV_{t-1} and TB_{t-1} by pressing the Genr button and entering "L_GDP=GDP(−1)," where (−1) is a lag operator. We apply this lag operator to all other variables. We now create a system object and specify the system of equations by choosing Objects/New Object. . . /System. In the System window, enter the equation and list the instrumental variables following a command INST. In this example, the same set of instrumental variables will be used for both equations because only one INST statement is included.[1]

> GDP = C(1) + C(2)*M + C(3)*I + C(4)*GOV
> M = C(5) + C(6)*GDP + C(7)*TB
> INST I GOV TB L_GDP L_M L_I L_GOV L_TB

Once we have created a system, we press the Estimate button on the toolbar. From the System Estimation dialog, we choose Three-Stage Least Squares for the estimation method.[2] The estimation results are shown in Output 8.1.

Output 8.1   3SLS estimation results

System: UNTITLED
Estimation Method: Three-Stage Least Squares
Sample: 1971 1994
Included observations: 24
Total system (balanced) observations 48
Linear estimation after one-step weighting matrix

	Coefficient	Std. Error	t-Statistic	Prob.
C(1)	−235.2532	88.24873	−2.635927	0.0118
C(2)	2.586984	0.365762	7.072865	0.0000
C(3)	−0.048738	0.468198	−0.104098	0.9176
C(4)	−5.164191	2.147285	−2.404986	0.0208
C(5)	98.80020	82.49873	1.197597	0.2380
C(6)	0.553648	0.013436	41.20764	0.0000
C(7)	6.150831	7.547730	0.814925	0.4198

Determinant residual covariance	33883037

Equation: GDP = C(1) + C(2)*M + C(3)*I + C(4)*GOV
Instruments: I GOV TB L_GDP L_M L_I L_GOV L_TB C
Observations: 24

R-squared	0.989395	Mean dependent var	3637.363
Adjusted R-squared	0.987804	S.D. dependent var	1852.258
S.E. of regression	204.5558	Sum squared resid	836861.8
Durbin-Watson stat	0.426578		

Equation: M = C(5) + C(6)*GDP + C(7)*TB
Instruments: I GOV TB L_GDP L_M L_I L_GOV L_TB C
Observations: 24

R-squared	0.986059	Mean dependent var	2156.796
Adjusted R-squared	0.984731	S.D. dependent var	1023.438
S.E. of regression	126.4640	Sum squared resid	335855.8
Durbin-Watson stat	0.365749		

Using *SAS*[3]

```
FILENAME F1 DDE 'EXCEL|[9-SEM.XLS]SEM!R2C1:R26C6';
DATA K; INFILE F1 LRECL=1000;
     INPUT YEAR GDP I GOV M TB;
     L_GDP= LAG(GDP); L_I= LAG(I); L_GOV= LAG(GOV);
     L_M= LAG(M); L_TB= LAG(TB);

PROC SYSLIN DATA=K 2SLS FIRST; <------- 3SLS or FIML
     ENDOGENOUS GDP M;
     INSTRUMENTS I GOV TB L_GDP L_M L_I L_GOV L_TB;
     INCOME: MODEL GDP = M I GOV;
     MONEY: MODEL M = GDP TB;
RUN;
```

(Note: FIML does not need instrumental variables.)

Notes

1 *EViews* has an option to apply different instrumental variables for each equation. See the *EViews* manual for more details.
2 The two-stage least squares (2SLS) results are shown in Output 6.1 in Chapter 6.
3 BASE SAS 9.4, SAS/ETS 13.1 and SAS/STAT 13.1. SAS Institute Inc., Cary, NC.

9 Vector autoregressive (VAR) models

Learning objectives

In this chapter, you should learn about:
- Differences between VAR models and simultaneous equations models;
- Importance of the lag order determination for VAR models;
- Use of VAR models for Granger-causality test, impulse-response analysis, variance decomposition analysis and forecasting.

9.1 VAR models

In simultaneous and structural econometric models, some variables are treated as endogenous and some as exogenous. This decision is often subjective and has been criticized by Sims (1980). According to Sims, if there exists a true simultaneity among a set of variables, they all have to be treated on an equal footing; there should not be any *a priori* distinction between endogenous and exogenous variables. In VAR models, all variables are treated as endogenous. Thus, VAR models can be viewed as unrestricted reduced-form equations of the correct but unknown structural models.[1] Considering that structural models are often misspecified in defining exogenous variables, use of VAR models may be an alternative approach.

VAR models are useful for analyzing dynamic relations among several time series and for forecasting their future values. The following is a simple VAR model with two variables and a lag order of two.

$$x_t = c_1 + a_{1,11}x_{t-1} + a_{1,12}y_{t-1} + a_{2,11}x_{t-2} + a_{2,12}y_{t-2} + u_{1t}$$

$$y_t = c_2 + a_{1,21}x_{t-1} + a_{1,22}y_{t-1} + a_{2,21}x_{t-2} + a_{2,22}y_{t-2} + u_{2t}$$

(9.1)

Re-expressing this using vector notations, we have

$$\begin{bmatrix} x_t \\ y_t \end{bmatrix} = \begin{bmatrix} c_1 \\ c_2 \end{bmatrix} + \begin{bmatrix} a_{1,11} & a_{1,12} \\ a_{1,21} & a_{1,22} \end{bmatrix} \begin{bmatrix} x_{t-1} \\ y_{t-1} \end{bmatrix} + \begin{bmatrix} a_{2,11} & a_{2,12} \\ a_{2,21} & a_{2,22} \end{bmatrix} \begin{bmatrix} x_{t-2} \\ y_{t-2} \end{bmatrix} + \begin{bmatrix} u_{1t} \\ u_{2t} \end{bmatrix},$$

$$Cov\begin{pmatrix} u_{1t} \\ u_{2t} \end{pmatrix} = \begin{bmatrix} \sigma_{11} & \sigma_{12} \\ \sigma_{21} & \sigma_{22} \end{bmatrix} = \Omega$$

or

$$Y_t = C + A_1 Y_{t-1} + A_2 Y_{t-2} + U_t$$

where $\sigma_{11} \equiv Cov(u_{1t}, u_{1t}) = Var(u_{1t})$, $\sigma_{22} = Var(u_{2t})$, and $\sigma_{12} = \sigma_{21} \equiv Cov(u_{1t}, u_{2t})$. The disturbances $U_t = [u_{1t}, u_{2t}]$ are serially uncorrelated; i.e., $Cov(u_{1t}, u_{1,t-s}) = 0$, $Cov(u_{2,t}, u_{2,t-s}) = 0$ and $Cov(u_{1,t}, u_{2,t-s}) = Cov(u_{1,t-s}, u_{2,t}) = 0$ for $s \geq 1$.[2]

A general form of VAR(p) models with k variables and a lag order of p is

$$Y_t = C + A_1 Y_{t-1} + \cdots + A_p Y_{t-p} + U_t$$

where Y_t is a $k \times 1$ vector of endogenous variables; C is a $k \times 1$ constant vector; $A_1, \cdots, A_p$ are $k \times k$ coefficient matrices; and U_t is a $k \times 1$ vector of innovations (or disturbances). If we include exogenous variables (Z_t), it will be

$$Y_t = C + A_1 Y_{t-1} + \cdots + A_p Y_{t-p} + B Z_t + U_t$$

where Z_t is a $d \times 1$ vector of exogenous variables; and B is a $k \times d$ coefficient matrix.

9.2 Estimation of VAR models

Each equation in a VAR model can be estimated by separately applying the OLS method.[3] Below are discussed some issues we need to consider in estimating VAR models.

Multicollinearity

Since the variables on the right-hand side are highly correlated in many cases, the standard errors of coefficient estimators tend to be large, implying that estimation of coefficients is not precise. However, it does not affect forecasting accuracy because forecasts are made by linear combinations of the variables on the right-hand side. Also, other VAR analyses (such as the impulse-response analysis, the variance decomposition analysis and the Granger-causality test) are little affected by the multicollinearity. Thus, VAR models are mainly used for these analyses and forecasting; individual coefficient estimates typically go unreported.

Over-parameterization

The number of parameters to be estimated increases rapidly as k and p increase; the number of VAR parameters increases as the square of the number of variables (k). For example, a ten-variable, five-lag VAR has 510 ($= 10 + 10^2 \times 5$) coefficients to be estimated including ten intercepts. As a result, the estimation could be inaccurate for a finite number of observations. Therefore, VAR models are often used for a small number of variables with short lag orders.

Determination of lag order

Several criteria have been suggested for the determination of lag order. Based on simulation results, Kilian (2001) concludes that the most accurate estimates of impulse-response functions and other VAR statistics can be obtained when the lag order is determined by the Akaike Information Criterion (AIC).

The lag order is chosen to minimize the value of the AIC over a range of alternative lag orders. According to Pindyck and Rubinfeld (1991, p. 217), however, a better practice would be to run the test for a few different lag structures and make sure that the results are not sensitive to the choice of lag length.

Alternatively, the lag order can be determined by a sequential likelihood ratio (LR) test. Starting with a sufficiently large lag, we size down to the right lag order by sequentially testing a null hypothesis that the coefficients on the last lag are jointly zero. If the null hypothesis is not rejected at a certain significance level (e.g., 5%), we decrease the lag order by one. We repeat this test until we first get a rejection. The lag order of the first rejected model is then selected for an optimal lag order.

Robustness check

If the lag order of a chosen VAR model is smaller than the *true* order, the disturbances are likely to be serially correlated. If so, the OLS estimator becomes inconsistent and also biased because of the endogeneity problem.[4] As a robustness check, you may test whether the serial correlations of disturbances are zero. *SAS* produces the *Chi*-square statistics and *p*-values of the Portmanteau test for the serial correlations of disturbances; its null hypothesis is $H_0 : \rho(1) = \cdots = \rho(s) = 0$ where $\rho(j)$ is the serial correlation between U_t and U_{t-j} ($j = 1, \cdots, s$).

9.3 Granger-causality test

Granger (2004) states that the causality has two components: (i) the cause occurs before the effect; and (ii) the cause contains information about the effect that is unique, and is in no other variable. A consequence of these two components is that the causal variable can help forecast the effect variable even after other variables have first been used. Thus, the idea of the Granger-causality test is to determine whether one time series is useful in forecasting another. Using a VAR model, it tests for zero restrictions on coefficients of lagged variables.

$$x_t = \alpha_0 + \alpha_1 x_{t-1} + \cdots + \alpha_k x_{t-k} + \beta_1 y_{t-1} + \cdots + \beta_k y_{t-k} + u_{1t}$$
$$y_t = \gamma_0 + \gamma_1 x_{t-1} + \cdots + \gamma_k x_{t-k} + \delta_1 y_{t-1} + \cdots + \delta_k y_{t-k} + u_{2t}$$

A joint null hypothesis $H_0 : \beta_1 = \cdots = \beta_k = 0$ implies that y does not Granger-cause x. Rejection of the null hypothesis concludes that the y values provide statistically significant information about future values of x in addition to lagged x values ($x_{t-1}, \cdots, x_{t-k}$). Similarly, a joint null hypothesis $H_0 : \gamma_1 = \cdots = \gamma_k = 0$ implies that x does not Granger-cause y.

When we test a simple hypothesis about one coefficient, e.g., $H_0 : \beta_1 = 0$, we use a *t*-statistic because the ratio of $\hat{\beta}_1 / se(\hat{\beta}_1)$ follows a Student-*t* distribution (thus called a *t* test). When we test a joint hypothesis about multiple coefficients, e.g., $H_0 : \beta_1 = \cdots = \beta_k = 0$, we use a test statistic which follows an *F*-distribution (thus called a *F* test).

Example 9.1 Spillover effects between the Korea and the US stock markets

---

An Excel file "9-var-spillover.xls" contains 461 daily observations on the NASDAQ, DOW Jones, KOSPI and KOSDAQ indices for the period from January 4, 2000 to December 28, 2001; a part of the

Excel file is shown below. In this example we will analyze the relations between the change rates of NASDAQ and KOSDAQ indices.

	A	B	C	D	
		KORdate	NASDAQ	DOW	KOSPI	KOSDAQ
1	KORdate	NASDAQ	DOW	KOSPI	KOSDAQ
2	20000104	4131.14	11357.5	1059.04	266
3	20000105	3901.68	10997.9	986.31	262.95
4	20000106	3877.54	11122.6	960.79	247.52
5	20000107	3727.12	11253.2	948.65	227.66

1 The data are daily observations, but their frequency is not regular because there were holidays when the stock markets were closed. So, when you import this file in *EViews*, choose Unstructured/Undated. Press the Genr button and generate change-rate variables by first-differencing the logarithms of the variables using a built-in function DLOG: DLN_NASDAQ = DLOG(NASDAQ) and DLN_KOSDAQ = DLOG(KOSDAQ).

2 Choose Quick/Estimate VAR . . . in the command window and enter appropriate information in the dialog box. Select Standard VAR for the VAR type and enter "DLN_NASDAQ DLN_KOS-DAQ" in the Endogenous variables section. For VAR(2), type "1 2" in the Lag Intervals for Endogenous box. Each pair of numbers defines a range of lags; "1 2" tells *EViews* to use the first through second lags of the variables included in the Endogenous variables section. The estimation results are shown in Output 9.1.

Output 9.1 Estimation results of VAR(2)

Vector Autoregression Estimates
Sample (adjusted): 4 461
Included observations: 458 after adjustments
Standard errors in ( ) & t-statistics in [ ]

	DLN_NASDAQ	DLN_KOSDAQ
DLN_NASDAQ(-1)	−0.067452	−0.090878
	(0.05153)	(0.06002)
	[−1.30890]	[−1.51413]
DLN_NASDAQ(-2)	−0.043714	0.150561
	(0.05138)	(0.05984)
	[−0.85087]	[2.51621]
DLN_KOSDAQ(-1)	0.105569	0.153924
	(0.04386)	(0.05109)
	[2.40676]	[3.01296]
DLN_KOSDAQ(-2)	−0.010954	−0.007454
	(0.04413)	(0.05140)
	[−0.24823]	[−0.14503]
C	−0.001370	−0.002153
	(0.00141)	(0.00165)
	[−0.96939]	[−1.30810]
R-squared	0.015297	0.035186
Adj. R-squared	0.006602	0.026666

	DLN_NASDAQ	DLN_KOSDAQ
Sum sq. resids	0.409115	0.554958
S.E. equation	0.030052	0.035001
F-statistic	1.759258	4.130091
Log likelihood	957.8502	888.0289
Akaike AIC	−4.160918	−3.856022
Schwarz SC	−4.115865	−3.810968
Mean dependent	−0.001471	−0.002690
S.D. dependent	0.030152	0.035477
Determinant resid covariance (dof adj.)		9.07E-07
Determinant resid covariance		8.88E-07
Log likelihood		1891.278
Akaike information criterion		−8.215188
Schwarz criterion		−8.125082

The estimated VAR(2) equations are

$$\hat{x}_t = -0.001370 - 0.067452\,x_{t-1} - 0.043714\,x_{t-2} + 0.105569\,y_{t-1} - 0.010954\,y_{t-2}$$
$$\hat{y}_t = -0.002153 - 0.090878\,x_{t-1} - 0.150561\,x_{t-2} + 0.153924\,y_{t-1} - 0.007454\,y_{t-2}$$

where $x_t = DLN\_NASDAQ_t$ and $y_t = DLN\_KOSDAQ_t$.

3 To determine the lag order (p), we need to estimate several models with different lag orders. After you make a table shown below, choose the model which has the smallest value of the AIC, as suggested by Kilian (2001).

p	1	2	3	4
AIC	−8.200	**−8.215188**	−8.2118	−8.2042

4 Alternatively, you may determine the lag order by testing down to the right lag order. After estimating a VAR model, you choose View/Lag Structure/Lag Length Criteria . . . in the VAR window. You will be prompted to specify the maximum lag order (m) to test for. The output displays the sequential likelihood ratio (LR) test results along with other information criteria for all lags up to the specified maximum (m). In Output 9.2, the selected lag is indicated by an asterisk (*).

Output 9.2 VAR lag order selection criteria

VAR Lag Order Selection Criteria
Endogenous variables: DLN_NASDAQ DLN_KOSDAQ
Exogenous variables: C
Sample: 1 461
Included observations: 456

Lag	LogL	LR	FPE	AIC	SC	HQ
0	1872.751	NA	9.37e-07	−8.205047	−8.186966*	−8.197925*
1	1877.882	10.19521	9.32e-07	−8.210009	−8.155766	−8.188642
2	1884.123	12.34442*	9.23e-07*	−8.219837*	−8.129431	−8.184224
3	1886.476	4.634809	9.30e-07	−8.212615	−8.086047	−8.162757
4	1888.550	4.066244	9.38e-07	−8.204168	−8.041438	−8.140065

* indicates lag order selected by the criterion
LR: sequential modified LR test statistic (each test at 5% level)
FPE: Final prediction error
AIC: Akaike information criterion
SC: Schwarz information criterion
HQ: Hannan-Quinn information criterion

5   Test for Causality (Spillover effects)

To define a group of two variables for a causality test, press Objects/New Object. . . /Group in the Workfile toolbar. And enter the variable names, "DLN_NASDAQ DLN_KOSDAQ." In the Group toolbar, choose View/Granger Causality . . . and enter the lag order.

Output 9.3   Granger causality tests

Pairwise Granger Causality Tests
Sample: 1 461
Lags: 2

Null Hypothesis:	Obs	F-Statistic	Probability
DLN_KOSDAQ does not Granger-Cause DLN_NASDAQ	458	2.89631	0.05625
DLN_NASDAQ does not Granger-Cause DLN_KOSDAQ		4.45857	0.01209

According to the test results in Output 9.3, the null hypothesis that KOSDAQ does not Granger-cause NASDAQ is not rejected (p-value = 0.05625) at a 5% significance level. In contrast, the p-value of 0.01209 for the other hypothesis indicates that NASDAQ Granger-causes KOSDAQ.

9.4 Forecasting

Forecasts of future values of a variable can be made using an estimated VAR model. Since forecasts by a VAR model are linear combinations of the variables on the right-hand side, multicollinearity does not matter. For a simple example, we use the following VAR(1) model.

$$\begin{bmatrix} x_t \\ y_t \end{bmatrix} = \begin{bmatrix} c_1 \\ c_2 \end{bmatrix} + \begin{bmatrix} a_{11} & a_{12} \\ a_{21} & a_{22} \end{bmatrix} \begin{bmatrix} x_{t-1} \\ y_{t-1} \end{bmatrix} + \begin{bmatrix} u_{1t} \\ u_{2t} \end{bmatrix}$$

Using the vector and matrix notations, the VAR(1) model is expressed as

$$Y_t = C + A_1 Y_{t-1} + U_t$$

The one-period-ahead forecasts made at period t are

$$Y_{t+1} = C + A_1 Y_t + U_{t+1}$$
$$\Rightarrow Y_{t+1|t} = E\left(Y_{t+1}|I_t\right) = C + A_1 Y_t$$

Substituting the OLS estimates for the coefficients, we can calculate the forecasts.

$$Y_{t+1|t} = \hat{C} + \hat{A}_1 Y_t$$

$$\Rightarrow x_{t+1|t} = \hat{c}_1 + \hat{a}_{11} x_t + \hat{a}_{12} y_t$$
$$y_{t+1|t} = \hat{c}_2 + \hat{a}_{21} x_t + \hat{a}_{22} y_t$$

The two-period-ahead forecasts made at period t are

$$Y_{t+2} = C + A_1 Y_{t+1} + U_{t+2}$$
$$\Rightarrow Y_{t+2|t} = C + A_1 Y_{t+1|t} = C + A_1 \left(C + A_1 Y_t\right) = C\left(1 + A_1\right) + A_1^2 Y_t$$

In the same way, multi-period-ahead forecasts can be made.

9.5 Impulse-response analysis

A shock to a variable in a VAR model directly affects the variable and is also transmitted to the other variables through the dynamic structure of a VAR model. An impulse-response function traces the effects of a shock to one variable on the current and future values of all variables included in a VAR model. With an interpretation of a shock as a policy-induced change, the impulse-response analysis can be used for estimating policy effects.

For this analysis, you need to specify the ordering of the variables in your VAR model. A somewhat arbitrary but common method is to put first the variable whose innovation is most independent (i.e., least influenced by the other innovations), to put second the variable whose innovation is second most independent and so on.[5]

The innovations, u_{1t} and u_{2t} in Eq. (9.1), are usually contemporaneously correlated, so that they have a common component which cannot be associated with a specific variable. One method is to attribute all of the effect of any common component to the variable that comes first, i.e., the variable which you think is most independent. To do this, we apply the Cholesky decomposition to the VAR models.

Cholesky decomposition

Suppose x is more exogenous than y in Eq. (9.1). The covariance matrix Ω can be transformed into a lower triangle form by applying the Cholesky decomposition.

$$\Omega = L \Lambda L' = \begin{bmatrix} l_{11} & 0 \\ l_{21} & l_{22} \end{bmatrix} \begin{bmatrix} \sigma_x^2 & 0 \\ 0 & \sigma_y^2 \end{bmatrix} \begin{bmatrix} l_{11} & 0 \\ l_{21} & l_{22} \end{bmatrix}'$$

Thus, the disturbances u_{1t} and u_{2t} are transformed into contemporaneously independent innovations ε_{xt} and ε_{yt} as follows.

$$U_t = LE_t \Rightarrow \begin{bmatrix} u_{1t} \\ u_{2t} \end{bmatrix} = \begin{bmatrix} l_{11} & 0 \\ l_{21} & l_{22} \end{bmatrix} \begin{bmatrix} \varepsilon_{xt} \\ \varepsilon_{yt} \end{bmatrix}, \text{ where } Cov \begin{pmatrix} \varepsilon_{xt} \\ \varepsilon_{yt} \end{pmatrix} = \begin{bmatrix} \sigma_x^2 & 0 \\ 0 & \sigma_y^2 \end{bmatrix}$$

Figure 9.1 shows how the Cholesky decomposition transforms the original disturbances.

The Cholesky decomposition transforms the contemporaneously correlated disturbances (u_{1t}, u_{2t}) into uncorrelated disturbances (ε_{xt}, ε_{yt}). In doing so, the common component is assigned to the variable (x) which comes first. Thus, x_t is influenced by its own disturbance ε_{xt} only while y_t is by both ε_{xt} and ε_{yt}; i.e., x_t is more independently determined than y_t.

Using the Cholesky-decomposed equations, the impulse-response analysis estimates the effects of a unit change in ε_{xt} (i.e., one standard deviation shock to ε_{xt}) on current and future values of x and y. To see how the impulse-response analysis works, we use the following VAR(1) which includes Cholesky-decomposed disturbances.

$$\begin{aligned} x_t &= a_{11}x_{t-1} + a_{12}y_{t-1} + l_{11}\varepsilon_{xt} \\ y_t &= a_{21}x_{t-1} + a_{22}y_{t-1} + l_{21}\varepsilon_{xt} + l_{22}\varepsilon_{yt} \end{aligned} \tag{9.2}$$

The contemporaneous responses, i.e., the effects of ε_{xt}, ε_{yt} on x_t, y_t are

$$\frac{\partial x_t}{\partial \varepsilon_{xt}} = l_{11} \qquad \frac{\partial x_t}{\partial \varepsilon_{yt}} = 0$$

$$\frac{\partial y_t}{\partial \varepsilon_{xt}} = l_{21} \qquad \frac{\partial y_t}{\partial \varepsilon_{yt}} = l_{22}$$

To calculate the impulse responses for one-period horizon, we rewrite Eq. (9.2) for x_{t+1}, y_{t+1}.

$$\begin{aligned} x_{t+1} &= a_{11}x_t + a_{12}y_t + l_{11}\varepsilon_{x,t+1} \\ &= a_{11} \times (a_{11}x_{t-1} + a_{12}y_{t-1} + l_{11}\varepsilon_{xt}) \\ &\quad + a_{12} \times (a_{21}x_{t-1} + a_{22}y_{t-1} + l_{21}\varepsilon_{xt} + l_{22}\varepsilon_{yt}) \\ &\quad + l_{11}\varepsilon_{x,t+1} \end{aligned}$$

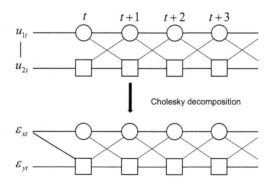

Figure 9.1 Cholesky decomposition

Note: Variables x and y are denoted by ○ and □, respectively.

$$y_{t+1} = a_{21}x_t + a_{22}y_t + l_{21}\varepsilon_{x,t+1} + l_{22}\varepsilon_{y,t+1}$$
$$= a_{21} \times (a_{11}x_{t-1} + a_{12}y_{t-1} + l_{11}\varepsilon_{xt})$$
$$+ a_{22} \times (a_{21}x_{t-1} + a_{22}y_{t-1} + l_{21}\varepsilon_{xt} + l_{22}\varepsilon_{yt})$$
$$+ (l_{21}\varepsilon_{x,t+1} + l_{22}\varepsilon_{y,t+1})$$

Then the one-period-horizon responses, i.e., the effects of ε_{xt}, ε_{yt} on x_{t+1}, y_{t+1} are

$$\frac{\partial x_{t+1}}{\partial \varepsilon_{xt}} = a_{11}l_{11} + a_{12}l_{21} \qquad \frac{\partial x_{t+1}}{\partial \varepsilon_{yt}} = a_{12}l_{22}$$

$$\frac{\partial y_{t+1}}{\partial \varepsilon_{xt}} = a_{21}l_{11} + a_{22}l_{21} \qquad \frac{\partial y_{t+1}}{\partial \varepsilon_{yt}} = a_{22}l_{22}$$

In the same way, we can derive the impulse responses for multiperiod horizons.

Example 9.2 Spillover effects (continued)

Choose Impulse from the VAR toolbar. In the Display section, choose Multiple graphs for graphical results and Table for tabulated results. In the Impulse Definition section, choose Cholesky-dof adjusted and specify the ordering of the variables in the box of Cholesky Ordering, according to the extent of their independence; the more independent variable comes first. We enter "DLN_NASDAQ DLN_KOSDAQ."

The impulse-response analysis shown in Figure 9.2 indicates that

1   the effect of NASDAQ shocks on the change rate of NASDAQ is immediate and disappears the next day;
2   NASDAQ does not respond to the shocks to KOSDAQ;
3   KOSDAQ responds to the shocks to NASDAQ for three days;
4   The effect of KOSDAQ shocks on the change rate of KOSDAQ is immediate and lasts until the next day.

9.6 Variance decomposition analysis

The variance-decomposition analysis decomposes variation (or forecast error, uncertainty) in each variable into the past shocks to the variables in a VAR model. It is useful for identifying the sources which have contributed to the changes of each variable.

According to Eq. (9.2), the one-period-ahead forecast error for x_t is $l_{11}\varepsilon_{xt}$.[6]

$$\text{Variance of the forecast error} = l_{11}^2 \sigma_x^2$$
$$\Rightarrow \quad \text{contribution by } \varepsilon_{xt} = 100\%$$
$$\text{contribution by } \varepsilon_{yt} = 0$$

The one-period-ahead forecast error for y_t is $l_{21}\varepsilon_{xt} + l_{22}\varepsilon_{yt}$.

$$\text{Variance of the forecast error} = l_{21}^2 \sigma_x^2 + l_{22}^2 \sigma_y^2$$
$$\Rightarrow \quad \text{contribution by } \varepsilon_{xt} = \frac{l_{21}^2 \sigma_x^2}{l_{21}^2 \sigma_x^2 + l_{22}^2 \sigma_y^2}$$

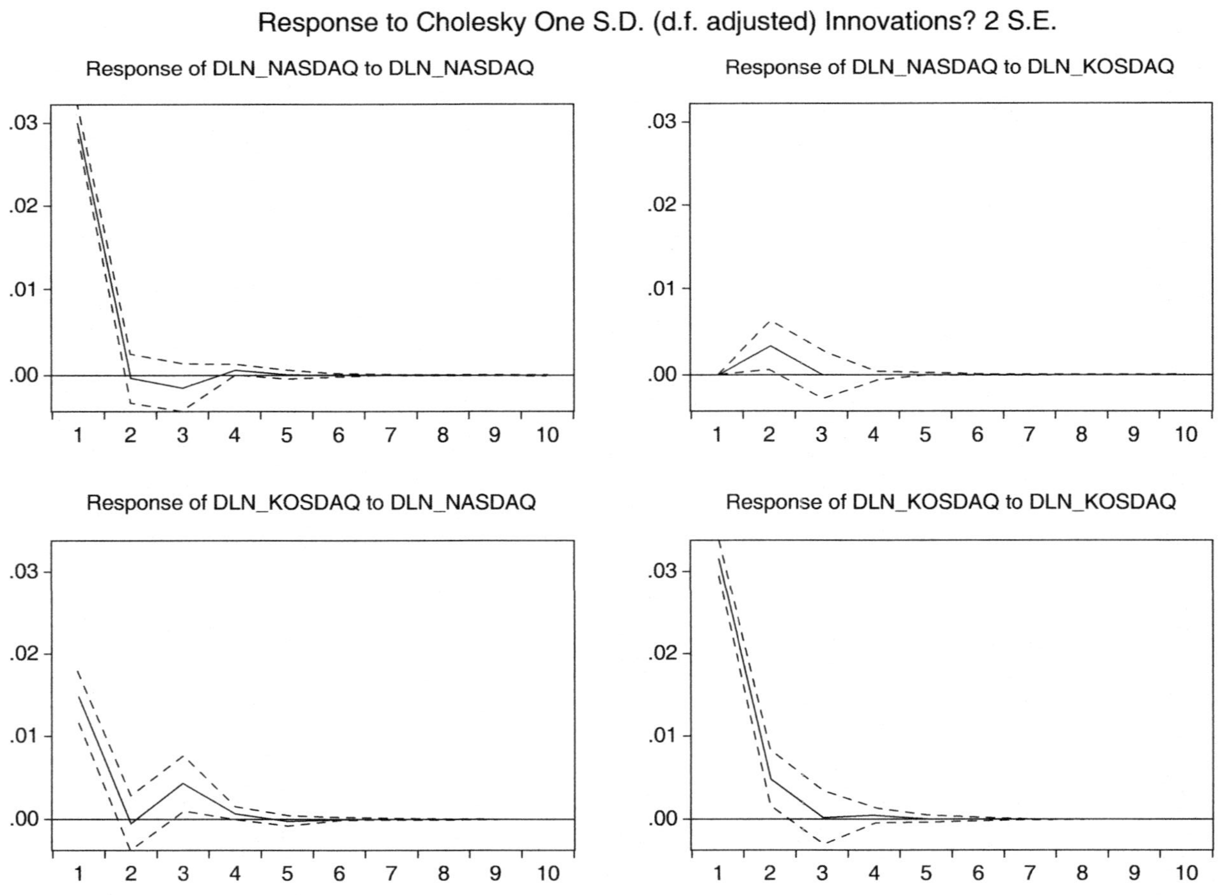
Response to Cholesky One S.D. (d.f. adjusted) Innovations? 2 S.E.
Response of DLN_NASDAQ to DLN_NASDAQ
Response of DLN_NASDAQ to DLN_KOSDAQ
Response of DLN_KOSDAQ to DLN_NASDAQ
Response of DLN_KOSDAQ to DLN_KOSDAQ
.03
.02
.01
.00
1
2
3
4
5
6
7
8
9
10

Figure 9.2 Impulse-response analysis

Notes: In the time horizon, '1' denotes the same day, '2' the next day and so on. The solid lines show mean values, and the dotted lines show 95% confidence intervals.

$$\text{contribution by } \varepsilon_{yt} = \frac{l_{22}^2 \sigma_y^2}{l_{21}^2 \sigma_x^2 + l_{22}^2 \sigma_y^2}$$

In the same way, we can decompose the variances of k-period-ahead forecast errors ($k > 1$).

Example 9.3 Spillover effects (continued)

To obtain the variance decomposition, select View/Variance Decomposition . . . from the VAR toolbar. We provide the same information as in the above impulse-response analysis.

Output 9.4 Variance decomposition analysis

Variance Decomposition of DLN_NASDAQ:

Period	S.E.	DLN_NASDAQ	DLN_KOSDAQ
1	0.030052	100.0000	0.000000
2	0.030241	98.77555	1.224445
3	0.030278	98.77817	1.221831
4	0.030284	98.77539	1.224615
5	0.030284	98.77493	1.225069

Variance Decomposition of DLN_KOSDAQ:

Period	S.E.	DLN_NASDAQ	DLN_KOSDAQ
1	0.035001	17.98342	82.01658
2	0.035342	17.65377	82.34623
3	0.035614	18.90272	81.09728
4	0.035626	18.93438	81.06562
5	0.035626	18.93673	81.06327

Cholesky Ordering: DLN_NASDAQ DLN_KOSDAQ

The tabulated results in Output 9.4 indicate that

a   the variation of the change rate of NASDAQ is caused mostly (over 98%) by its own disturbances; and

b   the variation of the change rate of KOSDAQ is caused by its own disturbances (about 81%) and also by NASDAQ disturbances (almost 19%).

9.7 Applications

9.7.1 Stock and Watson (2001)[7]

Sims (1980) provided a new macroeconometric framework that held great promise, vector autoregressions (VARs). A univariate autoregression is a single-equation, single-variable linear model in which the current value of a variable is explained by its own lagged values. A VAR is an n-equation, n-variable linear model in which each variable is in turn explained by its own lagged values, plus past values of the other $n-1$ variables. This simple framework provides a systematic way to capture rich dynamics in multiple time series. In data description and forecasting, VARs have proven to be powerful and reliable tools.[8]

This study estimates three-variable VARs using quarterly US data on the rate of price inflation (π_t), the unemployment rate (u_t) and the interest rate (R_t, specifically, the federal funds rate) from 1960:I–2000:IV.

(i) Granger-causality tests

It examines whether lagged values of each variable in the row labeled *Regressor* help to predict the variables in the column labeled *Dependent Variable*. Panel A of Table 9.1 shows that the unemployment

Table 9.1 VAR descriptive statistics for (π, u, R)

A. Granger-causality tests

Regressor	Dependent variable in regression		
	π	u	R
π	0.00	0.31	0.00
u	0.02	0.00	0.00
R	0.27	0.01	0.00

B. Variance decomposition from the recursive VAR ordered as π, u, R

B.i. Variance decomposition of π

Forecast horizon	Forecast standard error	Variance decomposition		
		π	u	R
1	0.96	100	0	0
4	1.34	88	10	2
8	1.75	82	17	1
12	1.97	82	16	2

B.ii. Variance decomposition of u

Forecast horizon	Forecast standard error	Variance decomposition		
		π	u	R
1	0.23	1	99	0
4	0.64	0	98	2
8	0.79	7	82	11
12	0.92	16	66	18

B.iii. Variance decomposition of R

Forecast horizon	Forecast standard error	Variance decomposition		
		π	u	R
1	0.85	2	19	79
4	1.84	9	50	41
8	2.44	12	60	28
12	2.63	16	59	25

Source: Stock and Watson (2001, Table 1 on page 105).

Notes: π denotes the rate of price inflation, u denotes the unemployment rate and R denotes the Federal Funds interest rate. The entries in Panel A show the p-values for F-tests that lags of the variable in the row labeled *Regressor* do not enter the reduced-form equation for the column variable labeled *Dependent variable*. The results were computed from a VAR with four lags and a constant term over the 1960:I–2000:IV sample period.

rate helps to predict inflation at the 5% significance level (the p-value is 0.02), but the federal funds rate does not (the p-value is 0.27). Inflation does not help to predict the unemployment rate, but the federal funds rate does. Both inflation and the unemployment rates help predict the federal funds interest rate.

(ii) Variance decompositions

Panel B of Table 9.1 shows the variance decomposition results obtained with the order of π_t, u_t, R_t. It suggests considerable interaction among the variables. For example, at the 12-quarter horizon, 75 (= 16+59) % of the variance of the federal funds interest rate is attributed to the inflation and unemployment shocks.

(iii) Impulse responses

Figure 9.3 shows the impulse responses when the order of π_t, u_t, R_t is used. The first row shows the effect of an unexpected 1 percentage point increase in inflation on all three variables, as it works

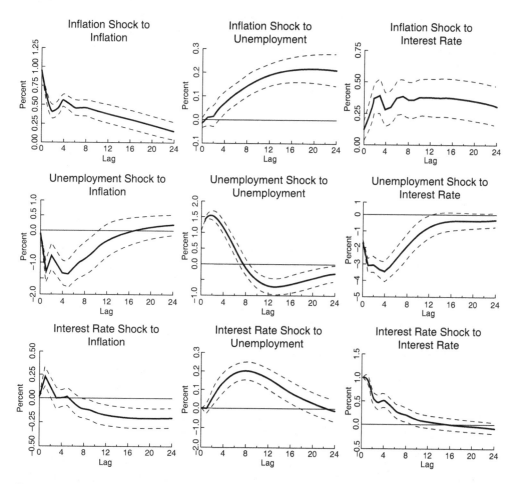

Figure 9.3 Impulse responses in the inflation-unemployment-interest rate recursive VAR

Source: Stock and Watson (2001, Figure 1 on page 107).

Note: The dotted lines indicate the 95% confidence interval bands.

through the VAR system with the coefficients estimated from actual data. The second row shows the effect of an unexpected increase of 1 percentage point in the unemployment rate and the third row shows the corresponding effect for the interest rate. Also plotted are ±1 standard error bands, which yield an approximate 66% confidence interval for each of the impulse responses. These estimated impulse responses show patterns of persistent common variation. For example, an unexpected rise in inflation slowly fades away over 24 quarters and is associated with a persistent increase in unemployment and interest rates.

(iv) Forecasting

The forecast h steps ahead is computed by estimating the VAR model through a given quarter, making the forecast h steps ahead, reestimating the VAR through the next quarter, making the next h-step-ahead forecast and so on through the forecast period.[9]

As a comparison, pseudo out-of-sample forecasts were also computed for a univariate autoregression with four lags (that is, a regression of the variable on lags of its own past values) and for a random walk forecast. Table 9.2 shows the root mean square forecast error for each of the forecasting methods.[10] It indicates that the VAR either does no worse than or improves upon the univariate autoregression and that both improve upon the random walk forecast.

9.7.2 Zhang, Fan, Tsai and Wei (2008)

The US dollar is frequently used as the invoicing currency of international crude oil trading. Hence, the fluctuation in the US dollar exchange rate is believed to underlie the volatility of crude oil price and especially its forecasting accuracy. This study examines the mean-price and the volatility **spillover effects** using VAR and ARCH-type models; the part on the mean-price spillover is introduced in this chapter and the part on the volatility spillover is in the next chapter.

(i) Data

Daily spot WTI crude oil price that is quoted in US dollars per barrel is used in this study. As the exchange of euro against US dollar accounts for the largest market trades in the total international

Table 9.2 Root mean squared errors of simulated out-of-sample forecasts, 1985:1–2000:IV

Forecast horizon	Inflation rate			Unemployment rate			Interest rate		
	RW	AR	VAR	RW	AR	VAR	RW	AR	VAR
2 quarters	0.82	0.70	0.68	0.34	0.28	0.29	0.79	0.77	0.68
4 quarters	0.73	0.65	0.63	0.62	0.52	0.53	1.36	1.25	1.07
8 quarters	0.75	0.75	0.75	0.12	0.95	0.78	2.18	1.92	1.70

Source: Stock and Watson (2001, Table 2 on page 108).

Notes: Entries are the root mean squared error of forecasts computed recursively for univariate and vector autoregressions (each with four lags) and a random walk ("no change") model. Results for the random walk and univariate autoregressions are shown in columns labeled *RW* and *AR*, respectively. Each model was estimated using data from 1960:I through the beginning of the forecast period. Forecasts for the inflation rate are for the average value of inflation over the period. Forecasts for the unemployment rate and interest rate are for the final quarter of the forecast period.

exchange, this study uses the daily spot (nominal) exchange rate of euro against US dollar. The data period is from January 4, 2000 to May 31, 2005.

(ii) VAR model

In terms of economics, mean spillover effect between two markets refers to the fact that the price in one market is affected not only by its own previous price movement but also by previous prices in other markets. In the long run, the test of mean spillover effect plays an important role in assessing whether the impact of change in the US dollar exchange rate on crude oil price is significant, and whether the change in the US dollar exchange rate can help to forecast future trends of the latter.

Mean spillover effect is based on a VAR model, that is, the standard Granger-causality test. After the optimal lagged order is set by the least values of AIC and SC, the Granger-causality test is carried out to detect the mean spillover effect between the crude oil price and the US dollar exchange rate. In order to use the notion of elasticity, the VAR model estimated in this study is expressed in logarithmic values.

$$\ln PE_t = \alpha_0 + \sum_{j=1}^{J} \alpha_{1j} \ln PE_{t-j} + \sum_{j=1}^{J} \alpha_{2j} \ln PO_{t-j} + u_t$$

$$\ln PO_t = \beta_0 + \sum_{j=1}^{J} \beta_{1j} \ln PE_{t-j} + \sum_{j=1}^{J} \beta_{2j} \ln PO_{t-j} + \varepsilon_t$$

where $\ln PE_t$ is the logarithmic US dollar exchange rate and $\ln PO_t$ is the logarithmic oil price in day t.

(iii) Mean spillover effect: Granger-causality test

The null hypothesis that changes of the oil price do not Granger-cause changes of the US dollar exchange rate, i.e., $H_0 : \alpha_{21} = \alpha_{22} = \cdots = \alpha_{2J} = 0$, is not rejected with a p-value of 0.9329. The null hypothesis that changes of the US dollar exchange rate do not Granger-cause changes of the international crude oil price, i.e., $H_0 : \beta_{11} = \beta_{12} = \cdots = \beta_{1J} = 0$, is rejected with a p-value of 0.0032. This implies that the international oil price is markedly affected by changes of the previous US dollar exchange rate, whereas the reverse does not work.

9.7.3 Trusov, Bucklin, and Pausels (2009)

The objective of this research is to develop and estimate a model that captures the dynamic relationships among new member acquisition, word-of-mouth (WOM) referrals and traditional marketing activities. WOM marketing is a particularly prominent feature on the Internet. The Internet provides numerous venues for consumers to share their views, preferences or experiences with others, as well as opportunities for firms to take advantage of WOM marketing. Thus, it is important to understand whether WOM is truly effective and, if so, how its impact compares with traditional marketing activities.

One of the fastest-growing arenas of the World Wide Web is the space of so-called social networking sites. A social networking site is typically initiated by a small group of founders who send out invitations to join the site to the members of their own personal networks. In turn, new members send invitations to their networks, and so on. Thus, invitations (i.e., WOM referrals) have been the foremost driving force for sites to acquire new members. As social networking sites mature, they may begin to increase their use of traditional marketing tools. Therefore, management may begin to question the relative effectiveness of WOM at this stage.

Modeling approach

The authors use the following approach to modeling the effects of WOM and traditional marketing on new member sign-ups.

a   They test for the potential dynamic relationships among WOM, marketing and new customer acquisition and for the potential permanent effects of these communication mechanisms.[11]

b   They specify a vector autoregressive (VAR) model that accounts for endogeneity and the dynamic response and interactions between marketing variables and outcomes.

c   They estimate the short-term and long-term responses of sign-ups to WOM and traditional marketing actions and compute the corresponding elasticities.

The VAR is used to describe the dynamic relationship of sign-ups (*S*), WOM referrals (*W*), media appearances (*M*) and promotional events (*E*).

$$Y_t = A + B \times t + \sum_{j=1}^{J} C^j Y_{t-j} + (dummies) + e_t \tag{9.3}$$

where $Y_t = | S_t, W_t, M_t, E_t |$ ', a 4x1 column vector of variables; *A* and *B* are 4x1 column vectors of parameters; *t* is included to capture a deterministic trend; C^j is a 4x4 coefficient matrix for lag *j*; dummy variables are included to indicate days of the week and holidays; and e_t is a 4x1 vector of disturbances with mean 0 and a 4x4 variance-covariance matrix Σ. Instantaneous effects among the variables (or endogeneity caused by simultaneous relation) are reflected in Σ; the diagonal elements in Σ are variances and the off-diagonal elements are covariances. If there exist instantaneous effects, the corresponding off-diagonal elements are nonzero. The lag order *J* is determined on the basis of the Akaike information criterion.

The parameters *A*, *B* and *C* are to be estimated. Because VAR model parameters are not interpretable on their own (Sims, 1980), effect sizes and significance are determined through the analysis of impulse-response functions (IRFs) and elasticities computed on the basis of the model. With regard to identification, the authors adopt the generalized IRF (i.e., simultaneous-shocking approach; Pesaran and Shin, 1998). This uses information in the residual variance-covariance matrix of the VAR model instead of requiring the researcher to impose a causal ordering among the endogenous variables (Dekipme and Hanssens, 1999). They also use IRFs to disentangle the short- and long-term effects of WOM and traditional marketing on sign-ups.

They translate IRFs into elasticities as follows: First, the IRF analysis yields the total change in number of sign-ups, ΔS, in response to a one-standard-deviation shock to, for example, WOM referrals. Second, using the data, they calculate the standard deviation for WOM referrals (σ_W) and mean values for sign-ups ($\bar{S}$) and WOM referrals ($\bar{W}$). Finally, they calculate the elasticity:

$$\text{elasticity} = \frac{\dfrac{\Delta S}{\bar{S}}}{\dfrac{\sigma_W}{\bar{W}}}$$

Note that this is a standard elasticity formula, except that σ_W is substituted for ΔW because σ_W is the change in *W* used to generate the IRF.

Data

The VAR model is applied to data from one of the major social networking sites, which prefers to remain anonymous. The dataset contains 36 weeks of the daily number of sign-ups and referrals (provided to the authors by the company) along with marketing events and media activity (obtained from third-party sources). The data cover the period in 2005 from February 1 to October 16.

Empirical results: Granger-causality test for dynamic relationship

This study begins empirical analysis by first testing for stationarity vs. evolution in each time series. The unit-root tests indicated trend stationarity in all series (i.e., all series appeared to be stationary after a deterministic trend is controlled for). This indicates that model estimations can be performed with all variables in levels, as depicted in Eq. (9.3). To investigate whether dynamic relationships are present among the variables, the authors conducted Granger-causality tests. Each cell in Table 9.3 gives the minimum *p*-value obtained from the causality tests as conducted from 1 lag to 20 lags.[12]

The results clearly show that dynamic relationships are present among the variables in the data. As expected, Granger-causality is detected for WOM referrals, media and events on sign-ups (the direct effects). In addition, Granger-causality is found for many of the other pairings. The results from the Granger-causality tests indicate the need to consider the full dynamic system, as in the above VAR model, and to account for the indirect effects of marketing actions.

Empirical results: short-term and long-term effects

To gauge the impact of WOM and the two traditional marketing variables on new sign-ups over time, the authors compute IRFs on the basis of the estimated VAR system parameters. The IRFs trace the incremental effect of a one-standard-deviation shock in WOM, events and media on the future values of sign-ups. These enable us to examine the carryover effects of each activity on sign-ups while fully accounting for the indirect effects of these activities in a dynamic system. Figure 9.4 plots the three IRFs for the effect of WOM referrals, media and events on new sign-ups over time.

The top panel in Figure 9.4 shows that the WOM effect on sign-ups remains significantly different from zero for approximately three weeks. In contrast, the effects of media and events (the middle and bottom panels of Figure 9.4) lose significance within just a few days. Compared with traditional marketing activities, the WOM referrals induce both a larger short-term response and a substantially longer carryover effect. These results highlight the need for researchers to employ models that can also account for the longer-term effects of WOM marketing.

The authors also calculate several short-term elasticities and a long-term elasticity for WOM, events and media. The immediate (one day) elasticity of WOM (0.068) is 8.5 times higher than those of events and media (0.008). The long-term elasticity of WOM referrals (0.532) is approximately 20 times higher than the elasticity for marketing events (0.532 vs. 0.026) and 30 times higher than the elasticity for media appearances (0.532 vs. 0.017). The estimated WOM elasticity of 0.532

Table 9.3 Results of the Granger-causality tests (minimum *p*-values across 20 lags)

Dependent variable is Granger-caused by	Sign-ups	WOM referrals	Media	Events
Sign-ups	–	0.02[a]	0.00	0.00
WOM referrals	0.00	–	0.22	0.08
Media	0.00	0.58	–	0.02
Events	0.02	0.00	0.01	–

Source: Trusov et al. (2009, Table 3 on page 95).
[a] WOM referrals are Granger-caused by sign-ups at the 0.02 significance level.

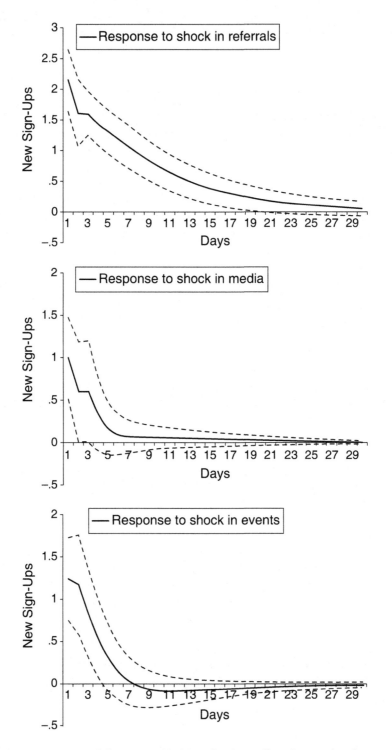

Figure 9.4 IRFs: Responses of sign-ups to shock in referrals, media and promotional events

Source: Trusov et al. (2009, Figure 4 on p. 96).

Note: The dotted lines indicate the 95% confidence interval bands.

substantially exceeds the range of values for advertising elasticities reported in the literature. Thus, these empirical findings support the notion that WOM may be among the most effective marketing communication strategies.

9.8 Summary

1   The VAR models treat all variables as endogenous variables and include their lagged variables on the right-hand side.
2   Since all explanatory variables in VAR models are lagged dependent variables $(Y_{t-1}, \cdots, Y_{t-p})$, they were predetermined before time period t and thus are not correlated with the disturbances in time period t, U_t. Therefore, the OLS estimation method produces consistent estimators. See Chapter 10 for an explanation about the OLS unbiasedness and consistency for dynamic models including VAR models.
3   It is important to carefully determine the lag order of VAR models. If a too small lag order is used (i.e., significant lagged dependent variables are omitted), the disturbances are likely to be serially correlated. If so, the OLS estimator becomes inconsistent and also biased; this belongs to the correlated-omitted-variable problem.
4   VAR models are useful for analyzing dynamic relations among several time series: Granger-causality test, impulse-response analysis and variance decomposition analysis. The VAR models are also useful for forecasting future values.

Review questions

1   We examine the causal relation between tax revenues and government expenditures in a country using the following VAR(3) model. In order to interpret estimates in terms of elasticity, the VAR model is expressed in logarithmic values.

$$\ln TAX_t = \alpha_0 + \sum_{j=1}^{3} \alpha_j \ln TAX_{t-j} + \sum_{j=1}^{3} \beta_j \ln EXP_{t-j} + u_t$$

$$\ln EXP_t = \gamma_0 + \sum_{j=1}^{3} \gamma_j \ln TAX_{t-j} + \sum_{j=1}^{3} \delta_j \ln EXP_{t-j} + \varepsilon_t$$

where $\ln TAX_t$ is the logarithmic tax revenue and $\ln EXP_t$ is the logarithmic government expenditure in year t. The test results of the Granger-causality are summarized in the following table.

Null hypothesis	F-statistic	p-value
$\ln TAX$ does not Granger-cause $\ln EXP$	5.78	0.007
$\ln EXP$ does not Granger-cause $\ln TAX$	1.25	0.321

(a)   We test if tax revenue changes lead government expenditure changes. For this Granger-causality test, write the null hypothesis using coefficients in the VAR model.
(b)   Make a conclusion about the causality in (a) at a 5% significance level.
(c)   We also test if government expenditures cause tax revenues. For this Granger-causality test, write the null hypothesis using coefficients in the VAR model.
(d)   Make a conclusion about the causality in (c) at a 5% significance level.

2   Suppose that the true model is the following VAR(2) model in which all coefficients are significantly different from zero, i.e., $a_{ij} \neq 0$ for $i = 1,2$ and $j = 1,2,3,4$.

$$x_t = a_{10} + a_{11}x_{t-1} + a_{12}y_{t-1} + a_{13}x_{t-2} + a_{14}y_{t-2} + u_{1,t}$$
$$y_t = a_{20} + a_{21}x_{t-1} + a_{22}y_{t-1} + a_{23}x_{t-2} + a_{24}y_{t-2} + u_{2,t}$$

The disturbances $\{u_{1,t}, u_{2,t}\}$ are serially uncorrelated; $Cov(u_{1,t}, u_{1,t-s}) = 0$, $Cov(u_{2,t}, u_{2,t-s}) = 0$ and $Cov(u_{1,t}, u_{2,t-s}) = Cov(u_{1,t-s}, u_{2,t}) = 0$ for $s \geq 1$. If we use the following under-specified VAR(1) model for estimation, its disturbances $\{w_{1,t}, w_{2,t}\}$ will be serially correlated.

$$x_t = b_{10} + b_{11}x_{t-1} + b_{12}y_{t-1} + w_{1,t}$$
$$y_t = b_{20} + b_{21}x_{t-1} + b_{22}y_{t-1} + w_{2,t}$$

(a) Explain that $\{w_{1,t}\}$ is autocorrelated, e.g., $Cov(w_{1,t}, w_{1,t-1}) \neq 0$.
(b) Explain that $\{w_{2,t}\}$ is autocorrelated, e.g., $Cov(w_{2,t}, w_{2,t-1}) \neq 0$.
(c) Explain that $\{w_{1,t}\}$ and $\{w_{2,t}\}$ are serially cross-correlated, e.g., $Cov(w_{1,t}, w_{2,t-1}) \neq 0$.
(d) Explain why the OLS estimators are not consistent.

3   An Excel file "9-var-spillover.xls" contains 461 daily observations on the Dow Jones and the BBB indices for the period from January 4, 2000 to December 28, 2001. Using the dataset, please answer the following questions about the relations between the change rates of the Dow Jones and the Kospi index. (You first need to create change-rate variables.)

(a) Identify a VAR model. In determining the lag order, two approaches (the AIC criterion and the sequential test) are widely used. Please use both approaches.
(b) Estimate the identified model.
(c) Do a robustness check for the estimated model. This is to test if the residuals from your estimated model in (b) show any significant autocorrelation. In your answer, please include the null hypothesis and p-values.
(d) Test if the Dow Jones index Granger-causes the Kospi index. Please include the null hypothesis and its p-value.
(e) Test if the Kospi index Granger-causes the Dow Jones index. Please include the null hypothesis and its p-value.
(f) Do an impulse-response analysis and interpret the results.
(g) Do a variance-decomposition analysis and interpret the results.
     For (f) and (g), assume that the Dow Jones index is more independent than the Kospi index.

4   Using the following VAR(2) model, we can test the Granger-causality between two stationary variables, x_t and y_t.

$$x_t = \alpha_0 + \alpha_1 x_{t-1} + \alpha_2 x_{t-2} + \beta_1 y_{t-1} + \beta_2 y_{t-2} + u_{1,t}$$
$$y_t = \gamma_0 + \gamma_1 x_{t-1} + \gamma_2 x_{t-2} + \delta_1 y_{t-1} + \delta_2 y_{t-2} + u_{2,t}$$

(a) Using the symbols in the above equations, write the null hypothesis that x does not Granger-cause y.
(b) Using the symbols in the above equations, write the null hypothesis that y does not Granger-cause x.

(c) Using the above VAR(2) model, make a one-period-ahead forecast for x_{t+1} given an information set $I_t = \{x_t, x_{t-1}, \cdots, y_t, y_{t-1}, \cdots\}$.

5 Using the following three-variable VAR(2) model, we can test the Granger-causality between three stationary variables; inflation rate (π_t), unemployment rate (U_t) and interest rate (R_t).

$$\pi_t = \alpha_0 + \alpha_1 \pi_{t-1} + \alpha_2 \pi_{t-2} + \alpha_3 U_{t-1} + \alpha_4 U_{t-2} + \alpha_5 R_{t-1} + \alpha_6 R_{t-2} + \varepsilon_{1,t}$$

$$U_t = \beta_0 + \beta_1 \pi_{t-1} + \beta_2 \pi_{t-2} + \beta_3 U_{t-1} + \beta_4 U_{t-2} + \beta_5 R_{t-1} + \beta_6 R_{t-2} + \varepsilon_{2,t}$$

$$R_t = \gamma_0 + \gamma_1 \pi_{t-1} + \gamma_2 \pi_{t-2} + \gamma_3 U_{t-1} + \gamma_4 U_{t-2} + \gamma_5 R_{t-1} + \gamma_6 R_{t-2} + \varepsilon_{3,t}$$

(a) Using the symbols in the above equations, write the null hypothesis that π does not Granger-cause U.

(b) Using the symbols in the above equations, write the null hypothesis that U does not Granger-cause π.

(c) Using the above VAR(2) model, make a one-period-ahead forecast for U_{t+1} given an information set $I_t = \{\pi_t, \pi_{t-1}, \cdots, U_t, U_{t-1}, \cdots, R_t, R_{t-1}, \cdots\}$.

Notes

1 Reduced-form equations are the ones whose right-hand-side variables are predetermined and thus uncorrelated with the disturbances (i.e., exogenous). In contrast, structural-form equations may include endogenous explanatory variables on the right-hand side.

2 If the disturbances are serially correlated, the OLS estimators will be inconsistent because of the lagged dependent variables on the right-hand side. Review question #2 shows why this inconsistency arises.

3 If the disturbance in one equation is contemporaneously correlated with the disturbance in the other equation, the SUR (seemingly unrelated regression) estimators are efficient. However, in this special case where each equation has the same set of independent variables, it can be shown that the SUR estimators are equivalent to the separately applied OLS estimators.

4 Serially correlated disturbances are correlated with lagged dependent variables on the right-hand side of the equation.

5 To avoid this arbitrary ordering, Pesaran and Shin (1998) develop a generalized impulse-response function which uses information in the residual variance-covariance matrix Ω without requiring the order of variables. Trusov et al. (2009), cited in a later section in this chapter, employs this method. *EViews* has a function for this method.

6 One-period-ahead forecast for x_t is made in period $t-1$. The information set in $t-1$ includes x_{t-1} and y_{t-1}, but not ε_{xt}. So, the one-period-ahead forecast for x_t is $a_{11}x_{t-1} + a_{12}y_{t-1}$ and its forecast error is $l_{11}\varepsilon_{xt}$.

7 Copyright American Economic Association; reproduced with permission of the *Journal of Economic Perspectives*.

8 Standard practice for data description by VARs is to report results from Granger-causality tests, impulse responses and variance decompositions.

9 Forecasts like these are often referred to as pseudo or "simulated" out-of-sample forecasts to emphasize that they simulate how these forecasts would have been computed in real time.

10 The mean squared forecast error is computed as the average squared value of the forecast errors over the 1985–2000 out-of-sample period, and the resulting square root is the root mean squared forecast error reported in the table; i.e., $\sqrt{\sum_{t=1}^{T}(y_t - f_t)^2 / T}$ where y_t is the actual value and f_t is the h-step-ahead forecast about y_t.

11 The original paper uses the word "endogeneity" when it means "dynamic relationship." Thus, we use "dynamic relationship" when it is a more appropriate expression.

12 Since the authors investigate the need for modeling a full dynamic system, they try to show that one variable significantly Granger-causes another variable at a certain lag. To do it, they run the

causality test for lags up to 20 and report the test results for the lag that has the highest significance for the Granger-causality. However, a wrong choice of too small lags may erroneously produce wrong results. Therefore, the causality test should be conducted starting from the lag order selected by the Akaike information criterion, not from lag one.

References

Dekipme, M.G. and D.M. Hanssens (1999), "Sustained Spending and Persistent Response: A New Look at Long-Term Marketing Profitability," *Journal of Marketing Research*, 36(4), 397–412.

Granger, C.W.J. (2004), "Time Series Analysis, Cointegration, and Applications," *American Economic Review*, 94(3), 421–425.

Kilian, L. (2001), "Impulse Response Analysis in Vector Autoregressions with Unknown Lag Order," *Journal of Forecasting*, 20, 161–179.

Pesaran, M.H. and Y. Shin (1998), "Generalized Impulse Response Analysis in Linear Multivariate Models," *Economics Letters*, 58(1), 17–29.

Pindyck, R.S. and D.L. Rubinfeld (1991), *Econometric Models and Economic Forecasts*, New York: McGraw-Hill.

Sims, C.A. (1980), "Macroeconomics and Reality," *Econometrica*, 48, 1–48.

Stock, J.H. and M.W. Watson (2001), "Vector Autoregressions," *Journal of Economic Perspectives*, 15, 101–115.

Trusov, M., R.E. Bucklin and K. Pauwels (2009), "Effects of word-of-Mouth Versus Traditional Marketing: Findings from an Internet Social Networking Site," *Journal of Marketing*, 73(5), 90–102.

Zhang, Y.J., Y. Fan, H.T. Tsai and Y.M. Wei (2008), "Spillover Effect of US Dollar Exchange Rate on Oil Prices," *Journal of Policy Modeling*, 30, 973–991.

Appendix 9 Estimation and analysis of VAR models using *SAS*[1]

One way of determining the lag order (p) is to choose the one which minimizes the value of information criteria, such as the AIC. To do it, you estimate VAR(p) models for a range of lag orders and obtain the AIC value for each p.

Alternatively, you can determine the lag order by sequentially testing a joint null hypothesis that the coefficients on the last lag are jointly zero. The following *SAS* codes sequentially apply the Wald test. In the TEST statement, each coefficient is expressed as AR(h, i, j) = coefficient of the lag h value of the j-th dependent variable to the i-th dependent variable.

If a joint null hypothesis is not rejected at a certain significance level, we decrease the lag order by one. We repeat this test until we first get a rejection. The alternative lag order from the first rejected test is then selected for an optimal lag order.

```
FILENAME SPILL DDE 'EXCEL|[10-VAR-SPILLOVER.xls]VAR1!R2C2:R462C5';
DATA K1; INFILE SPILL;
    INPUT NASDAQ DOW KOSPI KOSDAQ;
    LNNASDAQ= LOG(NASDAQ); LNDOW = LOG(DOW);
    LNKOSPI= LOG(KOSPI); LNKOSDAQ= LOG(KOSDAQ);
*----< Two ways of calculating the differences: DIF1(X) or X-LAG1(X) >-----;
    DLNASDAQ= DIF1(LNNASDAQ); DLDOW= DIF1(LNDOW);
    DLKOSPI= LNKOSPI - LAG1(LNKOSPI); DLKOSDAQ= LNKOSDAQ - LAG1(LNKOSDAQ);


***************************************************
* Determination of the lag order
***************************************************;

TITLE '< Determination of the lag order: Sequential Wald test >';
TITLE2 '----- Maximum lag order = 3 -----';
PROC VARMAX DATA=K1;
    MODEL DLNASDAQ DLKOSDAQ/P=3 ;
    TEST AR(3,1,1)=0, AR(3,1,2)=0, AR(3,2,1)=0, AR(3,2,2)=0; RUN;
TITLE2 '----- Maximum lag order = 2 -----';
PROC VARMAX DATA=K1;
    MODEL DLNASDAQ DLKOSDAQ/P=2 ;
    TEST AR(2,1,1)=0, AR(2,1,2)=0, AR(2,2,1)=0, AR(2,2,2)=0; RUN;
```

> < Determination of the lag order: Sequential Wald test >
>
> ----- Maximum lag order = 3 -----
>
> The VARMAX Procedure
>
> Number of Observations   460
>
> Number of Pairwise Missing   1

Simple Summary Statistics

Variable	Type	N	Mean	Standard Deviation	Min	Max
DLNASDAQ	Dependent	460	−0.00160	0.03020	−0.10168	0.13254
DLKOSDAQ	Dependent	460	−0.00283	0.03550	−0.22233	0.16046

The VARMAX Procedure

Type of Model	VAR(3)
Estimation Method	Least Squares Estimation

Model Parameter Estimates

Equation	Parameter	Estimate	Standard Error	t Value	Pr > |t|	Variable
DLNASDAQ	CONST1	−0.00132	0.00142	−0.93	0.3530	1
	AR1_1_1	−0.06933	0.05195	−1.33	0.1827	DLNASDAQ(t-1)
	AR1_1_2	0.10557	0.04466	2.36	0.0185	DLKOSDAQ(t-1)
	AR2_1_1	−0.05075	0.05176	−0.98	0.3274	DLNASDAQ(t-2)
	AR2_1_2	−0.01104	0.04443	−0.25	0.8038	DLKOSDAQ(t-2)
	AR3_1_1	−0.03649	0.05206	-0.70	0.4837	DLNASDAQ(t-3)
	AR3_1_2	0.01637	0.04419	0.37	0.7113	DLKOSDAQ(t-3)
DLKOSDAQ	CONST2	−0.00185	0.00165	−1.13	0.2609	1
	AR1_2_1	−0.07723	0.06021	−1.28	0.2003	DLNASDAQ(t-1)
	AR1_2_2	0.13301	0.05176	2.57	0.0105	DLKOSDAQ(t-1)
	AR2_2_1	0.13857	0.05999	2.31	0.0214	DLNASDAQ(t-2)
	AR2_2_2	−0.00598	0.05150	−0.12	0.9076	DLKOSDAQ(t-2)
	AR3_2_1	0.06953	0.06034	1.15	0.2498	DLNASDAQ(t-3)
	AR3_2_2	0.03200	0.05122	0.62	0.5324	DLKOSDAQ(t-3)

The estimated VAR(3) equations are

$$\hat{x}_t = -0.00132 - 0.06933x_{t-1} + 0.10557y_{t-1} - 0.05075x_{t-2} - 0.01104y_{t-2} - 0.03649x_{t-3} + 0.01637y_{t-3}$$
$$\hat{y}_t = -0.00185 - 0.07723x_{t-1} + 0.13301y_{t-1} + 0.13857x_{t-2} - 0.00598y_{t-2} + 0.06953x_{t-3} + 0.03200y_{t-3}$$

where $x_t = DLNASDAQ_t$ and $y_t = DLKOSDAQ_t$.

Testing of the Parameters

Test	DF	Chi-Square	Pr > ChiSq
1	4	4.79	0.3096

Covariances of Innovations

Variable	DLNASDAQ	DLKOSDAQ
DLNASDAQ	0.00091	0.00045
DLKOSDAQ	0.00045	0.00122

Information
Criteria

AICC	−13.8866
HQC	−13.8378
AIC	−13.8876
SBC	−13.7612
FPEC	9.305E-7

----- Maximum lag order = 2 -----

The VARMAX Procedure

Type of Model	VAR(2)
Estimation Method	Least Squares Estimation

Model Parameter Estimates

Standard

Equation	Parameter	Estimate	Error	t Value	Pr > |t|	Variable
DLNASDAQ	CONST1	−0.00137	0.00141	−0.97	0.3329	1
	AR1_1_1	−0.06745	0.05153	−1.31	0.1912	DLNASDAQ(t-1)
	AR1_1_2	0.10557	0.04386	2.41	0.0165	DLKOSDAQ(t-1)
	AR2_1_1	−0.04371	0.05138	−0.85	0.3953	DLNASDAQ(t-2)
	AR2_1_2	-0.01095	0.04413	-0.25	0.8041	DLKOSDAQ(t-2)
DLKOSDAQ	CONST2	−0.00215	0.00165	−1.31	0.1915	1
	AR1_2_1	−0.09088	0.06002	−1.51	0.1307	DLNASDAQ(t-1)
	AR1_2_2	0.15392	0.05109	3.01	0.0027	DLKOSDAQ(t-1)
	AR2_2_1	0.15056	0.05984	2.52	0.0122	DLNASDAQ(t-2)
	AR2_2_2	−0.00745	0.05140	−0.15	0.8847	DLKOSDAQ(t-2)

The estimated VAR(2) equations are

$$\hat{x}_t = -0.00137 - 0.06745x_{t-1} + 0.105569y_{t-1} - 0.04371x_{t-2} - 0.01095y_{t-2}$$
$$\hat{y}_t = -0.00215 - 0.09088x_{t-1} + 0.15392y_{t-1} + 0.15056x_{t-2} - 0.00745y_{t-2}$$

where $x_t = DLNASDAQ_t$ and $y_t = DLKOSDAQ_t$.

Testing of the Parameters

Test	DF	Chi-Square	Pr > ChiSq
1	4	13.38	0.0096

Covariances of Innovations

Variable	DLNASDAQ	DLKOSDAQ
DLNASDAQ	0.00090	0.00045
DLKOSDAQ	0.00045	0.00123

Information
Criteria

AICC	−13.8905
HQC	−13.8555
AIC	−13.8909
SBC	−13.8008
FPEC	9.273E-7

Once the lag order is determined, we can estimate the VAR model and perform other analysis as follows.

```
**************************************************
* Estimating the VAR(2): P=2
* Forecasting five periods ahead: LEAD=5
**************************************************;
TITLE '< Estimation and Forecasting of VAR(2) >'; TITLE2;
PROC VARMAX DATA=K1;
    MODEL DLNASDAQ DLKOSDAQ/P=2 PRINT=(DIAGNOSE);
    Output LEAD=5;
RUN;
**************************************************
* Granger causality test
* Null: Group2 does not Granger cause Group1
**************************************************;
TITLE '< Granger Causality test >';
PROC VARMAX DATA=K1;
    MODEL DLNASDAQ DLKOSDAQ/P=2 NOPRINT;
    CAUSAL GROUP1=(DLNASDAQ) GROUP2=(DLKOSDAQ);
    CAUSAL GROUP1=(DLKOSDAQ) GROUP2=(DLNASDAQ);
RUN;
```

```
**************************************************
* Impulse Response and Variance Decomposition
* The more independent variable comes first.
**************************************************;
TITLE '< Impulse Response and Variance Decomposition >';
PROC VARMAX DATA=K1;
    MODEL DLNASDAQ DLKOSDAQ/P=2 LAGMAX=10 PRINT=(IMPULSE=(ALL) DECOMPOSE)
        PRINTFORM=UNIVARIATE;
RUN;
```

< Estimation and Forecasting of VAR(2) > 1

The VARMAX Procedure

Type of Model   VAR(2)
Estimation Method   Least Squares Estimation

Model Parameter Estimates
Standard

Equation	Parameter	Estimate	Error	t Value	Pr > |t|	Variable
DLNASDAQ	CONST1	−0.00137	0.00141	−0.97	0.3329	1
	AR1_1_1	−0.06745	0.05153	−1.31	0.1912	DLNASDAQ(t-1)
	AR1_1_2	0.10557	0.04386	2.41	0.0165	DLKOSDAQ(t-1)
	AR2_1_1	−0.04371	0.05138	−0.85	0.3953	DLNASDAQ(t-2)
	AR2_1_2	−0.01095	0.04413	−0.25	0.8041	DLKOSDAQ(t-2)
DLKOSDAQ	CONST2	−0.00215	0.00165	−1.31	0.1915	1
	AR1_2_1	−0.09088	0.06002	−1.51	0.1307	DLNASDAQ(t-1)
	AR1_2_2	0.15392	0.05109	3.01	0.0027	DLKOSDAQ(t-1)
	AR2_2_1	0.15056	0.05984	2.52	0.0122	DLNASDAQ(t-2)
	AR2_2_2	−0.00745	0.05140	−0.15	0.8847	DLKOSDAQ(t-2)

Covariances of Innovations

Variable	DLNASDAQ	DLKOSDAQ
DLNASDAQ	0.00090	0.00045
DLKOSDAQ	0.00045	0.00123

Information
Criteria

AICC -13.8905
HQC   -13.8555
AIC   -13.8909

SBC   -13.8008

FPEC   9.273E-7

Robustness check

It is to ensure that enough lags are included in the estimation model. If too few lags are included, the disturbances are likely to be serially correlated and the autocorrelated disturbances will be correlated with lagged dependent variables on the right-hand side of the equation. This endogeneity problem causes the OLS estimators to be biased.

Portmanteau test for cross correlations of residuals:

$$H_0 : \rho(1) = \cdots = \rho(s) = 0 \text{ where } \rho(s) = corr\ coeff\ (U_t, U_{t-s})$$

Portmanteau Test for Cross Correlations of Residuals

Up To Lag (s)	DF	Chi-Square	Pr > ChiSq
3	4	4.30	0.3669
4	8	8.43	0.3924
5	12	9.34	0.6736
6	16	19.14	0.2614
7	20	27.48	0.1224
8	24	31.29	0.1456
9	28	35.93	0.1445
10	32	41.06	0.1308

Forecasts

Variable	Obs	Forecast	Standard Error	95%	Confidence Limits
DLNASDAQ	461	0.00174	0.03005	-0.05716	0.06064
	462	-0.00182	0.03024	-0.06110	0.05745
	463	-0.00145	0.03028	-0.06079	0.05789
	464	-0.00138	0.03028	-0.06074	0.05797
	465	-0.00147	0.03028	-0.06082	0.05789
DLKOSDAQ	461	0.00420	0.03500	-0.06440	0.07280
	462	-0.00076	0.03534	-0.07003	0.06851
	463	-0.00187	0.03561	-0.07168	0.06793
	464	-0.00258	0.03563	-0.07240	0.06725
	465	-0.00263	0.03563	-0.07245	0.06720

< Granger Causality test >

The VARMAX Procedure

Granger-Causality Wald Test

Test	DF	Chi-Square	Pr > ChiSq
1	2	5.79	0.0552
2	2	8.92	0.0116

Test 1: Group 1 Variables: DLNASDAQ
        Group 2 Variables: DLKOSDAQ

Test 2: Group 1 Variables: DLKOSDAQ
        Group 2 Variables: DLNASDAQ

< Impulse Response and Variance Decomposition >

Simple Impulse Response by Variable

Variable Response\Impulse	Lag	DLNASDAQ	DLKOSDAQ
DLNASDAQ	1	−0.06745	0.10557
	STD	0.05153	0.04386
	2	−0.04876	−0.00183
	STD	0.05156	0.04392
	3	0.02230	−0.00548
	STD	0.01205	0.00821
	4	0.00085	0.00206
	STD	0.00973	0.00264
DLKOSDAQ	1	−0.09088	0.15392
	STD	0.06002	0.05109
	2	0.14270	0.00664
	STD	0.06027	0.05136
	3	0.01692	0.01594
	STD	0.01264	0.01464
	4	−0.00783	0.00263
	STD	0.00965	0.00700

Proportions of Prediction Error

Covariances by Variable

Variable	Lead	DLNASDAQ	DLKOSDAQ
DLNASDAQ	1	1.00000	0.00000
	2	0.98776	0.01224
	3	0.98778	0.01222
	4	0.98775	0.01225
	5	0.98775	0.01225
DLKOSDAQ	1	0.17983	0.82017
	2	0.17654	0.82346
	3	0.18903	0.81097
	4	0.18934	0.81066
	5	0.18937	0.81063

Note

1 BASE SAS 9.4, SAS/ETS 13.1 and SAS/STAT 13.1. SAS Institute Inc., Cary, NC.

10 Autocorrelation and ARCH/GARCH

Learning objectives

In this chapter, you should learn about:
■ Autocorrealted disturbances in dynamic models;
■ Time-varying variances of disturbances.

10.1 Autocorrelation

When we analyze time-series data, the disturbances are often correlated with each other, particularly for time periods not too far apart. This property is known as *serial correlation* or *autocorrelation*. Symbolically, $Cov(u_t, u_s) \neq 0$ for $t \neq s$. This violates one of the OLS assumptions that the disturbances should not be correlated with each other.

The simplest form of autocorrelation is formally stated as follows: for $t = 1, \ldots, T$,

$$Y_t = \beta_0 + \beta_1 X_t + u_t$$
$$u_t = \rho u_{t-1} + \varepsilon_t, \qquad |\rho| < 1 \tag{10.1}$$

where ε_t is independently and identically distributed with zero mean and constant variance, called a *white noise* series. The restriction of $|\rho| < 1$ is required for the model to show stable processes. If $|\rho| \geq 1$, the processes of $\{u_t\}$ and $\{Y_t\}$ would explode without limit; such nonstationary cases are explained in Chapter 11.

The model Eq. (10.1) states that the error term u_t consists of two components: one is the previous period's error term multiplied by a parameter (ρu_{t-1}) and the other is a new change (ε_t). [1] FIGURES 10.1 and 10.2 show patterns of positive ($\rho > 0$) and negative ($\rho < 0$) autocorrelations.

In Eq. (10.1), u_t is related to one lagged disturbance (u_{t-1}) only and this process is called the first-order autocorrelation, denoted by AR(1). The autocorrelation can be extended to more lagged disturbances. For example, the *p*th-order autocorrelation AR(*p*) is

$$u_t = \rho_1 u_{t-1} + \rho_2 u_{t-2} + \cdots + \rho_p u_{t-p} + \varepsilon_t$$

10.1.1 Consequences of autocorrelation

Efficiency of the OLS estimator

The OLS estimator is not efficient because Assumption III in Chapter 2, no correlation between the disturbances, is violated. It is because the OLS estimation method ignores the autocorrelations when

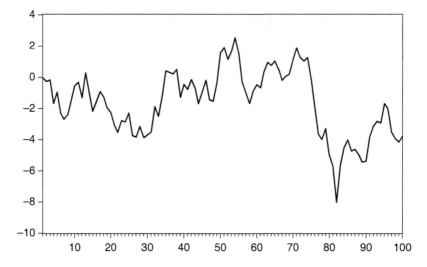

Figure 10.1 Positive autocorrelation

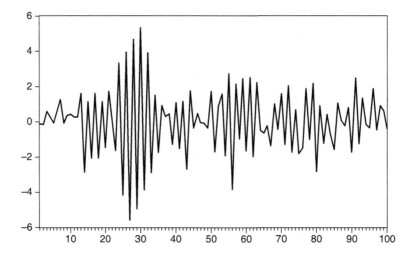

Figure 10.2 Negative autocorrelation

they exist. As a result, the OLS method yields incorrect standard errors, resulting in invalid *t*-statistics and *p*-values. Therefore, tests of hypotheses based on the OLS estimation are no longer valid.

Unbiasedness of the OLS estimator

The autocorrelation itself has nothing to do with the unbiasedness. The unbiasedness of the OLS estimator is subject only to the exogeneity of explanatory variables. Even in the presence of autocorrelated disturbances, the OLS estimator is still unbiased as long as $E(u_t | X_1, \cdots, X_T) = 0$; notice that the expectation is conditioned on the explanatory variables in *all* time periods. We say that such explanatory variable is *strictly exogenous*. For the OLS estimator to be unbiased, this strict exogeneity condition has to be satisfied.

The strict exogeneity implies that the disturbances are uncorrelated with explanatory variables in *all* time periods, $Cov(u_t, X_s) = 0$ for $s = 1, 2, \cdots, T$.[2] If this "no-correlation" condition is not satisfied, then the strict exogeneity is also not satisfied and the OLS estimator is therefore biased.

Now, we examine the consistency of the OLS estimator.

Dynamic models with no autocorrelation

In dynamic models which include lagged dependent variables as regressors, the no-correlation condition is violated. Consider the following simple autoregressive model.

$$Y_t = \beta_0 + \beta_1 Y_{t-1} + \varepsilon_t$$
$$Y_{t+1} = \beta_0 + \beta_1 Y_t + \varepsilon_{t+1} = \beta_0 + \beta_1(\beta_0 + \beta_1 Y_{t-1} + \varepsilon_t) + \varepsilon_{t+1}$$
$$\vdots$$

where ε_t s are white noise and thus $E(\varepsilon_t \varepsilon_s) = 0$ for $t \neq s$. The disturbance ε_t in the first equation is, however, correlated with the regressor Y_t in the second equation and all future dependent variables Y_{t+h} ($h = 1, 2, \cdots$) because they contain ε_t. This correlation has been caused by the lagged dependent variable. Since the no-correlation condition for all time periods is not satisfied, the OLS estimator becomes biased.

However, if $|\beta_1| < 1$, the correlation between ε_t and Y_{t+h} disappears as h increases to infinity. Using repeated substitution, we can express Y_{t+h} as a function of $\{\varepsilon_t\}$:

$$Y_{t+h} = \beta_0 + \beta_1 Y_{t+h-1} + \varepsilon_{t+h}$$
$$= \beta_0 + \beta_1(\beta_0 + \beta_1 Y_{t+h-2} + \varepsilon_{t+h-1}) + \varepsilon_{t+h}$$
$$\vdots$$
$$= \beta_0(1 + \beta_1 + \cdots + \beta_1^h) + \beta_1^{h+1} Y_{t-1} + (\beta_1^h \varepsilon_t + \cdots + \beta_1 \varepsilon_{t+h-1} + \varepsilon_{t+h})$$

The covariance between Y_{t+h} and ε_t is $Cov(Y_{t+h}, \varepsilon_t) = \beta_1^h Var(\varepsilon_t)$, which converges to zero if $|\beta_1| < 1$. These time series $\{Y_t\}$ and $\{\varepsilon_t\}$ are said to be *asymptotically uncorrelated* because their correlation disappears as h increases to infinity. If so, the influence of the correlation on the OLS bias diminishes and finally disappears. Therefore, the OLS estimator becomes consistent. In fact, it has been proven that if Y_{t+h} and ε_t are asymptotically uncorrelated, the *contemporaneous uncorrelatedness* in each period, i.e., $Cov(Y_{t-1}, \varepsilon_t) = 0$, is sufficient for the OLS estimator to be consistent.

Dynamic models with autocorrelation

In contrast, if the disturbances are autocorrelated in dynamic models, the OLS estimator cannot be consistent. Consider the following dynamic model with autocorrelated disturbances.

$$Y_t = \beta_0 + \beta_1 Y_{t-1} + u_t, \qquad u_t = \rho u_{t-1} + \varepsilon_t \tag{10.2}$$

The regressor Y_{t-1} includes u_{t-1} because $Y_{t-1} = \beta_0 + \beta_1 Y_{t-2} + u_{t-1}$ and the disturbance u_t includes u_{t-1} because of the autocorrelation. Thus, there exists a contemporaneous correlation between the regressor Y_{t-1} and the disturbance u_t. Furthermore, since the correlation exists in every period, its influence on the bias will not diminish even when the time period increases to infinity. Therefore, the OLS estimator is not consistent because of the lagged dependent variable and the autocorrelated disturbance.

However, this model itself is unnecessarily too complicated to be used in practice. Instead, we can transform Eq. (10.2) into a model whose disturbance is not autocorrelated. To do it, we multiply by ρ for the equation of Y_{t-1}.

$$\rho Y_{t-1} = \rho \beta_0 + \rho \beta_1 Y_{t-2} + \rho u_{t-1} \tag{10.3}$$

Subtracting Eq. (10.3) from Eq. (10.2) term-by-term, we can eliminate the autocorrelation of the disturbances.

$$Y_t = \gamma_0 + \gamma_1 Y_{t-1} + \gamma_2 Y_{t-2} + \varepsilon_t \tag{10.4}$$

where $\gamma_0 = \beta_0(1-\rho)$, $\gamma_1 = \beta_1 + \rho$, and $\gamma_2 = -\rho\beta_1$. This model belongs to the above case of dynamic models with no autocorrelation. Therefore, the OLS estimator for Eq. (10.4) is consistent.

In many applications, the autocorrelation disappears if lagged dependent and independent variables are included as regressors.[3] Furthermore, dynamic models provide more useful information than static models because they can describe dynamic effects of explanatory variables on the dependent variable. Therefore, a better solution to autocorrelation would be to include more lagged values of the dependent and explanatory variables until the disturbances become serially uncorrelated.

Autocorrelation vs. misspecification

Misspecified models often appear to have autocorrelated disturbances. Suppose that the true model includes lagged variables x_{t-1} and y_{t-1} but no autocorrelation.

$$Y_t = \alpha_0 + \alpha_1 X_t + \alpha_2 X_{t-1} + \alpha_3 Y_{t-1} + \varepsilon_t$$

If we omit X_{t-1} and Y_{t-1}, the disturbance of a misspecified model $Y_t = \beta_0 + \beta_1 X_t + u_t$ would be auto-correlated; $u_t \ (= \alpha_2 X_{t-1} + \alpha_3 Y_{t-1} + \varepsilon_t)$ is correlated with $u_{t+1} \ (= \alpha_2 X_t + \alpha_3 Y_t + \varepsilon_{t+1})$ because (X_{t-1}, Y_{t-1}) is correlated with Y_t, as specified in the true model. Thus, a significant autocorrelation in estimated residuals does not necessarily imply that we should estimate an autocorrelation model. Instead, a practically better solution is to include more lagged dependent and explanatory variables until the autocorrelation disappears.

10.1.2 Test for autocorrelation

Test for AR(1) with strictly exogenous regressors: Durbin-Watson test

The Durbin-Watson (DW) test can be applied only when all regressors are strictly exogenous, that is, the disturbance u_t at each period is uncorrelated with the regressors in *all* time periods. Thus, the DW test is limited in application.

The DW d statistic is defined as

$$d = \frac{\sum\limits_{t=2}^{n} (\hat{u}_t - \hat{u}_{t-1})^2}{\sum\limits_{t=1}^{n} \hat{u}_t^2} \tag{10.5}$$

where $\hat{u}_t = Y_t - \hat{\beta}_0 - \hat{\beta}_1 X_t$ is the residual from the OLS estimation without accounting for the autocorrelation. The DW d statistic is known to range between 0 and 4. For positively autocorrelated residuals, the numerator in Eq. (10.5) tends to be close to 0 because residuals at adjacent periods are similar in size; for negatively autocorrelated residuals, it becomes large and close to the upper bound 4 because residuals at adjacent periods tend to have opposite signs. This property of the DW d statistic is utilized to test for AR(1).

With positive autocorrelation as the alternative hypothesis,[4] the DW test concludes according to the lower and upper critical values (d_L and d_U) as follows; if H_0, we reject H_0 at a given significance level and conclude that the disturbance is positively first-order autocorrelated.

$$H_0 : \rho = 0 \quad vs. \quad H_1 : \rho > 0 \ (positive \ autocorrelation)$$

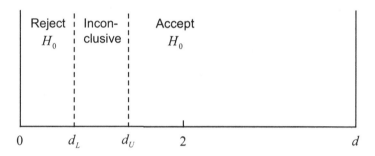

The lower and upper critical values can be obtained from a DW table, as demonstrated in an example below. *EViews* automatically produces the Durbin-Watson d statistic when you use the OLS method.

Test for AR(1) with any regressors: *t*-test

One main limitation of the Durbin-Watson test is that it cannot be used when regressors are not strictly exogenous; one such case is when lagged dependent variables are included as regressors. Consider the following dynamic model with an AR(1) error term.

$$Y_t = \beta_0 + \beta_1 Y_{t-1} + \gamma_1 X_{1t} + \cdots + \gamma_k X_{kt} + u_t$$
$$u_t = \rho u_{t-1} + \varepsilon_t, \quad |\rho| < 1$$

A test for AR(1) proceeds as follows:

a   Run the OLS regression of Y_t on the regressors ($Y_{t-1}, X_{1t}, \cdots, X_{kt}$) and calculate the OLS residuals $\hat{u}_t$s.

b   Run the OLS regression of $\hat{u}_t$ on $\hat{u}_{t-1}$ and all regressors ($Y_{t-1}, X_{1t}, \cdots, X_{kt}$), and obtain the coefficient estimate for $\hat{u}_{t-1}$, its t-statistic and p-value.

c   Using the t-statistic or p-value for the $\hat{u}_{t-1}$ coefficient, test the null hypothesis of $H_0 : \rho = 0$ against $H_1 : \rho \neq 0$ (or one-sided test $H_1 : \rho > 0$).

This test works for any regressors, as long as they are uncorrelated with the contemporaneous error term u_t.

Test for AR(p) autocorrelations: Lagrange multiplier (LM) test

We test for the following higher-order AR(p) autocorrelation of the disturbance.

$$u_t = \rho_1 u_{t-1} + \rho_2 u_{t-2} + \cdots + \rho_p u_{t-p} + \varepsilon_t$$

The null hypothesis is $H_0 : \rho_1 = \rho_2 = \cdots = \rho_p = 0$, meaning that there is no autocorrelation up to lag p. One widely used test is the LM test, also called the Breusch-Godfrey test. This LM test can be applied for any regressors, as long as they are uncorrelated with the contemporaneous error term u_t. It is an extension of the above AR(1) test; calculate the LM statistic after the OLS regression of $\hat{u}_t$ on ($\hat{u}_{t-1}, \cdots, \hat{u}_{t-p}$) and all regressors ($Y_{t-1}, X_{1t}, \cdots, X_{kt}$). Most computer packages including *EViews*, *SAS* and *R* produce the LM statistics and p-values; use of *EViews* and *SAS* is demonstrated in Appendix 10A and use of *R* is available at the e-Resource.

10.1.3 Estimation of autocorrelation

If a test concludes that the disturbance is autocorrelated, we need to estimate both the regression equation and the autocorrelation equation. Appendix 10A illustrates how to estimate autocorrelated regression models using *EViews* and *SAS*. For theoretical explanations about the estimation methods, refer to Greene (2003) or any econometrics textbooks.

10.2 ARCH-type models

Estimated regression functions can be used to predict future values of the dependent variable. When we use these predicted values for our decision making such as portfolio selection, we also need to know the uncertainty (or accuracy) of the prediction. There are two sources of uncertainty associated with the prediction; one is the uncertainty of coefficient estimates (measured by standard errors), and the other is the disturbance representing unexpected changes in the dependent variable. The standard errors of coefficient estimates can be incorporated for measuring the uncertainty of prediction in an easy way similar to constructing statistical confidence intervals. In contrast, virtually no method was available for modeling time-varying variances of the disturbance before the introduction of ARCH models.

In order to exploit the uncertainty, we need to predict future variances. Engle (2004, p. 405) states the need of forecasting models for time-varying variances as follows:

> There are some risks we choose to take because the benefits from taking them exceed the possible costs. Optimal behavior takes risks that are worthwhile. This is the central paradigm of finance; we must take risks to achieve rewards but not all risks are equally rewarded.

Recent analyses of financial data, such as exchange rates, stock prices and inflation rates, have found abundant evidence of clustering of large and small disturbances, similar to the graph below. It suggests a form of heteroscedasticity in which the variance depends on the size of preceding disturbances. When the disturbances are highly volatile, they are likely to remain so; when they are less volatile, they are likely to remain stable. Thus, in order to correctly evaluate the accuracy of prediction, these systematically time-varying variances need to be modeled.

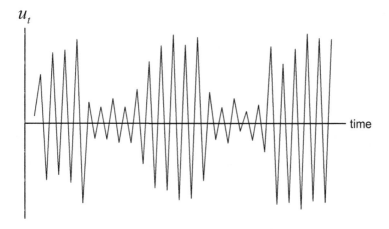

Engle (1982) suggests the AutoRegressive Conditionally Heteroscedastic (ARCH) model for this need. Since then, many extensions of the ARCH model have been proposed in the literature; among them, the Generalized ARCH (GARCH) model developed by Bollerslev (1986) is most widely used. The ARCH model and its extensions are surveyed in Bollerslev et al. (1992) and Bollerslev et al. (1994). This family of ARCH models provides useful measures and forecasts of time-varying variance.

10.2.1 ARCH model

Consider a regression model whose disturbance has a time-varying variance. Since the main use of the ARCH models is to forecast future variance, we express the model in terms of the next period's variables.

$$Y_{t+1} = \beta_0 + \beta_1 X_{t+1} + u_{t+1}$$
$$Var(u_{t+1}|I_t) \equiv \sigma_{t+1}^2 = E(u_{t+1}^2|I_t)$$

where I_t is the information set available at time t and includes observations on the dependent and explanatory variables; $I_t = \{Y_t, X_t, Y_{t-1}, X_{t-1}, \cdots\}$. The conditional variance σ_{t+1}^2 is based on the information set I_t and thus a one-period-ahead forecast made at t.

One simple method to estimate the conditional variance is a moving-window approach; it calculates the variance using a fixed number of the most recent residuals. For example, a forecast of the conditional variance σ_{t+1}^2 could be calculated every day using the most recent five-day residuals, that is,

$$\hat{\sigma}_{t+1}^2 = \frac{1}{5}(\hat{u}_t^2 + \hat{u}_{t-1}^2 + \hat{u}_{t-2}^2 + \hat{u}_{t-3}^2 + \hat{u}_{t-4}^2)$$

It assumes that the variance of Y_{t+1} (also u_{t+1}) is an equally weighted average of the squared residuals from the most recent five days. The use of equal weights seems unattractive as the more recent residuals would be more relevant. In addition, use of the window size of five days cannot be justified.

The ARCH model dose not impose such unattractive restrictions, but uses the estimated coefficients as weights. Below is shown an ARCH model of order q, ARCH(q) for the conditional variance σ_{t+1}^2.

$$Y_{t+1} = \beta_0 + \beta_1 X_{t+1} + u_{t+1}$$
$$Var(u_{t+1}|I_t) \equiv \sigma_{t+1}^2 = \gamma_0 + \gamma_1 u_t^2 + \cdots + \gamma_q u_{t+1-q}^2 \tag{10.6}$$

where the disturbances u_t s are assumed serially uncorrelated. Autocorrelation, if any, has to be corrected before an ARCH equation is applied.[5] If the disturbance follows a normal distribution, we have $u_{t+1}|I_t \sim N(0,\sigma_{t+1}^2)$. The lag order q can be selected by applying the Lagrange multiplier test proposed by Engle (1982).

To illustrate how to test for the existence and order of ARCH, let us use a dynamic model for company ABC's stock returns (*RET*) and market returns (*MKT*). An Excel file "10-returns.xls" contains 201 daily observations.

$$RET_t = \beta_0 + \beta_1 MKT_t + \beta_2 MKT_{t-1} + \beta_3 RET_{t-1} + \varepsilon_t \tag{10.7}$$

In *EViews*, import this Excel data file and generate lagged variables L1MKT and L1RET using the Genr function. After obtaining the OLS estimation results for "RET C MKT L1MKT L1RET," choose View/Residual Tests/ARCH LM Test . . . in the output window and enter the order of ARCH in the Lag Specification box. Using "1" for the lag to include, the following output tests a null hypothesis of H_0: No ARCH up to lag 1.

Output 10.1   Test for No ARCH up to lag 1

ARCH Test:

F-statistic	91.30620	Probability	0.000000
Obs*R-squared	63.02304	Probability	0.000000

The null hypothesis of no ARCH(1) is rejected at a 1% significance level with the *p*-value of 0.0000. It indicates that the disturbance shows a pattern of time-varying variance with at least one ARCH term. Thus, we need to estimate the regression model with an ARCH-type disturbance included. In determining the order of the ARCH term, we may test down by starting with a large number of ARCH terms.

To do it, choose Objects/New Object. . . /Equation and ARCH from the estimation method box and fill in the dialog window. In this example, we start with an ARCH(2) model by entering "2" for ARCH and "0" for GARCH.

Output 10.2   Estimates of an ARCH(2) model

Dependent Variable: RET
Method: ML – ARCH (Marquardt) – Normal distribution
Sample (adjusted): 2 201
Included observations: 200 after adjustments

Convergence achieved after 17 iterations
Variance backcast: ON
GARCH = C(5) + C(6)*RESID(-1)^2 + C(7)*RESID(-2)^2

	Coefficient	Std. Error	z-Statistic	Prob.
C	-0.009535	0.017985	-0.530141	0.5960
MKT	0.703441	0.003507	200.6067	0.0000
L1MKT	-0.104744	0.008379	-12.50088	0.0000
L1RET	0.511017	0.011070	46.16118	0.0000
Variance Equation				
C	0.038437	0.008231	4.669700	0.0000
RESID(-1)^2	0.826871	0.157779	5.240685	0.0000
RESID(-2)^2	0.015371	0.043053	0.357018	0.7211

The estimates in Output 10.2 show that the second-lagged ARCH term is not significant because its *p*-value is 0.7211. Now, we reduce the order of the ARCH terms to one.

Output 10.3   Estimates of an ARCH(1) model

Dependent Variable: RET
Method: ML – ARCH (Marquardt) – Normal distribution
Sample (adjusted): 2 201
Included observations: 200 after adjustments
Convergence achieved after 17 iterations
Variance backcast: ON
GARCH = C(5) + C(6)*RESID(-1)^2

	Coefficient	Std. Error	z-Statistic	Prob.
C	-0.012060	0.017277	-0.698024	0.4852
MKT	0.703750	0.003315	212.2779	0.0000
L1MKT	-0.104811	0.008230	-12.73475	0.0000
L1RET	0.511053	0.010755	47.51854	0.0000
Variance Equation				
C	0.039605	0.007430	5.330694	0.0000
RESID(-1)^2	0.834602	0.152377	5.477213	0.0000

Output 10.3 shows the estimates of an ARCH(1) model. The estimated ARCH equation is $\hat{\sigma}^2_{t+1} = 0.039605 + 0.834602 u^2_t$. The lag-one ARCH term is significant with a *z*-statistic of 5.477213 and a *p*-value of 0.0000, confirming the rejection of no ARCH(1) by the Lagrange multiplier test in Output 10.1.

Forecasts of the ARCH model can be obtained recursively. Consider an ARCH (q) model, Eq. (10.6). At period t, the one-period-ahead forecast of the disturbance variance is

$$Var(u_{t+1}|I_t) \equiv \sigma_{t+1}^2 = \gamma_0 + \gamma_1 u_t^2 + \gamma_2 u_{t-1}^2 + \cdots + \gamma_q u_{t+1-q}^2$$

where parameters γs and disturbances us are replaced with their corresponding estimates made in period t; i.e., $\hat{Var}(u_{t+1}|I_t) = \hat{\gamma}_0 + \hat{\gamma}_1 \hat{u}_t^2 + \hat{\gamma}_2 \hat{u}_{t-1}^2 + \cdots + \hat{\gamma}_q \hat{u}_{t+1-q}^2$. The information set at time t includes observations on $(Y_t, X_t, \cdots, Y_1, X_1)$. Using the observations we can obtain coefficient estimates $(\hat{\beta}_0, \hat{\beta}_1, \hat{\gamma}_0, \cdots, \hat{\gamma}_q)$ and residuals $(\hat{u}_t, \hat{u}_{t-1}, \cdots, \hat{u}_1)$. Therefore, we may say that $I_t = \{Y_t, X_t, Y_{t-1}, X_{t-1}, \cdots, Y_1, X_1; \beta_0, \beta_1, \gamma_0, \cdots, \gamma_q; u_t, u_{t-1}, \cdots, \hat{u}_1\}$.

The two-period-ahead forecast is

$$\begin{aligned}
Var(u_{t+2}|I_t) &= E\left[Var(u_{t+2}|I_{t+1})|I_t\right] = E(\sigma_{t+2}^2|I_t) \\
&= E(\gamma_0 + \gamma_1 u_{t+1}^2 + \gamma_2 u_t^2 + \cdots + \gamma_q u_{t+2-q}^2|I_t) \\
&= \gamma_0 + \gamma_1 E(u_{t+1}^2|I_t) + \gamma_2 u_t^2 + \cdots + \gamma_q u_{t+2-q}^2 \\
&= \gamma_0 + \gamma_1 Var(u_{t+1}|I_t) + \gamma_2 u_t^2 + \cdots + \gamma_q u_{t+2-q}^2
\end{aligned}$$

where $Var(u_{t+1}|I_t)$ is the one-period-ahead forecast as shown above.

In the same way, we can obtain the h-period-ahead forecast.

$$Var(u_{t+h}|I_t) = \gamma_0 + \gamma_1 Var(u_{t+h-1}|I_t) + \cdots + \gamma_q Var(u_{t+h-q}|I_t)$$

where $Var(u_{t+h-j}|I_t) = u_{t+h-j}^2$ if $t + h - j \le t$.

10.2.2 GARCH (Generalized ARCH) model

One useful generalization of the ARCH has been proposed by Bollerslev (1986) and is now most widely used in time-series analysis. Below is a GARCH model of order p and q, GARCH(p,q), where p denotes the number of lagged variances (GARCH terms) and q denotes the number of lagged squared residuals (ARCH terms).

$$\begin{aligned}
Y_{t+1} &= \beta_0 + \beta_1 X_{t+1} + u_{t+1} \\
Var(u_{t+1}|I_t) &\equiv \sigma_{t+1}^2 = E(u_{t+1}^2|I_t)
\end{aligned}$$

$$\sigma_{t+1}^2 = \gamma_0 + \sum_{i=1}^{q} \gamma_i u_{t+1-i}^2 + \sum_{j=1}^{p} \delta_j \sigma_{t+1-j}^2$$

With a normality assumption for the distribution, it follows $u_{t+1}|I_t \sim N(0, \sigma_{t+1}^2)$. The lag order of p and q can be selected by the Lagrange multiplier test in the same way as for the ARCH model. To better understand this model, consider a simple case, GARCH(1,1).

$$\sigma_{t+1}^2 = \gamma_0 + \gamma_1 u_t^2 + \delta_1 \sigma_t^2 \tag{10.8}$$

This specification indicates that the best forecast of the next period's (conditional on I_t) variance is a weighted average of the long-run variance (γ_0), the new information of the most recent residual (u_t^2) and the variance forecast made at the last period (σ_t^2) (Engle, 2001). When the forecast $\sigma_t^2 \equiv Var(u_t|I_{t-1})$ was made at the last period ($t-1$), the residual u_t^2 was not available. This model describes a learning process by which knowledge about the variance is updated with new information. Although it uses only one lagged residual (u_t^2), inclusion of a lagged variance forecast σ_t^2 makes this model equivalent to a weighted average of all past squared residuals.[6]

Below is shown how to estimate GARCH models. Using the above example of Eq. (10.7), choose Objects/New Object. . . /Equation and ARCH from the estimation method box. Then, enter "1" for ARCH and "1" for GARCH. The estimates of GARCH(1,1) are shown in Output 10.4.

Output 10.4   Estimates of the GARCH(1,1) model

Dependent Variable: RET
Method: ML – ARCH (Marquardt) – Normal distribution
Sample (adjusted): 2 201
Included observations: 200 after adjustments
Convergence achieved after 15 iterations
Variance backcast: ON
GARCH = C(5) + C(6)*RESID(-1)^2 + C(7)*GARCH(-1)

	Coefficient	Std. Error	z-Statistic	Prob.
C	−0.009835	0.017970	−0.547308	0.5842
MKT	0.703462	0.003488	201.6902	0.0000
L1MKT	−0.104771	0.008365	−12.52557	0.0000
L1RET	0.511039	0.011030	46.33161	0.0000
Variance Equation				
C	0.037985	0.009034	4.204942	0.0000
RESID(-1)^2	0.828252	0.157521	5.258039	0.0000
GARCH(-1)	0.015390	0.049043	0.313797	0.7537

Output 10.4 shows that the estimated GARCH equation is $\hat{\sigma}_{t+1}^2 = 0.037985 + 0.828252\,u_t^2 + 0.01539\,\sigma_t^2$. The lag-one GARCH term is not significant (p-value = 0.7537), while the lag-one ARCH term is significant (p-value = 0.0000).

The one-period-ahead forecast of the GARCH(1,1) model can be directly derived from Eq. (10.8).

$$Var(u_{t+1}|I_t) \equiv \sigma_{t+1}^2 = \gamma_0 + \gamma_1 u_t^2 + \delta_1 \sigma_t^2$$

where parameters and disturbance are replaced with their corresponding estimates made in period t; i.e., $\hat{Var}(u_{t+1}|I_t) \equiv \hat{\gamma}_0 + \hat{\gamma}_1 \hat{u}_t^2 + \hat{\delta}_1 \hat{\sigma}_t^2$ with $\hat{\sigma}_t^2 = \hat{Var}(u_t|I_{t-1})$.

The two-period-ahead forecast is

$$\begin{aligned}
Var(u_{t+2}|I_t) &= E\left[Var(u_{t+2}|I_{t+1})|I_t\right] = E(\sigma_{t+2}^2|I_t) \\
&= E\left[\gamma_0 + \gamma_1 u_{t+1}^2 + \delta_1 \sigma_{t+1}^2 | I_t\right] \\
&= \gamma_0 + \gamma_1 E\left[u_{t+1}^2|I_t\right] + \delta_1 E\left[\sigma_{t+1}^2|I_t\right] \\
&= \gamma_0 + (\gamma_1 + \delta_1) \times Var(u_{t+1}|I_t)
\end{aligned}$$

where $E\left[u_{t+1}^2|I_t\right] = E\left[\sigma_{t+1}^2|I_t\right] = Var(u_{t+1}|I_t)$, all of which are conditioned on I_t.

By repeated substitution, the *h*-period-ahead forecast is derived as

$$Var(u_{t+h}|I_t) = \gamma_0 + (\gamma_1 + \delta_1)Var(u_{t+h-1}|I_t)$$
$$= \gamma_0 + (\gamma_1 + \delta_1)\{\gamma_0 + (\gamma_1 + \delta_1)Var(u_{t+h-2}|I_t)\}$$
$$= \gamma_0\{1 + (\gamma_1 + \delta_1)\} + (\gamma_1 + \delta_1)^2 Var(u_{t+h-2}|I_t)$$
$$\vdots$$
$$= \frac{\gamma_0[1 - (\gamma_1 + \delta_1)^{h-1}]}{1 - (\gamma_1 + \delta_1)} + (\gamma_1 + \delta_1)^{h-1}Var(u_{t+1}|I_t)$$

Therefore, if $|\gamma_1 + \delta_1| < 1$,

$$Var(u_{t+h}|I_t) \rightarrow \frac{\gamma_0}{1 - (\gamma_1 + \delta_1)} \quad as \quad h \rightarrow \infty$$

10.2.3 TGARCH (Threshold GARCH) model

The GARCH model assumes that the conditional variance depends on the magnitude but not the sign of u_t. However, this assumption somewhat appears inconsistent with empirical evidence on the behavior of stock market prices; many studies present evidence on asymmetric effects between positive and negative shocks. A negative shock tends to increase future volatility more than a positive one of the same magnitude. One plausible explanation is the *leverage effect*, suggested by Black (1976). According to the leverage effect, a reduction in the equity price would lead to an increase of the debt-to-equity ratio, which in turn raises the riskiness of the firm as reflected in its future volatility. Thus, negative asset returns will have a bigger impact on the future volatility than positive ones do.

The TGARCH model can address the leverage effect; the volatility caused by unexpected decreases of the dependent variable (*Y*) is different from the one caused by unexpected increases. To consider this possible asymmetry, Zakoian (1994) proposes the following TGARCH(*p, q*) model.

$$Y_{t+1} = \beta_0 + \beta_1 X_{t+1} + u_{t+1}, \quad Var(u_{t+1}|I_t) \equiv \sigma_{t+1}^2$$

$$\sigma_{t+1}^2 = \gamma_0 + \sum_{i=1}^{q}(\gamma_i + \psi_i D_{t+1-i})u_{t+1-i}^2 + \sum_{j=1}^{p}\delta_j \sigma_{t+1-j}^2$$

where a dummy variable D_{t+1-i} is set to 1 if the value of the dependent variable unexpectedly decreased in the previous period (i.e., $u_{t+1-i} < 0$), and 0 otherwise. The model shows that a negative u_{t+1-i} has a large impact $(\gamma_i + \psi_i)u_{t+1-i}^2 > 0$ with $\psi_i > 0$, while a positive u_{t+1-i} has an impact $\gamma_i u_{t+1-i}^2$. Thus, the introduction of the dummy variables allows us to estimate asymmetric influence of residuals on its conditional variance (σ_{t+1}^2).

10.2.4 EGARCH (Exponential GARCH) model

Like the TGARCH model, the Exponential GARCH(*p,q*) model describes the conditional variance σ_{t+1}^2 as an asymmetric function of past u_ts (Nelson, 1990).

$$\log \sigma_{t+1}^2 = \gamma_0 + \sum_{i=1}^{q}\gamma_i g(z_{t+1-i}) + \sum_{j=1}^{p}\delta_j \log \sigma_{t+1-j}^2$$

$$g(z_{t+1-i}) = \varphi z_{t+1-i} + \theta\left[|z_{t+1-i}| - E(|z_{t+1-i}|)\right]$$

(10.9)

where $z_t = u_t/\sigma_t$, a standardized disturbance. Note that the disturbance u_ts (or z_ts) appear in the EGARCH function, not their squares u_t^2s; this is different from the GARCH model.

The function $g(\cdot)$ in Eq. (10.9) consists of two components, the "size effect" and the "sign effect" of the shocks on the volatility. The term $\theta\left[\left|z_{t+1-i}\right| - E\left(\left|z_{t+1-i}\right|\right)\right]$ depends only on the magnitude of shocks but not on their signs; that is, it represents the size effect. The sign effect is described by the first term φz_{t+1-i} in Eq. (10.9). As φ is typically negative, the term φz_{t+1-i} is negative for positive shocks and thus has an effect of decreasing future volatilities. In contrast, $\varphi z_{t+1-i} > 0$ for negative shocks, indicating that negative shocks increase future volatilities. Thus, the EGARCH model can describe the asymmetric relation with φz_{t+1-i}.

As the conditional variance σ_{t+1}^2 is expressed as an exponential function, i.e., $\log \sigma_{t+1}^2 = (\cdots) \rightarrow \sigma_{t+1}^2 = \exp(\cdots)$, it is always positive without any restriction on the parameters. This is another advantage of using the EGARCH over the ARCH and GARCH models.

10.2.5 GARCH-M model

The variance of the error term is introduced in the mean equation, therefore called the GARCH-in-Mean model.

$$Y_{t+1} = \beta_0 + \beta_1 X_{t+1} + \theta \sigma_{t+1}^2 + u_{t+1}$$

$$\sigma_{t+1}^2 = \gamma_0 + \sum_{i=1}^{q} \gamma_i u_{t+1-i}^2 + \sum_{j=1}^{p} \delta_j \sigma_{t+1-j}^2$$

This model is often used in financial applications where the expected return on an asset, $E(Y_{t+1}|I_t)$, is related to the expected asset risk σ_{t+1}^2. The coefficient θ on σ_{t+1}^2 is a measure of the risk-return tradeoff.

10.3 Applications

10.3.1 Wang, Salin and Leatham (2002)

Food safety issues have come to center stage as contamination incidents worldwide during the 1990s attracted press attention and US policy makers instituted the HACCP (Hazard Analysis Critical Control Point) regulatory process in 1996. There have been many studies which examine the impact on businesses of HACCP adoption. Another line of research is to highlight the existence of potential private incentives for firms to invest in food safety. The effectiveness of private incentives needs to be explored further, given their potential value in complementing government regulatory efforts.

The authors point to financial markets as a source of private incentive to promote food safety. Managers of publicly traded food companies seeking to maximize shareholders' wealth can be expected to align their tactics with the stock market valuation of food safety. One indicator of the market's valuation of food safety is the effect on stock returns associated with specific events of food bacterial contamination.

The authors used a financial market model (CAPM) adjusted for GARCH properties of the disturbances in the market model. The advantages of the GARCH approach are: (i) these estimates are more efficient, leading to better statistical properties; and (ii) direct investigation of possible changes in conditional variance of the stock returns is possible. Information about changes in volatility of stock returns is important for managers, shareholders and investors, given the role of the risk-return tradeoff in portfolio selection.

The basic market model relates the return on any given security (R_{it}) to the return on a market portfolio (R_{mt}). For any security i, the market model is

$$R_{i,t+1} = \alpha_i + \beta_i R_{m,t+1} + u_{i,t+1}$$

However, the validity of this model depends on strong assumptions: (i) the error term $u_{i,t+1}$ is serially uncorrelated; (ii) the error term follows a normal distribution with a constant variance. Since many previous studies have questioned and evidenced against these assumptions, this study extends the market model to allow for GARCH processes.

The mean equation now includes lag(s) of the dependent variable to account for possible serial correlation in the series of stock returns.

$$R_{i,t+1} = \alpha_i + \beta_i R_{m,t+1} + \sum_{h=1}^{H} \eta_h R_{i,t-h+1} + u_{i,t+1}$$

$$Var(u_{i,t+1} \mid I_t) = \sigma_{i,t+1}^2$$

The conditional variance equation in the GARCH(p,q) model is:

$$\sigma_{i,t+1}^2 = \gamma_{i0} + \sum_{s=1}^{q} \gamma_{is} u_{i,t-s+1}^2 + \sum_{h=1}^{p} \delta_{ih} \sigma_{i,t-h+1}^2$$

Using daily data, this study conducts an event study of food contamination incidents by adding dummy variables to the above model specification.

$$R_{i,t+1} = \alpha_i + \beta_i R_{m,t+1} \sum_{h=0}^{H} \eta_h R_{i,t-h+1}$$
$$+ \theta_{i1} D1_{t+1} + \theta_{i2} D2_{t+1} + \theta_{i3} D3_{t+1} + u_{i,t+1}$$

$$\sigma_{i,t+1}^2 = \gamma_{i0} + \sum_{s=1}^{q} \gamma_{is} u_{i,t-s+1}^2 + \sum_{h=1}^{p} \delta_{ih} \sigma_{i,t-h+1}^2 + \zeta_i D4_{t+1}$$

where $D1$ takes the value 1 two days before the event date and 0 otherwise; $D2$ equals 1 on the event day and 0 otherwise; $D3$ equals 1 two days after the event and 0 otherwise; and $D4$ equals 1 after the event day and 0 otherwise. While $D2$ is used to catch the effect of the event day, $D1$ is meant to summarize the potential for information leakage just prior to the event. $D3$ is used to take into account the possibility that the market may not be fully informed on the day of the announcement. The dummy $D4$ in the variance equation is used to assess if there is any change in the stock price volatility after the recall. If the market's valuation provides private incentives to promote food safety, it is expected that $\theta_{i1} < 0$, $\theta_{i2} < 0$, $\theta_{i3} < 0$ and $\zeta_i > 0$.

10.3.2 Zhang, Fan, Tsai and Wei (2008)

The volatility spillover effect between the US dollar exchange and the oil price is summarized here; their mean-price spillover effect was introduced in the previous chapter. The volatility spillover effect indicates that the price volatility magnitude in one market may be affected not only by its own previous volatility but also by the price volatility of foreign markets.

ARCH-type models are first used to test and measure the volatility clustering. According to the principle of least AIC value for model selection, a GARCH(1,1) model is chosen for the volatility clustering description of the US dollar exchange rate.

$$\ln PE_t = \alpha_0 + \sum_{j=1}^{J} \alpha_{1j} \ln PE_{t-j} + \sum_{j=1}^{J} \alpha_{2j} \ln PO_{t-j} + u_t$$

$$h_t^{PE} = \gamma_0 + \gamma_1 u_{t-1}^2 + \gamma_2 h_{t-1}^{PE}$$

where h_t^{PE} is the conditional variance of the residual, i.e., $Var(u_t | I_{t-1})$ with $I_{t-1} = \{\ln PE_{t-1}, \ln PO_{t-1}, \ln PE_{t-2}, \ln PO_{t-2}, \ldots\}$.

The current price volatility magnitude caused by its previous price increase and decrease could be quite asymmetric. This study suggests that the volatility in the oil market showed asymmetric responses and is thus well described by the following TGARCH(1,1) model.

$$\ln PO_t = \beta_0 + \sum_{j=1}^{J} \beta_{1j} \ln PE_{t-j} + \sum_{j=1}^{J} \beta_{2j} \ln PO_{t-j} + \varepsilon_t$$

$$h_t^{PO} = \delta_0 + \delta_1 \varepsilon_{t-1}^2 + \psi \varepsilon_{t-1}^2 D_{t-1} + \delta_2 h_{t-1}^{PO}$$

where a dummy variable D_{t-1} is set to 1 if $\varepsilon_{t-1} < 0$, and 0 otherwise. Due to the introduction of D_{t-1}, we can examine whether the influence of unexpected price increase ($\varepsilon_{t-1} > 0$) on the conditional variance (h_t^{PO}) is different from the one of price decrease ($\varepsilon_{t-1} < 0$). Specifically, when the oil price increases, the influence magnitude is measured by δ_1; whereas if the oil price decreases, the influence is by $\delta_1 + \psi$. In brief, so long as $\psi \neq 0$, it can be said that the influence concerned appears asymmetric.

Table 10.1 shows that significant GARCH effect occurs for the volatility of the US dollar exchange rate. In its variance equation, the sum of γ_1 and γ_2 depicts the decaying velocity of volatility shocks. The closer the sum is to 1, the slower its decaying velocity appears. In the GARCH(1,1) model here, the sum is equal to 0.9872 ($= 0.0339 + 0.9533$), which implies that the US dollar exchange rate holds finite variance with a weak stable process and the volatility of the US dollar exchange rate will be confronted with decaying ultimately, but its span will last for a relatively long time. Furthermore, the coefficient of h_{t-1}^{PE} is 0.9533, revealing that 95.33% of current variance shocks will still stay on the next day, hence the half-life of its decaying is 14 days.

The estimation of volatility model TGARCH(1,1) for the oil price shows that significant asymmetry can be identified from international oil price volatility, namely leverage effect. The leverage coefficient

Table 10.1 Parameter estimates of the GARCH and TGARCH models

PE Eq. (11.28)		PO Eq. (11.30)	
γ_0	6.43×10^{-7} (0.0733)	δ_0	0.0070 (0.0903)
γ_1	0.0339 (0.0015)	δ_1	0.0688 (0.0006)
γ_2	0.9533 (0.0000)	δ_2	0.9492 (0.0000)
		ψ	−0.0469 (0.0326)

Source: Adapted from Zhang et al. (2008, Table 4 on page 984).

Note: p-values are in parentheses.

ψ is negative, which means the influence of oil price rise on future oil price volatility appears larger than that of oil price fall with the same magnitude. Specifically, when oil price drops, the influence magnitude of ε_{t-1}^2 on h_t^{PO}, namely $\delta_1 + \psi$, is 0.0219 (=0.0688 − 0.0469); but when oil price upsurges, the influence magnitude, namely δ_1, is equal to 0.0688, which is about 3.1 times of that in the former scenario.

Based on the above models, a model is constructed to test the volatility spillover effect by appending a lagged conditional variance term of one market to the conditional variance equation of another market.

$$h_t^{PE} = \gamma_0 + \gamma_1 u_{t-1}^2 + \gamma_2 h_{t-1}^{PE} + \theta_1 h_{t-1}^{PO}$$

$$h_t^{PO} = \delta_0 + \delta_1 \varepsilon_{t-1}^2 + \psi \varepsilon_{t-1}^2 D_{t-1} + \delta_2 h_{t-1}^{PO} + \theta_2 h_{t-1}^{PE} \tag{10.10}$$

where $\theta_1 (\theta_2)$ can be viewed as the market volatility spillover term in the *PE* (*PO*) market. Specifically, if θ_1 is significantly different from zero, it may be said that volatility spillover effect from the *PO* market to the *PE* market does exist. According to the estimation results of Eq. (10.10), neither θ_1 nor θ_2 is significant. Therefore, it can be pointed out that, although significant unidirectional mean spillover effect can be found between oil price and US dollar exchange rate, their volatility spillover effect in any direction is insignificant.

10.3.3 Value at risk (VaR)

The concept of *value at risk* is defined as a measure of risk which one is expected to experience in worst cases. More formally, VaR_α is defined as the possible maximum loss over a given holding period within a $100(1-\alpha)\%$ confidence level. Suppose that at time period t, we assess the risk of a financial position for the next h periods. Let $\Delta V(h)$ be the value change of the assets in the financial position from time t to $t + h$. We define VaR_α of this position over the time horizon h with probability α as

$$\alpha = \Pr[\Delta V(h) \leq VaR_\alpha]$$

For example, the 1% value at risk, $VaR_{0.01}$, is the loss at the 1% worst case. In other words, the probability of experiencing more losses than $VaR_{0.01}$ is 1%. As we consider a loss, $\Delta V(h)$ and $VaR_{0.01}$ will be negative.

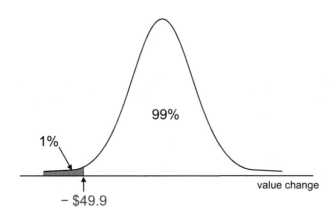

To calculate the *VaR*, we need to forecast the distribution of future returns R_{t+h}. Suppose a GARCH model predicts a mean 2% and a variance 9 for the next-period return, i.e., $\hat{R}_{t+1|t} \equiv E(R_{t+1} | I_t) = 2\%$ and $\hat{\sigma}^2_{t+1|t} \equiv E[(R_{t+1} - \hat{R}_{t+1|t})^2] = 9$. Assuming a normal distribution, the 1% percentile of R_{t+1} is -4.99%.[7]

$$0.01 = \Pr\left[\frac{R_{t+1} - 2}{\sqrt{9}} \leq -2.33\right] = \Pr[R_{t+1} \leq -4.99\%]$$

If the amount of the position is $1,000, its $VaR_{0.01}$ for one period is calculated as

$$VaR_{0.01} = \$1,000 \times (-0.0499) = -\$49.9$$

It indicates that the value can decrease more than $49.9 at a 1% probability.

Many authors have pointed out several conceptual problems with *VaR*. One important problem is that *VaR* disregards any loss beyond the *VaR* level. From the above graph, we can see that the *VaR* of $-\$49.9$ is the best outcome once the 1% worst case has been realized. Thus, the *VaR* measure under-estimates possible worst outcomes. To alleviate this problem, Artzner et al. (1997) proposed "expected shortfall," also called "beyond *VaR*." The expected shortfall is defined as the conditional expected loss given that the loss is beyond the *VaR* level.

$$ES_\alpha = E[\Delta V(h) \mid \Delta V(h) \leq VaR_\alpha]$$

Refer to Angelidis and Degiannakis (2009) and Yamai and Yoshiba (2005) for further explanations.

10.4 Summary

1   For time-series data, the disturbances in a regression model are often correlated between time periods. This property is known as *serial correlation* or *autocorrelation*. If so, the OLS estimator is no longer efficient because it violates one of the OLS assumptions that the disturbances should not be correlated with each other.

2   In static regression models where lagged dependent variables do not appear on the right-hand side as regressors, the autocorrelation itself does not affect the unbiasedness nor consistency of the OLS estimator. The unbiasedness requires the strict exogeneity of explanatory variables.

3   Since most economic time-series variables are not strictly exogeneous, the OLS estimator is biased. Note that this bias is caused by a violation of the strict exogeneity, but not by the presence of autocorrelation. However, if the disturbance and explanatory variables are contemporaneously and asymptotically uncorrelated, the OLS estimator is consistent.

4   For dynamic regression models which include lagged dependent variables as regressors, the auto-correlation makes the disturbance to be contemporaneously correlated with the lagged dependent variable. This contemporaneous correlation therefore causes the OLS estimator to be inconsistent.

5   A significant autocorrelation in estimated residuals does not necessarily imply that we should use a regression model with an autocorrelated disturbance. Because the disturbance is not observed, it is less interesting to interpret the autocorrelation. Instead, in many cases the autocorrelation disappears when more lagged dependent and independent variables are added as regressors. Further, this transformed model can provide useful information about dynamic relations of the variables.

6   A practical guideline for modeling: (i) Apply the Lagrange multiplier test for AR(*p*); (ii) If a significant autocorrelation is found, transform the regression model by including lagged-one

variables of the dependent and independent variables; (iii) Repeat (i) and (ii) until no autocorrelation is found.

7 Estimated regression functions can be used to predict future values of the dependent variable. When we use these predicted values for our decision making, we also need to know the uncertainty (or accuracy) of the prediction. The ARCH/GARCH-type models are useful for forecasting time-varying variances of the disturbance and thus the uncertainty associated with predicted values.

8 The GARCH model, an extension of the original ARCH model, is widely used in empirical analysis. The TGARCH and EGARCH models are useful in accounting for the asymmetric effects between positive and negative shocks.

Review questions

1 Consider the following autoregressive model of order one, AR(1), where ε_t is white noise with mean zero and variance σ^2.

$$y_t = \beta_0 + \beta_1 y_{t-1} + \varepsilon_t, \quad |\beta_1| < 1$$

Can the OLS method produce consistent estimates? Explain.

2 Consider the following dynamic model whose disturbance is autocorrelated of order one, where ε_t is white noise with mean zero and variance σ^2.

$$y_t = \beta_0 + \beta_1 y_{t-1} + u_t, \quad u_t = \rho u_{t-1} + \varepsilon_t \quad (\rho \neq 0)$$

(a) Explain why the OLS estimator is inconsistent.
(b) Explain how we can transform the model to obtain consistent estimates.

3 The following ARCH(1) model defines a one-period-ahead forecast made at period t, i.e., a conditional variance $\sigma_{t+1}^2 \equiv Var(u_{t+1}|I_t) = E(u_{t+1}^2|I_t)$.

$$\sigma_{t+1}^2 = \gamma_0 + \gamma_1 u_t^2$$

(a) Derive a two-period-ahead forecast made at period t, i.e., $Var(u_{t+2}|I_t)$.
(b) Explain how we can deal with the unobserved parameters and disturbance, ($\gamma_0, \gamma_1, u_t^2$).

4 Consider the following GARCH(1,1) model, where $\sigma_{t+1}^2 \equiv Var(u_{t+1}|I_t)$.

$$\sigma_{t+1}^2 = \gamma_0 + \gamma_1 u_t^2 + \delta_1 \sigma_t^2$$

(a) What is a one-period-ahead forecast made at period t?

(b) Explain how we can obtain forecasts when there are unobserved parameters and disturbance, ($\gamma_0, \gamma_1, \delta_1, \sigma_t^2, u_t^2$).

(c) Derive a two-period-ahead forecast made at period t, i.e., $Var(u_{t+2}|I_t)$.

5   Consider the following ARCH(1) model.

$$Y_{t+1} = \beta_0 + \beta_1 X_{t+1} + u_{t+1}$$
$$Var(u_{t+1}|I_t) \equiv \sigma_{t+1}^2 = \theta_0 + \theta_1 u_t^2$$

(a) Suppose that we want to test if the conditional variance of the disturbance is autoregressive. Using the parameters in the above model, express the null hypothesis that " H_0 : The conditional variance σ_{t+1}^2 is not autoregressive."

(b) In some cases, the effect of u_t^2 on σ_{t+1}^2 differs depending on whether u_t is positive or negative. One of the models which can examine such asymmetric relation is the following Threshold-ARCH(1) model.

$$\sigma_{t+1}^2 = \theta_0 + (\theta_1 + \varphi_1 D_t) u_t^2$$

where a dummy variable D_t is set to 1 if the value of the dependent variable unexpectedly decreased in the previous period (i.e., $u_t < 0$), and 0 otherwise.

(i) When u_t is negative, write the effect of u_t^2 on the conditional variance σ_{t+1}^2 using the parameters in the model.

(ii) When u_t is positive, write the effect of u_t^2 on the conditional variance σ_{t+1}^2 using the parameters in the model.

(iii) We want to test if there exists an asymmetric relation between u_t^2 and σ_{t+1}^2. Write the null hypothesis using the parameters in the model.

Notes

1   The new change (ε_t) can be interpreted as an unexpected change in Y_t (or a shock to Y_t). Then, the current value of Y_t is understood as the sum of the component related to the independent variable $(\beta_0 + \beta_1 X_t)$, the component related to the previous unexpected change (ρu_{t-1}) and the unexpected new change (ε_t).

2   The strict exogeneity $E(u_t|X_1, \cdots, X_T) = 0$ is stronger than the no-correlation condition. If the strict exogeneity is satisfied, the no-correlation is always satisfied.

3   On this ground, for vector autoregressive (VAR) models, lagged dependent variables are included until the disturbances show no autocorrelation; as explained in Chapter 9.

4   Since positive autocorrelation is much more commonly observed in economic time-series data than negative autocorrelation, our discussion is focused on positive cases.

5   Autocorrelation can be eliminated by including enough lagged values of the dependent and explanatory variables, as explained above in the previous section.

6   By repeated substitution for Eq. (10.8), we obtain

$$\begin{aligned}
\sigma_{t+1}^2 &= \gamma_0 + \gamma_1 u_t^2 + \delta_1 \{\gamma_0 + \gamma_1 u_{t-1}^2 + \delta_1 \sigma_{t-1}^2\} \\
&= \gamma_0(1 + \delta_1) + \gamma_1(u_t^2 + \delta_1 u_{t-1}^2) + \delta_1^2 \{\gamma_0 + \gamma_1 u_{t-2}^2 + \delta_1 \sigma_{t-2}^2\} = \cdots = \\
&= \gamma_0(1 + \delta_1 + \delta_1^2 + \delta_3^2 + \cdots) + \gamma_1(u_t^2 + \delta_1 u_{t-1}^2 + \delta_1^2 u_{t-2}^2 + \delta_1^3 u_{t-3}^2 + \cdots)
\end{aligned}$$

7   For the standard normal distribution, the 1% critical value on the left-hand side is -2.33; $Pr(Z \le -2.33) = 0.01$.

References

Angelidis, T. and S. Degiannakis (2009), *Econometric Modeling of Value-at-Risk*, New York: Nova Science Publishers, Inc.

Artzner, P., F. Delbaen, J.M. Eber and D. Heath (1997), "Thinking Coherently," *Risk*, 10(11), 68–71.

Black, F. (1976), "Studies in Stock Price Volatility Changes," *Proceedings of the 1976 Business Meeting of the Business and Economic Statistics Section*, American Statistical Association, 177–181.

Bollerslev, T. (1986), "Generalized Autoregressive Conditional Heteroskedasticity," *Journal of Econometrics*, 31, 307–327.

Bollerslev, T., R.Y. Chou and K.F. Kroner (1992), "ARCH Modeling in Finance: A Review of the Theory and Empirical Evidence," *Journal of Econometrics*, 52, 5–59.

Bollerslev, T., R.F. Engle and D.B. Nelson (1994), "ARCH Models" Chapter 49 in *Handbook of Econometrics*, Volume 4, Eds. R.F. Engle and D.L. McFadden, Amsterdam: North-Holland, 2959–3038.

Engle, R. (1982), "Autoregressive Conditional Heteroskedasticity with Estimates of the Variance of U.K. Inflation," *Econometrica*, 50, 987–1008.

Engle, R. (2001), "GARCH 101: The Use of ARCH/GARCH Models in Applied Econometrics," *Journal of Economic Perspectives*, 15, 157–168.

Engle, R. (2004), "Risk and Volatility: Econometric Models and Financial Practice," *American Economic Review*, 94, 405–420.

Greene, W.H. (2003), *Econometric Analysis*, 5th ed., Upper Saddle River, NJ: Prentice Hall.

Nelson, D.B. (1990), "Conditional Heteroskedasticity in Asset Returns: A New Approach," *Econometrica*, 59, 347–370.

Wang, Z., V. Salin, N.H. Hooker and D. Leatham (2002), "Stock Market Reaction to Food Recalls: A GARCH Application," *Applied Economics Letters*, 9, 979–987.

Yamai, Y. and T. Yoshiba (2005), "Value-at-Risk versus Expected Shortfall: A Practical Perspective," *Journal of Banking and Finance*, 29, 997–1015.

Zakoian, J.M. (1994), "Threshold Heteroskedastic Models," *Journal of Economic Dynamics and Control*, 18, 931–995.

Zhang, Y.J., Y. Fan, H.T. Tsai and Y.M. Wei (2008), "Spillover Effect of US Dollar Exchange Rate on Oil Prices," *Journal of Policy Modeling*, 30(6), 973–991.

Appendix 10A Test and estimation of autocorrelation using *EViews* and *SAS*

We illustrate the test and estimation of autocorrelated disturbances using a regression of company ABC's stock returns (*RET*) on market returns (*MKT*). An Excel file "10-returns.xls" contains 201 daily observations. First, we estimate the regression model by the OLS method.

$$RET_t = \beta_0 + \beta_1 MKT_t + u_t$$

Using *EViews*

After importing the file, select Objects/New Object. . . /Equation and enter the equation "RET C MKT" in the Equation Specification box. The OLS estimation results are in Output 10.5.

Output 10.5 OLS estimation results

Dependent Variable: RET
Method: Least Squares
Sample: 1 201
Included observations: 201

Variable	Coefficient	Std. Error	t-Statistic	Prob.
C	−0.143006	0.115982	−1.232999	0.2190
MKT	0.722365	0.022292	32.40450	0.0000

R-squared	0.840679	Mean dependent var	−0.392971
Adjusted R-squared	0.839878	S.D. dependent var	4.100162
S.E. of regression	1.640687	Akaike info criterion	3.838008
Sum squared resid	535.6791	Schwarz criterion	3.870877
Log likelihood	−383.7198	F-statistic	1050.051
Durbin-Watson stat	1.023533	Prob(F-statistic)	0.000000

Durbin-Watson test for AR(1)

Below is a part of the DW critical values for the 5% significance level. It shows that $d_L = 1.65$ and $d_U = 1.69$ when the number of observations is $n = 200$ and the number of regressors is $k = 1$.

n	$k = 1$	
	d_L	d_U
⋮	⋮	⋮
200	1.65	1.69
⋮	⋮	⋮

Since the DW *d* statistic from the OLS estimation is 1.023533, smaller than the lower critical value $d_L = 1.65$, the null hypothesis of no AR(1) is rejected at the 5% significance level.

Lagrange multiplier test for AR(*p*)

After you estimate the OLS regression of *RET* on *MKT*, select View/Residual Tests/Serial Correlation LM Test. . . . In the Lag Specification dialog box, you enter the highest order of autocorrelation to be tested. Below are the test results for AR(2); the estimated test regression of $\hat{u}_t$ is

$$\hat{u}_t = 0.003843 - 0.004668\, MKT_t + 0.444122\, \hat{u}_{t-1} + 0.091179\, \hat{u}_{t-2}$$

Output 10.6   Lagrange multiplier test for AR(2)

Breusch-Godfrey Serial Correlation LM Test:

F-statistic	31.59885	Probability	0.000000
Obs*R-squared	48.81956	Probability	0.000000

Test Equation:
Dependent Variable: RESID
Method: Least Squares
Presample missing value lagged residuals set to zero.

Variable	Coefficient	Std. Error	t-Statistic	Prob.
C	0.003843	0.101445	0.037887	0.9698
MKT	-0.004668	0.019725	-0.236667	0.8132
RESID(-1)	0.444122	0.071560	6.206250	0.0000
RESID(-2)	0.091179	0.071898	1.268167	0.2062

The null hypothesis is no autocorrelation up to lag 2, i.e., $H_0 : \rho_1 = \rho_2 = 0$ in $u_t = \rho_1 u_{t-1} + \rho_2 u_{t-2} + \varepsilon_t$. Since the Obs×R-squared statistic is 48.81956 with a *p*-value of 0.000000, we reject the null hypothesis at the 1% significance level. The estimates of the test equation shown in Output 10.6 indicate that the lag-one coefficient, RESID(−1), is significant with a *p*-value of 0.0000, but the lag-two coefficient, RESID(−2), is insignificant with a *p*-value of 0.2062.

t-test for AR(1)

Now, we drop the insignificant lag-two term and test for AR(1); the null hypothesis is $H_0 : \rho_1 = 0$ in $u_t = \rho_1 u_{t-1} + \varepsilon_t$. Since this is a special case of the Lagrange multiplier test, we can obtain all information for the *t*-test by following the above procedures. Select View/Residual Tests/Serial Correlation LM Test . . . and enter "1" for the Lag Specification dialog box.

Output 10.7   *t*-test for AR(1)

Breusch-Godfrey Serial Correlation LM Test:

F-statistic	61.40084	Probability	0.000000
Obs*R-squared	47.57721	Probability	0.000000

Breusch-Godfrey Serial Correlation LM Test:

Test Equation:
Dependent Variable: RESID
Method: Least Squares
Presample missing value lagged residuals set to zero.

Variable	Coefficient	Std. Error	t-Statistic	Prob.
C	0.001660	0.101586	0.016336	0.9870
MKT	−0.008238	0.019553	−0.421330	0.6740
RESID(-1)	0.488805	0.062381	7.835868	0.0000

Output 10.7 shows the estimated test regression of $\hat{u}_t$,

$$\hat{u}_t = 0.00166 - 0.008238\,MKT_t + 0.488805\,\hat{u}_{t-1}$$

The estimate of the lag-one coefficient, RESID(−1), is 0.488805 with a t-statistic of 7.835868 and a p-value of 0.0000, indicating that the disturbance is significantly autocorrelated with lag one. The same conclusion is obtained by applying the Lagrange multiplier test; the Obs×R-squared statistic is 47.57721 with a p-value of 0.000000.

Estimation of autocorrelation

Based on the test results, we now estimate the regression of *RET* on *MKT* with including the first-order autocorrelated disturbance. Press Estimate in the above output window to return to the Equation Specification dialog box. Then, specify the autocorrelation term AR(1) at the end of the list of independent variables, "RET C MKT AR(1)."[1]

Output 10.8 Estimation results with AR(1) error term

Dependent Variable: RET
Method: Least Squares
Sample (adjusted): 2 201
Included observations: 200 after adjustments
Convergence achieved after 14 iterations

Variable	Coefficient	Std. Error	t-Statistic	Prob.
C	−0.192514	0.314194	−0.612722	0.5408
MKT	0.592556	0.013817	42.88668	0.0000
AR(1)	0.722619	0.050134	14.41363	0.0000

R-squared	0.910962	Mean dependent var	-0.401953
Adjusted R-squared	0.910058	S.D. dependent var	4.108468
S.E. of regression	1.232140	Akaike info criterion	3.270268
Sum squared resid	299.0791	Schwarz criterion	3.319743
Log likelihood	-324.0268	F-statistic	1007.775
Durbin-Watson stat	1.557942	Prob(F-statistic)	0.000000
Inverted AR Roots	.72		

The estimated regression model is

$$\hat{RET}_t = -0.192514 + 0.592556 \ MKT_t$$
$$\hat{u}_t = 0.722619 \ u_{t-1}$$

An alternative solution to autocorrelation: adding lagged variables

A significant autocorrelation does not necessarily imply that the static model with autocorrelated disturbance is a correct model. Alternatively, we can examine whether a dynamic model with no autocorrelation fits the data well. To do this, we estimate the following dynamic model which includes lagged values of the dependent and independent variables.

$$RET_t = \beta_0 + \beta_1 MKT_t + \beta_2 MKT_{t-1} + \beta_3 RET_{t-1} + \varepsilon_t \tag{10A.1}$$

We need to generate lagged variables by clicking Genr from the Workfile menu and enter "L1RET= RET(−1)" and "L1MKT= MKT(−1)," where (−1) is a lag-one operator. To estimate Eq. (10A.1), select Objects/New Object. . . /Equation and enter "RET C MKT L1MKT L1RET" in the Equation Specification box. Since the lag-one variables are included for estimation, the effective number of observations will be reduced by one to 200. Output 10.9 shows that the estimated equation of Eq. (10A.1) is

$$\hat{RET}_t = 0.005.23 + 0.714326 MKT_t - 0.091446 MKT_{t-1} + 0.483708 RET_{t-1}$$

Output 10.9　Estimates of the dynamic model

Dependent Variable: RET
Method: Least Squares
Sample (adjusted): 2 201
Included observations: 200 after adjustments

Variable	Coefficient	Std. Error	t-Statistic	Prob.
C	0.005323	0.035882	0.148346	0.8822
MKT	0.714326	0.006850	104.2813	0.0000
L1MKT	−0.091446	0.017249	−5.301430	0.0000
L1RET	0.483708	0.021851	22.13695	0.0000

R-squared	0.985216	Mean dependent var	−0.401953
Adjusted R-squared	0.984990	S.D. dependent var	4.108468
S.E. of regression	0.503355	Akaike info criterion	1.484756
Sum squared resid	49.65982	Schwarz criterion	1.550722
Log likelihood	−144.4756	F-statistic	4353.855
Durbin-Watson stat	1.776917	Prob(F-statistic)	0.000000

Now, we test if the disturbance of the dynamic model Eq. (10A.1) is serially uncorrelated, i.e., $H_0: \rho = 0$ in $\varepsilon_t = \rho \varepsilon_{t-1} + \eta_t$. After obtaining the OLS results for Eq. (10A.1), select View/Residual Tests/Serial Correlation LM Test. . . . The test results for AR(1) are in Output 10.10. The estimated test regression is

Output 10.10   Lagrange multiplier test for AR(1)

Breusch-Godfrey Serial Correlation LM Test:

F-statistic	2.653195	Probability	0.104956
Obs*R-squared	2.684697	Probability	0.101316

Test Equation:
Dependent Variable: RESID
Method: Least Squares
Presample missing value lagged residuals set to zero.

Variable	Coefficient	Std. Error	t-Statistic	Prob.
C	−0.001657	0.035747	−0.046363	0.9631
MKT	0.000104	0.006822	0.015277	0.9878
L1MKT	0.008214	0.017902	0.458860	0.6468
L1RET	−0.011350	0.022848	−0.496751	0.6199
RESID(-1)	0.121661	0.074691	1.628863	0.1050

$$\hat{u}_t = -0.001657 - 0.000104\,MKT_t + 0.008214\,MKT_{t-1}$$
$$-0.01135\,RET_{t-1} + 0.121661\hat{u}_{t-1}$$

The *t*-test concludes that the disturbance is serially uncorrelated; the estimate of the lag-one coefficient, RESID(−1), is 0.121661 with a *t*-statistic of 1.628863 and a *p*-value of 0.1050, greater than a usual significance level of 10%. The same conclusion is obtained by the Lagrange multiplier test because the Obs×R-squared statistic is 2.684697 with a *p*-value of 0.101316. These test results show that we have eliminated the autocorrelation by adding lagged variables to the regression.

Using *SAS*[2]

```
FILENAME F1 DDE 'EXCEL|[10-RETURNS.XLS]RETURNS-ARCH!R2C1:R202C2';
TITLE '< Data: 10-RETURNS.xls >';
DATA DAT1; INFILE F1 LRECL=1000; INPUT RET MARKET;
*-----------------------------------------------------------------;
TITLE2 '------ DW test for AR(1) ------';
PROC AUTOREG; MODEL RET = MARKET/DW=1 METHOD=ML; RUN;

TITLE2 '------ LAGRANGE MULTIPLIER test for AR(2) ------';
PROC AUTOREG; MODEL RET = MARKET/GODFREY=2 METHOD=ML ; RUN;

TITLE2 '------ LAGRANGE MULTIPLIER test for AR(1) ------';
PROC AUTOREG; MODEL RET = MARKET/GODFREY=1 METHOD=ML ; RUN;
*-----------------------------------------------------------------;
```

```
TITLE2 '------ Estimation with AR(2) -------';
PROC AUTOREG; MODEL RET = MARKET/NLAG=2 METHOD=ML ; RUN;


TITLE2 '------ Estimation with AR(1) -------';
TITLE3 '--- Estimation method = ML (maximum likelihood) ---';
PROC AUTOREG; MODEL RET = MARKET/NLAG=1 METHOD=ML ; RUN;


TITLE3 '--- Estimation method = ULS (unconditional least squares) ---';
PROC AUTOREG; MODEL RET = MARKET/NLAG=1 METHOD=ULS ; RUN;



*----------------------------------------------------------------;
TITLE2 '------ Estimation of a dynamic model - ----';
TITLE3;


DATA DAT2; SET DAT1;
     L1RET=LAG(RET); L1MKT=LAG(MARKET); /**Create lagged variables**/


PROC AUTOREG;
     MODEL RET = MARKET L1MKT L1RET/GODFREY=1 METHOD=ML ;
RUN;
```

Note: SAS uses the following type of AR error models and reports AR coefficient estimates with the opposite sign to the ones by *EViews*.

$$u_t = -\rho_1 u_{t-1} - \rho_2 u_{t-2} - \cdots - \rho_p u_{t-p} + \varepsilon_t$$

The null hypothesis of the Godfrey test is no autocorrelation up to lag p; $H_0 : \rho_1 = \rho_2 = \cdots = \rho_p = 0$.

Appendix 10B Test and estimation of ARCH/GARCH models using *SAS*[3]

```
FILENAME F1 DDE 'EXCEL|[10-RETURNS.XLS]RETURNS-ARCH!R2C1:R202C2';

TITLE '< ARCH-type Models, 10-RETURNS.xls >';
DATA DAT1;
    INFILE F1 LRECL=1000; INPUT RET MARKET;
    L1RET= LAG(RET); L1MARKET= LAG(MARKET);


TITLE2 '----- Test for ARCH ------';
PROC AUTOREG;
    MODEL RET = MARKET L1MARKET L1RET/ARCHTEST; RUN;


TITLE2 '----- Estimation of ARCH(2) ------';
PROC AUTOREG;
    MODEL RET = MARKET L1MARKET L1RET/GARCH=(q=2); RUN;


TITLE2 '----- Estimation of GARCH(1,1) ------';
PROC AUTOREG;
    MODEL RET = MARKET L1MARKET L1RET/GARCH=(p=1,q=1);
```

Notes

1 For AR(2) autocorrelated disturbance, we enter "RET C MKT AR(1) AR(2)." For quarterly data, we might want to include u_{t-4}, i.e., $u_t = \rho_4 u_{t-4} + \varepsilon_t$, to account for the seasonality. If so, you enter AR(4) at the end of the list of independent variables, "RET C MKT AR(4)."
2 BASE SAS 9.4, SAS/ETS 13.1 and SAS/STAT 13.1. SAS Institute Inc., Cary, NC.
3 BASE SAS 9.4, SAS/ETS 13.1 and SAS/STAT 13.1. SAS Institute Inc., Cary, NC.

11 Unit root, cointegration and error correction model

Learning objectives

In this chapter, you should learn about:

- Spurious regression with integrated (unit root) time series;
- Tests for unit roots;
- Cointegration of several integrated variables and test for cointegration;
- Vector error correction model for cointegrated time series.

11.1 Spurious regression

If a dependent variable turns out to be significantly related with independent variables without any justifying reason, the relation is called a spurious or nonsense regression. To see what is meant by spurious regression, consider the following example.

Two times series Y_t and X_t are generated independently for $t = 1$ to 200 with the starting values of $Y_0 = 0$ and $X_0 = 0$:

$$Y_t = 0.2 + Y_{t-1} + \varepsilon_{yt} \qquad \varepsilon_{yt} \sim N(0,1)$$
$$X_t = 0.2 + X_{t-1} + \varepsilon_{xt} \qquad \varepsilon_{xt} \sim N(0,1)$$

where ε_{yt} and ε_{xt} are white noise drawn from the standard normal distribution.[1] Figure 11.1 shows that the two series fluctuate around upward trends.

As Y_t and X_t are by construction independent, the slope coefficient in a regression of Y_t on X_t should be insignificant. However, Output 11.1 shows that the OLS estimate of the slope coefficient is highly significant with the t value of 10.42512 and the p-value of 0.0000. The R^2 is very large (0.354383), but the Durbin-Watson d statistic is very low (0.024835), indicating highly autocorrelated disturbances. This is a typical case of spurious regression. As Granger and Newbold (1974) suggest, a good rule of thumb to suspect a spurious regression is that $R^2 > d$ (Durbin-Watson).

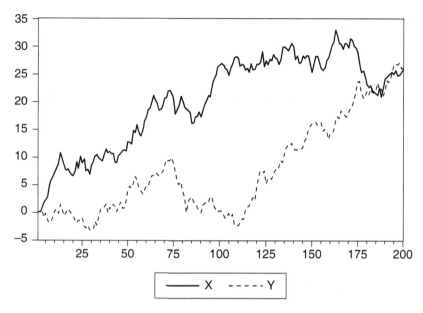

Figure 11.1 Plot of the generated series

Output 11.1 Regression of Y on X

Dependent Variable: Y
Method: Least Squares
Sample: 1 200
Included observations: 200

Variable	Coefficient	Std. Error	t-Statistic	Prob.
C	-4.917192	1.299047	-3.785230	0.0002
X	0.617655	0.059247	10.42512	0.0000

R-squared	0.354383	Mean dependent var		7.630083
Adjusted R-squared	0.351122	S.D. dependent var		8.582189
S.E. of regression	6.913209	Akaike info criterion		6.714695
Sum squared resid	9462.907	Schwarz criterion		6.747678
Log likelihood	-669.4695	F-statistic		108.6831
Durbin-Watson stat	0.024835	Prob(F-statistic)		0.000000

In order to correct this problem, let us generate first-differenced series from Y_t and X_t, respectively: $DY_t = Y_t - Y_{t-1}$ and $DX_t = X_t - X_{t-1}$. Output 11.2 shows the OLS estimation results of regressing DY on DX. Now, the estimate of the slope coefficient is correctly insignificant with the t value of 0.762072 and the p-value of 0.4469. And the R^2 is very small (0.002939) and the Durbin-Watson d statistic of 1.837398 indicates no autocorrelation.

Output 11.2 Regression of *DY* on *DX*

Dependent Variable: DY
Method: Least Squares
Sample (adjusted): 2 200
Included observations: 199 after adjustments

Variable	Coefficient	Std. Error	t-Statistic	Prob.
C	0.124682	0.065352	1.907867	0.0579
DX	0.047611	0.062476	0.762072	0.4469

R-squared	0.002939	Mean dependent var	0.130872
Adjusted R-squared	-0.002122	S.D. dependent var	0.913780
S.E. of regression	0.914749	Akaike info criterion	2.669666
Sum squared resid	164.8430	Schwarz criterion	2.702765
Log likelihood	-263.6318	F-statistic	0.580753
Durbin-Watson stat	1.837398	Prob(F-statistic)	0.446929

This example suggests that one should be careful when conducting regression analysis using *nonstationary* time series, particularly time series showing stochastic trends, to be explained below.

11.2 Stationary and nonstationary time series

A time series Y_t is said to be *strictly stationary* if the joint distribution of $(Y_{t_1}, \cdots, Y_{t_n})$ is the same as the joint distribution of $(Y_{t_1+\tau}, \cdots, Y_{t_n+\tau})$ for all $(t_1, \cdots, t_n)$ and τ; in other words, the distribution remains unchanged when shifted in time by an arbitrary value τ. However, the concept of strict stationarity is difficult to verify in practice because it is defined in terms of the distribution function.

The most commonly used form of stationarity is *weak stationarity* and defined as follows:

a   the mean of Y_t is constant over time;
b   the variance of Y_t is constant over time; and
c   the covariance between Y_t and $Y_{t-\tau}$ depends on the distance or lag(τ) between the two time periods, and not on the actual time at which the covariance is measured.

If a time series is weakly stationary, its mean and variance remain the same no matter when they are measured. Such a time series will not go too far away from the constant mean and therefore tend to return to the mean (i.e., "mean reverting").

If one or more of these conditions are not met, then the time series is called *nonstationary*. For example, a nonstationary time series has a time-varying mean and is not guaranteed to return to a certain value. The series in Figure 11.1 are examples of nonstationary series; they do not seem to return to a certain value and their variances increase over time.

The question is whether we may use nonstationary time series to estimate a regression model or whether the relationship of two nonstationary series can be described using constant coefficients, e.g., $Y_t = \alpha + \beta X_t + u_t$. Since the properties (such as mean, variance and covariance) of nonstationary time series change over time, the relationship between such series will not be constant. In fact, the two series in Figure 11.1 show a time-varying relation. Thus, the relation found in one period cannot be generalized to other time periods. It is therefore inappropriate to assume a constant regression equation for all time periods. Before we model for the time-series data, it is important to confirm that time series are stationary.

The most important types of nonstationary series are random walk models without and with drift:

$$Y_t = Y_{t-1} + u_t \tag{11.1}$$

$$Y_t = \alpha + Y_{t-1} + u_t \tag{11.2}$$

where u_t is white noise with mean 0 and variance σ^2, and α is the drift parameter. Using repeated substitution, we can confirm that these are nonstationary. In Eq. (11.1), random walk without drift, $Y_t = Y_0 + u_1 + \cdots + u_t$ and

$$E(Y_t) \ = Y_0 + E(u_1 + \cdots + u_t) = Y_0$$
$$Var(Y_t) = Var(u_1) + Var(u_2) + \cdots + Var(u_t) = t\sigma^2$$

Thus, the mean of Y_t is equal to its initial value of Y_0 for all t, and its variance $t\sigma^2$ increases over time, violating a condition of stationarity. In Eq. (11.2), random walk with drift, $Y_t = Y_0 + at + u_1 + \cdots + u_t$ and

$$E(Y_t) \ = Y_0 + at + E(u_1 + \cdots + u_t) = Y_0 + at$$
$$Var(Y_t) = Var(u_1) + Var(u_2) + \cdots + Var(u_t) = t\sigma^2$$

The mean of Y_t increases $(\alpha > 0)$ or decreases $(\alpha < 0)$ as time passes. Its variance $t\sigma^2$ is also time-varying. Thus, the random walk with drift is nonstationary.

These random walk models are a special case of autogressive regression, i.e., a case of $\rho = 1$ in $Y_t = \alpha + \rho Y_{t-1} + u_t$. Thus, these series are also known as *unit root processes* in the literature.

These random walk models belong to a more general class of stochastic processes known as *integrated processes*. If a time series is nonstationary but its first difference $(Y_t - Y_{t-1})$ is stationary, then the series is said to be *integrated of order 1*, denoted as $Y_t \sim I(1)$. The above random walk models are $I(1)$. Similarly, if a time series has to be differenced d times to become stationary, the series is said to be integrated of order d, denoted as $Y_t \sim I(d)$. If a series is stationary without differencing, it is integrated of order zero, $I(0)$.

11.3 Deterministic and stochastic trends

Many economic time series show upward trends reflecting economic growth. In this section, two most important models for trend are introduced. One model is to describe the trend as a linear function of time period, i.e.,

$$Y_t = \beta_0 + \beta_1 t + u_t \tag{11.3}$$

where u_t is white noise. For any t, $Var(Y_t \mid t) = Var(u_t \mid t) = \sigma^2$. The only uncertainty associated with predicting Y_t is from u_t, which is not a part of the trend. As such, the trend is completely predictable. Therefore, this series is said to have a *deterministic trend*. Although it is nonstationary because the mean $E(Y_t) = \beta_0 + \beta_1 t$ is not constant over time t, we can easily transform the series into a stationary one by eliminating the deterministic trend (if the coefficients are known; otherwise, their estimates are used):

$$u_t = Y_t - \beta_0 - \beta_1 t$$

This disturbance series is stationary around a deterministic trend and called a *trend-stationary* process. Thus, when the trend variable t is included, the regression of Y_t in Eq. (11.3) can be estimated by the OLS method in the same way as for a regression of a stationary dependent variable. Use of Y_t along with a time trend t does not cause a spurious regression problem.

In contrast, the other commonly observed trend causes a spurious regression. Consider the following random walk without drift.

$$Y_t = Y_{t-1} + u_t = Y_0 + (u_1 + \cdots + u_t)$$

Since each period's change $\{u_t\}$ persistently remains as a component of Y_t, the uncertainty associated with predicting Y_t comes from all current and past u_t s, i.e., $Var(Y_t) = Var(u_1 + \cdots + u_t) = Var(u_1) + \cdots + Var(u_t) = t\sigma^2$. As a result, the variation in this process is much more difficult to predict than the deterministic trend. This type of variation is called a *stochastic trend*. This integrated of order one series, $I(1)$, can be transformed into a stationary one by first-differencing and is said to be *difference-stationary*; $DY_t = Y_t - Y_{t-1} = u_t$.

Similarly, a random walk with drift contains both deterministic and stochastic trends.

$$Y_t = \alpha + Y_{t-1} + u_t$$
$$= Y_0 + \alpha\, t + (u_1 + \cdots + u_t)$$

The drift component represents a linear trend and exhibits an increasing ($\alpha > 0$) or decreasing ($\alpha < 0$) deterministic trend. The random walk component shows a stochastic trend.

The stochastic trend can cause a spurious regression problem; this is explained in Subsection 11.6.1. Therefore, before we use a time series, we need to test whether it is nonstationary containing a stochastic trend. If it is, we have to transform the nonstationary series into a stationary one by taking its first difference. The next section explains the test methods for the stochastic trend.

11.4　Unit root tests

The fact that there are many unit root tests in the literature indicates that there is no uniformly powerful test. In this section, only a couple of basic tests will be presented. In applying the tests, one should be careful because most unit root tests have low power, implying that the probability of correctly rejecting the null hypothesis of unit root is low.[2]

11.4.1　Dickey-Fuller (DF) test

$$Y_t = \alpha + \rho\, Y_{t-1} + \varepsilon_t \tag{11.4}$$
$$\Rightarrow\quad \Delta Y_t = \alpha + \gamma\, Y_{t-1} + \varepsilon_t$$

where $\Delta Y_t = Y_t - Y_{t-1}$, $\gamma = \rho - 1$, and ε_t is white noise. If $\rho < 1$ or $\gamma < 0$, the series Y_t is stationary. If $\rho = 1$ or $\gamma = 0$, then the series is integrated of order one, also called random walk or unit root process.

The Dickey-Fuller test formulates the following hypotheses based on Eq. (11.4):

$$H_0 : \gamma = 0 \quad \text{vs.} \quad H_1 : \gamma < 0$$

The null hypothesis means that there is a unit root. However, the OLS estimator for γ does not follow a Student-t distribution under the null hypothesis of unit root.[3] Instead, its critical values have been tabulated by Dickey and Fuller and considerably extended by others.

For a time series which shows a clear time trend, we need to extend the test equation to include a linear trend; this is to account for a possibility that the trend is deterministic.

$$\Delta Y_t = \alpha + \beta t + \gamma Y_{t-1} + \varepsilon_t$$

Under the alternative hypothesis $H_1 : \gamma < 0$, the time series Y_t is stationary around a deterministic trend βt because $Y_t = \alpha + \beta t + \rho Y_{t-1} + \varepsilon_t$. The null hypothesis for a unit root test is $H_0 : \gamma = 0$, that is, there is a unit root. The critical values for this test with a linear trend are different from the ones for the above DF test; *EViews* and *SAS* provide appropriate critical values.

11.4.2 Augmented Dickey-Fuller (ADF) test

The Dickey-Fuller test equation is also augmented with lagged dependent variables, i.e., ΔY_{t-j}, to control for possible autocorrelation of the disturbance:[4]

$$\Delta Y_t = \alpha + \beta t + \gamma Y_{t-1} + \sum_{j=1}^{m} \lambda_j \Delta Y_{t-j} + \varepsilon_t \qquad (11.5)$$

where ε_t is white noise. The hypotheses are $H_0 : \gamma = 0$ and $H_1 : \gamma < 0$. This test encompasses the above DF tests as a special case.

11.4.3 Example: unit root test using EViews

An Excel file "11-cointegration.xls" contains annual observations on the logarithmic values of real consumption (*LNCONS*) and real GDP (*LNGDP*) per capita of an Asian country, from 1961 until 2006. The plots in Figure 11.2 show clear increasing trends in both series.

After importing the variables in the order of "YEAR LNCONS LNGDP" from the Excel file, double click on the series name "LNCONS" and open the series window. To perform a unit root test for this series, choose View/Unit Root Tests/Standard Unit Test . . . in the Series window and specify the following.

1   Choose Augmented Dickey-Fuller for the Test type. From the pull-down menu for Test type, you can choose other tests including the Phillips and Perron (1988) test which uses the same regressions as the ADF test.
2   Specify whether to test for a unit root in the Level, 1st difference or 2nd difference of the series. If the test fails to reject the null hypothesis of unit root in the level but rejects the null in 1st difference, then the series contains one unit root in the level and is of integrated order one, $I(1)$.
3   Specify whether to include Intercept, Trend and intercept or None in the test equation. Since Figure 11.2 shows a nonzero intercept and a clear time trend, we choose to include Trend and intercept in the test equation.
4   For lag length, you may choose Automatic selection and a criterion such as Schwarz Info Criterion.

For the ADF test, the test statistic is the *t*-statistic for the lagged dependent variable Y_{t-1} in the test regression Eq. (11.5). The null hypothesis of unit root, $H_0 : \gamma = 0$, is rejected against the one-sided alternative if the *t*-statistic is less than the critical value given in the output. Output 11.3 shows the ADF test results for a series *LNCONS*.

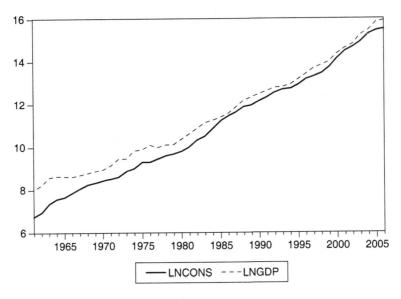

Figure 11.2 Plots of two time series

Output 11.3   ADF Unit Root Test for *LNCONS*

Null Hypothesis: LNCONS has a unit root
Exogenous: Constant, Linear Trend
Lag Length: 0 (Automatic based on SIC, MAXLAG = 9)

	t-Statistic	*Prob.* *
Augmented Dickey-Fuller test statistic	-1.089282	0.9196
Test critical values: 1% level	-4.175640	
5% level	-3.513075	
10% level	-3.186854	

*MacKinnon (1996) one-sided p-values.

Augmented Dickey-Fuller Test Equation
Dependent Variable: D(LNCONS)
Method: Least Squares
Sample (adjusted): 1962 2006
Included observations: 45 after adjustments

Variable	*Coefficient*	*Std. Error*	*t-Statistic*	*Prob.*
LNCONS(-1)	-0.069922	0.064191	-1.089282	0.2822
C	0.617292	0.416708	1.481356	0.1460
@TREND(1961)	0.014565	0.012219	1.191974	0.2400

The test results show that the value of the *t*-statistic is −1.089282 and its *p*-value is 0.9196, thus accepting the null hypothesis of unit root at a usual significance level. For the other series *LNGDP*, you follow the same procedures of the above ADF test.

11.5 Cointegration

If several variables are nonstationary but a linear combination of those variables becomes stationary, then they are defined as being cointegrated. For example, variables Y_{1t} and Y_{2t} are nonstationary, but if they have a common stochastic trend, a new variable $z_t = Y_{1t} - \lambda Y_{2t}$ can be stationary. If so, Y_{1t} and Y_{2t} are said to be *cointegrated*. The linear combination is called the *cointegrating equation* and λ the *cointegrating parameter*.

11.5.1 Tests for cointegration

To be cointegrated, $z_t (= Y_{1t} - \lambda Y_{2t})$ should be stationary. So, after first obtaining residuals ($\hat{z}_t = Y_{1t} - \hat{\lambda} Y_{2t}$) from a cointegrating regression of Y_{1t} on Y_{2t}, we can apply the ADF unit root test to the residuals.[5] A widely used alternative is the Johansen test. Examples below illustrate how to apply the Johansen test for cointegration using *EViews* and *SAS*.

Before we apply cointegration tests, we have to confirm that the variables tested for cointegration are integrated to the same order. The ADF test can be used for this confirmation.

11.5.2 Vector error correction models (VECMs)

The principle behind the VECMs is that there exists a long-run equilibrium relation among economic variables, such as the long-run average proportion of consumption in income. In the short run, however, they could be out of equilibrium.

Suppose that Y_{1t} and Y_{2t} are cointegrated in the form of $z_t = Y_{1t} - \lambda Y_{2t}$, where z_t is stationary. Since this cointegrating equation is equal to zero at the long-run equilibrium, we can treat any deviations from zero as the "(short-run) equilibrium errors." The time series Y_{1t} and Y_{2t} are expected to change in a way of correcting the equilibrium errors. The following is a VECM for two variables, including two lagged values of the dependent variables.

$$\Delta Y_{1,t} = \gamma_0 + \gamma_1 \Delta Y_{1,t-1} + \gamma_2 \Delta Y_{2,t-1} + \gamma_3 \Delta Y_{1,t-2} + \gamma_4 \Delta Y_{2,t-2} + \theta_1 z_{t-1} + \varepsilon_{1t}$$
$$\Delta Y_{2,t} = \delta_0 + \delta_1 \Delta Y_{1,t-1} + \delta_2 \Delta Y_{2,t-1} + \delta_3 \Delta Y_{1,t-2} + \delta_4 \Delta Y_{2,t-2} + \theta_2 z_{t-1} + \varepsilon_{2t} \qquad (11.6)$$
$$z_{t-1} = Y_{1,t-1} - \lambda Y_{2,t-1}$$

In the above equations, the error correction terms $\theta_1 z_{t-1}$ and $\theta_2 z_{t-1}$ capture the adjustments toward the long-run equilibrium and thus describe how the previous equilibrium error influences the next period's values of Y_{1t} and Y_{2t}. And θ_1 and θ_2 respectively tell us how sensitively Y_{1t} and Y_{2t} respond to the equilibrium error. This VECM has made the idea of cointegration practically useful for understanding the dynamics of economic variables.

Summary

When we analyze time series, we need to first test whether they are integrated, and if so, whether they are cointegraged. Here is an example of two variables.

After testing whether Y_{1t} and Y_{2t} have unit roots,

a   if $Y_{1t} \sim I(0)$ and $Y_{2t} \sim I(0)$, use VAR in Y_{1t} and Y_{2t};

b   if $Y_{1t} \sim I(0)$ and $Y_{2t} \sim I(1)$, use VAR in Y_{1t} and ΔY_{2t};

c   if $Y_{1t} \sim I(1)$ and $Y_{2t} \sim I(1)$, we need to test whether they are cointegrated.

If they are cointegrated, use a VECM in ΔY_{1t}, ΔY_{2t} and $z_{t-1}(= Y_{1,t-1} - \lambda Y_{2,t-1})$. Otherwise, use VAR in ΔY_{1t} and ΔY_{2t} only.

11.5.3 Example: test and estimation of cointegration using EViews

In the previous section, we have concluded that series *LNCONS* and *LNGDP* are integrated of order one, $I(1)$. Now, we test whether they are cointegrated by applying the Johansen test.[6]

(i) Johansen test for cointegration

To apply the Johansen (1988) test, you first need to group the variables whose cointegration is tested. Select Objects/New Object/Group from the Workfile toolbar. In the Group dialog box, enter the variable names "LNCONS LNGDP" and you will see a group window. Select View/Cointegration Test/ Johansen System Cointegration Test . . . from the group toolbar.

In the Cointegration Test Specification, you need to choose an appropriate assumption on the deterministic trends in the cointegrating equation (CE) and in the level variables Y_{1t} and Y_{2t}. It is because the asymptotic sampling distribution of the test statistic for cointegration depends on the assumptions made with respect to deterministic trends. In *EViews*, five assumptions are offered but assumptions 1 and 5 are rarely used in practice. The five assumptions can be illustrated in terms of Eq. (11.6). The point is whether an intercept and a linear deterministic trend are included in the CE or in the test VAR.[7]

Assumption 1: There is no intercept in the CE; there is no intercept in the test VAR (no deterministic trend in the level variables Y_{1t} and Y_{2t}):

$$z_{t-1} = Y_{1,t-1} - \lambda Y_{2,t-1}$$
$$\Delta Y_{1,t} = \gamma_1 \Delta Y_{1,t-1} + \gamma_2 \Delta Y_{2,t-1} + \theta_1 z_{t-1} + \varepsilon_{1t}$$
$$\Delta Y_{2,t} = \delta_1 \Delta Y_{1,t-1} + \delta_2 \Delta Y_{2,t-1} + \theta_2 z_{t-1} + \varepsilon_{2t}$$

Assumption 2: There is an intercept in the CE; there is no intercept in the test VAR (no deterministic trend in the level variables Y_{1t} and Y_{2t}):

$$z_{t-1} = Y_{1,t-1} - \lambda Y_{2,t-1} + \eta_0$$
$$\Delta Y_{1,t} = \gamma_1 \Delta Y_{1,t-1} + \gamma_2 \Delta Y_{2,t-1} + \theta_1 z_{t-1} + \varepsilon_{1t}$$
$$\Delta Y_{2,t} = \delta_1 \Delta Y_{1,t-1} + \delta_2 \Delta Y_{2,t-1} + \theta_2 z_{t-1} + \varepsilon_{2t}$$

Assumption 3: There is an intercept in the CE; there is an intercept in the test VAR (linear trends in the level variables Y_{1t} and Y_{2t}):

$$z_{t-1} = Y_{1,t-1} - \lambda Y_{2,t-1} + \eta_0$$
$$\Delta Y_{1,t} = \gamma_0 + \gamma_1 \Delta Y_{1,t-1} + \gamma_2 \Delta Y_{2,t-1} + \theta_1 z_{t-1} + \varepsilon_{1t}$$
$$\Delta Y_{2,t} = \delta_0 + \delta_1 \Delta Y_{1,t-1} + \delta_2 \Delta Y_{2,t-1} + \theta_2 z_{t-1} + \varepsilon_{2t}$$

Assumption 4: There are an intercept and a linear trend in the CE; there is an intercept in the test VAR (linear trends in the level variables Y_{1t} and Y_{2t}):

$$z_{t-1} = Y_{1,t-1} - \lambda Y_{2,t-1} + \eta_0 + \eta_1 t$$
$$\Delta Y_{1,t} = \gamma_0 + \gamma_1 \Delta Y_{1,t-1} + \gamma_2 \Delta Y_{2,t-1} + \theta_1 z_{t-1} + \varepsilon_{1t}$$
$$\Delta Y_{2,t} = \delta_0 + \delta_1 \Delta Y_{1,t-1} + \delta_2 \Delta Y_{2,t-1} + \theta_2 z_{t-1} + \varepsilon_{2t}$$

Assumption 5: There are an intercept and linear trend in the CE; there are an intercept and a linear trend in the test VAR (quadratic trends in the level variables Y_{1t} and Y_{2t}) :[8]

$$z_{t-1} = Y_{1,t-1} - \lambda Y_{2,t-1} + \eta_0 + \eta_1 t$$
$$\Delta Y_{1,t} = \gamma_0 + \gamma_1 t + \gamma_2 \Delta Y_{1,t-1} + \gamma_3 \Delta Y_{2,t-1} + \theta_1 z_{t-1} + \varepsilon_{1t}$$
$$\Delta Y_{2,t} = \delta_0 + \delta_1 t + \delta_2 \Delta Y_{1,t-1} + \delta_3 \Delta Y_{2,t-1} + \theta_2 z_{t-1} + \varepsilon_{2t}$$

A careful examination of individual series is required in choosing appropriate assumptions.[9] For the test variables *LNCONS* and *LNGDP*, we choose assumption 3. It is based on the observations in Figure 11.2 and Output 11.3: (i) Both series show linear deterministic trends; (ii) Both are integrated of order one; and (iii) The time trend term (@TREND) in the ADF test for *LNCONS* is not significant.

- The model to be tested does not have any exogenous variable.
- Enter "1 2" for lag intervals, the number of lagged $\Delta Y_{1,t-j}$ and $\Delta Y_{2,t-j}$ included in the model.

Output 11.4   Results of the Johansen cointegration test

Sample (adjusted): 1964 2006
Included observations: 43 after adjustments
Trend assumption: Linear deterministic trend
Series: LNCONS LNGDP
Lags interval (in first differences): 1 to 2

Unrestricted Cointegration Rank Test (Trace)

Hypothesized		Trace	0.05	
No. of CE(s)	*Eigenvalue*	*Statistic*	*Critical Value*	*Prob.***
None *	0.360233	21.65629	15.49471	0.0052
At most 1	0.055390	2.450281	3.841466	0.1175

Trace test indicates 1 cointegrating eqn(s) at the 0.05 level
* denotes rejection of the hypothesis at the 0.05 level
**MacKinnon-Haug-Michelis (1999) p-values

Unrestricted Cointegration Rank Test (Maximum Eigenvalue)

Hypothesized		Max-Eigen	0.05	
No. of CE(s)	*Eigenvalue*	*Statistic*	*Critical Value*	*Prob.***
None *	0.360233	19.20601	14.26460	0.0076
At most 1	0.055390	2.450281	3.841466	0.1175

Max-eigenvalue test indicates 1 cointegrating eqn(s) at the 0.05 level
* denotes rejection of the hypothesis at the 0.05 level
**MacKinnon-Haug-Michelis (1999) p-values

The Johansen test results are shown in Output 11.4. To determine the number (r) of cointegrating relations, we proceed sequentially from $r = 0$ to $r = 1$ until we fail to reject. The test results in Output 11.4 show that the null hypothesis of no cointegrating relation ($r = 0$) is rejected, but the null hypothesis of at most one cointegrating relation ($r \leq 1$) is not rejected with a p-value of 0.1175 (at the 5% or 10% significance level). Therefore, we conclude that there exists one cointegrating relation.[10]

For your information, Output 11.5 shows the output of an option "6 Summarize all 5 sets of assumptions" in the Cointegration Test Specification.

Output 11.5   Johansen cointegration test results of option 6

Sample: 1961 2006
Included observations: 43
Series: LNCONS LNGDP
Lags interval: 1 to 2

Selected (0.05 level*) Number of Cointegrating Relations by Model

Data Trend:	None	None	Linear	Linear	Quadratic
Test Type	No Intercept No Trend	Intercept No Trend	Intercept No Trend	Intercept Trend	Intercept Trend
Trace	2	2	1	1	1
Max-Eig	2	2	1	0	0

*Critical values based on MacKinnon-Haug-Michelis (1999)

Information Criteria by Rank and Model

Data Trend:	None	None	Linear	Linear	Quadratic
Rank or No. of CEs	No Intercept No Trend	Intercept No Trend	Intercept No Trend	Intercept Trend	Intercept Trend
Log Likelihood by Rank (rows) and Model (columns)					
0	73.92550	73.92550	80.39087	80.39087	84.85588
1	83.11624	85.10417	89.99387	90.08435	92.38827
2	87.07152	91.21901	91.21901	94.22473	94.22473
Akaike Information Criteria by Rank (rows) and Model (columns)					
0	−3.066302	−3.066302	−3.273994	−3.273994	−3.388645
1	−3.307732	−3.353682	−3.534599	−3.492295	−3.552943*
2	−3.305652	−3.405535	−3.405535	−3.452313	−3.452313
Schwarz Criteria by Rank (rows) and Model (columns)					
0	−2.738637	−2.738637	−2.864412	−2.864412	−2.897148
1	−2.816234	−2.821226	−2.961185*	−2.877923	−2.897613
2	−2.650322	−2.668289	−2.668289	−2.633150	−2.633150

(ii) Estimation of a VECM

To estimate a VECM, click Quick/Estimate VAR . . . from the main menu. Fill out the dialog box with appropriate information.

- In the Basics tab, choose Vector Error Correction for the VAR type.
- Enter the cointegrated series in the Endogenous Variables box: "LNCONS LNGDP."

- Number of lagged $\Delta Y_{1,t-j}$ and $\Delta Y_{2,t-j}$ included in the model; lag 2 ("1 2") is used in this example. If you want to estimate a VECM with no lagged ΔY, you need to enter "0 0."[11]
- The model in this example does not have any exogenous variable, other than the cointegrated variable.
- In the Cointegration tab, choose 3) Intercept (no trend) in CE and VAR.

Output 11.6 Estimates of ECM

Vector Error Correction Estimates
Sample (adjusted): 1964 2006
Included observations: 43 after adjustments
Standard errors in () & t-statistics in []

Cointegrating Eq:	CointEq1	
LNCONS(-1)	1.000000	
LNGDP(-1)	-1.067319	
	(0.02127)	
	[-50.1693]	
C	1.240251	

Error Correction:	D(LNCONS)	D(LNGDP)
CointEq1	-0.040629	0.353919
	(0.08351)	(0.08300)
	[-0.48654]	[4.26429]
D(LNCONS(-1))	0.236773	0.090418
	(0.16554)	(0.16453)
	[1.43030]	[0.54955]
D(LNCONS(-2))	-0.153758	-0.239851
	(0.15578)	(0.15483)
	[-0.98703]	[-1.54915]
D(LNGDP(-1))	0.255869	0.222482
	(0.13427)	(0.13345)
	[1.90564]	[1.66716]
D(LNGDP(-2))	-0.022495	0.399685
	(0.14410)	(0.14322)
	[-0.15611]	[2.79067]
C	0.132311	0.091837
	(0.04047)	(0.04023)
	[3.26908]	[2.28300]

As shown in Output 11.6, the estimated ECM is

$$\Delta LNCONS_t = -0.040629\, z_{t-1} + 0.236773\, \Delta LNCONS_{t-1} - 0.153758\, \Delta LNCONS_{t-2}$$
$$+ 0.255869\, \Delta LNGDP_{t-1} - 0.022495\, \Delta LNGDP_{t-2} + 0.132311$$

$$\Delta LNGDP_t = 0.353919\, z_{t-1} + 0.090418\, \Delta LNCONS_{t-1} - 0.239851\, \Delta LNCONS_{t-2}$$
$$+ 0.222482\, \Delta LNGDP_{t-1} + 0.399685\, \Delta LNGDP_{t-2} + 0.091837$$

where the cointegrating equation is

$$z_{t-1} = LNCONS_{t-1} - 1.067319 \Delta LNGDP_{t-1} + 1.240251$$

11.6 Applications

11.6.1 Stock and Watson (1988)

Using simulated data, the authors illustrate how regression analysis can be highly misleading when applied to variables containing stochastic trends. Based on the findings, they derive several rules of thumb for analysis of integrated variables. Below are introduced some of the rules of thumb.

For a simple regression $Y_t = \alpha + \beta X_t + u_t$, the probability limit of the OLS estimator for the slope coefficient is

$$\hat{\beta} = \beta + \frac{\sum_{t=1}^{T}(X_t - \bar{X})(u_t - \bar{u})/T}{\sum_{t=1}^{T}(X_t - \bar{X})^2/T} \quad \Rightarrow \quad plim \, \hat{\beta} = \beta + \frac{Cov(X,u)}{Var(X)}$$

Case 1: $Y \sim I(0)$, $X \sim I(0)$, $u \sim I(0)$

The OLS estimator is unbiased, consistent and efficient, i.e., BLUE, under the usual assumptions of the strict exogeneity, homoscedasticity and serial independence. Therefore, the t-statistic of the OLS $\hat{\beta}$ is valid.

Case 2: $Y \sim I(0)$, $X \sim I(1)$, $u \sim I(0)$,

The OLS estimator $\hat{\beta}$ converges much more quickly than in case 1 because the denominator $Var(X)$ explodes without a limit. In this case of *super consistency*, the usual critical values for the t-statistic are not correct. Instead, the Dickey-Fuller tables provide correct critical values.

Case 3: $Y \sim I(1)$, $X \sim I(1)$, $u \sim I(0)$

Y and X are cointegrated. And the OLS estimator $\hat{\beta}$ is super consistent. As in case 2, the Dickey-Fuller tables provide correct critical values for the t-statistic of $\hat{\beta}$.

Case 4: $Y \sim I(1)$, $X \sim I(1)$, $u \sim I(0)$

This is a case of spurious regression. Thus, the OLS estimator $\hat{\beta}$ is neither consistent nor meaningful.
The next two cases are for multiple regression models:

$$Y_t = \alpha + \beta X_t + \gamma Z_t + u_t$$

Case 5: $Y \sim I(1)$, $X \sim I(1)$, $Z \sim I(1)$, $u \sim I(0)$

The OLS coefficient estimator for a stationary variable, $\hat{\beta}$, is unaffected even though an integrated variable is included. In other words, the OLS $\hat{\beta}$ is consistent and its t-statistic is valid. It is because if the two regressors, X and Z, are uncorrelated, the estimator $\hat{\beta}$ from the multiple regression is the same as the one from a simple regression of Y on X.[12] To see why X and Z are uncorrelated, consider the covariance $Cov(X,Z)$. Since the stochastic trend in Z dominates the behavior of an integrated process, the sample covariance between an integrated variable and any mean-zero stationary variable tends to zero as the sample size increases.

On the other hand, the coefficient on the integrated regressor, Z, is super consistent.

Case 6: $Y \sim I(1),\ X \sim I(1),\ Z \sim I(1),\ u \sim I(0)$

We transform the multiple regression into

$$Y_t = \alpha + \beta(X_t - Z_t) + (\beta + \gamma)Z_t + u_t$$

Since the disturbance is stationary, the dependent variable Y is cointegrated with the regressors. If X and Z are cointegrated such that $(X-Z)$ is stationary, then the OLS estimator $\hat{\beta}$ is consistent and its t-statistic is valid: this belongs to case 5. It indicates that even if the coefficient of our interest is the coefficient on an integrated regressor, their OLS estimator will be valid as long as the regression equation can be rewritten in such a way that the coefficient of our interest becomes the coefficient on a stationary variable.

On the other hand, the coefficient ($\beta + \gamma$) on Z is super consistent because Z is integrated while u is stationary.

11.6.2 Baillie and Selover (1987)

This paper examines the econometric validity of some popular models of exchange rate determination that are widely used in forecasting nominal exchange rates. Use of the cointegration models gives extra insight into the reasons why the simple models of exchange rate determination have broken down and failed to give rise to successful forecasting. In this part we will focus on the purchasing power parity (PPP) model.

$$s_t = \alpha + \beta(p_t - p_t^*) + u_t \tag{11.7}$$

where s_t is the natural logarithm on the nominal exchange rate; p_t the natural logarithm of the domestic consumer price index; and asterisks (*) denote foreign quantities.

Table 11.1 shows the results of applying the ADF test to the variables used in the study. Notice that the null hypothesis is the existence of unit root and small positive values of the test statistic are suggestive of $I(1)$ variables.

The results indicate that the nominal exchange rate (s_t) and relative prices ($p_t - p_t^*$) appear to be $I(1)$. To evaluate the PPP model, Eq. (11.7), this study estimates a cointegrating relationship between s_t and $p_t - p_t^*$ and tests whether the residuals are stationary. According to Table 11.2, the hypothesis that the residuals are $I(1)$ can only be rejected for France; so that for the other countries, no cointegrating relationship can be found. Thus, exchange rates and relative prices will apparently drift apart without bounds. While PPP has been a convenient assumption in many models, permanent departures from PPP can arise from changes in productivity and tastes, shifts in comparative advantage, etc.

11.6.3 Granger (1988)

This study examines the relationship between causation and cointegration. The Granger-causality test explained in Chapter 10 evaluates whether the coefficients of lagged variables in a VAR model are

Table 11.1 Augmented Dickey-Fuller tests

Country	s_t	$(p_t - p_t^*)$
UK	−1.74	−2.01 (1)
Japan	−0.44	0.47 (0)
Germany	−0.36	−1.71 (2)
Canada	0.62	0.66 (4)
France	1.77	1.21 (3)

Source: Adapted from Baillie and Selover (1987, Table 5 on page 47).

Notes

(i)   Variables: s = (logarithm) nominal exchange rate; p = (logarithm) domestic consumer price index; and asterisks (*) denote foreign quantities.

(ii) Augmented DF test equation: $\Delta Y_t = \gamma Y_{t-1} + \sum_{j=1}^{q} \lambda_j \Delta Y_{t-j} + \varepsilon_t$.

(iii) The 1% and 5% significance levels of the above test statistic are −1.95 and −2.60, respectively. The number in parentheses besides the statistic is the value of q in the ADF equation in (ii).

Table 11.2 Estimates of $s_t = \alpha + \beta(p_t - p_t^*) + u_t$

Country	$\hat{\alpha}$	$\hat{\beta}$	DF statistic
UK	0.625	0.012	−1.17
Japan	−5.510	0.005	−1.49
Germany	−8.002	0.003	−1.31
Canada	−0.052	0.017	−1.35
France	−1.585	0.025	−2.23

Source: Baillie and Selover (1987, Table 8 on page 49).

Note

DF is the Dickey-Fuller statistic to test for a unit root in $\hat{u}_t$.

jointly significant. This Wald test based on *F*-statistics requires that the variables in the VAR model be stationary; otherwise, the *F*-statistics will have nonstandard distributions.

Granger (1988) considers a case where two variables x_t and y_t are integrated of order one but cointegrated. That is, $x_t \sim I(1)$, $y_t \sim I(1)$ but $z_t = x_t - \lambda y_t \sim I(0)$. For such cases he suggests to use error-correction models (ECMs) in testing the Granger-causality.

$$\Delta x_t = \theta_1 z_{t-1} + \sum_{\tau=1}^{p} \alpha_\tau \Delta x_{t-\tau} + \sum_{\tau=1}^{q} \beta_\tau \Delta y_{t-\tau} + \varepsilon_{1t}$$

$$\Delta y_t = \theta_2 z_{t-1} + \sum_{\tau=1}^{r} \gamma_\tau \Delta x_{t-\tau} + \sum_{\tau=1}^{s} \delta_\tau \Delta y_{t-\tau} + \varepsilon_{2t}$$

A consequence of the ECM is that either Δx_t or Δy_t (or both) must be caused by z_{t-1} which is itself a function of x_{t-1} and y_{t-1}. Thus, if a pair of series is cointegrated, then at least one of them must cause the other; either y_{t-1} causes in means x_t or x_{t-1} does y_t. This is a somewhat surprising result as cointegration is concerned with the long-run equilibrium, whereas the causality in mean is concerned with short-run forecastability. However, what it essentially says is that for a pair of series to have an attainable equilibrium, there must be some causation between them to provide the necessary dynamics. Granger points out that in the ECM, there are two possible sources of causation of x_t by $y_{t-\tau}$, either through the z_{t-1} term if $\theta_1 \neq 0$ (long-run causality), or through the lagged $\Delta y_{t-\tau}$ terms if they are significant (short-run causality).

If the error-correction term is not included in the VAR when the series is cointegrated, on some occasions one would not be able to detect causation when it is present. To see why, let's express the $I(1)$ variables as

$$x_t = \lambda q_t + u_t^x$$
$$y_t = q_t + u_t^y$$

where $x_t \sim I(1)$ and u_t^x, u_t^y are both $I(0)$. These are cointegrated through q_t. It is thus assumed that there exists only the long-run causality through q_t, but not the short-run causality between the two series. Suppose that for simplicity, q_t is a random walk, i.e., $\Delta q_t = \eta_t$, zero mean white noise, and u_t^x, u_t^y are white noise. Now consider Δx_t, which is given by

$$\Delta x_t = \lambda \eta_t + \Delta u_t^x = -u_{t-1}^x + \lambda \eta_t + u_t^x$$

The first term in the second line, $-u_{t-1}^x$, is the forecastable part of Δx_t and the final two terms will constitute the one-step forecast error of a forecast made at time $t-1$ based on x_{t-j}, y_{t-j} ($j \geq 1$). However, the first term, $-u_{t-1}^x$, is not directly observable, but is a component of x_{t-1} and thus cor related with $z_{t-1}(= x_{t-1} - \lambda y_{t-1})$, resulting in the long-run causation in mean. The above expression also shows that Δx_t has no direct relation with lagged $y_{t-\tau}$ or $\Delta y_{t-\tau}$. If z_{t-1} is not included in the VAR model, this will be misspecified and the possible value of lagged $y_{t-\tau}$ in forecasting x_t will be missed. In other words, causality of the cointegration type will not be captured by the Granger test without including error-correction terms. Thus, many of the papers discussing causality tests based on the "traditional" time-series modeling techniques could have missed some of the forecastability and hence reached incorrect conclusions about noncausality in mean. On some occasions, causation could be present but would not be detected by the testing procedures used.[13]

11.6.4 Dritsakis (2004)

This paper empirically examines the impact of tourism on the long-run economic growth of Greece by using causality analysis of (log) real gross domestic product (*LGDP*), (log) real effective exchange rate (*LEXR*) and (log) international tourism earnings (*LITR*). A three-variable VAR model with an error correction mechanism is applied for the period 1960:I – 2000:IV.

(i) Unit root tests

The augmented Dickey-Fuller (ADF) test is to check the significance of δ_2 in the following regression:

$$\Delta X_t = \delta_0 + \delta_1 t + \delta_2 X_{t-1} + \sum_{i=1}^{k} \alpha_i \Delta X_{t-i} + u_t \tag{11.8}$$

As shown in Table 11.3, the null hypothesis of a unit root is not rejected for all three variables, while it is rejected for their first-differenced variables. Therefore, the test results suggest that the three variables are integrated to the order of 1, $I(1)$.

(ii) Cointegration test

The maximum likelihood procedure of Johansen (1988) is employed to test for cointegration. To determine the number (r) of cointegrating relations, we proceed sequentially from $r = 0$ to $r \leq 2$ until we fail

Table 11.3 ADF tests for unit roots

	τ_τ	k
LGDP	−1.0461	2
LITR	−2.2231	4
LEXR	−2.3266	4
Δ*LGDP*	−3.7750**	4
Δ*LITR*	−9.4916***	4
Δ*LGDP*	−6.7897***	4

Source: Adapted from Dritsakis (2004, Table 1 on page 310).
Notes: τ_τ is the *t*-statistic for testing the significance of δ_2 when a time trend is included in Eq. (11.8). The critical values at 1%
and 5% are −4.21 and −3.53, respectively. The lag length (k) is determined using the Lagrange Multiplier autocorrelation test.
*** and ** indicate significance at the 1% and 5% levels, respectively.

to reject. The test results show that the null hypothesis of no cointegrating relation ($r = 0$) is rejected, but the null hypothesis of at most one cointegrating relation ($r \leq 1$) is not rejected at the 5% significance level. Thus, the results suggest that there exists one cointegrating relation which is estimated as

$$LGDP = 0.3129 \, LITR + 4.869 \, LEXR$$

This indicates that in the long run, tourist earnings and real exchange rate have a positive effect on gross domestic product.

(iii) Causality test

As the logarithms of the model variables are cointegrated, this study estimates a VAR model which includes a mechanism of error correction. Such error correction model (ECM) provides the short-run dynamic adjustment towards the long-run equilibrium, i.e., the estimated cointegrating relation shown above. The significance levels of the *F*-statistics for the lagged variables and the *t*-statistics for the coefficients ($\theta_1, \theta_2, \theta_3$) of EC_{t-1} are used to test for Granger-causality in the following ECM.

$$\begin{bmatrix} \Delta LGDP_t \\ \Delta LITR_t \\ \Delta LEXR_t \end{bmatrix} = A_0 + \sum_{i=1}^{q} A_i \begin{bmatrix} \Delta LGDP_{t-i} \\ \Delta LITR_{t-i} \\ \Delta LEXR_{t-i} \end{bmatrix} + \begin{bmatrix} \theta_1 \\ \theta_2 \\ \theta_3 \end{bmatrix} EC_{T-1} + \varepsilon_t$$

where A_0 is a 3×1 vector of constants, A_1 is a 3×3 coefficient matrix for lagged variables, $|\theta_1, \theta_2, \theta_3|'$ is a 3x1 vector of adjustment coefficients, e_t is a 3×1 vector of random errors and the estimated error correction term is $EC_{t-1} = LGDP_{t-1} - 0.3129 LITR_{t-1} - 4.869 LEXR_{t-1}$.

According to Granger (1988), there are two channels of causality: these may be called channel 1 and channel 2. If the lagged values of variables on the right-hand side (except the lagged values of the dependent variable) are jointly significant, then this is channel 1 and also called the "short-run" causality. If the lagged value of the error correction term is significant, then this is channel 2 and also called the "long-run" causality. The results are summarized in Table 11.4, where the numbers in parentheses are the lag lengths determined by using the Akaike criterion.

Table 11.4 shows that the coefficients of lagged variables are statistically significant when Δ*LGDP* is used as the dependent variable (channel 1), which means that international tourism earnings and real exchange rate affect economic growth in the short run. Regarding the long-run causality, the adjustment coefficients ($\theta_1, \theta_2, \theta_3$) are statistically significant only when economic growth (Δ*LGDP*) is used

Table 11.4 Causality test results based on a vector error correction model

Dependent variable	F-significance level for the lagged values of		
	$\Delta LGDP$	$\Delta LITR$	$\Delta LEXR$
$\Delta LGDP$	-	0.001*** (2)	0.008*** (1)
$\Delta LITR$	0.013** (3)	-	0.009*** (2)
$\Delta LEXR$	0.198 (2)	0.137 (2)	-

Source: Adapted from Dritsakis (2004, Table 3 on page 313).

Notes: *** and ** indicate significance at the 1% and 5% levels, respectively. Numbers in parentheses are lag lengths.

as a dependent variable; $H_0 : \theta_1 = 0$ is rejected at the 1% significance level. This significant causality of channel 2 implies that international tourism earnings (*LITR*) and real exchange rate (*LEXR*) affect economic growth through the error correction mechanism.

11.6.5 Ghosh (1993)

This study investigates whether the index spot and futures price changes are predictable with the concept of cointegration, a new econometric methodology which marries the short-run dynamic adjustment and long-run relationships between economic variables. It finds that index spot and futures prices are integrated processes. Further, as the two series are cointegrated, error correction models are developed and shown to be useful for forecasting index spot and futures prices.

11.7 Summary

1   If a regression model includes nonstationary (integrated) variables, the OLS method might produce wrong estimates; this is called the problem of spurious regression. Thus, it is important to make sure that the variables in a regression model are stationary.

2   If there are integrated variables in a regression model, we need to transform the variables into stationary ones by calculating their first differences.

3   If several variables are integrated of order one but a linear combination of those variables becomes stationary, then they are said to be cointegrated. If cointegrated, we have to use a vector error correction model (VECM) to incorporate the cointegrating relation (or the long-run equilibrium).

4   For the ADF unit root test and the VECM, it is important to carefully determine the lag order. If a too small lag order is used (i.e., significant lagged dependent variables are omitted), the disturbance is likely to be serially correlated. If so, the OLS estimator becomes inconsistent and also biased.

Review questions

1   Show if any deterministic and/or stochastic trends are included in the following series y_t, where x_t and ε_t are stationary series.

(a) $y_t = \alpha_0 + \beta x_t + \varepsilon_t$

(b) $y_t = \alpha_0 + \alpha_1 t + \beta x_t + \varepsilon_t$

(c) $y_t = \alpha + \rho y_{t-1} + \varepsilon_t, \quad |\rho| < 1$

(d) $y_t = \alpha + \beta t + \rho y_{t-1} + \varepsilon_t, \quad |\rho| < 1$

(e) $\Delta y_t = \varepsilon_t$

(f) $\Delta y_t = \alpha_0 + \varepsilon_t$

(g) $\Delta y_t = \alpha_0 + \alpha_1 t + \varepsilon_t$

2   The DF test uses the following equation and examines whether $\rho = 1$ vs. $\rho < 1$.

$$Y_t = \alpha + \beta t + \rho Y_{t-1} + \varepsilon_t$$

(a) If $\rho < 1$, what trends does the series show? Draw a possible time path.

(b) If $\rho = 1$, what trends does the series show? Draw a possible time path.

3   Below are shown the ADF test results.

Augmented Dickey-Fuller Unit Root Tests

Type	Lags	Tau	Pr < Tau
Single Mean	0	-12.04	0.0002
	1	-8.64	0.0211
	2	-1.49	0.5431
	3	-0.85	0.8041

(a) The p-values are very different depending on the lags included. Explain why this can happen.

(b) What is your conclusion from this ADF test?

4   The following is a regression equation for the ADF test.

$$\Delta Y_t = \alpha + \beta t + \gamma Y_{t-1} + \sum_{j=1}^{m} \lambda_j \Delta Y_{t-j} + \varepsilon_t$$

It is important to carefully determine the lag order.

(a) If a too small lag order is selected, what problem will there be?

(b) If a too large lag order is selected, what problem will there be?

5   The following regression is to test the Granger-causality and neutrality of money growth (Δm_t) on income growth (Δy_t)

$$\Delta y_t = \beta_0 + \beta(L)\Delta m_{t-1} + \alpha(L)\Delta y_{t-1} + \varepsilon_t$$

where $\beta(L) = \beta_1 + \beta_2 L + \beta_3 L^2 + \cdots + \beta_p L^{p-1}$, and similarly for $\alpha(L)$. The lag operator L is defined as $L^s x_t = x_{t-s}$ and $(1-L)x_t = x_t - x_{t-1} = \Delta x_t$.

(a) The Granger-causality test examines whether lagged values of money growth enter the income equation. Write this null hypothesis of the causality test using the parameters of the regression.

(b) The neutrality states that money growth will have no long-run (cumulative) effect on output growth. Thus, the sum of the coefficients on lagged money growth equals zero in the income-growth equation. Write a null hypothesis of this neutrality test using the parameters of the regression.

6   Answer the following questions about the Granger-causality test between two variables, x_t and y_t.

If the two variables are *stationary*, we can use the following VAR model where the lag order is 3.

$$x_t = \alpha_0 + \alpha_{x1}x_{t-1} + \alpha_{x2}x_{t-2} + \alpha_{x3}x_{t-3} + \alpha_{y1}y_{t-1} + \alpha_{y2}y_{t-2} + \alpha_{y3}y_{t-3} + u_{1t}$$

$$y_t = \beta_0 + \beta_{x1}x_{t-1} + \beta_{x2}x_{t-2} + \beta_{x3}x_{t-3} + \beta_{y1}y_{t-1} + \beta_{y2}y_{t-2} + \beta_{y3}y_{t-3} + u_{2t}$$

(a) Write the null hypothesis that x does not cause y.
(b) Write the null hypothesis that y does not cause x.

Suppose that the two variables are integrated of order one, $I(1)$, and *cointegrated*. Using the cointegrating relation of $z_t = y_t - \lambda x_t$ $(\lambda > 0)$, we can modify the above VAR model into the following vector error correction model (VECM).

$$\Delta x_t = \gamma_{x1}\Delta x_{t-1} + \gamma_{x2}\Delta x_{t-2} + \gamma_{y1}\Delta y_{t-1} + \gamma_{y2}\Delta y_{t-2} + \theta_1 z_{t-1} + \varepsilon_{1t}$$
$$\Delta y_t = \delta_{x1}\Delta x_{t-1} + \delta_{x2}\Delta x_{t-2} + \delta_{y1}\Delta y_{t-1} + \delta_{y2}\Delta y_{t-2} + \theta_2 z_{t-1} + \varepsilon_{2t}$$

(c) Write the null hypothesis that y does not cause x, both in the short and long run.
(d) It is expected that the two series will move toward the long-run equilibrium. The VECM specifies that any deviation from the long-run equilibrium is partly corrected in the following period. If so, what do you expect the sign of θ_1? Explain.
(e) What do you expect the sign of θ_2?

Suppose that the two variables are integrated of order one, $I(1)$, but *not cointegrated*.
(f) In order to test the Granger-causality, what form of VAR model can we use?

7 Below are several assumptions of the following simple regression model.

$$y_t = \beta_0 + \beta_1 x_t + u_t$$

(a) $y_t \sim I(1)$, $x_t \sim I(1)$, $u_t \sim I(0)$
  1) Is this case possible? If so, when?
  2) Is the OLS estimator for β_1 consistent?
(b) $y_t \sim I(0)$, $x_t \sim I(1)$, $u_t \sim I(0)$
  3) Is this case possible? If so, when?
  4) Is the OLS estimator for β_1 consistent?
(c) $y_t \sim I(1)$, $x_t \sim I(1)$, $u_t \sim I(1)$
  5) Is this case possible? If so, when?
  6) Is the OLS estimator for β_1 consistent?
(d) $y_t \sim I(1)$, $x_t \sim I(0)$, $u_t \sim I(0)$
  7) Explain if this case is possible.

8 Dritsakis (2004) empirically examines the impact of tourism on the long-run economic growth of Greece by using a causality analysis of real gross domestic product ($LGDP$), international tourism earnings ($LITR$) and real effective exchange rate ($LEXR$); all are in logarithmic values. A three-variable VAR model with an error correction mechanism is applied for the period 1960:I–2000:IV.

Based on the ADF unit root test and the Johansen cointegration test, he concludes that the three variables are integrated of order one and there exists one cointegrating relation.
(a) Write the VECM model which includes one lagged dependent variable and the error correction term, $z_{t-1} = LGDP_{t-1} - \lambda_1 LITR_{t-1} - \lambda_2 LEXR_{t-1}$.
(b) Using the notations in (a), write the null and alternative hypotheses which can test "Does tourism ($LITR$) cause economic growth ($LGDP$) in the short run?"
(c) Using the notations in (a), write the null and alternative hypotheses which can test "Is economic growth ($LGDP$) caused by tourism ($LITR$) and exchange rate ($LEXR$) in the long run?"

Notes

1 A stochastic process is called *white noise* if it has zero mean, constant variance, and is serially uncorrelated.

2 A hypothesis test is said to be *powerful* if at a chosen level of significance, it has the largest probability of rejecting the null when it is not correct. Thus, the power of a test indicates the extent to which an incorrect null hypothesis is rejected; in other words, an alternative hypothesis is concluded when it is correct.

3 In Eq. (11.4) the OLS estimator for the slope coefficient is $\hat{\gamma} = \sum y_{t-1} \Delta Y_t / \sum y_{t-1}^2$ $= \gamma + \sum y_{t-1} \varepsilon_t / \sum y_{t-1}^2$, where the small letters indicate deviations from mean values. Under the null hypothesis of unit root, the denominator $\sum y_{t-1}^2$ (the variance of Y_{t-1}) increases indefinitely and dominates the numerator, causing a faster convergence of $\hat{\gamma}$ to γ than for conventional stationary cases.

4 As explained in Chapter 10, the autocorrelation, if any, disappears when lagged dependent variables are included as regressors. Regarding the determination of m, the number of lagged dependent variables, you may test down to the right lag order by sequentially testing the significance of the last-lagged coefficient. Alternatively, you may use information criteria such as AIC and SBC.

5 For these residual-based tests using *EViews*, refer to *EViews* User's Guides.

6 A theoretical explanation of the Johansen test is given in Appendix 11B. Tests for cointegration and an estimation of VECM using *SAS* are illustrated in Appendix 11C.

7 The "test VAR" means the VAR of ΔY_{1t} and ΔY_{2t} in Eq. (11.6); see Appendix 11C for a graphical explanation of the assumptions.

8 For assumptions 3 and 4, the intercept in the CE may be dropped because it can be merged into the intercept γ_0 and δ_0 in the test VAR. Estimates of all other coefficients are unchanged with and without the intercept in the CE. In *SAS*, the CE equations do not include an intercept η_0 in the CE under assumptions 3 and 4; see Appendix 11C for an illustration of using *SAS*. Similarly, under assumption 5, the intercept and linear trend in the CE, $\eta_0 + \eta_1 t$, may be dropped.

9 As a rough guide, use assumption 2 if none of the series appears to have a deterministic trend. For linearly trending series, use assumption 3. If you are not sure which trend assumption to use, choose the "6) Summary of all 5 sets of assumptions" option. Refer to the *EViews* manual for more details.

10 When there are k variables, there can only be up to $k-1$ cointegrating relations; see Appendix 11B for an explanation. If the null of $r = 0$ is not rejected, it indicates that the $I(1)$ nonstationary variables are not cointegrated and a VAR model in their first differences is appropriate.

11 Regarding the determination of m, the number of lagged dependent variables, you may use the information criteria (e.g., AIC, SBC, etc.) or test down to the right lag order by sequentially testing the significance of the last-lagged coefficients. See Chapter 9 for an illustration of *EViews* and *SAS* for the determination of the lag order.

12 According to the Frisch-Waugh-Lovell Theorem, the OLS estimator $\hat{\beta}$ can also be obtained when the residuals from a regression of Y on Z are regressed on the residuals from a regression of X on Z. If X and Z are not correlated, nothing will be explained by Z in the regression of X on Z and thus the residuals are X themselves. In the regression of Y on Z, the Y-variation correlated with X will not be removed because Z is not correlated with X.

13 This is a Type II error situation. If you find causality with the Granger test, it is real. But if you fail to find it, causality of the cointegration type might still exist.

References

Baillie, R.T. and D.D. Selover (1987), "Cointegration and Models of Exchange Rate Determination," *International Journal of Forecasting*, 3, 43–51.

Dritsakis, N. (2004), "Tourism as a Long-run Economic Growth Factor: An Empirical Investigation for Greece Using Causality Analysis," *Tourism Economics*, 10(3), 305–316.

Engle, R. and C.W.J. Granger (1987), "Co-integration and Error Correction: Representation, Estimation and Testing," *Econometrica*, 35, 251–276.

Ghosh, A. (1993), "Cointegration and Error Correction Models: Intertemporal Causality Between Index and Futures Prices," *Journal of Futures Markets*, 12(2), 193–198.

Granger, C.W.J. and P. Newbold (1974), "Spurious Regressions in Econometrics," *Journal of Econometrics*, 2, 111–120.

Granger, C.W.J. (1988), "Some Recent Development in a Concept of Causality," *Journal of Econometrics*, 29, 199–211.

Johansen, S. (1988), "Statistical Analysis of Cointegration Vectors," *Journal of Economic Dynamics and Control*, 12, 231–254.

Phillips, P. and P. Perron (1988), "Testing for a Unit Root in Time Series Regression," *Biometrika*, 75, 335–346.

Stock, J.H. and M.W. Watson (1988), "Variable Trends in Economic Time Series," *Journal of Economic Perspectives*, 2, Summer, 147–174.

Appendix 11A Unit root test using *SAS*[1]

Augmented DF regressions and null hypotheses

$$Y_t = \alpha + \beta t + \rho Y_{t-1} + \sum_{j=1}^{m} \lambda_j \Delta Y_{t-j} + \varepsilon_t, \qquad H_0 : \rho = 1$$

$$\text{or} \quad \Delta Y_t = \alpha + \beta t + \gamma Y_{t-1} + \sum_{j=1}^{m} \lambda_j \Delta Y_{t-j} + \varepsilon_t, \qquad H_0 : \gamma = 0$$

```
**********************************************
* Augmented Dickey Fuller Test
**********************************************;
FILENAME F1 DDE 'EXCEL|[11-COINTEGRATION.XLS]COINTEGRATION!R2C1:R47C3';
DATA K; INFILE F1 LRECL=1000; INPUT YEAR LNCONS LNGDP;
TITLE '===== Augmented Dickey Fuller Test =====';
PROC ARIMA;
   IDENTIFY VAR=LNCONS STATIONARITY=(ADF=3); RUN;
/** (ADF=3) performs the ADF test with autoregressive orders 0,1,2 and 3. **/
```

===== Augmented Dickey Fuller Test =====

Augmented Dickey-Fuller Unit Root Tests

Type	Lags	Rho	Pr < Rho	Tau	Pr < Tau	F	Pr > F
Zero Mean	0	0.7829	0.8655	12.62	0.9999		
	1	0.7539	0.8591	3.96	0.9999		
	2	0.7249	0.8527	4.06	0.9999		
	3	0.7052	0.8481	2.89	0.9987		
Single Mean	0	0.2816	0.9665	1.04	0.9964	86.11	0.0010
	1	0.2353	0.9645	0.64	0.9892	9.11	0.0010
	2	0.4550	0.9727	1.49	0.9990	8.67	0.0010
	3	0.4659	0.9729	1.25	0.9980	4.39	0.0753
Trend	0	-3.1465	0.9247	-1.09	0.9197	1.26	0.9220
	1	-7.4021	0.5991	-1.72	0.7270	1.81	0.8171
	2	-7.1871	0.6172	-1.76	0.7061	3.01	0.5913
	3	-14.8087	0.1400	-2.28	0.4369	3.79	0.4440

(1) Two test statistics (Rho and Tau) are designed to account for possible autocorrelations and hetero-scedasticity of the error terms.

(2) Type of a deterministic trend

Zero Mean: $Y_t = \rho Y_{t-1} + \varepsilon_t$ (For simplicity, no lagged variables are included.)
   – Rho and Tau are to test $H_0 : \rho = 1$
   Under $H_1 : |\rho| < 1$, the series $\{Y_t\}$ has a zero mean.

Single Mean: $Y_t = \alpha + \rho Y_{t-1} + \varepsilon_t$
   – Rho and Tau are to test $H_0 : \rho = 1$
   Under $H_1 : |\rho| < 1$, the mean of $\{Y_t\}$ converges to a constant (single mean).
   – F is to test $H_0 : \alpha = 0$ and $\rho = 1$ (i.e., $Y_t = Y_{t-1} + \varepsilon_t$, random walk without drift)

Trend: $Y_t = \alpha + \beta t + \rho Y_{t-1} + \varepsilon_t$
   – Rho and Tau are to test $H_0 : \rho = 1$
   Under $H_1 : |\rho| < 1$, the mean of $\{Y_t\}$ shows a time trend of βt.
   – F is to test $H_0 : \beta = 0$ and $\rho = 1$ (i.e., $Y_t = \alpha + Y_{t-1} + \varepsilon_t$, random walk with drift).

(3) Guideline for selecting a deterministic trend in the test: Hamilton (1994, pp 501–503)
   – If a series does not show an increasing (or decreasing) trend, use Single Mean.
   Ex) interest rates, GDP growth rates, stock returns, etc.
   – If a series shows a trend, use Trend.
   Ex) GDP (level), stock prices, stock indices, etc.

Appendix 11B Johansen test for cointegration

Consider an autoregressive model of time series W_t.

$$W_t = \sum_{i=1}^{p} \Phi_i W_{t-i} + \varepsilon_t \tag{11A.1}$$

where W_t is a $k \times 1$ vector of order-one integrated variables, Φ_i is a $k \times k$ matrix and p is the order of the vector autoregressive process of the level variables. If the integrated variables are cointegrated, they can be represented by a vector error correction model according to the Granger representation theorem (Engle and Granger, 1987).

$$\Delta W_t = \Pi W_{t-1} + \sum_{i=1}^{p-1} \Gamma_i \Delta W_{t-i} + \varepsilon_t \tag{11A.2}$$

Where $\Delta W_t = W_t - W_{t-1}$, $\Pi = \sum_{i=1}^{p} \Phi_i - I = \alpha \beta'$, $\Gamma_i = -\sum_{j=i+1}^{p} \Phi_j$, α is a $k \times r$ matrix containing adjustment coefficients, β is a $r \times k$ matrix containing cointegrating (or long-run) parameters, In testing for cointegration, we may include an intercept in the above equation.

After estimating the Π matrix from an unrestricted VAR, Eq. (11A.1), the cointegration rank test determines the number of linearly independent columns (rank) of Π in Eq. (11A2). If $rank(\Pi) = 0$, there is no cointegrating relation in W_t. If $rank(\Pi) = r < k$, there are r stationary cointegrating relations. On the other hand, if the matrix Π has a full-rank ($r = k$), then it indicates no cointegrating relation; in other words, all components in W_t are stationary.[2] Therefore, there can only be up to $k-1$ linearly independent cointegrating equations.

For an easy understanding, consider a case where there are two variables, $W_t = [Y_{1,t}\ Y_{2,t}]'$. If $rank(\Pi) = 1$, it indicates that there is one cointegrating relation, e.g., $z_{t-1} = Y_{1,t-1} - \lambda Y_{2,t-1}$.

$$\begin{bmatrix} \Delta Y_{1t} \\ \Delta Y_{2t} \end{bmatrix} = \begin{bmatrix} \theta_1 \\ \theta_2 \end{bmatrix} z_{t-1} + \cdots = \begin{bmatrix} \theta_1 \\ \theta_2 \end{bmatrix} [1 - \lambda] \begin{bmatrix} Y_{1,t-1} \\ Y_{2,t-1} \end{bmatrix} + \cdots = \begin{bmatrix} \theta_1 & -\lambda\theta_1 \\ \theta_2 & -\lambda\theta_2 \end{bmatrix} \begin{bmatrix} Y_{1,t-1} \\ Y_{2,t-1} \end{bmatrix} + \cdots$$

$$= \Pi W_{t-1} + \cdots$$

$$\Rightarrow rank(\Pi) = rank \begin{bmatrix} \theta_1 & -\lambda\theta_1 \\ \theta_2 & -\lambda\theta_2 \end{bmatrix} = 1$$

If $rank(\Pi) = 2$ (full-rank), there is no cointegrating relation. One of the full-rank matrices is the identity matrix, so $\Pi = I_2$.

$$\begin{bmatrix} \Delta Y_{1t} \\ \Delta Y_{2t} \end{bmatrix} = \Pi W_{t-1} + \cdots = \begin{bmatrix} 1 & 0 \\ 0 & 1 \end{bmatrix} \begin{bmatrix} Y_{1,t-1} \\ Y_{2,t-1} \end{bmatrix} + \cdots = \begin{bmatrix} Y_{1,t-1} \\ Y_{2,t-1} \end{bmatrix} + \cdots$$

It implies that all components in $W_{t-1} = [Y_{1,t-1}\ Y_{2,t-1}]'$ are stationary. This is a contradiction because we are testing for cointegration of integrated variables. Notice that the unit root test has already confirmed that the variables $W_t = [Y_{1,t}\ Y_{2,t}]'$ are integrated of one.

Appendix 11C Vector error correction modeling (VECMs): test and estimation using *SAS*[3]

Consider an autoregressive model of time series W_t.

$$W_t = \sum_{i=1}^{p} \Phi_i W_{t-i} + \varepsilon_t$$

$$\Rightarrow \quad \Delta W_t = \alpha\beta' W_{t-1} + \sum_{i=1}^{p-1} \Gamma_i \Delta W_{t-i} + \varepsilon_t$$

where W_t is a $k \times 1$ vector, Φ_i is a $k \times k$ matrix, $\Delta W_t = W_t - W_{t-1}$, $\alpha\beta' = \sum_{i=1}^{p} \Phi_i - I$, $\Gamma_i = -\sum_{j=i+1}^{p} \Phi_i$,

α is a $k \times r$ matrix containing adjustment coefficients, β is a $r \times k$ matrix containing cointegrating (or long-run) parameters and p is the order of the vector autoregressive process of the level variables.

When $k = 2$ and $p = 3$, the above model can be expressed as follows.

$$\Delta Y_{1,t} = \theta_1 z_{t-1} + \gamma_1 \Delta Y_{1,t-1} + \gamma_2 \Delta Y_{2,t-1} + \gamma_3 \Delta Y_{1,t-2} + \gamma_4 \Delta Y_{2,t-2} + \varepsilon_{1t}$$
$$\Delta Y_{2,t} = \theta_2 z_{t-1} + \delta_1 \Delta Y_{1,t-1} + \delta_2 \Delta Y_{2,t-1} + \delta_3 \Delta Y_{1,t-2} + \delta_4 \Delta Y_{2,t-2} + \varepsilon_{2t}$$
$$z_{t-1} = Y_{1,t-1} - \lambda Y_{2,t-1}$$

where $W_t = \begin{bmatrix} Y_{1,t} \\ Y_{2,t} \end{bmatrix}$, $\Delta W_t = \begin{bmatrix} \Delta Y_{1,t} \\ \Delta Y_{2,t} \end{bmatrix}$ and $\alpha\beta' W_{t-1} = \begin{bmatrix} \theta_1 \\ \theta_2 \end{bmatrix} [1 - \lambda] \begin{bmatrix} Y_{1,t-1} \\ Y_{2,t-1} \end{bmatrix} = \begin{bmatrix} \theta_1 \\ \theta_2 \end{bmatrix} z_{t-1}.$

For the Johansen cointegration test, we need to specify the deterministic trends in the level variables Y_{1t} and Y_{2t}. The five assumptions made with respect to deterministic trends are given in Subsection "11.5.3 Example: Test and estimation of cointegration using *EViews*." The point is whether an intercept and a linear deterministic trend are included in the cointegrating equation (CE) or in the test VAR.

The CE describes the relative location of the level series. And the drifts and linear trends in the test VAR determine the deterministic trends of the level series. For your information, below are the graphs showing the deterministic trends of the level variables for assumptions 2, 3 and 4.[4]

Assumption 2

(CE) $\quad z_t = Y_{1t} - \lambda Y_{2t} + \eta_0 \quad \Rightarrow \quad Y_{1t} = \lambda Y_{2t} - \eta_0 + z_t$

(test VAR) $\quad \begin{aligned} \Delta Y_{1t} &= \gamma_1 \Delta Y_{1,t-1} + \gamma_2 \Delta Y_{2,t-1} + \theta_1 z_{t-1} + \varepsilon_{1t} \\ \Delta Y_{2t} &= \delta_1 \Delta Y_{1,t-1} + \delta_2 \Delta Y_{2,t-1} + \theta_2 z_{t-1} + \varepsilon_{2t} \end{aligned}$

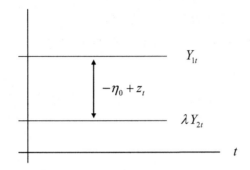

Assumption 3

(CE)　　　　　　　$z_t = Y_{1t} - \lambda Y_{2t} \;\Rightarrow\; Y_{1t} = \lambda Y_{2t} + z_t$

(test VAR)　　　$\Delta Y_{1t} = \gamma_0 + \gamma_1 \Delta Y_{1,t-1} + \gamma_2 \Delta Y_{2,t-1} + \theta_1 z_{t-1} + \varepsilon_{1t}$
　　　　　　　　$\Delta Y_{2t} = \delta_0 + \delta_1 \Delta Y_{1,t-1} + \delta_2 \Delta Y_{2,t-1} + \theta_2 z_{t-1} + \varepsilon_{2t}$

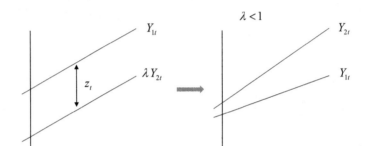

The left graph of the two parallel lines shows the relation between Y_{1t} and λY_{2t} while the right one shows the relation between Y_{1t} and Y_{2t} when $\lambda < 1$.

Assumption 4

(CE)　　　　　　　$z_t = Y_{1t} - \lambda Y_{2t} + \eta_1 t \;\Rightarrow\; Y_{1t} = \lambda Y_{2t} - \eta_1 t + z_t$

(test VAR)　　　$\Delta Y_{1t} = \gamma_0 + \gamma_1 \Delta Y_{1,t-1} + \gamma_2 \Delta Y_{2,t-1} + \theta_1 z_{t-1} + \varepsilon_{1t}$
　　　　　　　　$\Delta Y_{2t} = \delta_0 + \delta_1 \Delta Y_{1,t-1} + \delta_2 \Delta Y_{2,t-1} + \theta_2 z_{t-1} + \varepsilon_{2t}$

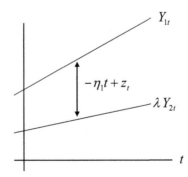

(1) Tests for cointegration: Johansen test (1988)

FILENAME F1 DDE 'EXCEL|[11-COINTEGRATION.XLS]COINTEGRATION!R2C1:R47C3';

DATA K; INFILE F1 LRECL=1000; INPUT YEAR LNCONS LNGDP;

TITLE '===== Test for Cointegration: Johansen =====';

PROC VARMAX;

    MODEL LNCONS LNGDP/P=3 CointTest=(Johansen= (NORMALIZE=LNCONS)); RUN;

===== Test for Cointegration: Johansen =====

The VARMAX Procedure

Number of Observations 46

Number of Pairwise Missing 0

Simple Summary Statistics

Variable	Type	N	Mean	Standard Deviation	Min	Max
LNCONS	Dependent	46	10.93601	2.56755	6.77040	15.53490
LNGDP	Dependent	46	11.43552	2.32858	8.00180	15.92480

Cointegration Rank Test Using Trace

HO: Rank=r	H1: Rank>r	Eigenvalue	Trace	5% Critical Value	Drift in ECM	Drift in Process
0	0	0.3602	21.6563	15.34	Constant	Linear
1	1	0.0554	2.4503	3.84		

Test statistics based on assumption 3[5]

    To determine the number (r) of cointegrating relations, we proceed sequentially from $r = 0$ to $r = 1$ until we fail to reject. The null of $r = 0$ is rejected (21.6563 > 15.34), but the null of $r = 1$ is not rejected (2.4503 < 3.84). Thus, we conclude that there exists one cointegrating relation.

Cointegration Rank Test Using Trace Under Restriction

HO: Rank=r	H1: Rank>r	Eigenvalue	Trace	5% Critical Value	Drift in ECM	Drift in Process
0	0	0.4054	34.5870	19.99	Constant	Constant
1	1	0.2475	12.2297	9.13		

Test statistics based on assumption 2

    The null of $r = 0$ is rejected (34.5870 > 19.99), and the null of $r = 1$ is also rejected (12.2297 > 9.13). These results indicate that the two variables are stationary $I(0)$, which is a contradiction to the results of the unit root tests. Notice that the maximum number of cointegrating relations is the number of variables less one; see Appendix 11B for an explanation.

Hypothesis of the Restriction

		Drift	Drift in
Hypothesis		in ECM	Process
HO(assumption 2)		Constant	Constant
H1(assumption 3)		Constant	Linear

Hypothesis Test of the Restriction

Rank	Eigenvalue	Restricted Eigenvalue	DF	Chi-Square	Pr > ChiSq
0	0.3602	0.4054	2	12.93	0.0016
1	0.0554	0.2475	1	9.78	0.0018

The above test results show which assumption is appropriate. The null hypothesis is assumption 2 and the alternative is assumption 3. For both ranks of 0 and 1, the null is rejected because the *p*-values are 0.0016 and 0.0018. Therefore, based on assumption 3, we conclude that there is one cointegrating relation.

Below are the estimates of α and β. Since the above test shows that there is one cointegrating relation, we use only the corresponding column in the output.

Long-Run Parameter Beta Estimates

Variable	1	2
LNCONS	1.00000	1.00000
LNGDP	-1.06732	-1.24188

Under assumption 3, the estimated cointegrating equation $z_{t-1}(= \beta' Y_{t-1})$ is

$$z_{t-1} = LNCONS_{t-1} - 1.06732\,LNGDP_{t-1}$$

The coefficient estimates for the error correction terms are $\hat{\alpha} = \begin{bmatrix} \hat{\theta}_1 \\ \hat{\theta}_2 \end{bmatrix} = \begin{bmatrix} -0.04063 \\ 0.35392 \end{bmatrix}$

Adjustment Coefficient Alpha Estimates

Variable	1	2
LNCONS	-0.04063	-0.07957
LNGDP	0.35392	-0.02836

(2) Estimation of VECM

TITLE '===== Estimating VECM =====';
TITLE2 '-- - assumption 3 ------';

PROC VARMAX;

   MODEL LNCONS LNGDP/P=3 ECM=(RANK=1 NORMALIZE=LNCONS)

    PRINT=(DIAGNOSE); RUN;

===== Estimating VECM =====

----- assumption 3 ------

The VARMAX Procedure

Type of Model		VECM(3)
Estimation Method	Maximum Likelihood Estimation	
Cointegrated Rank		1

Model Parameter Estimates

Standard

Equation	Parameter	Estimate	Error	t Value	Pr > |t|	Variable
D_LNCONS	CONST1	0.08192	0.10095	0.81	0.4224	1
	AR1_1_1	-0.04063	0.07746			LNCONS(t-1)
	AR1_1_2	0.04336	0.08268			LNGDP(t-1)
	AR2_1_1	0.23677	0.15356	1.54	0.1318	D_LNCONS(t-1)
	AR2_1_2	0.25587	0.12455	2.05	0.0473	D_LNGDP(t-1)
	AR3_1_1	-0.15376	0.14450	-1.06	0.2944	D_LNCONS(t-2)
	AR3_1_2	-0.02250	0.13367	-0.17	0.8673	D_LNGDP(t-2)
D_LNGDP	CONST2	0.53078	0.10033	5.29	0.0001	1
	AR1_2_1	0.35392	0.07699			LNCONS(t-1)
	AR1_2_2	-0.37774	0.08217			LNGDP(t-1)
	AR2_2_1	0.09042	0.15262	0.59	0.5573	D_LNCONS(t-1)
	AR2_2_2	0.22248	0.12379	1.80	0.0807	D_LNGDP(t-1)
	AR3_2_1	-0.23985	0.14362	-1.67	0.1036	D_LNCONS(t-2)
	AR3_2_2	0.39969	0.13285	3.01	0.0048	D_LNGDP(t-2)

The estimated VECM is

$$\Delta LNCONS_t = 0.08192 - 0.04063\, z_{t-1} + 0.23677\, \Delta LNCONS_{t-1}$$
$$- 0.15376\, \Delta LNCONS_{t-2} + 0.25587\, \Delta LNGDP_{t-1}$$
$$- 0.02250\, \Delta LNGDP_{t-2}$$
$$\Delta LNGDP_t = 0.53078 + 0.35392\, z_{t-1} + 0.09042\, \Delta LNCONS_{t-1}$$
$$- 0.23985\, \Delta LNCONS_{t-2} + 0.22248\, \Delta LNGDP_{t-1}$$
$$+ 0.39969\, \Delta LNGDP_{t-2}$$
$$z_{t-1} = \Delta LNCONS_{t-1} - 1.06732\, LNGDP_{t-1}$$

Expanding the z_{t-1} term, we obtain

$$\Delta LNCONS_t = 0.08192 - 0.04063\, LNCONS_{t-1} + 0.04336\, LNGDP_{t-1} + 0.23677\, \Delta LNCONS_{t-1}$$
$$- 0.15376\, \Delta LNCONS_{t-2} + 0.25587\, \Delta LNGDP_{t-1} - 0.02250\, \Delta LNGDP_{t-2}$$
$$\Delta LNGDP_t = 0.53078 + 0.35392\, LNCONS_{t-1} - 0.37774\, LNGDP_{t-1} + 0.09042\, \Delta LNCONS_{t-1}$$
$$- 0.23985\, \Delta LNCONS_{t-2} + 0.22248\, \Delta LNGDP_{t-1} + 0.39969\, \Delta LNGDP_{t-2}$$

To estimate VECM under other assumptions, use the following:

TITLE2 '-- - assumption 2 ------';

PROC VARMAX;

    MODEL LNCONS LNGDP/P=3 ECM=(RANK=1 NORMALIZE=LNCONS ECTREND); RUN;

    /***(ECTREND moves the intercept inside the CE equation)***/

TITLE2 '-- - assumption 4 ------';

PROC VARMAX;

    MODEL LNCONS LNGDP/P=3 ECM=(RANK=1 NORMALIZE=LNCONS ECTREND)
    TREND=LINEAR ; RUN;

    /***(ECTREND moves the linear trend inside the CE equation)***/

(3) Diagnostic checks for white-noise residuals

An option "PRINT=(DIAGNOSE)" prints residual diagnostics.

Portmanteau Test for Cross
Correlations of Residuals

Up To Lag	DF	Chi-Square	Pr > ChiSq
4	4	5.32	0.2558
5	8	6.77	0.5614
6	12	10.40	0.5805
7	16	15.80	0.4668
8	20	21.70	0.3569
9	24	26.08	0.3493
10	28	29.79	0.3732
11	32	35.05	0.3255
12	36	38.30	0.3655

Univariate Model White Noise Diagnostics

Variable	Durbin Watson	Normality Chi-Square	Pr > ChiSq	ARCH F Value	Pr > F
LNCONS	1.74821	0.78	0.6755	0.06	0.8156
LNGDP	1.98397	0.78	0.6766	0.66	0.4214

Univariate Model AR Diagnostics

Variable	AR1		AR2		AR3		AR4	
	F Value	Pr > F	F Value	Pr > F	F Value	Pr > F	F Value	Pr > F
LNCONS	0.28	0.5983	0.13	0.8808	0.09	0.9624	0.11	0.9787
LNGDP	0.00	0.9726	0.06	0.9454	0.04	0.9895	0.04	0.9969

According to the above output, the residuals for both variables are serially uncorrelated up to lag 12. Further, the residuals follow normal distributions, have no ARCH effect, and have no AR effect up to lag 4 for each variable.

(4) Test for weak exogeneity

The significance of the adjustment coefficients $\alpha = [\theta_1\ \theta_2]'$ can be tested. This is called a test for weak exogeneity.

TITLE '===== Testing weak exogeneity =====';
TITLE2 '-- - assumption 3 ------';
PROC VARMAX;
    MODEL LNCONS LNGDP/P=3 ECM=(RANK=1 NORMALIZE=LNCONS);
    COINTEG RANK=1 EXOGENEITY;
RUN;

Testing Weak Exogeneity of Each Variables

Variable	DF	Chi-Square	Pr > ChiSq
LNCONS	1	0.25	0.6202
LNGDP	1	15.04	0.0001

The above results show that the adjustment coefficient in the LNCONS equation (θ_1) is not significantly different from zero (p-value = 0.6202) but the one in the LNGDP (θ_2) is significant (p-value = 0.0001).

Notes

1 BASE SAS 9.4, SAS/ETS 13.1 and SAS/STAT 13.1. SAS Institute Inc., Cary, NC.
2 The full-rank of $rank(\Pi) = k$ indicates that there exist k linearly independent cointegrating vectors. Since a $k \times k$ identity matrix I_k is also a full-rank matrix, we may use I_k for Π . If so, each stationary variable ΔW_{jt} in ΔW_t includes its corresponding level variable W_{jt}. It implies that all components in W_t are stationary. This is a contradiction because we are testing for cointegration of integrated variables W_t . Notice that before this cointegration test is applied, the unit root test has already confirmed that the variables are integrated of the same order.
3 BASE SAS 9.4, SAS/ETS 13.1 and SAS/STAT 13.1. SAS Institute Inc., Cary, NC.
4 Assumptions 1 and 5 are rarely used in practice.
5 The *linear* Drift in Process indicates an intercept in the test VAR of ΔY_{1t} and ΔY_{2t}, thereby the level variables Y_{1t} and Y_{2t} showing linear trends; this is assumption 3. In contrast, the *constant* Drift in Process indicates no intercept in the test VAR, thereby the level variables Y_{1t} and Y_{2t} showing no trend; this is assumption 2. Since our focus is on assumptions 2 and 3 in many applications, which assumption to choose depends on the existence of linear trends in the level variables.

12 Qualitative and limited dependent variable models

Learning objectives

In this chapter, you should learn about:

- Probit and logit regression models which are used for examining binary decisions;
- Differences between these binary-choice models and the linear regression model;
- Tobit model which is used for censored dependent variables;
- Self-selection bias when a self-selected choice variable is included as a regressor.

In previous chapters, we have studied regression models which include qualitative (or dummy) explanatory variables. In this chapter, we consider models in which the dependent variable is qualitative. These models can be used to examine the determinants of economic agents' binary decisions. For example, a person makes a decision every morning regarding whether he or she should bring an umbrella. Every year firm managers decide whether they keep the incumbent auditors or replace them with new ones. In cases of such binary choice options, the dependent variable can be expressed as

$$Y_i = 1 \quad \text{if the } i\text{th agent chooses option } 1$$
$$= 0 \quad \text{otherwise}$$

Leaving advanced models to more specialized books, this chapter will introduce widely used models for a binary dependent variable: the linear probability model, the probit model and the logit model.

For cases of limited dependent variables in which the dependent variable is fully observed only for some observations, the Tobit model will be introduced. The self-selection bias problem will also be explained as an application of the probit model.

12.1 Linear probability model

The linear probability model is introduced to outline the issues associated with qualitative dependent variables, although it has some theoretical problems and is rarely used. The linear probability model is very simple and appears like a standard linear regression model, except that the dependent variable is a binary variable. Suppose that the dependent variable Y takes only two values, 1 if the subject belongs to the outcome of our interest and 0 otherwise. The probability of observing $Y = 1$ may be modeled as a linear function of explanatory variables:

$$P_i = \Pr(Y_i = 1 \mid X_{2i}, X_{3i}) = \beta_1 + \beta_2 X_{2i} + \beta_3 X_{3i}$$

Since the probability P_i is not observable, we replace P_i with observations on Y_i ($= 0$ or 1) to estimate the coefficients.

$$Y_i = \beta_1 + \beta_2 X_{2i} + \beta_3 X_{3i} + u_i \tag{12.1}$$

where u_i represents the difference between P_i and Y_i, and $E(u_i \mid X_{2i}, X_{3i}) = 0$ is assumed. The conditional expected value of Y_i in Eq. (12.1) is

$$
\begin{aligned}
E(Y_i \mid X_{2i}, X_{3i}) &= 1 \times \Pr(Y_i = 1 \mid X_{2i}, X_{3i}) + 0 \times \Pr(Y_i = 0 \mid X_{2i}, X_{3i}) \\
&= \Pr(Y_i = 1 \mid X_{2i}, X_{3i}) \\
&= P_i
\end{aligned}
$$

$E(Y_i \mid X_{2i}, X_{3i})$ can be interpreted as P_i, the conditional probability that the subject belongs to the outcome of interest ($Y_i = 1$) given X_{2i} and X_{3i}. Thus, Eq. (12.1) fits in the multiple regression model.

$$
\begin{aligned}
Y_i &= E(Y_i \mid X_{2i}, X_{3i}) + u_i \\
&= P_i + u_i
\end{aligned}
$$

Using the OLS estimates for Eq (12.1), we can obtain the probability of $Y_i = 1$:

$$\hat{P}_i = \hat{\beta}_1 + \hat{\beta}_2 X_{2i} + \hat{\beta}_3 X_{3i} \tag{12.2}$$

However, the linear probability model has some problems. Predicted values of P_i in Eq. (12.2) are not guaranteed to be bounded between 0 and 1. Further, the error term u_i in Eq. (12.1) takes only two values, far from the normal distribution, and its variance is heteroscedastic.[1] Therefore, this linear probability model is not appropriate for analyzing binary dependent variables.

12.2 Probit model

Assume that there is an underlying latent variable Y^* which is related to explanatory variables as follows:

$$Y_i^* = \beta_1 + \beta_2 X_{2i} + \beta_3 X_{3i} + u_i \tag{12.3}$$

where u_i follows a normal distribution. The latent variable Y_i^* is *unobservable*, but can be related to an observable variable Y_i in the following way.

$$
\begin{aligned}
Y_i &= 1 \quad && \text{if} \quad Y_i^* > c \\
&= 0 \quad && \text{if} \quad Y_i^* \le c
\end{aligned}
\tag{12.4}
$$

where c is a prescribed constant (usually zero). In the example of making a decision about auditors, the latent variable Y_i^* can be interpreted as a measure of the extent of the managers' preference for new auditors. However, we as outside analysts cannot observe the latent variable, but can observe Y_i only, i.e., whether the managers had kept the incumbent auditors or replaced with new ones.

When the error term u_i in Eq. (12.3) is assumed to follow a normal distribution, this model is called the **probit** model. The probability of $Y_i = 1$, i.e., P_i, can be expressed as follows (with setting c to 0):

$$
\begin{aligned}
P_i &= \Pr\left(Y_i = 1 \mid X_{2i}, X_{3i}\right) = \Pr\left(Y_i^* > 0\right) \\
&= \Pr\left(\beta_1 + \beta_2 X_{2i} + \beta_3 X_{3i} + u_i > 0\right) \\
&= \Pr\left[u_i > -(\beta_1 + \beta_2 X_{2i} + \beta_3 X_{3i})\right] \\
&= \Pr\left[u_i \leq \beta_1 + \beta_2 X_{2i} + \beta_3 X_{3i}\right]
\end{aligned}
$$

Then

$$
P_i = F(\beta_1 + \beta_2 X_{2i} + \beta_3 X_{3i}) \tag{12.5}
$$

or

$$
F^{-1}(P_i) = \beta_1 + \beta_2 X_{2i} + \beta_3 X_{3i}
$$

where F is the cumulative normal distribution function and F^{-1} is the inverse of the cumulative normal distribution function. The probit model may be expressed either as Eqs. (12.3) and (12.4), or as Eq. (12.5).

Since the probit model does not belong to the linear regression models, the OLS method cannot be used for estimating the parameters. Instead, the maximum likelihood estimation (MLE) is used. The likelihood function is

$$
\begin{aligned}
L &= \prod_{Y_i=0} \Pr(Y_i^* > 0) \times \prod_{Y_i=1} \Pr(Y_i^* \leq 0) \\
&= \prod_{Y_i=0} [1 - F(\beta_1 + \beta_2 X_{2i} + \beta_3 X_{3i})] \times \prod_{Y_i=1} F(\beta_1 + \beta_2 X_{2i} + \beta_3 X_{3i})
\end{aligned}
$$

where $\Pr(\cdot)$ denotes a probability conditioned on the explanatory variables X_2 and X_3. Maximum likelihood estimates are the values of coefficients which maximize the likelihood function. See Appendix 12 for an explanation about the MLE.

12.2.1 Interpretation of the coefficients

Since the probit model involves a function of $F(\cdot)$, the marginal effect of a unit change in a regressor is a derivative of the composite function. Thus, the marginal effect $\partial P / \partial X$ is the product of a coefficient (β) and the density function $f(\cdot)$ by the chain rule.

$$
\frac{\partial P_i}{\partial X_{2i}} = \beta_2 \times f(\beta_1 + \beta_2 X_{2i} + \beta_3 X_{3i})
$$

$$
\frac{\partial P_i}{\partial X_{3i}} = \beta_3 \times f(\beta_1 + \beta_2 X_{2i} + \beta_3 X_{3i})
$$

where $f(\cdot)$ is the normal density function, the derivative of $F(\cdot)$. The marginal effect on the probability of a unit change in a regressor ($\partial P / \partial X_2$ or $\partial P / \partial X_3$) depends on the observed values of all regressors. Thus, the coefficients β_js do not have an immediate interpretation of the net effects. However, since $f(\cdot)$ is always positive, we can interpret the sign of a coefficient. Positive values of $\beta_2(\beta_3)$

imply that increasing $X_2(X_3)$ will increase the probability of observing $Y = 1$; negative values imply the opposite.

Example 12.1 Estimation using *EViews*

To illustrate how to estimate a probit model using *EViews*, consider the data analyzed in Spector and Mazzeo (1980). They examine what factors determine students' final grades in an intermediate macroeconomics course.

$$\Pr(GRADE_i = 1) = F(\beta_1 + \beta_2 GPA_i + \beta_3 TUCE_i + \beta_4 PSI_i)$$

	A	B	C	D	E	F
	OBS	GPA	TUCE	PSI	GRADE	LETTER
1	1	2.66	20	0	0	C
2	2	2.89	22	0	0	B
3	3	3.28	24	0	0	B
4	4	2.92	12	0	0	B
5	5	4.00	21	0	1	A
6	6	2.86	17	0	0	B

Import an Excel file "12-spector.xls." It contains 32 observations on the variables "OBS GPA TUCE PSI GRADE."

OBS = observation number;
GPA = entering grade point average;
TUCE = score on an examination given at the beginning of the term to test entering knowledge of macroeconomics;
PSI = personal system of instruction (dummy variable), 1 if the new method is used, 0 otherwise;
GRADE = 1 if the letter grade is A, 0 otherwise;
LETTER = letter grade.

Choose Objects/New Object. . . /Equation. In the Equation Estimation dialog, select BINARY for estimation method. In the Equation specification field, type the name of the binary dependent variable followed by a list of regressors: "GRADE C GPA TUCE PSI" to estimate the following model. Click the **Probit** button for Binary estimation method.

The estimation results of the probit model are shown in Output 12.1.

Output 12.1 Estimation results of a probit model

Dependent Variable: GRADE
Method: ML – Binary Probit (Quadratic hill climbing)
Sample: 1 32
Included observations: 32
Convergence achieved after 5 iterations
Covariance matrix computed using second derivatives

Variable	Coefficient	Std. Error	z-Statistic	Prob.
C	-7.452320	2.542472	-2.931131	0.0034
GPA	1.625810	0.693882	2.343063	0.0191
TUCE	0.051729	0.083890	0.616626	0.5375
PSI	1.426332	0.595038	2.397045	0.0165
Mean dependent var	0.343750	S.D. dependent var		0.482559
S.E. of regression	0.386128	Akaike info criterion		1.051175
Sum squared resid	4.174660	Schwarz criterion		1.234392
Log likelihood	-12.81880	Hannan-Quinn criter.		1.111906
Restr. log likelihood	-20.59173	Avg. log likelihood		-0.400588
LR statistic (3 df)	15.54585	McFadden R-squared		0.377478
Probability(LR stat)	0.001405			
Obs with Dep = 0	21	Total obs		32
Obs with Dep = 1	11			

12.2.2 Measuring the goodness-of-fit

For the probit model, the R^2 is not meaningful. An analog to the R^2 in a conventional regression is McFadden's R^2 (or likelihood ratio index). This measure has an intuitive appeal in that it is bounded by 0 and 1. Although McFadden's R^2 increases as the fit of the model improves, the values between 0 and 1 have no natural interpretation.

Expectation-Prediction (Classification) Table

Alternatively, we can evaluate the goodness-of-fit of a probit model using a 2×2 table of correct and incorrect classification. After you obtain estimation results, choose View/Expectation-Prediction Evaluation. In the Prediction evaluation box, enter a prediction cutoff value of your choice. Each observation will be classified depending on whether the predicted probability is greater or smaller than this cutoff. See the *EViews* manual for more details and interpretations of the table.

The predicted probabilities are calculated using the fitted probit equation for all observations $(i = 1,2,\cdots,31)$.

$$\hat{P}_i = F(-7.452320 + 1.625810 \, GPA_i + 0.051729 \, TUCE_i + 1.426332 \, PSI_i)$$

where F is the cumulative normal distribution function. Below is shown a part of the predicted probabilities (GRADE_F).

OBS	GPA	TUCE	PSI	GRADE	GRADE_F
1	2.66	20	0	0	0.018171
2	2.89	22	0	0	0.053080
3	3.28	24	0	0	0.189926
4	2.92	12	0	0	0.018571
5	4.00	21	0	1	0.554575
6	2.86	17	0	0	0.027233

With a cutoff probability of 0.4, we can obtain the following table. The classification rate is 84.38% $[= 100 \times (18+9) / 32]$.

		Actual GRADE		Total
		0	1	
Predicted probability is	≤ 0.4 (GRADE = 0)	**18**	2	20
	> 0.4 (GRADE = 1)	3	**9**	12
Total		21	11	32

12.3 Logit model

If we assume a logistic distribution for u_i in Eq. (12.3), the probability of $Y_i = 1$, i.e., P_i, can be expressed as

$$P_i = G(\beta_1 + \beta_2 X_{2i} + \beta_3 X_{3i}) = \frac{1}{1 + e^{-(\beta_1 + \beta_2 X_{2i} + \beta_3 X_{3i})}}$$

Then,

$$\log\left(\frac{P_i}{1 - P_i}\right) = \beta_1 + \beta_2 X_{2i} + \beta_3 X_{3i}$$

where G is the cumulative logistic distribution function, and $\dfrac{P_i}{1 - P_i}$ is called the *odds* in favor of an event $Y_i = 1$ (i.e., the ratio of the probability that an event will occur divided by the probability that the same event will not occur). The left-hand side variable, $\log\left(\dfrac{P_i}{1 - P_i}\right)$, is called the *logit*.

Since the logit model does not belong to the linear regression models, the OLS method cannot be used for estimating the parameters. Instead, the maximum likelihood estimation (MLE) is used to estimate the nonlinear logit model. Its likelihood function is

$$L = \prod_{Y_i = 0} \Pr(Y_i^* > 0) \times \prod_{Y_i = 1} \Pr(Y_i^* \leq 0)$$

$$= \prod_{Y_i = 0} [1 - G(\beta_1 + \beta_2 X_{2i} + \beta_3 X_{3i})] \times \prod_{Y_i = 1} G(\beta_1 + \beta_2 X_{2i} + \beta_3 X_{3i})$$

where $\Pr(\cdot)$ denotes a probability conditioned on the explanatory variables X_2 and X_3.

12.3.1 Interpretation of the coefficients

Similar to the probit model, the marginal effect of a unit change in a regressor ($\partial P / \partial X$) is a derivative of the composite function and is therefore the product of a coefficient (β) and the derivative of $G(\cdot)$ by the chain rule.

$$\frac{\partial P_i}{\partial X_{2i}} = \beta_2 \times P_i(1 - P_i), \qquad \frac{\partial P_i}{\partial X_{3i}} = \beta_3 \times P_i(1 - P_i)$$

where $\partial G / \partial X_{2i} = \partial G / \partial X_{3i} = P_i(1 - P_i)$ is utilized. The net effects involve not only its coefficient but also the level of probability at which the change is measured. Thus, the coefficients β s do not have an immediate interpretation of the net effects. However, since $P_i(1 - P_i)$ is always positive, we can interpret their signs. Positive values of $\beta_2(\beta_3)$ imply that increasing $X_2(X_3)$ will increase the probability of observing $Y = 1$; negative values imply the opposite.

Example 12.2 Estimation using *EViews*

Click the Logit button for Binary estimation method in the Equation Specification dialog box. Output 12.2 shows the estimation results.

Output 12.2 Estimation results of a logit model

Dependent Variable: GRADE
Method: ML – Binary Logit (Quadratic hill climbing)
Sample: 1 32
Included observations: 32
Convergence achieved after 5 iterations
Covariance matrix computed using second derivatives

Variable	Coefficient	Std. Error	z-Statistic	Prob.
C	-13.02135	4.931317	-2.640541	0.0083
GPA	2.826113	1.262940	2.237725	0.0252
TUCE	0.095158	0.141554	0.672235	0.5014
PSI	2.378688	1.064563	2.234426	0.0255

Mean dependent var	0.343750	S.D. dependent var		0.482559
S.E. of regression	0.384716	Akaike info criterion		1.055602
Sum squared resid	4.144171	Schwarz criterion		1.238819
Log likelihood	-12.88963	Hannan-Quinn criter.		1.116333
Restr. log likelihood	-20.59173	Avg. log likelihood		-0.402801
LR statistic (3 df)	15.40419	McFadden R-squared		0.374038
Probability(LR stat)	0.001502			
Obs with Dep = 0	21	Total obs		32
Obs with Dep = 1	11			

Similar to the probit model, you can also evaluate the goodness-of-fit of the logit model using the expectation-prediction (classification) table.

Estimation Using *SAS*[2]

```
FILENAME F1 DDE 'EXCEL|[12-SPECTOR.XLS]Spector!R2C1:R33C6';
DATA DAT1; INFILE F1; INPUT OBS GPA TUCE PSI GRADE1 LETTER $;
*----------------(Three ways of estimating probit models)-------------;
PROC SORT DATA=DAT1; BY DESCENDING GRADE1;
TITLE '< PROBIT MODEL >';
```

```
PROC LOGISTIC DATA=DAT1 ORDER=DATA;
    CLASS GRADE1;
    MODEL GRADE1 = GPA TUCE PSI/ LINK=PROBIT RSQ; RUN;
PROC PROBIT DATA=DAT1 ORDER=DATA;
    CLASS GRADE1;
    MODEL GRADE1 = GPA TUCE PSI/ D=NORMAL; RUN;
PROC QLIM DATA=DAT1;
    MODEL GRADE1 = GPA TUCE PSI;
    ENDOGENOUS GRADE1 ~ DISCRETE(DISTRIBUTION=NORMAL ORDER=DATA); RUN;
*----------------(Three ways of estimating logit models)-------------;
TITLE '< LOGIT MODEL >';
PROC LOGISTIC DATA=DAT1 ORDER=DATA;
    CLASS GRADE1;
    MODEL GRADE1 = GPA TUCE PSI/LINK=LOGIT RSQ;
PROC PROBIT DATA=DAT1 ORDER=DATA;
    CLASS GRADE1;
    MODEL GRADE1 = GPA TUCE PSI/ D=LOGISTIC; RUN;
PROC QLIM DATA=DAT1;
    MODEL GRADE1 = GPA TUCE PSI;
    ENDOGENOUS GRADE1 ~ DISCRETE(DISTRIBUTION=LOGISTIC ORDER=DATA); RUN;
```

12.3.2 Logit vs. probit

In most applications, the logit and probit models produce similar results. The choice between the two models is one of convenience. If a researcher believes that movement towards probability of one or zero occurs quickly after certain values of the regressors, then the probit model provides a better approximation to the data-generating process, as shown in Figure 12.1. Otherwise, the logit model is preferred and more commonly used.

12.3.3 Adjustment for unequal sampling rates: Maddala (1991), Palepu (1986)

One of the common issues in the analysis of discrete choices is that of unequal sampling rates from the two groups. Consider a population of N firms consisting of N_1 in group 1 and N_2 in group 2 ($N_1 + N_2 = N$). We obtain a sample of n firms. Instead of drawing a random sample, we draw a choice-based sample, that is, n_1 from group 1 and n_2 from group 2 ($n_1 + n_2 = n$). Typically, n_1 and n_2 are set equal. In a case of bank failures, the number of failed banks N_1 is usually much smaller than the number of nonfailed banks N_2, so, n_1 is often chosen to be equal to N_1 (all failed banks are included in the sample) and only n_2 banks are chosen from the total N_2 nonfailed banks.

The question is whether there is anything wrong with using this choice-based sample to estimate the logit model. The answer to this question is that there is nothing wrong with the logit model. The coefficients of the explanatory variables are not affected by unequal sampling rates from two groups. It is only the constant term that is affected.

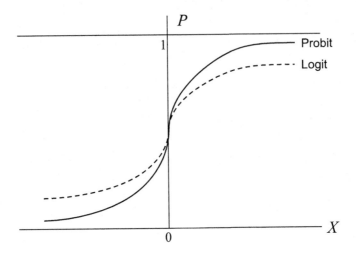

Figure 12.1 Probit and logit cumulative distributions

However, this result cannot be applied to the probit model. The unequal sampling causes a complicated problem for the probit model and affects estimation of the coefficients as well. This is one reason why the logit model is preferred to the probit model. See Maddala (1991) and Palepu (1986) for more details.

12.4 Tobit model

Consider a case of examining consumption expenditures on inexpensive goods, e.g., the amount of monthly alcohol consumption. Depending on consumers' preference for alcohol, many consumers spend positive amount. However, a nontrivial fraction of consumers might spend zero because their *desired* amount of alcohol consumption is zero or negative. For this group of consumers, we observe zero amount at the least, but cannot observe their desired (negative) amount of alcohol consumption. Thus, the desired alcohol consumption is unobserved (or censored) if it is less than zero. When we analyze observations of zero consumption, we need to consider that their desired consumption levels may not be identical.

12.4.1 The Tobit model

The Tobit model has been developed for this type of data and is also called a *censored* regression model because the dependent variable is censored. In the alcohol consumption example, we define a latent variable Y^* as the desired level of alcohol consumption and relate it to a possible determinant X.

$$Y_i^* = \beta_1 + \beta_2 X_i + u_i$$

where $u_i \sim iid\ N(0, \sigma^2)$. Due to the censoring, the observed alcohol consumption Y_i is related to the underlying variable Y_i^* as follows:

$$
\begin{aligned}
Y_i &= Y_i^* && \text{if } Y_i^* > c \\
&= 0 \text{ or } c && \text{if } Y_i^* \le c
\end{aligned}
$$

where c is a prescribed constant (often zero). This is a case of being *left censored* at c.[3] In the probit and logit models, our interest is to identify the determinants of the *probability* of observing $Y_i = 1$. In contrast, our interest with the Tobit model is to identify the determinants of the *level* of Y_i with correcting for the unobservability of censored observations.

The maximum likelihood estimates (MLEs) for parameters β_1, β_2, σ can be obtained by finding values which maximize the following likelihood function.

$$
\begin{aligned}
L &= \prod_{Y_i=0/c} \Pr(Y_i^* \le 0) \times \prod_{Y_i>c} f(Y_i \mid Y_i^* < c) \cdot \Pr(Y_i^* > c) \\
&= \prod_{Y_i=0/c} \Pr(Y_i^* \le 0) \times \prod_{Y_i>c} f(Y_i) \\
&= \prod_{Y_i=0/c} \Phi(Z_i) \times \prod_{Y_i>c} \left(\frac{1}{\sigma}\right) \times \phi\left(\frac{Y_i - \beta_1 - \beta_2 X_i}{\sigma}\right)
\end{aligned}
$$

where $\Pr(\cdot)$ denotes a probability conditioned on the explanatory variable X; $f(\cdot)$ is the normal density with mean $\beta_1 + \beta_2 X_i$ and variance σ^2; $\phi(\cdot)$ and $\Phi(\cdot)$ are the density and distribution functions of the standard normal distribution; and $Z_i = (c - \beta_1 - \beta_2 X_i)/\sigma$. Notice that the actual value of Y (i.e., 0 or c) when $Y^* \le c$ has no effect on the likelihood function because the likelihood function is defined using the censoring value c only. What matters is the fact that those observations have been censored. Thus, for an application of the Tobit model, we are required to know the censoring value and which observations are censored.[4] The MLE can incorporate the information about the censored observations and therefore produce consistent estimates.

Maddala (1991) points out that there are more examples of inappropriate use of the Tobit model than of its correct use. Researchers are tempted to use the Tobit model when they have a bunch of zero (or other limit) observations. This is often inappropriate. He emphasizes that in the Tobit model, Y^* can be less than c but these observations with $Y^* < c$ are not observed and thus recorded as c because of the censoring. Thus, the limit observations arise because of *nonobservability*.

However, the limit observations can also arise by *individual choices* in some cases. For instance, in the case of automobile expenditures, the zero observations arise because some individuals choose not to make any expenditures; it is not because negative values of Y^* are not observed.[5] Another case is to model hours worked in labor markets. The hours worked cannot be negative, and the zeros are a consequence of individual choices not to work. In these cases, the proper estimation method is to model the choice, to be explained in the next section about the choice-based model. Amemiya (1984) classifies this choice-based model as the Type 2 Tobit model and the above Tobit model as the standard (Type 1) Tobit model.

12.4.2 Applications of the Tobit model

APPLICATION 1: The Tobit model is suitable for a case of minimum wage law where observed wages are censored from the bottom. Some of the employees are not affected by the law because their equilibrium wages are higher than the minimum wage set by the law. For those whose equilibrium wages without the law are below the minimum wage, their observed wages are equal to the minimum wage if they are nonetheless employed or equal to zero if they are not employed.

$$
\begin{aligned}
W_i &= W_i^* && \text{if } W_i^* > W_{\min} \\
&= 0 \text{ or } W_{\min} && \text{if } W_i^* \le W_{\min}
\end{aligned}
$$

where W_i is the observed wage, W_i^* is the equilibrium wage if the minimum wage law had not been enforced and $W_{\min}$ is the minimum wage and the censoring value.

APPLICATION 2: Another application is to a stock market where a ceiling has been imposed on the foreign investors' shareholdings. If foreign investors' ownership in one company is not allowed to exceed a ceiling (e.g., 20% of the outstanding shares), their desired level of shareholdings is not observable beyond the ceiling and thus right-censored.

$$S_i = S_i^* \qquad \text{if } S_i^* < S_{ceiling}$$
$$= S_{ceiling} \qquad \text{if } S_i^* \geq S_{ceiling}$$

where S_i is the observed shareholdings of foreign investors for firm i, S_i^* is their desired level of shareholdings and $S_{ceiling}$ the ceiling on the foreign investors' shareholdings.

APPLICATION 3: For a study of unemployment, we can observe the unemployed length of time. But, some of these cases could be ongoing unemployment at the time of observation. If so, their duration of unemployment is observed only until the time of observation and thus right-censored.

12.4.3 Estimation using EViews *and* SAS

Using *EViews*

First, import an Excel file "12-censored.xls." It contains 15 observations on the variables "Y Z1 Z2 BOTTOM" where BOTTOM is the variable containing the censoring points.

	A	B	C	D
1	Y	Z1	Z2	BOTTOM
2	0	2.1	3.1	0
3	0	2.3	3.3	0
4	0	1.2	2.3	0
5	0	1.3	2.1	0
6	1.7	2.7	3.6	1
7	2.8	2.9	4.5	1
8	1.9	2.3	3.5	1
9	2.5	3.2	4.2	1
10	3.1	3.2	4.9	3.1

Choose Object/New Object. . . /Equation. In the Equation Estimation dialog, select CENSORED for estimation method. Enter the name of the censored dependent variable followed by the list of regressors, "Y C Z1 Z2." You can choose Logistic or Normal for the distribution of the error term. You must also provide information about the censoring points of the dependent variable. If the limit point is known for all individuals, specify them appropriately. In this example, the left censoring value is 0 for all observation. Below are shown the estimation results (Output 12.3).

Output 12.3   Censored regression

Dependent Variable: Y
Method: ML – Censored Normal (TOBIT) (Quadratic hill climbing)
Sample: 1 15

Included observations: 15
Left censoring (value) at zero
Convergence achieved after 7 iterations
Covariance matrix computed using second derivatives

	Coefficient	Std. Error	z-Statistic	Prob.
C	-6.560200	0.865637	-7.578463	0.0000
Z1	0.584308	0.658915	0.886772	0.3752
Z2	1.724908	0.501846	3.437124	0.0006
		Error Distribution		
SCALE:C(4)	0.476320	0.105262	4.525082	0.0000
R-squared	0.948741	Mean dependent var		2.526667
Adjusted R-squared	0.934762	S.D. dependent var		1.840600
S.E. of regression	0.470122	Akaike info criterion		1.764456
Sum squared resid	2.431164	Schwarz criterion		1.953269
Log likelihood	-9.233421	Hannan-Quinn criter.		1.762445
Avg. log likelihood	-0.615561			
Left censored obs	4	Right censored obs		0
Uncensored obs	11	Total obs		15

EViews also allows more general specifications where the censoring points are known but differ across observations. Simply enter the variable name (here BOTTOM) in the appropriate field which contains the censoring points. Refer to the *EViews* manual for other options.[6]

Using *SAS*[7]

```
FILENAME F1 DDE 'EXCEL|[12-CENSORED.XLS]TOBIT!R2C1:R16C4';
DATA DD; INFILE F1; INPUT Y Z1 Z2 BOTTOM;
TITLE '< CENSORED REGRESSION (TOBIT MODEL) >';
PROC QLIM DATA=DD;
    MODEL Y = Z1 Z2;
    ENDOGENOUS Y ~ CENSORED(LB=0); RUN;
PROC QLIM DATA=DD;
    MODEL Y = Z1 Z2;
    ENDOGENOUS Y ~ CENSORED(LB=BOTTOM); RUN;
```

Note:
(1) You may include a lower bound, an upper bound, or both as options:
     CENSORED(LB=0 UB=100), TRUNCATED(LB=0 UB=100).
(2) When the censoring (or truncating) points are known but differ across observations, enter the name of the variable containing the censoring (or truncating) values.
     CENSORED(LB = *var1* UB = *var2*), TRUNCATED(LB = *var1* UB = *var2*)

12.5 Choice-based models

The choice-based (or selection-based) models consist of two equations. One equation is for the choice decision, and the other is for the response variable of the main interest. Depending on the outcome from the choice equation, the response equation is defined accordingly. In what follows, two widely used models are introduced: the self-selection model and the choice-based Tobit model.

12.5.1 Self-selection model

This self-selection model belongs to the **switching regression** model. Depending on binary selections (or choices) by individual subjects in a sample, they are assigned to one of two different regression equations. In doing so, the assignment is not randomly done but choice-based. Suppose that managers must choose between options, for example, whether to replace the incumbent audit firms with new ones. Managers do not choose randomly from available alternatives, but rather on the basis of the firms' characteristics and the expected net benefits from each option. If this nonrandomness in the sample is ignored, the OLS estimation is biased in most applications, called the **self-selection bias**. In this example, the nonrandomness has arisen from individual managers' choices.

Consider the following example where there are two options, denoted by 0 and 1. We can model for the managers' decision using a latent variable d_i^* :

$$d_i^* = \delta_1 + \delta_2 W_i - \varepsilon_i \tag{12.6}$$

for which we observe a binary indicator $D_i = 0$ if $d_i^* \leq 0$ (or $\varepsilon_i \geq \delta_1 + \delta_2 W_i$), and $D_i = 1$ if $d_i^* > 0$ (or $\varepsilon_i < \delta_1 + \delta_2 W_i$).

Now, the main regression includes a dummy variable which represents the choice of options.[8]

$$Y_i = \gamma_1 + \gamma_2 D_i + \gamma_3 X_i + u_i \tag{12.7}$$

where ε_i and u_i have a joint normal distribution with mean zero, variances σ_ε^2 and σ_u^2 and a (possibly) nonzero covariance $\sigma_{u\varepsilon}$. It follows that

$$E(Y_i|D_i = 0, X_i) = \gamma_1 + \gamma_2 X_i + E(u_i|D_i = 0, X_i)$$
$$E(Y_i|D_i = 1, X_i) = \gamma_1 + \gamma_2 + \gamma_3 X_i + E(u_i|D_i = 1, X_i)$$

The expected value of the error term is conditioned on the value of the dummy variable:

$$E(u_i|D_i = 0, X_i) = E(u_i|\varepsilon_i \geq \delta_1 + \delta_2 W_i, X_i)$$
$$= \sigma_{u\varepsilon} \times \frac{\phi(\delta_1 + \delta_2 W_i)}{1 - \Phi(\delta_1 + \delta_2 W_i)} \tag{12.8}$$
$$E(Y_i|D_i = 1, X_i) = E(u_i|\varepsilon_i < \delta_1 + \delta_2 W_i, X_i)$$
$$= \sigma_{u\varepsilon} \left(-\frac{\phi(\delta_1 + \delta_2 W_i)}{\Phi(\delta_1 + \delta_2 W_i)} \right)$$

where $\phi(\cdot)$ and $\Phi(\cdot)$ are the density and distribution function of the standard normal distribution. If $\sigma_{u\varepsilon} \neq 0$, i.e., ε_i and u_i are correlated, then $E(u_i|D_i = 0, X_i) \neq 0$ and $E(u_i|D_i = 1, X_i) \neq 0$, leading to $E(u_i|X_i) \neq 0$ in Eq. (12.7). Since this violates the Assumption I in Chapter 2, the OLS estimator for Eq. (12.7) becomes biased; this is called the self-selection bias.[9]

Estimation should account for this self-selection bias. In what follows, the two-stage estimation method developed by Heckman (1976) is introduced. This method is based on the above derivation of the self-selection bias.[10]

In the first stage of the two-stage estimation method, the choice model is estimated for the total observations using the probit model. The estimated value $\hat{\delta}_1 + \hat{\delta}_2 W_i$ from the probit model is then used to generate nonzero conditional expected values in Eq. (12.8) for all observations: $\phi(\hat{\delta}_1 + \hat{\delta}_2 W_i)/[1 - \Phi(\hat{\delta}_1 + \hat{\delta}_2 W_i)]$ for $D_i = 0$ and $-\phi(\hat{\delta}_1 + \hat{\delta}_2 W_i)/\Phi(\hat{\delta}_1 + \hat{\delta}_2 W_i)$ for $D_i = 1$. These are called the **inverse Mills ratios**.

In the second stage, we can obtain consistent estimates by applying the OLS estimation method to Eq. (12.7) with the inverse Mills ratios added:

$$Y_i = \gamma_1 + \gamma_2 D_i + \gamma_3 X_i + \sigma_{u\varepsilon} inverseMills_i + u_i^*$$

where

$$
\begin{aligned}
inverseMills_i &= \left(\frac{\phi(\hat{\delta}_1 + \hat{\delta}_2 W_i)}{1 - \Phi(\hat{\delta}_1 + \hat{\delta}_2 W_i)} \right) && \text{for} \quad D_i = 0 \\
&= \left(-\frac{\phi(\hat{\delta}_1 + \hat{\delta}_2 W_i)}{\Phi(\hat{\delta}_1 + \hat{\delta}_2 W_i)} \right) && \text{for} \quad D_i = 1
\end{aligned}
$$

and u_i^* is a disturbance after the inverse Mills ratio is included; therefore, $E(u_i^* | X_i = 0)$. The covariance $\sigma_{u\varepsilon}$ is estimated as the coefficient for the *inverse Mills* variable.

A more general case is when each option leads to a different relation for the response variable Y:

$$
\begin{aligned}
Y_i &= \alpha_1 + \alpha_2 X_i + v_i && \text{for} \ D_i = 0, \text{firms which selected option 0} && (12.9) \\
&= \beta_1 + \beta_2 Z_i + w_i && \text{for} \ D_i = 1, \text{firms which selected option 1}
\end{aligned}
$$

It is assumed that the errors (ε_i, v_i, w_i) have a trivariate normal distribution with mean zero, and variances ($\sigma_\varepsilon^2, \sigma_v^2, \sigma_w^2$), and possibly nonzero covariances. We have n observations, of which n_0 belong to option 0 and n_1 to option 1. In this situation, we cannot estimate α_1 and α_2 using only the n_0 observations from option 0 because a nonzero expected value $E(v_i | D_i = 0, X_i) \neq 0$ causes the OLS estimator biased, which is the self-selection bias:

$$
\begin{aligned}
E(v_i | D_i = 0, X_i) &= E(v_i | \varepsilon_i \geq \delta_1 + \delta_2 W_i, X_i) \\
&= \sigma_{v\varepsilon} \times \frac{\phi(\delta_1 + \delta_2 W_i)}{1 - \Phi(\delta_1 + \delta_2 W_i)} \\
&\neq 0
\end{aligned}
$$

where $\phi(\cdot)$ and $\Phi(\cdot)$ are the density and distribution function of the standard normal distribution, and $\sigma_{v\varepsilon}$ is a nonzero covariance. For the same reason, we cannot apply the OLS method to the second equation in Eq. (12.9) because $E(w_i | D_i = 1, Z_i) \neq 0$:

$$
\begin{aligned}
E(w_i | D_i = 1, Z_i) &= E(w_i | \varepsilon_i < \delta_1 + \delta_2 W_i, Z_i) \\
&= \sigma_{w\varepsilon} \times \left(-\frac{\phi(\delta_1 + \delta_2 W_i)}{\Phi(\delta_1 + \delta_2 W_i)} \right) \\
&\neq 0
\end{aligned}
$$

where $\sigma_{w\varepsilon}$ is a nonzero covariance. Notice that if v_i and w_i are not correlated with ε_i, i.e., $\sigma_{v\varepsilon} = 0$ and $\sigma_{w\varepsilon} = 0$, then there is no self-selection bias because $E(v_i | D_i = 0, X_i) = 0$ and $E(w_i | D_i = 1, Z_i) = 0$. However, this special case is very unlikely in real data.

In the first stage of the two-stage estimation method, we estimate the choice equation for the total sample n using the probit model and calculate the inverse Mills ratio for each observation:

$\phi(\hat{\delta}_1 + \hat{\delta}_2 W_i)/[1 - \Phi(\hat{\delta}_1 + \hat{\delta}_2 W_i)]$ for option 0 and $-\phi(\hat{\delta}_1 + \hat{\delta}_2 W_i)/\Phi(\hat{\delta}_1 + \hat{\delta}_2 W_i)$ for option 1. In the second stage, after including appropriate inverse Mills ratios into Eq. (12.9), we apply the OLS method.

$$
\begin{aligned}
Y_i &= \alpha_1 + \alpha_2 X_i + \sigma_{v\varepsilon} \times \left(\frac{\phi(\hat{\delta}_1 + \hat{\delta}_2 W_i)}{1 - \Phi(\hat{\delta}_1 + \hat{\delta}_2 W_i)} \right) + v_i^* \quad \text{for } D_i = 0 \\
&= \beta_1 + \beta_2 Z_i + \sigma_{w\varepsilon} \times \left(-\frac{\phi(\hat{\delta}_1 + \hat{\delta}_2 W_i)}{\Phi(\hat{\delta}_1 + \hat{\delta}_2 W_i)} \right) + w_i^* \quad \text{for } D_i = 1
\end{aligned}
\tag{12.10}
$$

where v_i^* and w_i^* are disturbances after the inverse Mills ratios are added. Since $E(v_i^* | D_i = 0, X_i) = 0$ and $E(w_i^* | D_i = 1, Z_i) = 0$, the OLS estimators for Eq. (12.10) are consistent. The covariances $\sigma_{v\varepsilon}$ and $\sigma_{w\varepsilon}$ are estimated as the coefficients for the *inverse Mills* ratios.

The MLE estimation can also produce consistent estimates by finding values which maximize the following likelihood function:

$$
L = \prod_{D_i = 0} f_0(Y_i \mid d_i^* \le 0) \cdot \Pr(d_i^* \le 0) \times \prod_{D_i = 1} f_1(Y_i \mid d_i^* > 0) \cdot \Pr(d_i^* > 0)
$$

where $\Pr(\cdot)$ denotes a probability conditioned on the explanatory variable W in the first-stage choice model, Eq. (12.6); $f_0(\cdot)$ and $f_1(\cdot)$ are normal density functions corresponding to $D = 0$ and $D = 1$, respectively, in the switching regression Eq. (12.9).

Example 12.3   Do hospitals make people healthier?

An incorrect approach is to simply compare the health status of those who have been to the hospital with the health of those who have not. This simple approach is similar to comparing apples to oranges. People are not randomly assigned to hospitals, but decide to go to hospitals if they need to go. People who go to hospitals are probably less healthy to begin with. Even after hospitalization, people who have sought medical care are not as healthy, on average, as those who were never hospitalized in the first place, though they may well be better off than they otherwise would have been.

12.5.2 Choice-based Tobit model

This model is defined as follows:

$$
\begin{aligned}
d_i^* &= \delta_1 + \delta_2 W_i - \varepsilon_i \\
Y_i &= \beta_1 + \beta_2 X_i + u_i \quad \text{if } d_i^* > 0 \\
&= 0 \quad \text{if } d_i^* \le 0
\end{aligned}
\tag{12.11}
$$

where the disturbances (ε_i, u_i) follow a bivariate normal distribution with mean zero, variances σ_ε^2 and σ_u^2, and a possibly nonzero covariance $\sigma_{\varepsilon u}$. It is assumed that only the sign of the choice variable d_i^* is observed. As the response variable Y_i is recorded as zero when $d_i^* \le 0$, there are usually a significant number of zero observations. It is also assumed that the values of W_i in the choice equation are observed for all i but the values of X_i need not be observed if $d_i^* \leq 0$. This model is an extension of the standard Tobit model and classified as the Type 2 Tobit model in Amemiya (1984). The difference is the inclusion of the choice equation in this choice-based Tobit model.

If we use only the observations with nonzero values of Y_i and apply the OLS estimation to the response equation in Eq. (12.11), this can cause a bias for the same reason explained in the previous section.

In a study on working hours of wives by Mroz (1987), the selection (or choice) equation is for working/nonworking decision and the response equation is for the working hours of wives. The variables used for W_i in the selection equation are age, education, job experience, number of pre-school children of age less than 6, number of schooling children of age between 6 and 18, local unemployment rate, education of the mother and education of the father. For X_i in the response equation, all the variables except education years of the mother and the father are included. The same set of explanatory variables may be used in both the selection and the response equation. However, the two equations would have different coefficient estimates because the selection equation is estimated by the probit model but the response equation is by a linear regression model.

The two-stage estimation technique developed by Heckman (1976) can be applied to correct for the bias, as explained in the previous section. The MLE method can also produce consistent estimates using the following likelihood function:

$$L = \prod_{D_i = 0} \Pr(d_i^* \leq 0) \times \prod_{D_i = 1} f(Y_i \mid d_i^* > 0) \cdot \Pr(d_i^* > 0)$$

where $\Pr(\cdot)$ denotes a probability conditioned on the explanatory variable W; $f(\cdot)$ is the normal density with mean $\beta_1 + \beta_2 X_i$ and variance σ^2. In fact, this likelihood function is the same as the one for the sample selection model.

12.5.3 Estimation using SAS[11]

```
*********************************************************
* SELF SELECTION/ Switching Regression
*********************************************************;
DATA K1;
    DO I=1 TO 200;
        W= RANUNI(12345); V= RANNOR(12345); U= RANNOR(12345);
        E= RANNOR(12345); X1= RANUNI(12345); X2= RANUNI(12345);
        DSTAR= 1-2*W + E;
        Y1=1 + 3*X1-2*X2 + 0.5*E + V;
        Y2 = -2 + 2*X1 + X2 + 0.3*E + U;
        IF DSTAR > 0 THEN D=1; ELSE D=0;
        IF D=0 THEN Y=Y1; ELSE Y=Y2;
        OUTPUT;
    END;
KEEP Y D DSTAR W X1 X2 ; RUN;
```

```
TITLE '========== Self-Selection Model/ Switching Regression ==========';
TITLE2 '---------- MLE ----------';
PROC QLIM DATA=K1;
    MODEL D = W/DISCRETE;
    MODEL Y = X1 X2 / SELECT(D=0); RUN;

PROC QLIM DATA=K1;
    MODEL D = W/DISCRETE;
    MODEL Y = X1 X2 / SELECT(D=1); RUN;

*-----------------------------------------------------------;
TITLE2 '-------- Two-stage estimation using inverse Mills ratio - ------';

PROC SORT data=K1 ; by descending D;
/***** First Stage: Probit *****/
/* note use of order=data to get coefficients with right signs */
/* will save predicted gammaw's to dataset MILLS for calculation of
    inverse mills ratio; note that all variables from dataset a
    will also be saved in dataset MILLS */
PROC LOGISTIC order=data ;
    class D;
    model D = W/LINK=PROBIT RSQ;
    output out=MILLS xbeta=gammaw p=pred;
RUN;
DATA MILLS; set MILLS;
    /* create inverse mills ratio */
    if (D eq 1) then
        lambda=(1/sqrt(2*3.141592654)*exp(-1*gammaw**2/2))/probnorm(gammaw);
    else if (D eq 0) then
        lambda=(1/sqrt(2*3.141592654)*exp(-1*gammaw**2/2))/(probnorm(gammaw)-1);
    else lambda=.;

PROC SORT; BY D;
PROC REG; MODEL Y = X1 X2 LAMBDA; BY D; RUN;

****************************************************
* Choice-based censored (Type 2 Tobit)
****************************************************;
DATA K1;
    DO I=1 TO 200;
        W= RANUNI(12345);     E= RANNOR(12345);
```

```
        X1= RANUNI(12345);     X2= RANUNI(12345); U= RANNOR(12345);
        DSTAR= 1-2*W + 2.5*X1 + E;     Y = 10 + 3*X1 -X2 +0.5*E + U;
        IF DSTAR > 0 THEN D=1;   ELSE D=0;
        IF D=0 THEN Y=0;             /*** censored ***/
        OUTPUT;
    END;
KEEP Y D DSTAR W X1 X2 ; RUN;

TITLE '------- Choice-based Censored (Type 2 Tobit) ---------';
PROC QLIM DATA=K1 METHOD=QN;
    MODEL D = W X1 / DISCRETE;
    MODEL Y = X1 X2 / SELECT(D=1);
RUN;
```

12.6. Applications

12.6.1 Bushee (1998)

This paper examines whether institutional investors create or reduce incentives for corporate managers to reduce investment in research and development (R&D) to meet short-term earnings goals. Many critics argue that the frequent trading and short-term focus of institutional investors encourage managers to engage in such myopic investment behavior. It is because managers have incentives to reduce R&D in order to avoid an earnings disappointment that would trigger large-scale institutional investor selling and lead to a temporary misvaluation of the firm's stock price. Others argue that the large stockholdings and sophistication of institutions allow them to monitor and discipline managers, ensuring that managers choose investment levels to maximize long-run value rather than to meet short-term earnings goals. Bushee examines these competing views by testing whether institutional ownership affects R&D spending for firms that could reverse a decline in earnings with a reduction in R&D.[12] The following two hypotheses are tested:

H_{1a} : *Ceteris paribus*, a higher percentage of institutional holdings in a firm *increases* the likelihood that its manager cuts R&D to meet short-term earnings goals.

H_{1b} : *Ceteris paribus*, a higher percentage of institutional holdings in a firm *decreases* the likelihood that its manager cuts R&D to meet long-term earnings goals.

The dependent variable used to test for myopic investment behavior is an indicator (*CUTRD*) that equals one if the firm cuts R&D relative to the prior year, and zero if the firm maintains or increases R&D. Bushee uses an indicator variable rather than the magnitude of the change in R&D because theory does not address how the level of institutional ownership should affect the magnitude of the increases in R&D, and because the magnitude of decreases in R&D should be based on the amount of the earnings decline. Thus, the magnitude of the change in R&D is unlikely to be a linear function of the level of institutional ownership.

To test hypotheses H_{1a} and H_{1b} on the influence of institutional ownership on myopic investment behavior, the author uses a logit model to regress *CUTRD* on the level of the firm's institutional ownership and a set of control variables that proxy for changes in the R&D investment opportunity set, differences in the costs of cutting R&D and proxies for other earnings management incentives:

$$\Pr(CUTRD_i = 1) = F\left[\alpha + \beta_1 PIH_i + (other\ factors)\right]$$

where $F[\cdot]$ is the logistic cumulative distribution function; $CUTRD = 1$ if R&D is cut relative to the prior year, 0 otherwise; and $PIH =$ percentage of institutional holdings.

Table 12.1 presents results for the logit regression of the indicator for cuts in R&D ($CUTRD$) on the control variables and the percentage of institutional ownership (PIH). The coefficient estimates and p-values are presented for the SD sample.[13] The coefficient on the PIH variable is significantly negative. This result supports H_{1b}, suggesting that institutional investors are sophisticated investors who serve a monitoring role, relative to individual investors, in reducing the incentives of managers to reverse a decline in earnings through cuts in R&D. This finding does not support the concern, expressed in H_{1a}, that institutional investors cause underinvestment in R&D based on their expected reactions to disappointing current earnings news.

The last column of Table 12.1 presents the estimated impact of a change in each independent variable across its interquartile range on the probability of cutting R&D. To obtain this impact, the author multiplies the marginal effect of a one-unit change in the independent variable (which is calculated as the estimated coefficient times the logit density function evaluated at the sample means of the independent variables) by the interquartile range for each variable. A change in institutional holdings across the interquartile range (from 5% to 38%) reduces the probability that a manager cuts R&D by 6.9%. This effect appears economically significant, given that about 30% of all firms cut R&D in any given year.

12.6.2 *Leung, Daouk and Chen (2000)*

It is often observed that a prediction with little forecast error does not necessarily lead to capital gain. Leitch and Tanner (1991) found that traditional measures of forecasting performance, such as the root mean squared errors (RMSE), were not as strongly correlated with profits from a trading strategy based on a set of predictions as was a measure of the directional accuracy. Given this notion, the authors compare trading rules which are based on a probit model (direction of the return) and a vector autoregressive (VAR) model (level of the return).

The trading rules are:

1   Probit model: If the probability of positive excess return is greater than 0.5, purchase index fund and short T-bill. Otherwise, short index fund and purchase T-bill.

Table 12.1 Logit regression of indicator for cut in R&D ($CUTRD$) on control variables and institutional holdings, using the SD sample

Variable	Expected sign	Coefficient	p-value	Marginal effects
Intercept		−0.158	0.323	
PIH	+/	−0.928	0.001	−0.069
other factors		Included		
pseudo-R^2		0.122		
Number of observations		2,469		

Source: Adapted from Bushee (1998, Table 4 on page 321).

2   VAR: If a forecast of excess return is positive, purchase index fund and short T-bill. Otherwise, short index fund and purchase T-bill.

The empirical results are:

1   The number of times a forecasting model correctly predicts the direction of the index excess return over the 60 out-of-sample forecast periods from January 1991 through December 1995.

	US S&P 500		UK FTSE 100		Japan Nikkei 225	
	Number	Ratio	Number	Ratio	Number	Ratio
Probit (direction)	36	0.60	36	0.60	38	0.63
VAR (level)	32	0.53	32	0.53	35	0.58

2   Excess returns from index trading guided by the probit and VAR forecasts

	US S&P 500	UK FTSE 100	Japan Nikkei 225
Probit (direction)	40.7	28.1	84.1
VAR (level)	14.2	10.5	49.4

The empirical results suggest that the focus should be on accurately predicting the direction of movement as opposed to minimizing the forecasts' deviations from the actual observed values.

12.6.3 Shumway (2001)

In order to forecast bankruptcy probabilities, most economists have been estimating single-period (static) logit models with multiple-period bankruptcy data. That is, only one observation for each firm is used for analysis. However, the characteristics of most firms change from year to year. By ignoring the fact that firms change through time, static models produce bankruptcy probabilities that are biased and inconsistent.

In contrast, hazard models use all available information to determine each firm's bankruptcy risk at each point in time and therefore resolve the problems of static models by explicitly accounting for time. These hazard models are equivalent to a multiperiod logit model that is estimated with data on each firm in each year of its existence as if each firm-year were an independent observation. The dependent variable (Y_i) in the multiperiod logit model is set equal to one only in the year (t_i) in which a bankruptcy filing occurred. Since a multiperiod logit model is estimated with the data from each firm-year as if they were separate observations, its likelihood function is

$$L = \prod_{i=1}^{n}\left[F(t_i, X_i; \beta)^{Y_i} \times \prod_{j<t_i}\{1 - F(j, X_i; \beta)\}\right]$$

where F is the cumulative distribution function for bankruptcy.

12.6.4 Robinson and Min (2002)

When entering a new market, the first entrant typically faces the greatest market and technical uncertainties. Do market pioneers have unusually low survival rates? Unusually low survival rates can offset the pioneer's market share reward that often arises for surviving businesses and surviving brands.

Unusually low survival rates can also deter investing in the costly and risky attempt to pioneer a new market. The authors' study compares survival rates for 167 first-entrant market pioneers vs. 267 early followers.

Hypotheses: first-mover advantages and survival

Market pioneers typically face the greatest market and technological uncertainties. Market uncertainty arises because it is unusually difficult to forecast sales for a pioneering product. Because an early follower has more time to learn about customer needs and wants, reduced uncertainty should increase its survival chance.

H_1: When pioneer lead time is held constant, market pioneers have a lesser chance than early followers of surviving.

However, if first-mover advantages more than offset market and technological uncertainties, we have the following alternative hypothesis:

$H_{1, alt}$: When pioneer lead time is held constant, market pioneers have a greater chance than early followers of surviving.

Hypotheses: pioneer lead time and survival

Increasing pioneer lead time should increase the pioneer's chance of survival. A short-term benefit arises from the pioneer's monopoly before the second entrant's arrival. If the market pioneer does not face any competitors, its survival should be easier. A long-term benefit arises because increasing lead time tends to strengthen first-mover advantages. By lengthening the pioneer's temporary monopoly and strengthening its first-mover advantages, we have the following:

H_2: Increasing pioneer lead time increases the market pioneer's chance of surviving.

Because increasing pioneer lead time makes the pioneer stronger, to the extent that the pioneer and early followers are competing for scarce resources, an early follower's chance of surviving should decrease. By strengthening the pioneer's first-mover advantages, even a short delay hurts an early follower. This yields the following:

H_3: Delayed market entry decreases an early follower's chance of surviving.

An alternative hypothesis for H_3 points to an inverted-U relationship. In the first year or two of the market's evolution, decreased market and technology uncertainties yield substantial benefits for an early follower. If so, a short delay can help an early follower's chance of survival. As time goes by, an early follower's learning yields diminishing marginal returns. With diminished learning and a pioneer that is developing stronger first-mover advantages, a long delay should hurt an early follower's survival chance. This yields the following:

$H_{3, alt}$: Delayed market entry initially increases an early follower's chance of survival. Any additional delay decreases an early follower's chance of surviving.

Data

The *Thomas Register* provides detailed coverage of domestic manufacturing for nonfood products in regional and national markets.

Model

The model's dependent variable equals 1 if the business survived, 0 otherwise. Survival is evaluated at both five and ten years after the *Thomas Register*'s first listing; 87% of the market pioneers vs. 70% of the early followers survived five years. The corresponding ten-year survival rates are 66% and 48%. Both differences are statistically significant.

The full model specification includes the hypothesis testing variables and other control variables. For H_1 and $H_{1, alt}$, a market pioneer dummy variable equals 1 for the market pioneer and 0 for an early follower. For H_2, H_3 and $H_{3, alt}$, interaction terms estimate a different lead time impact for market pioneers and early followers. Each interaction term multiplies pioneer lead time (in logarithm) by the respective dummy variable.

Table 12.2 presents the logit regression results which can be expressed as follows: for the market pioneers whose dummy variables are *Market pioneer* = 1 and *Early follower* = 0,

$$\hat{Pr}(Survive) = F[13.69 + 1.60 + 0.72(\text{Ln } lead \ time) + (other \ factors)]$$

and for the early followers whose dummy variables are *Market pioneer* = 0 and *Early follower* = 1,

$$\hat{Pr}(Survive) = F[13.69 + 1.01(\text{Ln } lead \ time) - 0.60(\text{Ln } lead \ time)^2$$
$$+ (other \ factors)]$$

Statistical significance is based on conservative two-tailed tests. The hypothesis testing results are from the year-of-entry models that explain five- and ten-year survival from the year of entry (number of observations = 434). Because market pioneering significantly increases a pioneer's chance of surviving both five and ten years, $H_{1, alt}$ is supported.[14] Because increasing pioneer lead time increases pioneer survival rates significantly, H_2 is supported. This indicates that the combined impact of the pioneer's temporary monopoly plus stronger first-mover advantages helps increase its chance of survival.

Table 12.2 Logit regression results that explain five-year and ten-year survival

Variable	Five-year survival		Ten-year survival	
	Coefficient	t-statistic	Coefficient	t-statistic
Constant	13.69**	2.17	4.08	0.77
Market pioneer	1.60**	2.19	1.42**	2.54
(Market pioneer) (Ln lead time)	0.72*	1.76	0.62**	2.41
(Early follower) (Ln lead time)	1.01*	1.70	1.57***	2.86
(Early follower) (Ln lead time)²	−0.60**	−2.00	−0.83***	−2.94
Other factors	Included		Included	

Source: Adapted from Robinson and Min (2002, Table 5 on page 126).
Variable definition: Market pioneer = 1 for the market's first entrant, 0 otherwise; Early follower = 1 for each entrant in the year the second entrant entered, 0 otherwise; Ln lead time = the natural logarithm of the lead time in years over the second entrant.
Asterisks denote significance levels: * = 10%, ** = 5% and *** = 1%.

We test the potential inverted-U relationship between pioneer lead time and early follower survival using a squared term. The results consistently support the inverted-U relationship predicted in $H_{3,\,alt}$ since the coefficient estimate for the squared term is negative (-0.60) and significant at the 5% level. When we set the first derivative equal to zero, early follower survival rates peak when pioneer lead time equals roughly two years.[15] Thus, some delay appears to help an early follower resolve market and technological uncertainties, but an additional delay hurts an early follower's survival changes.

12.6.5 Leuz and Verrecchia (2000)

The authors examine whether a commitment by a firm to increased levels of disclosure lowers the information asymmetry component of the firm's cost of capital. They analyze data on German firms which have switched from the German to an international reporting regime (IAS), thereby committing themselves to increased levels of disclosure.

Since the information asymmetry component is not observable, the authors use proxy variables such as the bid-ask spread, trading volume and share price volatility. Then the alternative hypothesis is that a switch to an international reporting regime leads to a lower bid-ask spread, more trading volume and less share price volatility.

The key problem in estimating the cross-sectional regression is that firms *choose* their reporting strategy considering the costs and benefits of international reporting. An OLS regression of the proxy for cost of capital on firm characteristics and a dummy for the firm's reporting strategy would suffer from self-selection bias. In response to the self-selection problem, the authors estimate the following two-equation model: the first is a model for disclosure decision, and the second is a model for cost of capital.

$$d_i^* = \gamma_0 + \sum \gamma_s z_{si} + \varepsilon_i$$
$$y_i = \delta\, d_i + \beta_0 + \sum \beta_k x_{ki} + u_i$$

where $d_i = 1$ if $d_i^* > 0$ and $d_i = 0$ otherwise; d_i^* is the firm's unobservable net benefit of international reporting; d_i is its reporting choice; z_{si}s are variables determining the firm's reporting strategy; y_i is the information asymmetry component of the firm's cost of capital; x_{ki}s are exogenous variables determining this component; and ε_i and u_i are normally distributed disturbances.

The first equation specifies a probit regression and models the firm's reporting decision in order to control for self-selection. The second equation models the link between the information asymmetry component of the firm's cost of capital, its disclosure strategy and other firm characteristics. This specification takes into account that the reporting variable is endogenous and measures the marginal effect of the disclosure proxy.

The cross-sectional sample is composed of 102 firms during 1998. This study considers the firms' disclosure policy for the fiscal year ending between 7/1/97 and 6/31/98 and uses a dummy variable ($IR97$).

Panel A of Table 12.3 reports a probit regression of the international reporting dummy ($IR97$). The likelihood ratio statistic indicates that the disclosure model has significant explanatory power. All explanatory variables have the expected signs and are significant, except the coefficient of *Firm Value* (size) and *Free Float*. Firm size and listing in the United Kingdom or the United States, however, are highly correlated ($\rho = 0.62$). Without the foreign listing dummy, the coefficient of firm size is positive and highly significant ($p = 0.0001$), while the coefficient of free float is positive but remains insignificant ($p = 0.315$). We are not concerned about this apparent multicollinearity in the data since we estimate the disclosure model only to control for self-selection bias. Moreover, the results reported below are qualitatively unchanged if the foreign listing dummy is excluded from the model.

Panel B of Table 12.3 presents the results from the second-stage estimation using inverse Mills ratios from the probit model in panel A to account for the self-selection problem with the firm's disclosure strategy. The dependent variable is the firm's average percentage bid-ask spread from June to December 1998. The model is highly significant and explains more than 80% of the variation in relative bid-ask spreads, which is similar to the R^2 obtained in other cross-sectional studies. The coefficient of the international reporting dummy is negative as predicted and statistically significant. Moreover, the marginal effect of the dummy is economically significant. Taking the antilogarithm of the coefficient, our model suggests that an international reporting strategy is associated with an average

Table 12.3 Two-stage cross-sectional regressions, using the bid-ask spread for the information asymmetry component

Panel A: Disclosure probit model (first stage)

$$Pr(IR97) = F[\alpha_0 + \alpha_1 \log(FirmValue) + \alpha_2 ROA + \alpha_3 (FreeFloat) + \alpha_4 (CapitalIntensity)$$
$$+ \alpha_5 (UK / US.Listing)]$$

Variable	Coefficient	Std. error	z-statistic	p-value (two-sided)
Constant	−5.651	2.344	−2.411	0.016
Firm Value	0.208	0.153	1.361	0.173
ROA	0.067	0.038	1.778	0.075
Free Float	−0.047	0.885	−0.053	0.958
Capital Intensity	1.662	0.919	1.808	0.071
U.K./US Listing	1.579	0.472	3.345	0.001
LR statistic (5 df)	42.347		McFadden R^2	0.408
p-value (LR statistic)	0.0000	Within sample classification rate		89.22

Panel B: Bid-ask spread model (second stage)

$$\log(spread) = \beta_0 + \beta_1 IR97 + \beta_2 \log(FirmValue) + \beta_3 (Volume) + \beta_4 \log(Volatility) + \beta_5 \log(FreeFloat)$$
$$+ \beta_6 InverseMills + \varepsilon$$

Variable	Coefficient	Std. error	z-statistic	p-value (two-sided)
Constant	2.806	0.939	2.988	0.003
IR97	−0.471	0.223	−2.114	0.035
Log(Firm Value)	−0.449	0.036	−12.441	0.000
Log(Volume)	−0.360	0.087	−4.164	0.000
Log(Volatility)	0.631	0.238	2.647	0.008
Log(Free Float)	−0.223	0.097	−2.300	0.022
Inverse Mills ratio	0.306	0.145	2.106	0.035
R^2	0.816	F-statistic		70.393
Adj. R^2	0.806	p-value (F-statistic)		0.0000

Source: Adapted from Leuz and Verrecchia (2000, Table 4 on page 107).

Variable definition: IR97 = 1 if the firm follows an international reporting; *Firm Value* = market value of the firm's equity as of 1/1/98; *ROA* = average return on assets over the past five years; *Free Float* = percentage of shares that are not closely held; *Capital Intensity* = long-term assets divided by total assets; *UK/US Listing* = 1 if the firm is listed on the London or the New York Stock Exchanges; *Volume* = average daily turnover on the Frankfurt Stock Exchange in 1998; *Volatility* = standard deviation of daily returns in 1998.

reduction in the bid-ask spread of more than 35%. All other variables have the expected signs and are highly significant. Furthermore, the significance of the inverse Mills ratio confirms that it is important to adjust for selection bias.

12.7 Summary

1   The probit and logit regression models are used to examine the determinants of binary decisions.
2   Different from the linear regression models, the dependent variable for these models is the probability for choosing one out of two choices. Thus, the dependent variable is related to possible determinants through a link function so that the value of the right-hand side is bounded between 0 and 1. The link functions used are the cumulative normal distribution function (probit) and the cumulative logistic distribution function (logit). Because of the link function, each regression coefficient does not have the meaning of net effect of the corresponding regressor on the probability.
3   The Tobit model is employed when the dependent variable in a regression model is not fully observed but censored below a limit value, for example. In such cases, a bunch of the limit value will be observed because the *true* values below the limit cannot be observed. Thus, the observed limit value does not have the same meaning for the observational units. The Tobit model accounts for the possible differences in their true values among the observational units located at the limit.
4   In regression models which include a binary choice variable as an explanatory variable, the binary choice might not be assigned randomly but selected by the observational units themselves. With such self-selection, the OLS estimators are inconsistent and biased. The two-stage estimation method developed by Heckman (1976) can account for the self-selection bias and produce consistent estimators.

Review questions

1   Use an Excel file "12-loan-approval.xls" for the following questions. A question of our interest is whether there has been a discrimination against minorities (i.e., nonwhites) in the mortgage loan market. A binary dependent variable (*APPROVE*) represents the decision about loan applications, and a binary independent variable (*WHITE*) is the key variable for the question.

APPROVE = 1 if a loan application was approved, 0 otherwise
WHITE = 1 if the applicant is white, 0 otherwise

The other control variables are:

MARRIED = 1 if the applicant is married, 0 otherwise
DEP = the number of dependents
HEXP = housing expenditures, % of the total income
DEBT = other obligations, % of the total income
UNEMP = unemployment rate by industry
MALE = 1 if the applicant is male, 0 otherwise
The Excel data file contains observations collected from 500 applicants. The variables in the file are named as "*APPROVE MARRIED DEP HEXP DEBT UNEMP MALE WHITE*."
(a)   Estimate a logit model of *APPROVE* on *WHITE*. Is there evidence of discrimination against nonwhites?

$$\Pr(APPROVE_i = 1) = G\,(\beta_0 + \beta_1 WHITE_i)$$

(b) Estimate a logit model of *APPROVE* on *WHITE* and the control variables. Is there still evidence of discrimination against nonwhites?

$$\text{Pr}\,(APPROVE_i = 1) = G\,(\beta_0 + \beta_1 WHITE_i + \beta_2 MARRIED_i + \beta_3 DEP_i$$
$$+\,\beta_4 HEXP_i + \beta_5 DEBT_i + \beta_6 UNEMP_i + \beta_7 MALE_i)$$

(c) Are there insignificant control variables? If so, eliminate one at a time to get a simpler model. Does your final model produce a different result on the discrimination?

(d) Reestimate the final model using the probit function. Does the probit model produce a different result from the logit model?

2 The following graph describes a case of a censored dependent variable. The observed values of a dependent variable are depicted by ●, but the underlying values of the censored observations are depicted by ○. Explain why the OLS estimator based on the observed values (●) is biased.

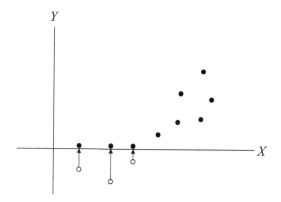

3 The following logit regression model is from Robinson and Min (2002), "Is the First to Market the First to Fail? Empirical Evidence for Industrial Goods Businesses," *Journal of Marketing Research*, Vol. 39, 120–128.

$$\text{Pr}\,(Survive = 1) = G\,[\,\beta_0 + \beta_1 (P) + \beta_2 (P)(\text{Ln } lead) + \beta_3 DEP_i$$
$$+\,\beta_3 (F)(\text{Ln } lead) + \beta_4 (F)(\text{Ln } lead)^2 + X\gamma\,]$$

where *Survive* is a dummy variable set to 1 if the business survived for five (or ten) years after the *Thomas Register*'s first listing, 0 otherwise; *P* a dummy for market pioneers; *F* a dummy for early followers; Ln *lead* the logarithmic value of the lead time; and *X* a vector of other factors for the survival.

(a) Dose increasing pioneer lead time increase the market pioneer's chance of surviving?
    Using the coefficients in the above model, write the null and alternative hypotheses.

(b) What is the impact of delayed market entry on an early follower's chance of surviving? Is the relation linear or inverted-U shaped?
    (The linear relation means that delayed market entry *continuously* decreases an early follower's chance of surviving. In contrast, the inverted-U relation indicates that delayed market entry *initially* increases an early follower's chance of survival, but any additional delay decreases the chance.)

(c) If $\beta_4 = 0$ (linear), what do you expect about the sign of β_3?

If $\beta_4 < 0$ (inverted U), what do you expect about the sign of β_3?

(d) Write the estimated logit model using the estimates in Table 12.2.

(e) Based on the estimation results in Table 12.2, make a conclusion about the arguments in (a) and (b). (Use a significance level of 10%.)

4   The following logit regression model has been modified from the one in Robinson and Min (2002), "Is the First to Market the First to Fail? Empirical Evidence for Industrial Goods Businesses," *Journal of Marketing Research*, Vol. 39, 120–128.

$$\Pr(S = 1) = G[\alpha_0 + \alpha_1(\text{Ln } lead) + \alpha_2(F) + \alpha_3(F)(\text{Ln } lead)]$$

where S is a dummy variable set to 1 if the business survived for five years after the *Thomas Register*'s first listing, 0 otherwise; F is a dummy for early followers; and ($\text{Ln } lead$) is the logarithmic value of the lead time.

(a) Write $\Pr(S = 1)$ for early followers $(F = 1)$.

(b) Write $\Pr(S = 1)$ for pioneers $(F = 0)$.

Using the coefficients in the above model, write the null and alternative hypotheses which can answer the following questions:

(c) When the effect of the pioneer lead time is held constant, do market pioneers have a greater chance of surviving than early followers?

(d) Dose increasing pioneer lead time decrease the early followers' chance of surviving?

(e) Dose increasing pioneer lead time increase the market pioneer's chance of surviving?

5   We examine whether there exists a difference in medical expenditures between the insured ($INSURANCE = 1$) and the uninsured ($INSURANCE = 0$).

$$Y = \beta_0 + \beta_1 INSURANCE + X\gamma + u$$

where Y is the medical expenditures and X is a vector of other factors.

(a) Can we estimate the regression using the OLS method? If not, explain how we can obtain consistent estimates.

(b) Why do we need to include the other factors (X)?

Explain what other factors we need to include in the regression.

6   [2SLS for a dummy endogenous variable]

In applications with a dummy endogenous regressor, Angrist and Krueger (2001) warn against using probit or logit models to generate first-stage predicted values. Plugging in fitted values from a logit or probit equation *directly* in the second stage does not generate consistent estimates unless the first-stage model of probit or logit happens to be exactly right. Thus, the OLS estimates of the following regression are not consistent in most cases.

$$Y_i = \beta_1 + \beta_2 \hat{D}_i + \beta_3 Z_{1i} + u_i$$

where the dummy endogenous variable D_i is replaced by the fitted values by a probit or logit model, i.e., $\hat{D}_i = F(\hat{\gamma}_0 + \hat{\gamma}_1 Z_{1i} + \hat{\gamma}_2 Z_{2i} + \cdots + \hat{\gamma}_s Z_{si})$, using instrumental variables $(Z_{1i}, Z_{2i}, \cdots, Z_{si})$.

(a) Explain why the above estimates are consistent if the first-stage model is correctly specified.

(b) Using an example, show why the above estimates are not consistent if the first-stage model is not correct.

(c) An alternative method is to use the fitted values $\hat{D}_i$ from a probit or logit equation as instruments, instead of plugging in the fitted values directly in the second-stage regression (Angrist and Pischke, 2009, p. 191). Explain how this method can produce consistent estimates.

(d) In fact, the consistency of the 2SLS estimator does not depend on getting the first-stage functional form right. Kelejian (1971) shows that 2SLS based on a Taylor-series expansion using the linear terms, higher powers and cross products of instrumental variables will be consistent. That is, consistent 2SLS estimates can be obtained by using the OLS fitted values from the first-stage linear regression of D on $Z_1,$ $\cdots, Z_s,$ $Z_1^2,$ $\cdots, Z_s^2,$ $Z_1 Z_2,$ $\cdots, Z_{s-1} Z_s,$ etc.[1] Explain why this method produces consistent estimates.

Notes

1 Since Y_i takes on only two values of 1 or 0, the error term u_i also takes only two values: $u_i = 1 - \beta_1 - \beta_2 X_{2i} - \beta_3 X_{3i}$ when $Y_i = 1$ and $u_i = -\beta_1 - \beta_2 X_{2i} - \beta_3 X_{3i}$ when $Y_i = 0$, with probabilities P_i and $1 - P_i$, respectively. The variance of u_i (or Y_i) is $P_i(1 - P_i)$. Since $P_i = E(Y_i | X_{2i}, X_{3i}) = \beta_1 + \beta_2 X_{2i} + \beta_3 X_{3i}$ the variance of u_i depends on the values of X_{2i} and X_{3i}, therefore being heteroscedastic.

2 BASE SAS 9.4, SAS/ETS 13.1 and SAS/STAT 13.1. SAS Institute Inc., Cary, NC.

3 The censoring can be made on the right-hand side, called *right censored* at the known value c: $Y_i = Y_i^*$ if $Y_i^* < c$, and $Y_i = c$ if $Y_i^* \geq c$. The censoring can also be made on both sides: $Y_i = c_1$ if $Y_i^* \leq c_1$, $Y_i = Y_i^*$ if $c_1 < Y_i^* < c_2$, and $Y_i = c_2$ if $Y_i^* \geq c_2$.

4 If we ignore qualitative differences among the zero observations ($Y = 0$), the OLS estimator is biased. If we use only the uncensored observations ($Y > 0$), the OLS estimator is also biased for the same reason. For a more detailed explanation, see Chapter 24 in Greene (2008).

5 In the consumption of expensive durable goods, even the cheapest price is substantially high. For example, when consumers go shopping for a new car, they first decide whether they are willing to pay a minimum of about $10,000. In this first-stage decision, they will consider other alternatives, such as purchasing a used car. If they choose not to buy a new car, their observed amount paid for a new car will be recorded as zero. Using data only from those who have purchased a new car, we can examine what have determined their observed expenditures. Thus, two stages of decision are involved, whether to buy and how much to pay. In contrast, the consumption of inexpensive goods does not require the first-stage decision because consumers can consume any small amount. They just determine how much to purchase. If their desired amount is less than zero, their amount purchased will be recorded as zero.

6 If we use "BOTTOM" as the censoring points on the Left edit field, the first four ($Y = 0$) and the ninth ($Y = 3.1$) observations are treated as censored observations because the Y values are equal to or less than their censoring points given by BOTTOM.

7 BASE SAS 9.4, SAS/ETS 13.1 and SAS/STAT 13.1. SAS Institute Inc., Cary, NC.

8 The analysis of "treatment effects" also belongs to this self-selection model. Let the dependent variable Y denote wage and the dummy D indicate whether or not the individual received post-graduate education (treatment). Then the dummy coefficient γ_2 measures the effect of the post-graduate education. As potentially high-earners are likely to receive more education, the OLS estimation of this regression model will be biased; the OLS estimate for γ_2 tends to be larger than its true value.

9 This self-selection bias can be understood in terms of the endogeneity of the dummy variable D_i. There could exist *unobserved omitted factors* which affect the decision d_i^* through ε_i and also the final outcome Y_i through u_i. Because of the common omitted factors, ε_i is correlated with u_i. Since ε_i is a part of D_i, D_i will be correlated with u_i and become endogenous. This endogeneity causes the self-selection bias in Eq. (12.7). However, if there is no such common factor and ε_i is not correlated with u_i ($\sigma_{u\varepsilon} = 0$), there will be no self-selection bias, as can be understood in Eq. (12.8).

10 An alternative approach to control for the self-selection bias includes the maximum likelihood estimation (Lee and Trost, 1978). The propensity score matching is also often employed although this is not an alternative approach but addresses a different self-selection bias (Armstrong et al., 2010).

11 BASE SAS 9.4, SAS/ETS 13.1 and SAS/STAT 13.1. SAS Institute Inc., Cary, NC.

12 US accounting rules require that R&D expenditures be immediately and fully expensed. Critics argue that this accounting treatment creates the managerial myopia problem because the US capital markets have a short-term focus that creates pressure on managers to sacrifice R&D to maintain short-term earnings growth.

13 The SD sample consists of all firm-years for which $-RD_{t-1} < (EBTRD_t - EBTRD_{t-1}) < 0$, where RD = research and development per share, EBTRD = earnings per share before taxes and R&D.

14 The coefficient estimate of *Market pioneer* is positive (1.60) and significant at the 10% level. Notice that the coefficient estimate of (Ln *Lead time*) is 0.72 for the pioneers but 1.01 for the early followers. Since they are different, the effect of the lead time on survival is different although the lead time is held constant. Therefore, the hypothesis $H_{1, alt}$ should be "When the effect of the lead time on survival is held constant, market pioneers have a greater chance than early followers of surviving."

15 Taking the derivative of the follower's Pr(*Survive*) with respect to (Ln *Lead time*) and setting to zero, we can solve for (Ln *Lead time*) = $1.01/(2 \times 0.6)$ = 0.842. Thus, the peak (*Lead time*) = $\exp(0.842)$ = 2.32.

16 Since fitted values $\hat{D}_i$ s are calculated only in the range of data, most of the fitted values are expected to lie between 0 and 1. Thus, use of a Taylor-series approximation does not face the problem that predicted probabilities can be greater than 1 or smaller than 0.

References

Amemiya, T. (1984), "Tobit Models: A Survey," *Journal of Econometrics*, 24, 3–61.

Armstrong, C.S., A.D. Jagolinzer and D.F. Larcker (2010), "Chief Executive Officer Equity Incentives and Accounting Irregularities," *Journal of Accounting Research*, 8(2), 225–271.

Angrist, J.D. and A.B. Krueger (2001), "Instrumental Variables and the Search for Identification: From Supply and Demand to Natural Experiments," *Journal of Economic Perspectives*, 15, 69–85.

Angrist, J.D. and J.S. Pischke (2009), *Mostly Harmless Econometrics: An Empiricist's Companion*, Princeton, NJ: Princeton University Press.

Bushee, B.J. (1998), "The Influence of Institutional Investors on Myopic R&D Investment Behavior," *The Accounting Review*, 73, 305–333.

Greene, W.H. (2008), *Econometric Analysis*, 6th ed., Upper Saddle River, NJ: Prentice Hall.

Heckman, J.J. (1976), "Sample Selection bias as a Specification Error," *Econometrica*, 47(1), 153–61.

Kelejian, H.H. (1971), "Two-Stage Least Squares and Econometric Systems Linear in Parameters but Nonlineaer in the Endogenous Variables," *Journal of the American Statistical Association*, 66, 373–374.

Lee, L.F. and R.P. Trost (1978), "Estimation of Some Limited Dependent Variable Models with Application to Housing Demand," *Journal of Econometrics*, 8, 357–382.

Leitch, G. and J.E. Tanner (1991), "Economic Forecast Evaluation: Profits Versus the Conventional Error Measures," *American Economic Review*, 81, 580–590.

Leung, M.T., H. Daouk and A.S. Chen (2000), "Forecasting Stock Indices: A Comparison of Classification and Level Estimation Models," *International Journal of Forecasting*, 16, 173–190.

Leuz, C. and R.E. Verrecchia (2000), "The Economic Consequences of Increased Disclosure," *Journal of Accounting Research*, 38, 91–124.

Maddala, G.S. (1991), "A Perspective on the Use of Limited-Dependent and Qualitative Variables Models in Accounting Research," *The Accounting Review*, 66, 788–807.

Mroz, T.A. (1987), "The Sensitivity of an Empirical Model of Married Women's Hours of Work to Economic and Statistical Assumptions," *Econometrica*, 5, 765–799.

Palepu, K.G. (1986), "Predicting Takeover Targets: A Methodological and Empirical Analysis," *Journal of Accounting and Economics*, 8, 3–35.

Robinson, W.T. and S. Min (2002), "Is the First to Market the First to Fail? Empirical Evidence for Industrial Goods Businesses," *Journal of Marketing Research*, 39, 120–128.

Shumway, T. (2001), "Forecasting Bankruptcy More Accurately: A Simple-Hazard Model," *Journal of Business*, 74, 101–124.

Spector, L. and M. Mazzeo (1980), "Probit Analysis and Economic Education," *Journal of Economic Education*, 11, 37–44.

Appendix 12 Maximum likelihood estimation (MLE)

To understand the idea of the maximum likelihood estimation, consider the following Bernoulli trial. There are two possible outcomes, i.e., $Y = 0$ or 1. Let p be the probability of $Y = 1$. Then $Pr(Y=0) = 1-p$. Suppose we have observed (1,1,0) in three independent consecutive trials. The probability of having these observations is $L = p^2(1-p)$, which is the likelihood function. This likelihood function is maximized when $p = 2/3$, which is the ML estimate given the observations. Thus, the ML estimates are the values of parameters which maximize the likelihood (or probability) of having the realized outcome. This approach to estimating parameters is based on the idea that, out of all the possible values for the parameter p, the value that makes the likelihood of the observed outcome largest should be chosen.

One strength is that the MLE is generally the most asymptotically efficient estimator when the probability distribution is correctly specified. Notice that in order to specify the likelihood function, we need to know (or assume) the probability distribution of the outcome.

Now, we apply the MLE to a linear regression model which includes three parameters ($\beta_1, \beta_2, \sigma^2$).

$$Y_i = \beta_1 + \beta_2 X_i + u_i, \qquad u_i \sim iid\ N(0, \sigma^2)$$

where *iid* denotes "*i*ndependently and *i*dentically *d*istributed." As the disturbance is assumed to follow a normal distribution, the dependent variable also has a normal distribution:

$$Y_i \sim iid\ N(\beta_1 + \beta_2 X_i, \sigma^2)$$

We can define the likelihood function which is the joint probability density of observing the random sample. Since the observations are mutually independent, the joint density is just the product of individual densities.

$$L(\beta_1, \beta_2, \sigma^2 \mid Y, X) = \prod_{i=1}^n f(Y_i \mid \beta_1, \beta_2, \sigma^2, X_i)$$

While the density $f(\cdot)$ for Y is conditioned on the parameters ($\beta_1, \beta_2, \sigma^2$), the likelihood function $L(\cdot)$ is expressed as a function of the unknown parameters conditioned on the sample data. It is usually simpler to work with the log of the likelihood function:

$$\ln L(\beta_1, \beta_2, \sigma^2 \mid Y, X) = \sum_{i=1}^n \ln f(Y_i \mid \beta_1, \beta_2, \sigma^2, X_i)$$

$$= -\frac{1}{2} \sum_{i=1}^n \left\{ \ln \sigma^2 + \ln(2\pi) + (Y_i - \beta_1 - \beta_2 X_i)^2 / \sigma^2 \right\}$$

To find the values which maximize the log likelihood function, we take its derivatives with respect to the parameters and set them to zero.

$$\frac{\partial \ln L}{\partial \beta_1} = \frac{1}{\sigma^2} \sum_{i=1}^n (Y_i - \beta_1 - \beta_2 X_i) = 0$$

$$\frac{\partial \ln L}{\partial \beta_2} = \frac{1}{\sigma^2} \sum_{i=1}^n (Y_i - \beta_1 - \beta_2 X_i) X_i = 0$$

$$\frac{\partial \ln L}{\partial \sigma^2} = -\frac{n}{2\sigma^2} + \frac{n}{2\sigma^4} \sum_{i=1}^n (Y_i - \beta_1 - \beta_2 X_i)^2 = 0$$

The first two equations are the same as the normal equations from the OLS method in Chapter 2. Thus, for this linear regression model with a normally distributed error term, the MLE estimators for the coefficients β_1 and β_2 are the same as the OLS ones. However, the estimator for σ^2 is slightly different in the denominator: $\hat{\sigma}^2_{MLE} = \sum_{i=1}^{n} (Y_i - \beta_1 - \beta_2 X_i)^2 / n$ but $\hat{\sigma}^2_{OLS} = \sum_{i=1}^{n} (Y_i - \beta_1 - \beta_2 X_i)^2 / (n-2)$. The difference becomes smaller and finally vanishes as the sample size increases.

INDEX

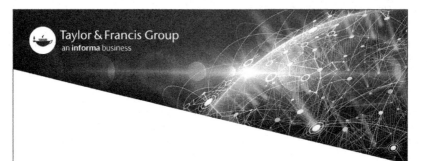

Printed in the United States
by Baker & Taylor Publisher Services